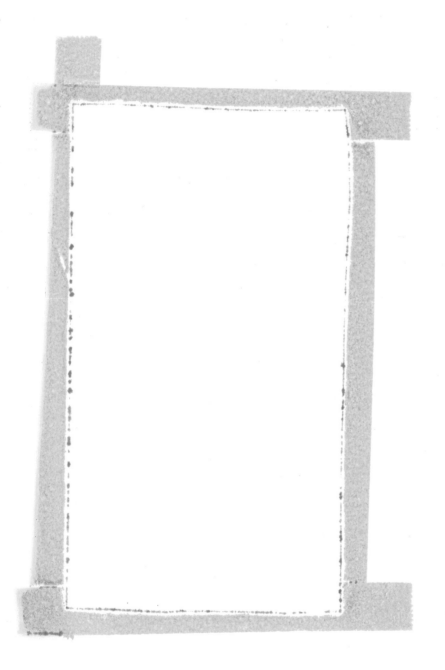

new birth of
FREEDOM

PETER C. HODGSON

new birth of
FREEDOM

A Theology of Bondage
and Liberation

Fortress Press
Philadelphia

The author gratefully acknowledges permission to make use of some material contained in his article, "Freedom, Dignity, and Transcendence: A Response to B. F. Skinner," *Soundings: An Interdisciplinary Journal,* vol. 55 (Fall 1972), pp. 347-358, © 1972 by the Society for Religion in Higher Education and Vanderbilt University.

Biblical quotations from the Revised Standard Version of the Bible, copyrighted 1946, 1952, © 1971, 1973 by the Division of Christian Education of the National Council of the Churches of Christ in the U.S.A., are used by permission.

Biblical quotations from *The New English Bible,* copyrighted © The Delegates of the Oxford University Press and The Syndics of the Cambridge University Press 1961, 1970, are reprinted by permission.

Library of Congress Catalog Card Number 75-37145

ISBN 0–8006–0437–7 cloth
ISBN 0–8006–1437–2 paper

		1-0437 cloth
5358K75	Printed in U.S.A.	1-1437 paper

To

EVA, DAVID, and JENNIFER

CONTENTS

PREFACE

This book, while taking its start from the experience of freedom and oppression in America, is intended primarily as an exercise in systematic theology, which seeks to develop an interpretation of the symbols of Christian faith as a whole in terms of the story of human bondage and liberation, which is also the story of God's worldly suffering and redemptive power.

In the first chapter, I attempt to designate certain themes and dilemmas emerging from the American experience, for which theological answers must be found and to which the remainder of the work is addressed. The book does not purport, however, to be primarily an "American" theology of freedom. I draw upon Anglo-, Afro-, and Latin-American literature to a much greater extent than I did in earlier work, but find important resources for developing the constructive argument in German idealism, in French and German existential and social phenomenology, and in contemporary Continental theology and biblical scholarship. Good theology, it seems to me, must transcend regional and national identities, although it may well arise out of the determinate situation of a people, a place, or an epoch.

The work is intended as a foundational theology of freedom and should not be identified, therefore, with any one of the specific liberation theologies—third world, black, woman's—although I have drawn extensively from the literature arising out of these movements. In *Children of Freedom: Black Liberation in Christian Perspective* (Fortress Press, 1974) I sought to enter in a special way into the perspective of one of these movements and to share therefore a particular way of experiencing bondage and liberation in America. Without such a prolegomenon the present book could not have been written. But in the final analysis I cannot *do* black theology, or feminist theology, or third world

xiii

theology. *My* situation, as a white American male, is one shaped by forefathers who sought to bring forth on this continent "a new nation, conceived in liberty," and who enslaved blacks, dispossessed Indians, and subjugated women in the process. It is to this broader paradox or contradiction in the American experience that I must address myself—the contradiction between the ideals of freedom and equality envisioned by the Declaration of Independence, and the realities of racial, class, sexual, as well as economic, political, and technological domination. To penetrate this paradox, I have found it necessary to undertake a theological interpretation of bondage and liberation at the most fundamental and inclusive level attainable. For this reason a theology of freedom has emerged from the attempt to understand what has happened to liberty in America and how humanity as a whole might experience "a new birth of freedom."

In order to set this theology in a context that exposes significant alternatives, the second chapter develops a typology of rival understandings of freedom (ancient and modern) and specifies distinctive features of the Christian view. Included among the modern alternatives are Marxism, Freudianism, existentialism, the counter culture, behaviorism, and technology. I hope that this typology will prove useful for a study of the perennial issues relating to the question of human freedom. The third chapter offers a phenomenological description of essential structures of human freedom, drawing especially upon resources provided by Ricoeur, Heidegger, and Hegel.

On these foundations the constructive argument of the last four chapters is built. Christianity, it is argued, is the religion of freedom par excellence. In accord with the Hebraic tradition, it perceives bondage to be a dimension of freedom itself—a freedom that enslaves itself by an interior act of self-deception and that objectifies this act, demonically intensifying it, in law, death, and oppressive sociopolitical and ideological powers. Jesus is "the radically free person" who proclaimed and enacted a gospel of liberation from these internal and external forms of bondage. Moreover, this Jesus, it is believed, has been raised from the dead and is now at work in the world actualizing the freedom he once engendered. His resurrection is the energizing force in the dialectics of emancipation and redemption by which liberation occurs historically. The positive meaning of freedom is understood by Christian faith neither as autonomy nor as membership in a privileged group, but as openness to the liberating power of God, which engenders new and transformed understandings of subjectivity and community. This transformation is consummated by the vision of a coming, true communion of free subjects—the "kingdom of freedom" proclaimed by Jesus as the rule of God and the true destiny of humankind. (A more complete summary of the constructive argument is found at the end of Chapter II, pp. 105–112.)

Throughout I have attempted to avoid masculine nouns, pronouns, and adjectives where the reference is to human beings in the generic sense. But adherence to such a principle is especially difficult when it comes to language about God—whose being is personal though beyond sexual distinctions—unless one is satisfied to refer to God in the neuter, or repeat the divine name constantly, or use such awkward expressions as "he/she" and "him/her." I have not found a satisfactory solution to this problem.

I am indebted to the John Simon Guggenheim Memorial Foundation for a Fellowship that made possible a full year of writing, study, and travel in 1974–75. Vanderbilt University granted sabbatical leave during this period, and the University Research Council provided secretarial funds. Students who for several years attended my course on Theology of Freedom in Vanderbilt Divinity School have made a notable contribution to the development of the work. The doctoral dissertations of Warren McWilliams, Aquin O'Neill, and John Shelley have enriched my understanding on several points. Discussions with my colleagues Edward Farley and Peter Paris on the structure and content of the argument have been especially helpful. Barbara Andolsen and Howard Harrod assisted with bibliographic resources, and Pam Damron Knight and Linda Tober helped with proofreading and indexing. Norman Hjelm, Director and Senior Editor of Fortress Press, has been a source of constant support and encouragement. Criticisms of an earlier version of Chapter III by Daniel Dugan, Peter Manchester, and other friends in the Society for Religion in Higher Education, to whom this material was presented as a paper, are much appreciated. Some of the material in Chapters II and III relating to Skinner and Ricoeur was first published in the Fall 1972 issue of *Soundings,* and is reused by permission. Portions of Chapter V were presented as a lecture at the Perkins School of Theology, Southern Methodist University, where I benefited greatly from the ensuing discussion with colleagues and students. A series of lectures to the Huntsville-Vanderbilt Study Forum in 1973–74 provided a stimulating context for the discussion of many of my ideas. To the then Director of the Study Forum, Townsend Walker, I am especially grateful.

PETER C. HODGSON

The Divinity School
Vanderbilt University
September 1975

PART ONE

ON THE EXPERIENCE AND
INTERPRETATION OF FREEDOM

Chapter I

Freedom in America:
The Vision, the Fault,
the Unfinished Work

1. THE VISION:
"A NEW NATION, CONCEIVED IN LIBERTY"

The European settlers who immigrated to the New World in the seventeenth century were motivated by a vision, a sense of purpose and calling, that became the basis for what Sidney Mead has called the "creative idea" of America, namely, "the potential capacity of mankind to be 'free.' "[1] This idea was elaborated in biblical, indeed Hebraic, images of creation, election, and mission. Americans were to be an elect people, a new Israel, chosen by God to redeem the Old World, prepared for a role of struggle, sacrifice, and eventual triumph.[2] This sense of continuity with ancient Israel, its exodus from Egypt and its entry into a promised land where the human potential for freedom under divine sovereignty was to be fulfilled, was given classical expression in the public addresses of Abraham Lincoln at the precise moment when the legitimacy of that vision was being tested by the fault that lay within.

Given seventeenth century Protestantism's preoccupation with divine sovereignty and with the theocratic ideal of ancient Israel, it is not surprising that the central religious symbol by which the Puritans, Pilgrims, Quakers, Separatists, and others interpreted their experience in the New World should have been that of the "kingdom of God"—a symbol which in its characteristic form oc-

1. Sidney E. Mead, "American History as a Tragic Drama," *Journal of Religion*, 52 (October 1972): 342.
2. J. F. Maclear, "The Republic and the Millennium," in Elwyn A. Smith, ed., *The Religion of the Republic* (Philadelphia: Fortress Press, 1971), p. 183; cf. p. 188. See also Robert N. Bellah, "Civil Religion in America," in William G. McLoughlin and Robert N. Bellah, eds., *Religion in America* (Boston: Beacon Press, 1968), pp. 9–10, 12.

curs repeatedly in the sayings of Jesus, although its roots are traceable to Old Testament prophecy and apocalyptic. We are indebted to H. Richard Niebuhr for the definitive study of this image in American Protestantism.[3] Niebuhr has shown that the concept itself includes several aspects and has undergone an evolution during the course of the American experience. In the earliest period, down to the middle of the eighteenth century, it was a realistic rather than an idealistic or utopian image. It referred to the reality of God's sovereign rule rather than to an ideal society established progressively through human effort. Rather than presupposing the beneficence and perfectibility of persons, it presupposed their bondage to sin, their inability to liberate themselves. Its real starting point, says Niebuhr, was the free God, not the human passion for freedom.[4]

The dilemma faced by this way of thinking was how the freedom of God and his sovereign power could be efficaciously actualized in a transformed and liberated human community. "As a theory of *divine* construction the Protestant movement was hard put to provide principles for human construction."[5] It did so primarily in negative terms, providing the basis for the principle of the limitation of powers and the relativization of human claims to power. God alone is sovereign, and all human pretensions to sovereignty must be checked and balanced by constitutional safeguards.[6] In this fashion the Puritan doctrine of the kingdom of God served as a critical backdrop for the constitutional theories of the Founding Fathers and later for the emergence of what Ralph Gabriel calls the American democratic faith.[7]

Under the impact of the Great Awakening and subsequent revivals, a different aspect of the kingdom concept came to the fore

3. H. Richard Niebuhr, *The Kingdom of God in America* (New York: Harper & Brothers, 1935). On the centrality of this motif for all Protestant groups, see pp. 18–19, 45–46, 87.
4. Ibid., pp. 51, 24; also pp. 46–49, 56, 79, 98.
5. Ibid., pp. 27–30.
6. Ibid., pp. 62, 65, 69, 75–80, 84–87.
7. Ralph Gabriel, *The Course of American Democratic Thought* (New York: Ronald Press, 1940), pp. 28–29. See also Richard Hofstadter, *The American Political Tradition and the Men Who Made It* (New York: Vintage Books, 1960), pp 3–10.

in evangelical and liberal Protestantism. The redemption from sin and servitude accomplished by Christ on behalf of the sovereign God meant that a new realm of peace, justice, and freedom was to be established upon the earth. This motif had been present from the beginning in Puritanism, but it was now given a more historical and perfectionist cast with the emergence of the belief that the return of Christ and the beginning of his earthly reign was to be preceded by a preparatory millennial period, which human beings had the responsibility to establish in progressive stages. This view was known as *post*millennialism because of its belief that Christ would return only *after* the millennial period. The place of inauguration for the latter was, of course, to be the new republic in America, which would serve as a beacon and standard for humankind as a whole.[8]

In a recent essay M. Darrol Bryant has analyzed the relationship of Jonathan Edwards, the greatest American theologian, to the millennial optimism of the Great Awakening.[9] In his early writings, notably *A History of the Work of Redemption* (1738–39), Edwards supported the postmillennialist vision of the building of God's redemptive kingdom in America, primarily through a great renewal of the proclamatory and missionary work of the church. But in his middle period, beginning with the treatise on *Religious Affections* (1746), Edwards shifted to a premillennialist critique of the Awakening: the kingdom would still come, but it would be solely the work of Christ and the Holy Spirit, in which human effort would play no significant role. In effect Edwards had returned to the view of the kingdom characteristic of Puritan orthodoxy in the seventeenth century. Finally, in his post-1750 writings —*The Nature of True Virtue, The Doctrine of Original Sin Defended, The Freedom of the Will, The End for Which God Created the World*—Edwards developed a transhistorical critique of all forms of millennialism. Human beings are radically sinful;

8. Niebuhr, *The Kingdom of God in America*, pp. 90–99, 124, 150 ff.; Maclear, "The Republic and the Millennium," pp. 184–186, 189–190, 194–200.
9. M. Darrol Bryant, "America as God's Kingdom," in *Religion and Political Society* (New York: Harper & Row, 1974), pp. 49–94.

an autonomous, self-determining, and self-liberating individualism is an illusion; true virtue is oriented to the glorification of God as the ground of being; and human destiny finds its fulfillment not in a political but a "spiritual" realm, "a glorious society of created beings." The question, of course, is whether these three stages in Edwards's thought are mutually exclusive, so that it becomes impossible to sustain the millennialist vision of a redeemed and transfigured earth in the context of a transhistorical critique. Bryant seems to think that all millennial tendencies must be expunged from "proper" theological work.[10] Hence his position, and perhaps also Edwards's, ultimately prove to be undialectical: a theology of the glory of God relates to political and historical realities only in the sense that a tangent touches a circle (to adopt Karl Barth's image). In Chapter VI, I shall address this issue and offer a way of understanding how God's kingdom is actualized historically, a way of holding in tension both the millennial and critical elements by means of a dialectics of emancipation and redemption.

To summarize thus far: in the prevailing view the kingdom of God in America was to be a "kingdom of freedom"—or in Lincoln's eloquent image, "a new nation, conceived in liberty, and dedicated to the proposition that all men are created equal." Freedom was in the first instance a function of *dependence,* of belonging to a covenant community, which in turn was based on God's sovereign rule in nature and history. This rule of God constituted a world of coherence and meaning, with transcendent structures of right and wrong, a world not of humanity's own making but experienced rather as a gift, a world in which human beings could dwell. To safeguard this dwelling, peoples were to establish political constitutions in accordance with the divine governance, which would exclude any form of human tyranny and assure equality, justice, and liberty to all citizens of the state. In the second place, this "realm of freedom" assumed for Americans an important *spatial* dimension, in view of the seemingly illimitable land, which permitted unconfined movement and growth.

10. Ibid., pp. 86–87.

Such an attitude toward space undergirded the compulsion to explore and civilize the continent—the "errand into the wilderness," as the Puritans expressed it—as well as the typical American tendency to "move on" when conditions became too settled, crowded, or undesirable. The *temporal* aspects of freedom were not lacking either, for there existed a strong sense of new beginning in a New World, of being able (in the words of Robert Benne and Philip Hefner) "to shake free of the limiting past in a struggling ascent toward the realization of promise in a gracious future." Finally, and in partial conflict with the original Puritan consciousness of a covenant community under the sovereign will of God, as well as Edwards's later strictures against freedom of the will, there emerged in America a strong sense of *voluntary action,* undoubtedly shaped by the distinctive ways that space and time had been experienced. The quintessence of freedom for most Americans came to mean choosing, initiating, deciding.[11]

In due course I shall note that each of these aspects of the American experience of freedom was subject to exaggeration and distortion. The sense of belonging to a divinely established covenant community could stifle human responsibility and lead to authoritarian forms of polity; or conversely, it could provide the basis for assuming a divine mandate to claim the entire continent on behalf of white civilization. The freedom based on illimitable land could lead to unrestrained growth, the rapid depletion of resources, and the tendency to take flight before undesirable conditions rather than to face and resolve them. The lack of established traditions and the sense of a new future at human disposal could degenerate into purposeless innovation and ceaseless change, explaining the tendency to discard still useful products while acquiring new ones with only superficial "improvements." It

11. For this brief portrayal of motifs in the American experience of freedom, see Gibson Winter, "The Question of Liberty in a Technologized World," *Anglican Theological Review,* Supplementary Series, no. 1 (July 1973), pp. 78–80, 88–89; Sidney Mead, *The Lively Experiment: The Shaping of Christianity in America* (New York: Harper & Row, 1963), pp. 5–7, 12–13; Robert Benne and Philip Hefner, *Defining America: A Christian Critique of the American Dream* (Philadelphia: Fortress Press, 1974), pp. 8–16.

also accounts for the assumption of technological mastery over the flow of time, including the human ability to rationalize and control the future through planning. Finally the strong tradition of voluntary action (the privilege primarily of white males, of course) could lead to mastery, domination, and exploitation—not only of nature and things but also of human beings.

So powerful was the American vision of freedom, in both its creative and destructive dimensions, that it became part of the national ideology, clearly perceptible in what Robert Bellah and others have described as the American "civil religion." This religion was intended to provide a foundation for and give direction and purpose to the American sense of mission and national destiny. The foundation was located in the divine election of Americans as a chosen people to carry forth God's purposes in the world. Such a belief could and often did serve as a legitimation, of course, for self-serving national interests and for claims to authority and leadership. The symbols and rites of a civil religion have the function, at least in part, of unifying public opinion and enhancing support for the governing authorities and their policies. But, according to Bellah, the civil religion can also introduce a transcendent dimension into the political process, providing a criterion of right and wrong, a source of human rights, a basis for prophetic judgment, and a goal for the nation demanding sacrifice and self-dedication that lies beyond the people and their rulers. God alone is the ultimate sovereign, thus relativizing human claims to authority and placing issues in a broader perspective. Bellah acknowledges that the civil religion is also subject to abuse and distortion; in the hands of Richard Nixon, for example, it became a form of national self-worship, extolling American innocence and the virtue of individual self-reliance, without any sense of higher judgment. But in Bellah's view these distortions need not falsify the validity and central thrust of the civil religion, based as it is on an authentic grasp of the American vision of a new land of freedom, blessed by divine favor and subject to divine judgment.[12]

2. THE FAULT: "THE BOND-MAN'S . . . UNREQUITED TOIL"

A. FLAWED DEFINITIONS OF FREEDOM

In all the Indo-European languages "freedom" has been defined in contrast to the institution of slavery. The Greek word *eleutheria* (from the Indo-Germanic root *leudh,* to grow, rise, ascend) designated the freedom enjoyed by the "ascendant" male citizens of the *polis,* in contrast to the subjugation of slaves, foreigners, women, and children. The free man was able to move about and to speak and act freely without physical or legal hindrance. Thus freedom for the Greek citizen meant self-disposal, power over oneself, autonomy, and participation in a privileged community. The slave, by contrast, was not at his own disposal, did not enjoy autonomy, was powerless, had no citizenship rights, and belonged to no "realm" of freedom (the *polis*). Women, of course, were not slaves (although they could *be* enslaved along with men when captured in battle or condemned as debtors), but their proper place was the household or *oikia,* not the public sphere or *polis,* and they enjoyed none of the rights of citizenship, such as free speech, the vote, and ownership of property.[13] The same root meanings are true of the Latin and Anglo-Saxon words for freedom. *Libertas* derives from *liberi,* "children," and was probably originally intended to distinguish the sons (*liberi*) in the family from the slaves and from women. The sons would inherit the property, and liberty was rooted in the ownership of property, while slaves and married women were excluded from property

12. See especially Bellah's programmatic article of 1967, "Civil Religion in America," in McLoughlin and Bellah, *Religion in America,* pp 3–23, and its somewhat more sober sequel, "American Civil Religion in the 1970's," *Anglican Theological Review,* Supplementary Series, no. 1 (July 1973), pp. 8–20. Bellah's affirmative assessment of the civil religion is supported by Benne and Hefner, *Defining America,* pp. 115–20, and challenged by Sydney E. Ahlstrom, "Requiem for Patriotic Piety," *Worldview,* 15 (August 1972): 9–11. See also the earlier critical comments by Peter Berger in *The Noise of Solemn Assemblies: Christian Commitment and the Religious Establishment in America* (New York: Doubleday, 1961). The debate over the civil religion is continued by several of the contributors to Elwyn A. Smith, ed., *The Religion of the Republic* (Philadelphia: Fortress Press, 1971).
13. For further discussion of the Greek understanding of freedom, see Chap. II, Sec. 2A.

rights. Finally, the Anglo-Saxon *frēo,* from which our word *freedom* derives, meant "to be fond of," "to hold dear," and probably designated the men who were "dear to [i.e., akin to] the chief," hence not enslaved.

The Hebrew language represents a partial contrast to the Indo-European tradition. The Hebrews made an essential contribution to the cause of freedom by rejecting the tribalism, cultic deities, and sacred monarchies of other ancient peoples. The Aramaean nomads developed a passion for independence and were impatient with external controls of any sort. The Israelites experienced Yahweh as their Liberator from bondage in Egypt. At the same time, they shared in the practice of slavery common to the ancient Near East, according to which debtors and captives in battle could be placed in servitude, but usually only for stated periods and under strict legal safeguards (cf. Ex. 21:1–11; Deut. 15:12–18). The prophets condemned social injustice, envisioning a future messianic kingdom of peace, justice, and freedom on earth; and Jeremiah in particular, reminding the people of their release from Egyptian bondage, demanded the liberation of all Hebrew slaves (34:8–16). Yet the Hebraic language lacked a specific concept of freedom. The root *chāphaš,* meaning "free" in the sense of free from slavery, free of charge, released from obligation, willing, occurs some twenty-four times in the Old Testament. But the substantive formed from it, *chuphᵉšāh,* is found only once, and in a context where slavery is accepted: "If a man lies carnally with a woman who is a slave, betrothed to another man and not yet ransomed or given her freedom [*chuphᵉšâh*], an inquiry shall be held" (Lev. 19:20). Without a specific and common terminology, the problematic of freedom did not emerge in ancient Israel. The freedom of the individual, though presupposed, was subordinated to the interests of the covenant community; and democratic political institutions did not develop as in the Greek city-states.

One may conclude by saying that the concept of freedom has been flawed on the basis of its linguistic heritage because

it presupposes and even sanctions the distinction between ascendant and oppressed peoples, the distinction between master and
slave, citizen and alien, male and female. Linguistically, the
word freedom is a product of those who are masters and who
define their mastery vis-à-vis slavery.

> The conception of freedom implies its antithesis. Free men only
> exist where there are unfree men. The awareness of freedom
> could only arise in a place where men lived together with others
> who were not independent but had a master over them whom
> they served and who controlled their lives. . . . Historically it
> was the existence of the unfree, the slaves, that first gave the
> others the feeling that they themselves were free.[14]

The concept of freedom is flawed, not only because it has been
accommodated to the institution of slavery, but also because, by
defining freedom as autonomy and as membership in an exclusive
clan or caste, it tended to mean the right to exploit the natural
environment and other human beings to one's own gain and the
gain of one's group. This possibility was not fully realized until
the modern era. John Hope Franklin notes that the sort of freedom which came to light in the Renaissance and again on the
American frontier—namely, "the freedom to destroy freedom,
the freedom of some to exploit the rights of others"[15]—created the
modern institution of slavery and the slave trade. It is no accident that the white aristocracy of the antebellum South sensed a
peculiar affinity to the classical world. The white column became
the symbol of a certain type of freedom, founded upon slavery:
behind the white columns lived a free man, but behind the house
with the white columns dwelled the slaves who made the freedom
of the man possible.

B. THE HERITAGE OF EXPLOITATION
    AND ESTRANGEMENT IN AMERICA

The American experiment in freedom was unable to escape
the fault, contradiction, and failure that have characterized the

14. Max Pohlenz, *Freedom in Greek Life and Thought: The History of an Ideal*,
trans. Carl Lofmark (Dordrecht: D. Reidel Publishing Co., 1966), p. 3.
15. John Hope Franklin, *From Slavery to Freedom: A History of Negro Americans*
(3d ed.; New York: Vintage Books, 1969), pp. 43, 173–174.

human struggle to be free. What was already clear to Jonathan Edwards in the middle of the eighteenth century, and should have become evident to American leadership in the course of the nineteenth century, is now indelibly a part of the national consciousness in the year of the Bicentennial of the Republic. During the sixties and early seventies, the last vestiges of American innocence were lost, and it is difficult for us to dream any more, to remember what America might have been, or to imagine what it might still become. The traumas of the last few years tend to obscure the fact that the loss of innocence and the faulting of freedom are not recent phenomena but rather were present, embryonically at least, almost from the beginning of the American experience. The fault as such is not peculiar to the American people but is a universal affliction of the human condition. What is distinctive about America has been its grandeur of vision and greatness of promise, combined with a tragic heritage of exploitation and estrangement.

In the next few pages I shall examine this heritage—not exhaustively but representatively—by calling attention to four major points at which the vision of a new nation, conceived in liberty, has been faulted through exploitation and an ensuing estrangement: *the land, American Indians, blacks,* and *women.* Then I shall analyze certain common patterns in this fourfold heritage, especially as they bear upon the problems of today.

(1) The Land

The environmental crisis did not begin with the technological revolution. It had its origin with the attitude toward the land on the part of the first white explorers and settlers. This attitude stood in stark contrast to that of the native Americans whom the Europeans encountered in the wilderness. The Indians had no concept of private property, and land was not a merchantable commodity. It could be occupied and used by tribes or other communal groups, and boundary lines demarcating the territory of tribes could be established, but land could not be owned or possessed by individuals. The white colonists brought with them

European notions of the private ownership of property; lands could be bought and sold through the exchange of money and paper titles. In their dealings with Indians, whites kept imposing *their* view of land on the former, not recognizing alternative possibilities, and accusing the Indians of bad faith when presumably "legal" contracts were violated.[16] Since the Indians had not "taken possession" of more than a tiny fraction of the land by settling, cultivating, and "subduing" it, it was assumed that the vast wildernesses of the New World were "vacant," available for the taking by white civilizers. The theological justification for this possession of the land was succinctly stated in a sermon by John Cotton in 1630:

> [It is] a Principle in Nature, That in a vacant soyle, he that taketh possession of it, and bestoweth culture and husbandry upon it, his Right it is. And the ground of this is from the grand Charter given to *Adam* and his posterity in Paradise, *Gen.* 1, 28. *Multiply, and replenish the earth, and subdue it.* If therefore any sonne of *Adam* come and finde a place empty, he hath liberty to come, and fill, and subdue the earth there.[17]

On this basis, then, frontiersmen moved up the rivers to hunt animals and trap furs, settlers followed to claim the land for their farms, agricultural entrepreneurs established great plantations to raise lucrative cash crops in the frontier lands of the South and Southwest, speculators moved westward in the quest for gold and other precious metals, coastal cities grew in population with new waves of immigrants, and towns began to dot the interior of the continent. The immensity of the land seemed to protect it from damage; no sense dawned of the limits and fragility of nature; and prodigal attitudes developed that have prevailed ever since. In his Second Annual Message to Congress (1830), Andrew Jackson epitomized the prevailing atitude:

16. See D'Arcy McNickle, "Indian and European: Indian-White Relations from Discovery to 1887," in *American Indians and American Life,* ed. G. E. Simpson and J. M. Yinger, vol. 311 of *The Annals of the American Academy of Political and Social Science* (May 1957), pp. 5–6.
17. Wilcomb E. Washburn, ed., *The Indian and the White Man* (Documents in American Civilization Series; New York: Anchor Books, 1964), p. 103. Another frequently cited text, and one reflected in Cotton's last sentence, was Ps. 115:16: "The heavens are the Lord's heavens, but the earth he has given to the sons of men."

. . . true Philanthropy could not wish to see this continent restored to the condition in which it was found by our forefathers. What good man would prefer a country covered with forests and ranged by a few thousand savages to our extensive Republic, studded with cities, towns, and prosperous farms, embellished with all the improvements which art can devise or industry execute, occupied by more than twelve million happy people, and filled with all the blessings of liberty, civilization, and religion? [18]

Jackson could scarcely have foreseen that the "twelve million happy people" would grow to some 215 million not so happy ones by 1976, and that the vast increase in population, combined with the advent of technological power, would produce an environmental crisis that threatens to ravish irretrievably a beautiful and once virgin continent.

Modern science and technology have fostered attitudes toward the natural world that encourage what Roszak calls the rape of the earth: nature is an object to be measured, calculated, controlled, and if necessary exploited for human benefit. Urban-industrial society has created both the need and the means of exploitation: depletion of natural resources in order to sustain ever-higher living standards; pollution of air, soil, and water; development of wilderness areas for tourism, travel, camping, and industry; the increasing urbanization of life and creation of an artificial living environment for human beings. Symptomatic of our arrogance is the assumption that technology will be able to solve whatever problems it creates, and hence that there are no limits to what the human species can know, do, and achieve.[19]

Together with the exploitation of the land has gone an increasing estrangement from it. Most Americans are no longer able to enter into an unmediated relationship with nature. This is the case not only because of our extreme reliance on protective, labor-saving, and recreational devices, but also because of a changed attitude toward nature itself. Gibson Winter points out that from the point of view of scientific technology, nature is un-

18. Quoted in McNickle, "Indian and European," p. 9.
19. Theodore Roszak, *Where the Wasteland Ends* (New York: Anchor Books, 1973), pp. 3–22, 212–216.

derstood merely as a complex of energies to be analyzed and controlled. "The reduction of everything to energy leaves no place for mediation of holiness and grace in places, things, persons, and communities. Nothing is left to elicit commitment or trust." The result is that the world is evacuated of meaning and coherence, and men and women are left alone in a boundaryless void, in a state of "technologized worldlessness."[20]

(2) American Indians

The attitude of white Europeans toward the Indians of North America may be taken as prototypical in some degree of their later treatment of other native or seminative American groups (Latin Americans, Puerto Ricans, Chicanos, Eskimos, etc.), and indeed of their attitude toward peoples of the third world generally. The first white men to conquer North America were not the Pilgrim settlers in New England but the Spaniards who entered Mexico in 1519 and then moved northward in quest of gold and fabled Indian treasures. The atrocities of the conquistadors were vividly described by Bishop Bartolomé de las Casas in 1552. He reported that they baptized the Indians, then enslaved them, exploited their labor, plundered their riches, and in the course of forty years had murdered some twelve to fifteen million men, women, and children. All that was accomplished by this senseless tyranny was to ravage the ancient civilization of the Aztec, Maya, Pueblo, and other Indian peoples, which was considerably higher and more refined than that of the conquistadors.[21]

Awareness that the first Americans were not displaced white Europeans, and indeed that the latter were preceded by vast, ancient, and mysterious civilizations in the "new" world, dawned gradually upon the English colonists and constituted a peculiar surd in an otherwise unambiguous sense of destiny. These native

---

20. Winter, "The Question of Liberty in a Technologized World," pp. 81–82, 90–92.
21. C. W. Ceram, *The First American: A Story of North American Archaeology* (New York: Mentor Books, 1971), pp. 32, 55–59, 77–79, 82–85. Joseph Comblin suggests that the freedom of the conquistador epitomized "the self-affirmation of the isolated and autonomous individual." "Freedom and Liberation as Theological Concepts," in *The Mystical and Political Dimension of the Christian Faith*, ed. C. Geffré and G. Gutiérrez, *Concilium*, vol. 96 (New York: Herder and Herder, 1974), p. 99.

peoples were misnamed, being neither "red" nor "Indian." "Some of the clergy," writes Ceram, "were of the opinion that the Indians were not human beings at all, since there was no mention of them in the Bible. . . . Cotton Mather . . . asserted, not metaphorically but literally, that *the devil in person* had brought these Red Men to America."[22]   Indians were commonly referred to as "savages" (wild men), "red devils," sometimes even as "beasts" or "animals." [23]

Thomas Jefferson was among the first to engage in a scientific archaeological study of Indian remains, and in his *Notes on Virginia* (1781) he propounded what later proved to be the correct theory that the Indians first migrated to America from Asia via the Bering Straits.[24]   By contrast with some of his compatriots, Jefferson sought to minimize what appeared to be the immense cultural and ethnic differences between native Indians and white Europeans, even envisioning a mixture of blood and a joint conquest of the continent. He did this, however, as Winthrop Jordan points out, "by transforming the Indian into a degraded yet basically noble brand of white man." The degradation he attributed to the harshness of the environment, which, if overcome through civilizing contact with the West, would allow Indians to become essentially white in behavior, physical characteristics, and mental ability.[25]   In fact, many early colonists believed that they had a mission "to make Europeans out of the New World inhabitants, in social practices and in value concepts."[26]   This was to be accomplished not only by educating and Christianizing the Indians, but also by inducing them to change from subsistence to commercial hunting and to agriculture, since it was assumed that the latter represented a more "civilized" mode of life. Moreover,

22. Ceram, *The First American*, pp. 249–250; cf. p. 88.
23. Especially revealing is a letter written by Hugh Henry Brackenridge (c. 1782) in which reference is made to "the animals, vulgarly called Indians." Later in the letter Brackenridge acknowledges that "they have the shapes of men and may be of human species, but certainly in their present state they approach nearer the character of Devils. . . ." *The Indian and the White Man*, pp. 111, 116.
24. Ceram, *The First American*, pp. 26–32.
25. Winthrop D. Jordan, *White Over Black: American Attitudes Toward the Negro, 1550-1812* (Baltimore: Penguin Books, 1969), pp. 477–478.
26. McNickle, "Indian and European," p. 2.

efforts were made during the early years to maintain peaceful relations with the tribes, entering into trade agreements with them, and taking special care not to occupy their lands without their consent or the purchase of their "title" to it. Treaties were signed establishing boundaries beyond which white settlers could not move.[27]

But the government found it increasingly difficult to adhere to this policy after the population began moving inexorably westward following independence from Great Britain. Not only was there an insatiable hunger for land, but also the confidence that Indians could be peacefully "civilized" was fading. By 1830, writes McNickle, the possibility "of allowing the Indian people a chance to maintain their integrity as a people" was gone forever. "From the latter date onward, it became a question of how soon, and by what devices, the extinguishment of the Indian past would be effected." On May 28, 1830, Andrew Jackson signed the Indian Removal Act, which gave the president authority to remove all Indian tribes east of the Mississippi River to new lands in the West, title to which would be guaranteed in perpetuity. Forced evacuations followed, during which hundreds of thousands of Indians were dislocated and many thousands died.[28]

Once the process of dispossession had begun, however, it would be carried to its logical conclusion. The General Allotment Act of 1887 (the Dawes Act) provided the legal basis for breaking up the communal land ownership of the tribes, dividing their reservations, assigning a parcel to each man, woman, and child (thus presumably transforming Indians from "nomads" into farmers and cattlemen), and declaring all the rest "surplus" lands, which were opened for white homesteading at $2.50 per acre. By this means, the Indians were dispossessed of some 91 million acres, or two-thirds of their land base, between 1887 and 1933, and 90,000 persons were left landless. Justification for this policy was provided

27. Ibid., pp. 2–6; Francis P. Prucha, *American Indian Policy in the Formative Years: The Indian Trade and Intercourse Acts 1790–1834* (Cambridge: Harvard University Press, 1962), chap. I.
28. McNickle, "Indian and European," pp. 9–10; Prucha, *American Indian Policy*, chaps. IX–X.

on several grounds: Indians could not claim to *own* the land over which they ranged; they were violent and bloodthirsty by nature; and civilization has bestowed upon the white man a special burden to uplift weaker peoples—the latter view being reinforced by the growing popularity of Social Darwinism.[29]   On the remaining reservations, programs of forced acculturation were launched, the logic of which was concisely stated by the Commissioner of Indian Affairs in 1901:

> To civilize . . . is to educate, and to educate means breaking up of tribal customs, manners, and barbarous usages, and the assumption of the manners, usages, and customs of the superior race with whom they are thereafter to be thrown into contact.[30]

The effects on Indian life of nearly two centuries of exploitation were of course devastating. The aboriginal Indian population of North America at the time of the first white settlements is estimated at 750,000 to one million, but by 1850 it had been reduced to 250,000 as a result of disease, dissipation, starvation, massacre, removal, and maladaptation; and Indians appeared to be a dying race. By 1900 the population had dropped to 237,000, but then it began a slow climb, which accelerated rapidly after 1950.[31]   Today there are over 800,000 Indians in the United States, which means that the population has been rebuilt to the approximate level of some three centuries ago. This reflects considerable improvement in medical, educational, and living conditions, but Indians as a whole continue to be a destitute and exploited minority, still subject to repressive policies of the Bureau of Indian Affairs.

Despite this tragic history, Indians have not suffered as much as African slaves and their descendants in America. Indians proved

29. Theodore H. Haas, "The Legal Aspects of Indian Affairs from 1887 to 1957," in *American Indians and American Life*, pp. 12–15. The arguments of Theodore Roosevelt are especially instructive in this regard; see *The Indian and the White Man*, pp 131–136. See also D. S. Otis, *The Dawes Act and the Allotment of Indian Lands*, ed. Francis P. Prucha (Norman: University of Oklahoma Press, 1973).
30. Cited by Howard L. Harrod, *Mission Among the Blackfeet* (Norman: University of Oklahoma Press, 1971), p. 83. In chaps. IV–VII Harrod describes the effects of forced acculturation on the Blackfeet Indians of Montana.
31. See J. Nixon Hadley, "The Demography of the American Indians," in *American Indians and American Life*, pp. 23–30.

not readily adaptable to servitude—although attempts were made to enslave them—because of their autonomous culture, familiarity with the environment, and hostility toward the chattel slavery practiced by Englishmen in America. Indians were capable of defending themselves and of exacting a bloody price for their exploitation, and they had to be dealt with as nations or tribes rather than as isolated individuals. They resisted assimilation into white society and retained an autonomy and mystique that exacted grudging respect. The ideology of color prejudice did not apply quite so unambiguously to Indians as to Africans (in other words, the "black" African was *darker* than the "red" Indian). Most important, as Jordan points out,

> The Indian became for Americans a symbol of their American experience. . . . Confronting the Indian in America was a testing experience, common to all the colonies. Conquering the Indian symbolized and personified the conquest of the American difficulties, the surmounting of the wilderness. To push back the Indian was to prove the worth of one's own mission, to make straight in the desert a highway for civilization. With the Negro it was utterly different.[32]

(3) Black Slaves and White Prejudice[33]

Our attention might well focus on the special brutality, by contrast with other cultures, of the North American institution of slavery, which required black slaves to be held in perpetual servitude instead of for stated periods, and regarded them as property or chattel, with no civil rights and virtually no legal

32. Jordan, *White Over Black*, pp. 89–91. Jordan notes in the Preface that his study of "American Attitudes Toward the Negro" deals also with Indians, "for it is impossible to see clearly what Americans thought of Negroes without ascertaining their almost invariably contrary thoughts concerning Indians" (p. xiv).
33. This section presupposes my earlier study, *Children of Freedom: Black Liberation in Christian Perspective* (Philadelphia: Fortress Press, 1974). I do not intend to repeat the results of that book but to build upon them, drawing especially on the excellent work by Winthrop D. Jordan, *White Over Black: American Attitudes Toward the Negro, 1550–1812.* The subject of black oppression and white racism is one that very few white Americans can address with a clear conscience. Since writing *Children of Freedom*, I have become aware in new ways of my own complicity in the very problems that I sought to elucidate. I find myself, with many others, confronted by a tragic situation, which is objectified institutionally in ways that tend both to entrap individuals and to magnify their personal responsibility. Such is the character of human bondage, for which only a saving deliverance will suffice.

protections.[34]   However, I shall be concerned primarily with the shaping of white attitudes toward blacks, and with the contradiction between these attitudes and the ideals of the Declaration of Independence.   Although "bond slavery" was a "memory trace of long standing" in their heritage, the English had no clear model for chattel slavery, and they were drawn into slave trading by the example of the Spanish and the Portuguese,[35] for whom, however, well-established traditions assured a more humane treatment of slaves and their eventual emancipation.   Unfortunately, these traditions were not transferred to the West Indies, Virginia, Maryland, and the Carolinas, where the institution of slavery developed with a logic and completeness unparalleled elsewhere, partially because of the way in which an unrestrained capitalism responded to economic exigencies.[36]   Although the fact of slavery, economically induced, tended to generate prejudice toward the enslaved person, clearly a prior disposition (or "prejudice") to enslave certain groups of people and not others must have existed.   According to Jordan,

> *difference,* surely, was the indispensable key to the degradation of Negroes in English America. . . . It may be taken as given that there would have been no enslavement without economic need, that is, without persistent demand for labor in underpopulated colonies.   Of crucial importance, too, was the fact that for cultural reasons Negroes were relatively helpless in the face of European aggressiveness and technology.   In themselves, however, these two elements will not explain the enslavement of Indians and Negroes. . . . What was it about Indians and Negroes which set them apart, which rendered them *different* from Englishmen, which made them special candidates for degradation?[37]

We have already noted that the "difference" of Indians from whites was relativized in the minds of the latter, and that the Indians resisted enslavement.   But the alleged difference of

34. On this subject, see in particular Stanley M. Elkins, *Slavery: A Problem in American Institutional and Intellectual Life* (2d ed.; Chicago: University of Chicago Press, 1968) , chap. II.
35. Jordan, *White Over Black,* pp. 52, 56.
36. See Elkins, *Slavery,* pp. 43–52, 61–62.
37. Jordan, *White Over Black,* p. 91; cf. the whole of chap. II, pp. 44–98.

Negroes remained absolute and undoubtedly continues to be the major factor in white attitudes toward blacks in America, although the reasons for viewing blacks as different have shifted to some degree. At the outset, the "heathenism" of African slaves was a factor of considerable importance in the minds of the English colonists, for whom the word "Christian" was synonymous with white, English, civilized, and free. Christians could not be enslaved but heathens could be, and one of the reasons given for their enslavement was to convert them to Christianity—although later it was necessary to assert that the conversion of slaves did not entail their manumission.[38] This suggests that the appeal to heathenism was more of a rationale than a real motive for enslavement, although the alien character of African religion has always seemed to alarm white Americans. Together with the heathenism of black Africans was a belief in their savage (i.e., uncivilized) behavior and above all their sexual passion. Many interpreters have regarded the attribution of unusually potent and primitive sexual powers to Negroes as representing the displacement of white libidinal drives, which could not be openly acknowledged; likewise, the repulsion toward blacks would be the obverse of a powerful sexual attraction for them.[39]

Beneath all these differences lay the irreducible fact of the Negro's dark skin color, which by the end of the seventeenth century had become an independent rationale for enslavement. Well before their contact with dark-skinned people, the concept of *black* had accumulated an intensely negative connotation for Englishmen, as evidenced by this definition of pre-sixteenth century usage in the *Oxford English Dictionary*: "Deeply stained with dirt; soiled, dirty, foul. . . . Having dark or deadly purposes; malignant; pertaining to or involving death, deadly; baneful, disastrous, sinister. . . . Foul, iniquitous, atrocious, horrible, wicked. . . . Indicating disgrace, censure, liability to punishment,

38. Ibid., pp. 20–24, 91–97; John Hope Franklin, *From Slavery to Freedom: A History of Negro Americans*, pp. 75–76, 86–87.
39. Jordan, *White Over Black*, pp. 24–28, 458–459, 467, 471, 491, 578–579, 582; Gibson Winter, *Being Free: Reflections on America's Cultural Revolution* (New York: Macmillan, 1970), pp. 122–123.

etc." These negative meanings of *black* were inherited from the symbolism for good and evil deeply imbedded in the collective unconscious of Indo-European peoples—light versus dark, white versus black, purity versus stain—but they seem to have attained a special potency in the English language. The description of Africans as "black," for which we have the early English voyagers to thank, represents an exaggeration of their actual complexion (just as "white" exaggerates the color of light-skinned peoples), thus betraying the significance attributed to this physiological characteristic. Other distinctive traits, such as hair, lips, and nose, while often mentioned, were of lesser importance. The outcome of all these factors—economically induced exploitation, lack of a "humane" tradition of slavery, accentuation of cultural and physiological differences—led to a *chattel racial slavery* in the American colonies, which had no parallel in the ancient or modern worlds, and which stood in the starkest contradiction to the principle of equality and unalienable human rights.[40]

The contradiction runs as a faulted vein through the whole of American history. It stands forth clearly personally as well as institutionally, and perhaps can be seen in its most tragic dimension in the struggle with the problem of slavery on the part of two great architects of American democracy, Thomas Jefferson and Abraham Lincoln. Jefferson serves as a kind of paradigm of white American attitudes. His "central dilemma," according to Jordan, was that "he hated slavery but thought Negroes inferior to white men." His personal entanglement in slavery was genuinely tragic, for as a Virginia planter he found himself economically dependent upon a system he hated, and his precarious financial condition precluded the possibility of freeing more than a few of his slaves. Thus at best he sought to be a benevolent and solicitous slave master; but this, together with what was very likely a continuing liaison with one of his own slaves, Sally Hemings, must only have increased his sense of guilt.

40. Jordan, *White Over Black,* pp. 4–11, 96–98, 458, 509, 512 ff.; cf. also Frantz Fanon, *Black Skin, White Masks,* trans. Charles Markmann (New York: Grove Press, 1967), pp. 183, 188–191.

Jefferson was thoroughly and personally committed to the natural rights philosophy, to which he gave classic expression in the opening words of the Declaration of Independence: "We hold these truths to be self-evident, that all men are created equal, that they are endowed by their Creator with certain unalienable Rights, that among these are Life, Liberty, and the pursuit of Happiness." Since Negroes are unquestionably human, they cannot rightfully be deprived of their liberty, and the system of slavery is profoundly wrong, a violation of the laws of God and nature. Jefferson knew this and felt it deeply—although more, to be sure, as a philosophical principle than as a concrete matter involving the particular Negroes he held in bondage. At the same time, he was unable to rid himself of the belief that Negroes were mentally inferior to white men, and that this innate difference could never be overcome by education and changes in environment. His writings on the subject later provided some of the best ammunition for the proslavery argument. He was able to avoid outright contradiction with his egalitarian principles only by means of a bit of casuistry: Negroes fully possess what is essential to being human, namely, a "moral sense," and in this respect are perfectly equal to whites; but persons who are morally equal are gifted with different mental endowments—not only individually, it seems, but by race as well. Jefferson never used this argument to justify slavery; rather, aware of his own intellectual confusion and of the practical political difficulties that stood in the way of emancipation, he grew increasingly silent on the subject.[41]

Lincoln's attitude toward Negroes and slavery has been the subject of much scholarly discussion in recent years.[42] He was not

41. Jordan, *White Over Black*, chap. XII; Hofstadter, *The American Political Tradition*, pp. 18–44. Many of the details are spelled out in Fawn M. Brodie, *Thomas Jefferson: An Intimate History* (New York: Norton, 1974).
42. Of the many books on this subject, see especially Benjamin Quarles, *Lincoln and the Negro* (New York: Oxford University Press, 1962). Others include William O. Douglas, *Mr. Lincoln and the Negro* (New York: Atheneum, 1963); Ernest S. Cox, *Lincoln's Negro Policy* (Los Angeles: Noontide, 1968) ; John S. Wright, *Lincoln and the Politics of Slavery* (Reno: University of Nevada Press, 1970) ; and Arthur Zilversmit, ed., *Lincoln on Black and White: A Documentary History* (Belmont, Calif.: Wadsworth, 1971). In this section I have been especially helped by William J. Wolf, *Lincoln's Religion* (Philadelphia: Pilgrim Press, 1970), and by the chapter on Lincoln in Hofstadter's *The American Political Tradition*, pp. 93–136.

free of racial prejudice, as evidenced by remarks made during the debates with Douglas, and he appeared to remain publicly indifferent to slavery until it became a political issue that he could exploit. But he was capable of transcending earlier perspectives and of deepening his awareness of what must be done. When he was finally drawn into the debates over whether to extend slavery into new territories that were not part of the old South, he attacked the proslavery arguments with brilliance, force, and deep conviction. His argument against slavery had two main components. The first was based on his conviction that the Declaration of Independence had the force of divine revelation, especially its great affirmation that "all men are created equal." God's law of freedom in the creation of man was to be progressively embodied in the positive legislation of states, which meant that slavery must disappear from the face of the earth. In the second place, he regarded slavery as a form of stealing, a deprecation of human work, a denial of the biblical injunction, "In the sweat of *thy* face"—not that of others—"shalt thou eat bread."

Thus Lincoln was persuaded that slavery was manifestly unjust and opposed to the will of God and our "national axioms." But at the same time he believed that the Constitution protected the right to hold slaves in the original slave states and to have the fugitive slave law enforced. The only constitutional means of attacking slavery was by preventing its spread into new territories and states, thereby assuring its ultimate extinction "in God's good time." The Constitution itself took a compromising position on the question of slavery, and Lincoln's interpretation may well have been correct—although he must have agonized over the contradiction between the principles of the Declaration and the practical politics of the Constitution. In any case, his strict constitutionalism caused him to oppose the abolitionists and to proceed with great caution even after he assumed the presidency. The Emancipation Proclamation is a case in point. Because the federal government had no constitutional power to interfere with the practice of slavery in the states, the emancipation of slaves could be legally justified only as a war measure, designed to disrupt the social fabric of the Confederacy and to rob it of its greatest wartime resource, slave labor. At the same time, Lincoln's decision to free the slaves was made in response to what he regarded God's will to be; he had long sought divine guidance on the matter, and by the fall of 1862 was persuaded that the proper time and circumstances for the act had arrived. It is true that the Proclamation had little practical effect, for it applied only to slaves in the Confederate states, who for the moment were beyond the ken of federal authority. But it laid the foundation for the ultimate abolition of slavery throughout the United States by means of the Thirteenth Amendment, which Lincoln conceived and skillfully guided through Congress in 1864–65. For a while he had toyed with the possibility of a compensated emancipation (again because of constitutional safeguards for property) and a voluntary colonization of former slaves abroad, but eventually put these fanciful notions aside in favor of the only genuine solution. Such were the personal, political, and institutional ambiguities in which the greatest American president found himself entangled.

Lincoln was profoundly aware of the tragic and fateful significance of slavery in the context of American history and institutions. Slavery must be destroyed to save not only the Union but also democracy, "the last, best hope of earth." If some are enslaved, none can be free: "In giving freedom to the slave, we assure freedom to the free." More than this, Lincoln viewed the Civil War as God's judgment on and punishment for the nation's refusal to put slavery "in process of ultimate extinction." In the Second Inaugural, his profoundest address, he had a vision of the price that must be paid by the American people for their terrible offense against humanity:

> If we shall suppose that American slavery is one of those offenses which, in the providence of God, must needs come, but which, having continued through His appointed time, He now wills to remove, and that He gives to both North and South this terrible war as the woe due to those by whom the offense came, shall we discern therein any departure from those divine attributes which

the believers in a Living God always ascribe to Him? Fondly do we hope, fervently do we pray, that this mighty scourge of war may speedily pass away. Yet, if God wills that it continue, until all the wealth piled by the bond-man's two hundred and fifty years of unrequited toil shall be sunk, and until every drop of blood drawn with the lash, shall be paid with another drawn with the sword, as was said three thousand years ago, so still it must be said, "The judgments of the Lord, are true and righteous altogether."

The war was to end within the year. But perhaps even Lincoln could not have foreseen that the offense would not yet be repaid in a hundred years, and that its scourge would continue to burden Americans, black and white, well beyond the second centennial of the founding of the Republic.

(4) Women

The vision of a new nation did not hold much promise of a new beginning for the women who accompanied the first settlers to America. Of the eighteen married women who arrived with the other *Mayflower* passengers on the shores of Massachusetts in 1620, only four survived the first rugged winter. It would take three centuries to attain basic human rights for women, culminating in the ratification of the Nineteenth Amendment in 1920. Even then the work would be far from finished. The colonists brought with them attitudes toward women long established in English common law and in Western culture and religion. It was a man's world: woman's *place* was in the home; her *role* was defined in relation to the needs of man as mother, wife, sex-object and cult-object; her *subordination* was justified not only because of the frailty of her body and mind, but also as a punishment for the sin of Eve and because of biblical injunctions that she remain silent, subordinate, and obedient.[43] Puritan New England was as rigid

43. See Eleanor Flexner, *Century of Struggle: The Woman's Rights Movement in the United States* (Cambridge: Harvard University Press, 1959), pp. 4, 8 and Elizabeth Janeway, *Man's World, Woman's Place: A Study in Social Mythology* (New York: Dell Publishing Co., 1971), p. 7–20. On psychological and theological factors in the male domination of women, see the discussion of "sexism" in Chap. IV, Sec. 3c (1).

a theocratic patriarchy as has ever existed on the face of the earth.[44]

For at least two centuries, women in the New World were treated as virtual slaves. Married women in particular suffered what Elizabeth Cady Stanton called "civil death." They had no legal existence apart from their husbands, who in effect "owned" them and who by law could deprive them of liberty or punish them. They could not own property, had no title to their own earnings, could not sign contracts, had no claim to their children in the case of legal separation, and very limited means of redress by which to seek divorce. "Civil death" applied to single as well as married women in political, economic, and educational matters. They were of course denied the franchise (along with blacks, Indians, and nonpropertied white males), and were expected not to speak in public. In addition, women were paid very low wages (in 1833 it was estimated that they earned no more than one-fourth of men's wages and averaged $1.25 per week or less), were limited to unskilled jobs, were excluded from the professions on the grounds of incompetence, were provided virtually no opportunities for education outside the home until private schools for girls began to be established in the middle third of the nineteenth century (even then the opportunity was limited to the daughters of affluent families), and were expected to adhere to a more rigid code of moral conduct than men.[45]

The fates of blacks and women were linked together at several critical points in the history of the Republic: the antislavery movement of the 1830s and 1840s, the drive for woman suffrage in the first two decades of the twentieth century, and the civil

44. This was made clear by the challenge of Anne Hutchinson, who eventually was banished from the Massachusetts Bay Colony and excommunicated. Flexner, *Century of Struggle*, pp. 10–11.
45. Ibid., pp. 7–8, 23, 28, 44, 53–56, 63–64. An exhaustive catalog of these abuses, modeled after the Declaration of Independence, was drawn up in the form of a "Declaration of Sentiments" by Elizabeth Cady Stanton and Lucretia Mott for a Convention on Woman's Rights held in Seneca Falls, New York, July 1848. The text is reprinted in Aileen S. Kraditor, ed., *Up from the Pedestal: Selected Writings in the History of American Feminism* (Chicago: Quadrangle Books, 1968), pp. 184–188. The origin of the woman's rights movement is commonly dated from the Seneca Falls Convention. On the Convention, see Flexner, pp. 71–77.

rights movement of the 1960s. In the first and last of these, women who initially became involved in the struggle for black liberation moved on to address their own rights. Just the opposite occurred in the case of the suffrage movement, which achieved final success through an accommodation to white supremacy and Jim Crow laws. Regarding the first, the women who were drawn into the antislavery movement

> were the first conscious feminists, who would go to school in the struggle to free the slaves and, in the process, launch their own fight for equality. It was in the abolition movement that women first learned to organize, to hold public meetings, to conduct petition campaigns. As abolitionists they first won the right to speak in public, and began to evolve a philosophy of their place in society and of their basic rights. For a quarter of a century the two movements, to free the slave and liberate the woman, nourished and strengthened one another.[46]

The women who joined the American Anti-Slavery Society had never intended to tack feminism onto abolitionism, but the two issues became conjoined because it happened that the most interesting lecturers on slavery in the late 1830s were women—notably the Grimké sisters, Angelina and Sarah, who paved the way for many others: Lucy Stone, Lucretia Mott, Abby Kelley Foster, Susan B. Anthony (who became the leading organizer of the woman's movement for over half a century), and Sojourner Truth and Frances Harper (the first black women abolitionists). The Grimkés were true pioneers, and Angelina—a brilliant, naturally gifted orator who addressed large audiences throughout New England for a three-year period—once commented prophetically, "We Abolition Women are turning the world upside down." [47] Indeed they were, in ways that even they could only dimly foresee. Sarah in her writings and Angelina in her speeches insisted on *universal human* rights, regardless of race, color, or sex; for they perceived

46. Flexner, *Century of Struggle*, p. 41; cf. pp. 42–50. On the role of women in the abolition movement, see Aileen S. Kraditor, *Means and Ends in American Abolitionism* (New York: Pantheon Books, 1969), chap. 3; also Alma Lutz, *Crusade for Freedom: Women in the Antislavery Movement* (Boston: Beacon Press, 1968).
47. In a letter to a Negro friend, Sarah Douglass. Quoted in Lutz, *Crusade for Freedom*, p. 131.

that the arguments used against women's speaking (by other abolitionists) were very similar to those used against the Negro's
equality by slaveholders. Human rights are indivisible; and the
logic that leads to the oppression of one group can be used against
others as well.

However, the effect of an oppressive social structure is such as
to turn the interests of oppressed groups against each other, causing them to compete for the available concessions. Some progress
had been made prior to the Civil War in changing laws regarding
property, earnings, and guardianship of children, but not the vote.
Some feminist leaders were disappointed when, after the war, they
sensed that the interests of women were being put aside by their
former black and abolitionist allies in the effort to secure passage
of the Fourteenth Amendment, which guaranteed citizenship
rights to all citizens of the United States, but introduced the word
"male" into the Constitution for the first time (in such a way that
it qualified the word "citizen"). When Frederick Douglass, the
black abolitionist who from the beginning had been a staunch
advocate of women's rights as well, was challenged on this matter,
he replied by citing the rising violence against newly freed
Negroes in the South, and then told the women in effect: To you
the vote is desirable, to us it is vital.[48] With the ratification of the
Fifteenth Amendment, which guaranteed the right to vote for all
citizens regardless of "race, color, or previous condition of servitude," but not *sex*, it became apparent that a separate woman
suffrage amendment would be necessary, and there began a half-
century of work to secure its adoption.

As these labors progressed it seemed increasingly necessary to
the women that they must separate their struggle for the suffrage
from any continuing association with the cause of Negro rights.
Several factors conspired to bring this about. First, the suffrage
movement reached its height during the period of 1890–1920,
which was precisely when white racism was more virulent and

48. Aileen S. Kraditor, *The Ideas of the Woman Suffrage Movement 1890–1920*
(New York: Anchor Books, 1971), p. 140; see also Flexner, *Century of Struggle*, pp.
142–149.

widespread than at any other time since the Civil War (encouraged by Darwinism, the first migration of blacks to Northern cities,
the fears of Eastern and Southern European immigrants, etc.).
Moreover, it was during this period that Southern constitutional
conventions were adopting a variety of stratagems to deprive
Negroes of political power. The new generation of leaders in the
suffragist movement, who were almost all native-born middle-class
whites, shared the dominant race-consciousness of the time. In
the second place, they had shifted their strategy from arguments
based on justice (universal human rights, the consent of the
governed, etc.) to arguments based on expediency (society would
benefit in various ways from the vote of women). Obviously, it
would be "expedient" if the voting power of the "intelligent"
portion of the population (i.e., white Anglo-Saxon, mostly Protestant, men and women) could be increased, thus neutralizing the
influence of foreign-born immigrants and the "poor, ignorant,
and immoral" elements of society, whose access to the franchise
ought perhaps to be limited by educational and other voting re-
quirements. Finally, Southern support would be necessary to
secure the votes for a suffrage amendment in the Congress and
in the state legislatures, and women suffrage was sold in the South
principally by arguing that the enfranchisement of women would
insure the permanency of white supremacy in the South and the
salvation of Anglo-Saxon civilization generally.[49] In this fashion
two exploited groups, whose interests should have coincided since
they were both victims in different ways of white male domination, found themselves opposed to each other; and suspicion,
sometimes even outright hostility, continues to characterize relations between the black and women's liberation movements.[50]

The arguments against female suffrage used by the opponents of
the Nineteenth Amendment are significant for our purposes, for
they typify male attitudes toward women generally and help to

49. These factors are detailed brilliantly in Kraditor, *The Ideas of the Woman
Suffrage Movement,* chaps. 3, 7.
50. On this point, see Rosemary Ruether, "Crisis in Sex and Race: Black Theology
vs. Feminist Theology," *Christianity and Crisis,* 34 (April 15, 1974): 67–73.

account for male domination of women in other periods of
American history as well. "It was the link of woman to the home
that underlay the entire ideology," writes Kraditor.[51] "The [anti-
suffragists] regarded each woman's vocation as determined not by
her individual capacities or wishes but by her sex. Men were
expected to have a variety of ambitions and capabilities, but all
women were destined from birth to be full-time wives and
mothers." This ideology was defended by three arguments, theological, biological, and sociological. Theologically, it was asserted
that God had ordained different functions for man and woman,
that the place of the latter was the home where she was to obey her
husband, and that in public she was to remain seen, not heard.
Biologically, it was claimed that feminine psychological and physiological characteristics render women unsuitable for voting (they
are too emotional) and political life (they are too delicate to
withstand its turbulence). The sociological argument was the
most subtle, declaring that "social peace and the welfare of the
human race depended upon woman's staying home, having children, and keeping out of politics." Women would vote as a bloc,
causing conflict between the sexes; their femininity would be
destroyed by the rough and tumble of political life, causing them
to become aggressive and unladylike; besides, they can exercise a
greater and more wholesome influence on politics through the
proper rearing of their sons in the home; and finally women do
not really *want* to vote, as evidenced by the small minority of
active suffragists. The last two arguments, the biological and the
sociological, reflect what Elizabeth Janeway calls the myths of
female weakness and female power, the latter of which has always
proved more threatening to males, evoking the counter-myth of
weakness.[52] These myths are still with us, and the struggle for
woman's liberation continues today, focused more on psychological
and cultural factors than on basic political and economic rights.

51. Kraditor, *The Ideas of the Woman Suffrage Movement,* p. 12. Chap. 2 of this
book, on which I rely heavily, describes "the rationale of antisuffragism" in considerable detail.
52. Janeway, *Man's World, Woman's Place,* pp. 51–57, 279–285.

C. Common Patterns in the Faulting of the American Vision

From the exploitation of the land, Indians, blacks, and women, it is possible to deduce certain common patterns in the way that freedom has been faulted in America—perhaps even to speak of "a flaw inherent in these 'almost chosen people' themselves." [53] These patterns have helped to shape American attitudes toward other ethnic and social groups, the peoples of the third world, the poor of all lands, the youthful counter culture—indeed, all those who seem to stand outside the main stream of white middle-class values. Now even the middle class finds itself threatened by the very technology and material prosperity it has prized so highly. I shall attempt to isolate and describe the following patterns: (1) a triple idolatry of nation, untrammeled individualism, and private property; (2) an apotheosis of force, violence, and competition; (3) a fear of cultural, racial, and sexual "difference"; and finally (4) an accentuation of flawed forms of freedom by modern technology.

(1) The most characteristic idolatry resulted from an undialectical overextension of the symbolic framework in which Americans initially understood their divinely given mission to establish a kingdom of freedom. It was the prideful presumption that the American Republic *is* the unambiguous realization of this kingdom. From this presumption developed an elaborate mythology of the white man's destiny to subdue and civilize the continent, allowing nothing to stand in the way of progress. This myth permitted no recognition of finitude and limit, and completely lacked a sense of prophetic judgment. Protestant Christianity took on the worst aspects of a civil religion, providing ideological sanction for policies presumed to be in the national interest, extolling American innocence, virtue, and self-worship. It was this sort of national idolatry that Jonathan Edwards foresaw as implicit in the Great Awakening, causing him to withdraw his support from it, and to seek to regain his orientation through an act of "humbling"

53. Mead, "American History as a Tragic Drama," p. 349.

by living with the Indians.[54]   The quest for a creative, non-idolatrous way of relating the nation to the kingdom, the political to the transpolitical, the human struggle to create a free society to the divine gift of redemption, has been a perennial problem in American religious and institutional history, one which I shall address theologically in the chapters on the dialectics of liberation and the symbolics of freedom (Chapters VI, VII).

Edwards also perceived the possibility of an idolatrous individualism, predicated on the notion of a sinless, innocent, autonomous free will.[55]   This "American Adam," as R. W. B. Lewis described him,[56] stood at the beginning of a new epoch in human history, untrammeled by the burdens of the past, free to make of himself whatever he could, free to seek fortune and glory in a land of inexhaustible riches.   It was self-evident, of course, that the American Adam did not include Indians and Negroes, nor for that matter the latter-day immigrants from Eastern and Southern Europe.   And it is no accident that an American Eve never joined the mythical scene.   The understanding of freedom primarily in terms of individual autonomy is one of several points at which the American experience parallels that of the ancient Greeks.   In my analysis of the way in which the structures of freedom are transfigured by Christian faith, I shall seek a "decentering" of the autonomous individual, shifting the emphasis away from the self to intersubjective and transsubjective relations of freedom, which provide the foundation for authentic subjectivity (see Chapters III, VII).

Closely related to the autonomy of privileged white males was the idolatry of privatism and private property.   Perhaps the most grievous and persistent failing of American society has been the tendency to neglect the well-being of the social whole to the

54. See Bryant, "America as God's Kingdom," pp. 56, 79, 87; also Bellah, "American Civil Religion in the 1970's," pp. 11–13; and Benne and Hefner, *Defining America,* pp. 108–112.
55. Bryant, "America as God's Kingdom," pp. 82–83.
56. R. W. B. Lewis, *The American Adam: Innocence, Tragedy and Tradition in the Nineteenth Century* (Chicago: University of Chicago Press, 1955), pp. 1–10.

advantage of private property and capital.[57] This flaw can be traced back to the distrust, on the part of the authors of the Constitution, of the common man, democratic rule, and the revolutionary principles espoused in the Declaration of Independence. Richard Hofstadter points out that the Constitution was a product of the propertied classes and that the Fathers were not interested in extending liberty to slaves and indentured servants. Rather they were concerned with freedom from fiscal uncertainty and from attacks on property by popular insurrection.[58] The predominant freedom in America was to be a freedom for property, and the concepts of freedom and private property became inextricably linked. Jordan notes the Lockean source of this notion: ". . . men possessed a 'property' in both themselves and their possessions; they had a natural right to their life, liberty, and 'estates.' "[59] When the two conflicted, the right to property outweighed the right to human freedom, as the fugitive slave laws demonstrated. We have observed that the early settlers assumed that land and other natural resources could and should be privatized; this assumption continues today when private energy companies are permitted to buy up natural resources such as coal, oil, and gas. In short, the sanctity of private property is an unquestioned dogma of the American tradition. Unrestrained capitalism, predicated on private ownership of wealth and resources, has led to the exploitation of land and labor for personal gain and profit. Against the idolatry of privatism and the concomitant neglect of social well-being, I shall argue for a communal understanding of freedom that is not based on the special privileges of private ownership and private membership.

(2) Chapter IV will examine the foundation of all forms of idolatry in an apotheosis of the human will-to-power, which entails a refusal to recognize the limits of finite, creaturely being and the tendency to set oneself up as an omnipotent god. Gibson

---

57. Cf. Mead, "American History as a Tragic Drama," pp. 354–358; Benne and Hefner, *Defining America*, pp. 109–111.
58. Hofstadter, *The American Political Tradition*, pp. 4–5, 10–16.
59. Jordan, *White Over Black*, pp. 350–351.

Winter regards white will-to-power as the underlying source of slavery and racism, and as the root of a tendency toward violence and force in American life.[60] In the arguments opposing woman suffrage, an attitude surfaced that tells something significant about the American fault. Women should not vote, it was said, because they lack the physical strength to enforce their mandate through the use of arms. Force, in other words, was believed to be the ultimate basis of government in America; peace was insured because minority elements knew that revolt or resistance could not succeed. "Only those who possessed the *might* to secure the vote had the *right* to vote." [61] It is only a short step from this view to the philosophy that might makes right—or, as Theodore Roosevelt expressed it in justifying the dispossession of Indian lands, ". . . it was wholly impossible for any government to evolve order out of such chaos without resort to the ultimate arbitrator—the sword." [62] Such attitudes reflect a lingering distrust of democratic rule, the violence of frontier life, and the cutthroat competition of laissez-faire capitalism.

(3) The sanction of force and violence in political affairs reflects an underlying fear—the fear of weakness and impotence,[63] above all the fear of cultural, racial, and sexual "difference." Despite the great ethnic diversity of the people as a whole, Americans have been insensitive to and have tended to reject genuine cultural and racial difference. "The others" must become like us or remain permanently alien; and it is upon "the others" that both the libidinal drives and the sense of impotence of the dominant white class have been projected.[64] The inheritance of color prejudice from our European forebears exacerbated the problem of "difference" with respect to Indians and especially blacks, who have remained beyond the ken of acceptability for most Americans. The alleged differences between the sexes, which serve to justify male domina-

60. Winter, *Being Free,* pp. 121, 125, 132.
61. Kraditor, *The Ideas of the Woman Suffrage Movement,* pp. 19–22.
62. Washburn, ed., *The Indian and the White Man,* p. 134.
63. In Chapter IV, I shall argue that flight, sloth, and fear are the dialectical opposites to the sin of idolatry.
64. Cf. Winter, *Being Free,* pp. 122–123.

tion, probably reflect a subconscious awareness of the primordial power of women—the power over birth and childrearing—and the attempt by males to overcome their fear of the mother-figure by laying claim to a mental and physical superiority. Taken together, these fears of difference are related elements of a common syndrome,[65] and they have had the effect of segregating groups by class, race, and sex.

(4) In light of factors such as these, Gibson Winter argues that the original meaning of freedom in America has undergone a subtle corruption: the freedom based on illimitable land came to mean unrestrained growth; voluntary action took on the form of mastery, domination, and exploitation; and the dream of a divinely given new beginning was transmuted into the merely human power to innovate. Growth, mastery, and innovation are forms of freedom whose flaws are accentuated by technology. Indeed, technology itself came to be equated with freedom, "the apotheosis of the voluntary," as Winter puts it. Of course the irony is that technology, instead of actualizing freedom, threatens to destroy it.

> The technologized form of liberty—growth, mastery, and change— has become counterproductive. The infinite expansiveness is destroying the environment and exhausting resources. The mastery of nature is proving not only unattainable but undesirable. The insatiable drive for novelty has left human communities in a state of disorder and each new program extends the damage. So technologizing liberty has miscarried in its own terms of quantitative and qualitative improvement.

Worst of all, technology has subverted the American dream of a voluntary society by creating a bureaucratic process that regulates most aspects of human behavior, heightens social alienation, and robs persons of the freedom to initiate actions and choose genuine alternatives. "More and more individuals find themselves caught in a web of pointless consumerism or poverty, endless commuting or ghettoized immobility, hyperactivity with no time for human

65. Cf. Ruether, "Crisis in Sex and Race," pp. 67–68, 71–72.

relationships, or hopeless inactivity and dependence." Technology, the ultimate expression of the human will-to-power, now threatens to enslave its creator.[66]

3. THE UNFINISHED WORK:
"A NEW BIRTH OF FREEDOM"

Thus far we have surveyed both the original vision of freedom in America and the faulting of that vision by an exploitation of the land, Indians, blacks, and women, as well as certain common and persistent patterns that might lead to the assumption of a flaw inherent in the American people and their institutions. The story of America bears obvious similarities not only to the rise and fall of ancient civilizations, but also to the biblical drama of creation and fall. Precisely the latter analogy, however, raises an as yet unanswered question and points to an unfinished work. Is there to be a third chapter to this story, a moment of restoration and redemption, a new birth of freedom in America? The question remains unanswered and the work unfinished, not only because the evidence is ambiguous, but also because redemption always transcends merely human, historical possibilities. The experience of evil and fault has an undeniable empirical facticity; but redemption demands a different angle of vision, a "poetics of the will," as Paul Ricoeur puts it, which in the nature of the case cannot be verified by appeal to the empirical facts, but is based on the act of *poieisis,* the imaginative engendering of a new and liberated world. It is only possible to *hope* for redemption, whereas it is easy enough to *demonstrate* the reality of the fault.

We can, however, approach the question of redemption negatively and by indirection, and we can point to religious aspects of the American experience that are capable of being recovered. We may start by asking what we have learned about liberty and

66. Winter, "The Question of Liberty in a Technologized World," pp. 81–86 (quotations from pp. 85–86); see also his earlier work, *Being Free,* chaps. I and II. A similar analysis is advanced by Richard Goodwin in *The American Condition* (New York: Doubleday, 1974), a book whose central theme concerns the loss of freedom. I return to the question of technology and bureaucracy in Chap. II, Sec. 6B.

liberation from the history of exploitation in America. We have learned, suggests Winter, that human beings cannot remain free in splendid isolation and radical autonomy, but only

> in dependence upon nature and through the gifts of community and society. . . . We usually think of the free as the voluntary and consider dependence or belonging as unfree. Technology, however, discloses that the voluntary is reciprocal to the involuntary gift of belonging. The American preoccupation with the voluntary has concealed this full meaning of liberty as a reciprocity of dependence and independence, belonging and initiative.[67]

The gift of belonging is mediated through nature and human communities, but it does not originate there. Precisely its gratuitous, nonmanipulable, yet liberating character indicates that it cannot arise from any human project or from sheer matter, organic or inorganic, but rather from a transcendent, holy source, which is reducible neither to nature nor to human spirit. The Western world experiences the absence of this source as an eclipse of God, a "withdrawing of the giving in which world comes to pass before the sweep of man's projects." The very coherence of the world in which human beings dwell is dependent upon the granting of this source, for otherwise the world becomes a function of merely human projects and calculations. Our problem, Winter concludes, "is one of finding our way through and beyond technologized worldlessness into a realm of belonging and initiating that can reestablish authentic liberty." This "work of foundations" will entail a rediscovery of grace and a recovery of the authentic religious dimensions of the American experience.

The word "authentic" is important, for there are some aspects of our religious heritage that accentuate divine sovereignty at the cost of free human participation, and others that so stress the initiative and manifest destiny of Americans as to exclude any

---

67. Winter, "The Question of Liberty in a Technologized World," pp. 87–88. Jonathan Edwards already recognized this in his criticism of the great stress placed on voluntarism by the Great Awakening, his advocacy of "general benevolence," and his "humbling" encounter with nature (see Bryant, "America as God's Kingdom," pp. 82–84, 87). I shall discuss the reciprocity of the voluntary and the involuntary in Chap. III, Sec. 2B.

sense of divine judgment and limit. What is needed is a creative mediation of the voluntary and involuntary elements of our religious experience. We must learn that the true source of belonging liberates rather than enslaves, and that our freedom increases precisely in accord with our openness to it, our acceptance of it through the mediation of nature, persons, communities, and events. "The source of belonging which addresses us in things and others is the non-paradoxical source of liberty, for in responding to the Mystery our freedom arises. This is the grace of the Mystery which is attested in our biblical heritage. In belonging to the Mystery man is liberated to partnership in creation." [68]

The sense of belonging to a source that grants freedom was preserved in the Puritan doctrine of the kingdom of God. Democracy itself was to be subject to God's sovereign rule in the world, which provides a principle of limitation relevant to all spheres of human governance. "The converse of dependence on God," writes Niebuhr, "is independence of everything less than God." This principle was applicable to the conscience of the individual as well as to the pretensions of the community, to economic life as well as to church and state. The kingdom of God provided the foundation for a permanent revolution of freedom, which would rest content with no human accomplishment and continue until the end of time. Its presupposition, says Niebuhr, was not liberty as a self-evident right of people but the human bondage to sin; the Puritans were "thoroughly convinced that no liberty could last or be beneficial which was not the liberty of men who had been brought somehow to fall in love with a universal goodness and to love it for its own sake alone. The permanent revolution in which [these Puritans] were engaged was designed to make men fit for ever greater freedom." [69]

Robert Bellah believes that elements of the principle of limitation and of a transcendent critique of American culture have been

68. Ibid., pp. 90–93. The Heideggerian roots of this interpretation are acknowledged by Winter. I shall advance a similar thesis on my own terms in Chapters III and VII.
69. Niebuhr, *The Kingdom of God in America*, pp. 69, 75–87, 98.

preserved in the civil religious tradition, although in other respects this tradition has been subject to demonic perversion.[70] Whether or not Bellah is right about American civil religion, it remains unlikely that true judgment and a genuine rebirth of freedom could arise solely from what, after all, is a political religion, serving the interests of the state and culture that have sanctioned it. Redemptive criticism must infuse a culture, to be sure, but it can emanate only from a source that transcends it. A *critical* political religion requires a political *theology* that stands radically over against all national mythologies and is founded upon an independent source of revelation.[71] We have already observed that Jonathan Edwards offered a transhistorical critique of all religious and political projects in a theology of the glory of God.[72] The problem in Edwards's case was that the critical, eschatological perspective tended to expunge the political dimension of theology entirely, which in his final phase was restricted to the purely spiritual realm, by contrast with his earlier endorsement of the millennial vision of God's kingdom in America.

Political and critico-eschatological elements are held in a more fruitful tension by Abraham Lincoln, who, though in no sense a formal theologian, was one of the most creative religious thinkers of America. Lincoln's speeches and writings represent the critical civil religious tradition at its best; they are profoundly informed by the biblical motifs of creation, fall, judgment, and redemption or rebirth. I have selected the Gettysburg Address and the Second Inaugural to furnish the leitmotifs for this chapter. The former begins with Hebraic images of creation and election: ". . . our fathers brought forth on this continent a new nation, conceived in liberty, and dedicated to the proposition that all men are created

70. See Sec. 1 above. More recently Bellah has called attention to what he regards as the potential for renewal in the emergence of a new religious consciousness in America. *The New Republic*, 171 (November 23, 1974) : 33–41.
71. Cf. Jürgen Moltmann, "The Cross and Civil Religion," in *Religion and Political Society*, pp. 9–47. The essays by Willi Oelmüller and J. B. Metz in this volume are also relevant. A shorter version of Moltmann's article appears under the title, "Political Theology," in *Theology Today*, 28 (April 1971): 6–23. I shall attempt to provide the foundations of a critical political theology oriented to the theme of liberation in Chapters V–VI.
72. Bryant, "America as God's Kingdom," pp. 84–86.

equal." The speech then turns to the moment of fall and judgment: "Now we are engaged in a great civil war, testing whether
that nation, or any nation so conceived and so dedicated, can long
endure." In this address Lincoln does not elaborate on the reason
for the war and for the testing of the nation. But this reason is
specified with prophetic judgment in the Second Inaugural
(above, pp. 24–25): it is the "offense" of American slavery, "the
bondman's two hundred and fifty years of unrequited toil," for
which this "scourge of war" is part of the terrible price that must
now be paid.

The larger portion of the Gettysburg Address is concerned with
the third motif, that of redemption. Now the Christian imagery
of death and resurrection, sacrifice and rebirth, predominates.
The question is how those who died on the battlefield at Gettysburg are to be properly honored.

> The world will little note nor long remember what we say here,
> but it can never forget what they did here. It is for us the living,
> rather, to be dedicated here to the unfinished work which they
> who fought here have thus far so nobly advanced. It is rather
> for us to be here dedicated to the great task remaining before us
> —that from these honored dead we take increased devotion to that
> cause for which they gave the last full measure of devotion; that
> we here highly resolve that these dead shall not have died in vain;
> that this nation, under God, shall have a new birth of freedom;
> and that government of the people, by the people, for the people,
> shall not perish from the earth.

The imagery of "new birth" may reflect the well-known passage
in the Gospel of John, where Jesus says to Nicodemus that "unless
one is born anew, he cannot see the kingdom of God" (Jn. 3:3, 7).
Whereas the Fourth Gospel has in mind the new birth of individuals through the Spirit of God (3:5–6), Lincoln refers to the
new birth of a nation "under God." Given Lincoln's frequent
use of biblical images, this connection is not implausible.

The eloquent phrase, "a new birth of freedom," captures many
of the significant motifs. It suggests that freedom, once granted
to humankind in the original act of creation, has been lost and

must now be reborn.   This birth, like all births, is a painful one, entailing suffering, dedication, sacrifice.   The symbolism of Jesus' death on the cross, and of his resurrection from the dead, is just below the surface.   The new birth of freedom occurs "under God," meaning that liberation from bondage, like resurrection from the dead, is not an autonomous human achievement.   The finishing of freedom is the work of God, but "under God" it is also to become a human work.   Finally, an eschatological orientation underlies the entire address.   That to which we now dedicate ourselves is not merely a return to an original condition but rather something qualitatively new: namely, that freedom itself shall become "imperishable," that it shall be irrevocably embodied in the institutions and structures of human government, that the earth shall become a realm of justice, equality, and freedom.[73]

Lincoln must have known that this work would remain long unfinished—painfully so in the more than a century since the end of the Civil War, and in the two centuries since the Declaration of Independence—but he would have continued to hold this vision before us.   In contemporary America, the possibilities for both bondage and liberation have been greatly heightened.   The issue hangs in the balance, and we do not yet know whether in our time we shall experience a new birth of freedom.   We know, by faith, that "in God's good time" it shall be so.

73. On the Gettysburg Address and the motifs of sacrifice and redemption in Lincoln's thought, see especially Wolf, *Lincoln's Religion*, pp. 123–124, 148, 161–172, 185; and Reinhold Niebuhr, "The Religion of Abraham Lincoln," in Allan Nevins, ed., *Lincoln and the Gettysburg Address* (Urbana: University of Illinois Press, 1964), pp. 72–87.   In the same collection of papers, Robert Lowell calls attention to the "curious, insistent use of birth images" in the Gettysburg Address (pp. 88–89) .   See also Hofstadter, *The American Political Tradition*, pp. 93–95, 134–136; and Benne and Hefner, *Defining America*, chap. IV, esp. pp. 103–108.

Chapter II

Rival Freedoms

1. RIVAL MEANINGS OF FREEDOM AND THE SPIRAL OF LIBERATION

Historically, the Christian religion provided an alternative to the definition of freedom oriented to the concepts of mastery, autonomy, private property, privileged community, and divinely sanctioned state—an alternative that remains as valid and necessary for modern America as for the ancient world. Born among a people who were themselves not masters but subjects of the Roman Empire, the Christian movement came upon the scene in the context of a rivalry over the meaning of freedom in Hellenistic and Roman culture, and offered its own distinctive point of view. Christianity, it has been said, is the religion of freedom par excellence.[1] In accord with the Hebraic tradition, it perceived bondage to be a dimension of freedom itself, not something imposed by alien, suprahuman powers—a freedom that enslaves itself through the interior act of self-deception and that objectifies this act, demonically intensifying it, in the oppressive powers and dehumanizing conventions of culture, society, and politics.

Jesus was the radically free person who proclaimed a gospel of liberation: liberation from law and religious piety, from social and political powers, from sin and death. Moreover, this Jesus, it was believed, had been raised from the dead and was now at work in the world actualizing the freedom he once proclaimed. Freedom for Christians entailed not merely a liberation *from* bondage but also *to* or *for* something. However, this positive sense was understood neither as autonomy nor as membership in a privileged group, but as openness to liberating power ("faith"), which was not at the disposal of men and women but was the gift

1. G. W. F. Hegel, *Encyclopedia of the Philosophical Sciences*, § 482 (for full bibliographical citation, see Chapter III, n. 23).

of the transcendent yet near God. The pagan views were not simply abandoned but transformed into what might be called non-privatistic, non-autonomous subjectivity ("life") and non-separated, non-alienated community ("love"). The transformation was founded on and consummated by the vision of (or "hope" for) a coming, true communion of free subjects—the "kingdom of freedom" proclaimed by Jesus as the rule of God and the true destiny of humankind.

Such, at least, is the thesis of this book, the elaboration of which will be the concern of the ensuing chapters. But before the constructive argument can be broached it will be necessary to enlarge the interpretive context by analyzing, in the present chapter, various rival understandings of freedom, which will permit distinctive aspects of the Christian view to stand out. Such an analysis will carry us well beyond the American experience into the broad sweep of Western intellectual and cultural history.

"Freedom" is one of those root words of human experience—like "being," "truth," "beauty," "goodness"—for which a finally satisfying and universally accepted definition can never be found. Because freedom approximates the distinctive essence of human nature itself, different perceptions of what the human being is have led to fundamental rivalries over the meaning of freedom. Christianity enters the lists as one possibility among many, sharing certain characteristics with other views, yet advancing a distinctive logic of its own. In order to isolate this logic, it will be necessary to develop a hermeneutical framework that exposes root options and permits meaningful comparisons. But what such a framework might be is by no means self-evident.

One attractive approach would be to assume that the several liberation movements of our time—third world, radical left, black, woman's, counter cultural—each illustrate basic optional understandings of freedom. But such is not necessarily the case. The liberation movements are programmatic in orientation, concerned to develop agendas for action to alleviate specific oppressions, and for the most part they have not reflected in a fundamental, systematic way on the meaning of freedom and the reasons for its loss in human experience. Although, as I shall argue shortly, certain correlations do in fact exist, the liberation movements tend to cut across fundamental philosophical possibilities; and given their practical function, it is necessary for them to shift their focus as the fronts on which they are struggling move forward. I shall draw upon the literature of the liberation movements at various points throughout this book, but shall not rely upon the movements themselves to provide the interpretive setting for the theological argument.

Another method would be to develop a fundamental philosophical anthropology oriented to certain universal structures of freedom. But such a procedure, although essential in the course of our argument (Chapter III), does not expose at the outset basic hermeneutical options with respect to such questions as: Why a particular set of structures and not others? What is the proper sequence and interrelation of structures? Is freedom a possibility at all in light of the determining laws of nature and human behavior? Any phenomenology of freedom will already reflect a specific tradition and have made certain fundamental choices.

Thus at the outset, in order to provide a hermeneutical framework for the ensuing discussion, I shall propose a historico-typological rather than a philosophico-structural scheme, by means of the following typology of parallels between ancient and modern views of freedom in Western culture.

	Parallels	
Types of Freedom	*Ancient*	*Modern*
Political-Economic Freedom	Greek Democracy (*Polis*)	Marxism (*Oikonomia*)
Rational-Psychoanalytic Freedom	Stoicism (*Logos*)	Freudianism (*Erōs*)
Tragic-Existential Freedom	Classical Tragedy	Existentialism (Camus, Sartre)
Ecstatic-Vitalistic Freedom	Pagan Religions of Nature	Romanticism (Nietzsche) Counter Culture
Pragmatic-Technocratic Freedom		Behaviorism (Skinner) Natural Science Technology

Such a scheme has certain limitations. For one thing, the parallels are not exact. Within the types, shifts of emphasis occur, but not sufficiently to destroy the continuity within types and the usefulness of the comparison. In the first type, *polis* (the "city-state") is replaced by *oikonomia* ("economy") as the central concept, but freedom continues to be defined primarily in terms of *objective* political and socioeconomic structures. According to Marx, by contrast with ancient Greek and modern democratic political theory, the political structure is determined by the system of economic relations rather than vice versa.

As one moves from the first to the second type, a clear shift of emphasis occurs from an objective to a *subjective* basis for freedom, but within that broad scheme many variations are possible. For Freud, by contrast with the ancient Stoics as well as with post-Cartesian rationalism, *erōs* replaces *logos* as the fundamental reality, although for Freud *logos* remains the key to the analytic process by which *erōs* is liberated; psychoanalysis is a highly rational therapeutic.

In the third type, classical tragedy presupposes a theistic world view, specifically, the existence of an inscrutable or capricious god who predestines the hero to an evil fate, which he can and must resist but not ultimately escape. Modern existentialist literature lacks this theistic assumption but nonetheless retains certain neotragic motifs. This is evident from the writings of Camus and Sartre, according to whom human beings find themselves in an absurd situation that ultimately will destroy them, but which they can freely resist, thereby constituting a meaning for their existence within the limits of finitude. Like the second type, existentialism stresses the basically subjective character of human freedom, but at the same time extends it in the direction of *intersubjective* relations, as is evident from the analysis of intersubjectivity by philosophers such as Sartre, Scheler, Buber, and Marcel.

The last two types differ structurally from the first three. With respect to ecstatic-vitalistic freedom, no shift of emphasis occurs from "ecstasy" to "vitalism" (as, e.g., from the political to the

economic in the first type), since these are defining characteristics
of both the ancient nature religions and modern romanticism.
Neither Nietzsche nor the counter culture has sought to repristi-
nate nature religion, but certain motifs of an essentially pagan,
polytheistic world view are retained. Moreover, in both cases we
discover a *transsubjective* basis for liberation, by contrast with the
stress upon objective structures in the first type, and as a transcendental extension of the subjectivity and intersubjectivity of
freedom in the second and third types. As such, ecstatic-vitalistic
freedom poses a pagan alternative to liberation understood in a
biblical framework, which is transsubjective in a different sense.
(In Chapter III, I shall note that certain parallels exist between
essential structures of human freedom—objective, subjective, intersubjective, and transsubjective—and the *rival types* being considered in this chapter.)[2]

The final type, pragmatic-technocratic freedom, lacks a clear
parallel in antiquity. To be sure, the key terms *pragma* and
technē are rooted in Greek culture and science, but their sense is
quite different from modern pragmatism and technology. Moreover, both the behavioral and the natural sciences have called
traditional views of freedom into question on the basis of a
thoroughgoing determinism, and what they offer in their place—
e.g., scientifically managed human behavior, technologically controlled environments—may no longer deserve the name "freedom."
Nevertheless, both behaviorism and technology understand themselves to be providing a scientific basis for the liberation of objective social relations. Hence with the fifth type we return to an
objective understanding of freedom, but the operative framework
is no longer *politics* or *economics* but scientific *technique*—which
may actually expunge freedom rather than engender it.

The parallel typologies mentioned here are by no means exhaustive. The most fundamental limitation is to Western con-
ceptualities. A genuine cross-cultural analysis would complicate
and enlarge the picture well beyond the limits of this book. Even

2. See Chap. III, Sec. 2c, esp. p. 130.

within the domain of Western culture, several significant figures
and schools either are not represented or cut across the designated
types. For example, the rationalist philosophy of freedom from
Descartes to Kant could be added to the second type, but its view
of the human psyche differs profoundly from the Freudian. The
idealist and phenomenological literature on human freedom of
the past two centuries shares characteristics drawn from the first
three types and cannot be aligned with any one of them. Thus
despite the great significance of this literature for our subject, I
shall not be able to discuss it within the typology of this chapter.
Rather, I shall turn to several of its major representatives (Kant,
Hegel, Husserl, Heidegger, and especially Ricoeur) for the elaboration of essential structures of freedom in Chapter III.

The types of freedom selected for consideration in this chapter
are roughly parallel to several phases in the struggle for human
liberation, which, according to an observation by Gibson Winter,[3]
tends to move in a spiral. At first the stress falls on the material
goods and cultural capacities of a productive society—economic
liberation we shall call it, following Marx. But then it becomes
apparent that, if one has no voice in controlling the system in
which one participates, freedom is illusory—hence the demand for
political liberation in addition to economic. Moreover, freedom
must mean not only material well-being but also liberation from
psychic repression (cf. rational-psychoanalytic freedom), and the
liberation of personal existence vis-à-vis physical, social, and cosmic environments (cf. tragic-existential freedom). Finally liberation must issue in "the process of becoming a whole person who
can rejoice in nature, respond to beauty, share in poetic visions
and participate in intimate human communities"—a cultural liberation relating to our second and third types as well as to the
ecstatic-vitalistic freedom of the counter culture. The point of
the spiral imagery is twofold. First, there is a specific process or
sequence in the movement toward liberation: economic-political-

3. Gibson Winter, *Being Free: Reflections on America's Cultural Revolution* (New
York: Macmillan, 1970), p. 7. Winter is here influenced by the sociological categories of Talcott Parsons.

psychic-personal-cutural; and second, each of the phases in the liberation process must be incorporated or preserved at higher levels of the spiral, so that full freedom is to be understood as a rich and complex phenomenon, encompassing many dimensions. Liberation in a biblical perspective may be seen as adding another level to the spiral—that of religious transcendence or of openness to God as the power of freedom, thereby casting the other levels into a new light, but by no means negating them.

The contemporary liberation movements may be correlated to a certain extent with one or more of the phases in the spiral of liberation. Each is, for the moment, "at" a certain point more than at another, although each must ultimately move through all the phases, as the following schema suggests.

Rival Freedoms	*Spiral of Liberation*	*Liberation Movements*
Political-Economic Freedom (Greek Democracy, Marxism)	Economic Liberation	Third World Liberation
	Political Liberation	
Pragmatic-Technocratic Freedom (Behaviorism, Science, Technology) [4]		Black Liberation
Rational-Psychoanalytic Freedom (Stoicism, Freudianism)	Psychic Liberation	
		Woman's Liberation
Tragic-Existential Freedom (Classical Tragedy, Existentialism)	Personal Liberation	
	Cultural Liberation	
Ecstatic-Vitalistic Freedom (Religions of Nature, Romanticism)		Counter Culture
	Religious Liberation	
Biblical Freedom [5] (Judaism, Christianity)		

4. For purposes of correlation, pragmatic-technocratic freedom appears in second place, since it purports to provide a scientific basis for the liberation of objective structures, both economic and political.

5. Biblical freedom is not being considered among the rival types of this chapter, but it serves as the foundation for the rest of the book. It seems appropriate, therefore, to include it in this schema.

The liberation of the peoples of the third world finds itself chiefly at the first level of the spiral, the struggle for socioeconomic justice (hence the significance of Marxist analysis in much of Latin America and Asia today), but is also moving increasingly into the political arena. Black liberation has shifted from a primary focus on basic social, economic, and civil rights to a more political and psychic phase—the consolidation of political power in the black ghettos of the inner cities, and the raising of black consciousness through a sense of identity and self-affirmation. The oppression of women has always been primarily a psychological phenomenon, rooted in male sexual domination, but with unmistakable socioeconomic and political ramifications. The woman's movement too first concentrated on social and economic rights, from about the middle of the nineteenth century onward, then shifted to political action as momentum for the suffrage amendment grew; but only now in the third phase of woman's liberation (in the 1960s and 1970s) is it coming to terms with the underlying psychological and personal factors. Both it and black liberation are pushing toward the cultural spiral, with its stress upon aesthetic, vitalistic, and communal experiences. The counter culture occupies a unique place in this discussion because it can be considered both as a representative of one of the types of freedom (ecstatic-vitalistic) and as a contemporary liberation movement (although less defined or organized than the others). These correlations are, of course, very imprecise because of the fluidity of the liberation movements in relation to the fundamental types of freedom; for this reason the latter provide a better framework for illustrating the hermeneutical issues.

In the final section of this chapter, significant aspects of the Christian view[6] of freedom will be sketched in an anticipatory way by comparison with the other types. My purpose at that point will be to argue not that the Christian view is "true" while the others are "false," but that it draws authentic elements from all the types, transposing these elements into its own distinctive

6. The reason for limiting this work primarily to one of the biblical religions, Christianity, is indicated below, p. 105.

logic.   From the Christian point of view, the rival types of freedom are not mutually exclusive options.   Rather each calls to light
in its own way different yet essential aspects of a complex total
phenomenon.   But each alone is also inadequate.

2. POLITICAL-ECONOMIC FREEDOM

A. THE GREEK POLIS

It was in ancient Greece that the reality of freedom was clearly
conceptualized for the first time.   Moreover, freedom became the
basic ideal of *life* for the Greeks.   It was the central existential as
well as conceptual reality, analogous to the role played by the
mystery of nature in the ancient Near East and by faith in Israel.[7]
Nonetheless, it must be remembered that from the beginning
freedom was defined for the Greeks by and in contrast to the
institution of slavery.   Their word *eleutheria* derived from the
Indogermanic root *leudh* (to grow, rise, ascend), designating those
who belong to an ascendant people or are citizens of the *polis,* by
contrast with oppressed subjects or slaves.   The citizen was able
to move about freely and to speak and act as he chose without
being hindered by physical necessities or the will of another
human being.   Thus freedom meant both self-determination or
autonomy and membership in a privileged community.   But of
course citizenship rights were restricted to adult males.   Women
and children were excluded, and foreigners taken captive in battle
as well as debtors were enslaved or imprisoned, although (in the
case of males) usually for stated periods, after which they could be
manumitted or earn their freedom.[8]

The ultimate rationale for the practice of slavery on the part of
the Greeks, according to Hannah Arendt, was not the exploitation

7. Cf. Kurt Niederwimmer, *Der Begriff der Freiheit im Neuen Testament* (Berlin:
Verlag Alfred Töpelmann, 1966), pp. 1–2; and Herbert J. Muller, *Freedom in the
Ancient World* (New York: Harper & Row, 1961), p. 145.
8. On the etymological and historical details, see Niederwimmer, *Der Begriff der
Freiheit*, pp. 2–3; and Gerhard Kittel, ed., *Theological Dictionary of the New Testa-
ment*, trans. G. W. Bromiley (6 vols.; Grand Rapids: Eerdmans Publishing Co.,
1964–1974), II, 487–488. See also Max Pohlenz, *Freedom in Greek Life and
Thought: The History of an Ideal*, trans. Carl Lofmark (Dordrecht: D. Reidel
Publishing Co., 1966), pp. 3–6.

of cheap labor for profit, but rather the attempt to exclude labor, by which the necessities of life were provided, from the distinctively human realm. She writes:

> The ancients . . . felt it necessary to possess slaves because of the slavish nature of all occupations that served the needs for the maintenance of life. It was precisely on these grounds that the institution of slavery was defended and justified. To labor meant to be enslaved by necessity, and this enslavement was inherent in the conditions of human life. Because men were dominated by the necessities of life, they could win their freedom only through the domination of those whom they subjected to necessity by force. The slave's degradation was a blow of fate and a fate worse than death, because it carried with it a metamorphosis of man into something akin to a tame animal.[9]

The political conception of freedom that emerged in the classical era of Greece (c. 594–431 B.C.) presupposed this distinction between the realm of necessity and a realm of freedom. The free Greek was a citizen *(politēs)* of a city-state *(polis)*, whose freedom, in turn, was based on independence from foreign domination and from preoccupation with the physical necessities of life. Aristotle expressed it beautifully: the *polis* is the *koinōnia tōn eleutherōn,* the "community of the free." [10] According to Aristotle, writes Arendt,

> the *bios politikos* denoted explicitly only the realm of human affairs, stressing the action, *praxis,* needed to establish and sustain it. Neither labor nor work was considered to possess sufficient dignity to constitute a *bios* at all, an autonomous and authentically human way of life; since they served and produced what was necessary and useful, they could not be free, independent of human needs and wants.[11]

9. Hannah Arendt, *The Human Condition* (Chicago: University of Chicago Press, 1958), pp. 83–84, cf. p. 12. She cites Aristotle's discussion of slavery in *Pol.* III. 4, 1253b25. This analysis is related to her own seminal distinction among labor, work, and action, which is the central theme of the book.
10. *Pol.*, III.4, 1279a21. Niederwimmer, *Der Begriff der Freiheit,* pp. 6–7; *Theological Dictionary of the New Testament,* II, 488; Rudolf Bultmann, "Der Gedanke der Freiheit nach antikem und christlichem Verstädis," *Glauben und Verstehen,* IV (Tübingen: J. C. B. Mohr, 1965), 44; and Bultmann, "The Significance of the Idea of Freedom for Western Civilization," *Essays Philosophical and Theological,* trans. James Greig (New York: Macmillan, 1955) , p. 306.
11. Arendt, *The Human Condition,* p. 13.

Indeed, there were only two distinctively political activities: action *(praxis)* and speech *(lexis),* which meant not only that most political action, apart from violence, was transacted in words, but also that finding the right words at the right time was the quintessence of politics. Thereby a place of action and relationship was cleared in which human beings could dwell as authentically human, disclosing themselves by the creative use of imagination, deciding policies and settling disputes through words and persuasion rather than force and violence. The true *polis* was not a physical entity but a quality of relationship. "Not Athens, but the Athenians were the *polis,*" notes Arendt; the walls and the laws of the city secured the space and the structure within which free political actions could transpire.[12] It is not by accident that, in addition to *eleutheria,* the other common Greek words designating "freedom" referred precisely to these definitive qualities of the political life, namely, action and speech: *exousia* (freedom to act, power, authority) and *parrēsia* (ability to say anything, hence freedom of opinion, expression, speech).[13]

Despite its paradigmatic significance, the freedom of the city-states proved highly fragile and did not survive beyond the end of the fifth century. For one thing, the *polis* depended for its success on a small population (Plato considered five thousand citizens the ideal number, thus permitting a direct participative democracy) and a high level of rationality. When these conditions changed, the fragile structure of the *polis* was shaken. Moreover, the Peloponnesian War (431–404 B.C.) drained the city-states of material and spiritual resources. The war was caused by their inability to form a lasting union, to transform the *polis* into a *cosmopolis.*

Of greater significance is the fact that the Greeks were unable to resolve the inherent tension between the individual and the state. On the one hand, their impulse toward individual freedom was likely to become reckless, lawless, or selfish because it was neither sanctioned nor disciplined by a higher principle. It was rooted

12. Ibid., pp. 25–27, 175–180, 193–198.
13. Niederwimmer, *Der Begriff der Freiheit,* pp. 4–5.

in the Homeric tradition of personal fame and glory and was nourished by habitual competition. In this respect, freedom was understood purely in terms of self-assertion, autonomy, personal power. Hence it needed the constant restraint of the law, and when that restraint was removed it tended to become anarchic. Plato was aware of this, but he saw the root of the problem only in the insatiability of the will-to-freedom, not in the will itself. As Niederwimmer points out, "that an element of destruction is already contained in the impulse for self-realization as such . . . remained hidden from the Greeks." [14]

On the other hand, the law that needed to restrain individualism tended itself to become despotic because of the absence of any sense for civil liberties or the rights of individuals *against* the state on the basis of a higher law. "The Greeks," says Muller,

> never made a clear distinction between the state and society, or drew up bills of rights protecting "the people" against the state, because the *polis* was virtually indistinguishable from society or the people, embracing all their major interests and constituting their highest interest. They were not so much citizens with abstract rights as members of a community with status, as in a family.[15]

The possibilities for the despotic idealism of the state were clearly present in Plato's alternative to anarchy in *The Republic,* modeled on Sparta. Thus the law that needed to sustain freedom itself became a form of bondage: this paradox, which lies at the heart of the Pauline theology of law, was also hidden from the Greeks.

Finally, the limitation of freedom to citizenship on the part of adult males, and the exclusion of women, slaves, foreigners, and very often the poor, was a fatal flaw. This practice was condoned by the great philosophers (Plato, Aristotle), but was attacked for the first time by Euripides in the fourth century.[16] A freedom defined in terms of self-mastery and privileged caste, and predicated on the institution of slavery—despite the magnificent concep-

14. Ibid., pp. 8–12; Muller, *Freedom in the Ancient World,* pp. 202–203.
15. Muller, *Freedom in the Ancient World,* pp. 167–168, 212, 216–218.
16. Ibid., p. 190.

tion of the *polis* as the *koinōnia tōn eleutherōn*—does not correspond to the true concept of freedom and contains the seeds of its
own destruction.

B. MARX: THE BASIS OF FREEDOM IN POLITICAL ECONOMY

The Greeks drew a sharp distinction between the public realm
of the *polis* and the private domain of the household or *oikia*.
The household was the place of necessity and labor, the *polis* the
sphere of freedom and action.   Slaves and women were restricted
to the household, while the citizen had to leave his *oikia* and enter
the *polis* in order to engage in free action.   Of these two realms,
the *polis* was clearly superior, although it depended upon the life-
sustaining labor of the *oikia*: it was precisely because the citizen
did not have to concern himself with the latter that he was free
to enter politics.   This division yielded the purest form of politics
known to history, but at a high cost in terms of human dignity.

In the modern world, this distinction between politics and
economics has been largely obliterated and the priority between
them reversed.   With the rise of "society," economic activities
have entered the public realm, and nations find themselves primarily concerned with the collective, centralized administration of
housekeeping.   Behavior has replaced action as the foremost mode
of human relationship, and the modern science of economics is
based on uniform behavior, subject to statistical analysis, rather
than individual, free action.   Political science has yielded the
place of preference to "political economy," which would have
been a contradiction in terms for antiquity.   Karl Marx did not
invent political economy but learned it from the liberal economists
of his day; he simply added the reality of class conflict to their
fiction of social harmony.   Today "political economy" is known
as the science of economics, and it is no accident that economists,
not political scientists, are the favored consultants of modern
governments.   Politics, as practiced by the politicians, tends to be
a matter of strategy, image, power and personality, rather than of
free humanizing action.[17]

17. For these two paragraphs, see Arendt, *The Human Condition*, pp. 28–49.

Marx contended, in opposition to Hegel and the Greeks, that the human person is a corporeal, natural being whose essential activity consists in the production of objects of value by means of labor.[18]   This person is also a historical being, i.e., a being-for-itself and for-others in historical, social relations—a species-being *(Gattungswesen)*, as Marx put it.   In his "Theses on Feuerbach," he writes: "The essence of man is no abstraction inhering in each single individual.   In its actuality it is the ensemble of social relationships." [19]

These two factors—humankind's material objectivity and historical sociality—mean that *political economy* is the most appropriate science for the study of human beings: not just politics, for the essential human act is the economic one of producing objects to meet needs; not just economics, which could be construed on its classical model as referring to the individual, private household; but political economy, the study of the economic conditions that lie at the root of all social and political structures.   Marx's most famous formulation of this position is found in the Introduction to his *Critique of Political Economy:*

> In the social production of their subsistence men enter into determined and necessary relations with each other which are independent of their wills—production relations. . . . The sum of these production-relations forms the economic structure of society, the real basis upon which a juridical and political superstructure arises, and to which definite social forms of consciousness correspond.   The mode of production of the material subsistence conditions the social, political, and spiritual life-processes in general. It is not the consciousness of men which determines their existence, but on the contrary it is their social existence which determines their consciousness.[20]

18. Karl Marx, "Economic and Philosophic Manuscripts," in *Writings of the Young Marx on Philosophy and Society*, ed. and trans. Loyd D. Easton and Kurt H. Guddat (New York: Anchor Books, 1967), pp. 325–326.   See also the labor theory of value elaborated in the first volume of *Capital;* and, for an analysis of this theory, Jean Hyppolite, *Studies on Marx and Hegel*, trans. John O'Neill (New York: Basic Books, 1969) , pp. 137–144.
19. *Writings of the Young Marx*, p. 402; cf. pp. 293–294, 305–306, 326–327.
20. In *Capital, The Communist Manifesto, and Other Writings*, ed. Max Eastman (New York: Modern Library, 1932) , pp. 10–11.   A similar statement is found in *The Communist Manifesto*, ibid., p. 341.   It is not surprising that, in the latter work, Marx should take an entirely negative attitude toward politics as such, describing it as "merely the organized power of one class for oppressing another" (p. 343).

The basic reality confronting political economy is not simply the production of material objects in a nexus of social relations, but the alienation and exploitation of human labor in the productive system. People are found in a condition of bondage or oppression from which they must be liberated. Unfortunately, Marx was never very clear about the origins of alienation. In "Money and Alienated Man," written in 1844, he suggests that the problem first arises with the use of money as the means of exchange, which replaces the direct mediation between human beings by a material thing. Money, in turn, gives rise to private property because, in making monetary exchanges, persons do not relate to one another as human beings; things thereby lose the significance of being "truly human and social property" and become *private* property, which can be surrendered only in exchange for an abstract monetary value. Private property in turn leads to alienated labor and its attendant ills in capitalist economies: private ownership of the means of production, alienation of the worker from the products of his labor by the payment of wages, and the extortion of surplus value by increasing productivity without returning an equivalent value to the worker.[21]

But in another writing of the same year, the "Economic and Philosophic Manuscripts," Marx suggests that the relation between private property and alienated labor is more dialectical than this:

> We have obtained the concept of externalized [alienated] labor
> . . . from political economy as a result of the movement of private
> property. But the analysis of this idea shows that though private
> property appears to be the ground and cause of externalized labor,
> it is rather a consequence of externalized labor, just as gods are
> originally not the cause but the effect of an aberration of the
> human mind. Later this relationship reverses. Only at the final
> culmination of the development of private property does this, its
> secret, reappear—namely, that on the one hand it is the product

21. "Excerpt-Notes of 1844," *Writings of the Young Marx*, pp. 266–267, 273–276; also pp. 290, 296–299. On the theory of surplus value, which constitutes the most original and revolutionary aspect of his analysis of capitalism, see *Capital*, vol. I, trans. Samuel Moore and Edward Aveling (New York: Modern Library, 1906), pts. III–V; and vol. III, trans. Ernest Untermann (Chicago: Charles H. Kerr & Co., 1909), p. 953. Also Arendt, *The Human Condition*, p. 88; and Hyppolite, *Studies on Marx and Hegel*, pp. 127, 142, 145–148.

of externalized labor and that secondly it is the means through which labor externalizes itself, the realization of this externalization.[22]

If private property is the *product* of alienated labor, then what causes the alienation of labor in the first place? The manuscript breaks off before an answer can be provided. But at the very end, and elsewhere in his writings, Marx hints that the problem resides in the very dynamics of labor itself. Labor is intrinsically alienating because, under the conditions of *scarcity* at least, human beings labor or produce objects to satisfy their own *selfish* needs.[23] Arendt points out that Marx speaks repeatedly of labor as an "eternal necessity imposed by nature." [24] Thus it is consistent for Marx to maintain, at the end of *Capital,* that labor remains eternally bound to the kingdom of necessity, and that the kingdom of freedom can only lie beyond labor entirely—a point to which I shall return shortly.[25]

Thus at the root of the alienation endemic to production relations lies what appears to be a *primordial human flaw,* namely, *selfishness,* which is, nonetheless, a factor of the penuriousness intrinsic to nature. Hyppolite refers to this flaw as "a certain *will to power,* which one can hardly imagine will disappear with the disappearance of capital." [26] If we may follow Marx's scenario, then the alienation engendered by will-to-power leads to the use of money and the privatizing of property. Private property, in turn, intensifies and institutionalizes this alienation. It becomes the *actual* cause of the estrangement, exploitation, and domination that have characterized production relations throughout history.

At this point Marx makes a crucial assumption. The abolition of private property and the establishment of a socialist economic system will eliminate the alienation of labor, which originally

22. *Writings of the Young Marx,* p. 298.
23. See the statements to this effect at the beginning of the essay called "Free Human Production" in the "Excerpt-Notes of 1844," ibid., pp. 277–278.
24. Arendt, *The Human Condition,* pp. 99, 103; cf. *Capital,* I, 50, 201, 205; III, 873–874.
25. *Capital,* III, 954.
26. Hyppolite, *Studies on Marx and Hegel,* pp. 127, 129–130, 137, 140–141. He notes that this is not a strictly Marxist concept.

gave rise to private property and is now caused by it. In other words, an alteration in economic relations will have a reformatory impact on human nature itself, overcoming the primordial selfishness that engendered alienation in the first place. It might appear illogical that an effect (private property) should alter its cause (alienation), but Marx's point seems to be that the relation between the two has reversed, so that now private property and capitalist economy cause or at least reinforce alienation, rather than vice versa. In any case, the strategy for liberation is clearly that of economic-political revolution: a radical change in humankind's outward social circumstances will transform the psychic quality of life. Just because of the institutional objectification of alienation, Marx makes it clear that nothing short of forcible revolutionary action will succeed in producing changes. He criticizes the Utopian Socialists for hoping to attain their ends by peaceful means and small experiments. But not only will the bourgeois class not yield its capital voluntarily; it also is locked into an alienating economic structure that it is powerless to alter.[27]

It should be observed in passing that for Marx religion has lost whatever liberating significance it might once have had. At its best, religion is an expression of and protest against real suffering —"the opium of the people," offering illusory happiness in place of real happiness;[28] at its worst it is an ideology justifying class divisions and social oppression.

Despite his rejection of religion, Marx's description of the liberated society has overtones of a utopian religious vision—a vision informed by the biblical image of the kingdom of God as a kingdom of freedom. In the early manuscripts he envisions a community of "free human production" in which each individual produces to satisfy, not only his or her own needs, but the needs of others as well, and in which each finds fulfillment in the other as well as in him- or herself. In such a community,

27. *The Communist Manifesto,* in *Capital and Other Writings,* pp. 352–353, 355.
28. Introduction to "Critique of Hegel's Philosophy of Right," *Writings of the Young Marx,* p. 250.

I would have been the mediator between you and the species and you would have experienced me as a redintegration of our own nature and a necessary part of your self; I would have been affirmed in your thought as well as your love. In my individual life I would have directly created your life; in my individual activity I would have immediately confirmed and realized my true human and social nature.[29]

In the *Communist Manifesto*, a similar utopianism follows the necessarily harsh and violent measures by which private property will be abolished and power transferred from the bourgeoisie to the proletariat. The latter, in turn, must eliminate its own supremacy as a class, at which time society will enter upon a genuinely "postpolitical" phase, public power having lost its "political character." "In place of the old bourgeois society, with its classes and class antagonisms, we shall have an association in which the free development of each is the condition for the free development of all."[30]

Surprisingly, we learn that this utopianism is based, initially at least, on an increase in productive capacities to the point that society is able to adopt the principle, "From each according to his abilities, to each according to his needs." Capitalism, then, by stimulating productivity through the extraction of surplus value, unwittingly contributes to the birth of the new society![31] But in fact, continues Marx, because labor remains bound to the necessity imposed by nature, "the kingdom of freedom [*Reich der Freiheit*] does not commence until the point is passed where labor under the compulsion of necessity and of external utility is required. In the very nature of things it lies beyond the sphere of material production in the strict meaning of the term."[32] By suspending labor "under the compulsion of necessity," the kingdom of freedom might be able to change all work into absolutely free "self-activ-

29. "Excerpt-Notes of 1844," *Writings of the Young Marx*, p. 281, cf. pp. 272, 278–280; "Economic and Philosophic Manuscripts," pp. 293, 304–306, 312–313.
30. *The Communist Manifesto*, in *Capital and Other Writings*, pp. 342–343. On the concept of the postpolitical, see below, pp. 86–87, 352–353.
31. *Capital*, III, 953; *The Criticism of the Gotha Program*, in *Capital and Other Writings*, pp. 5–7.
32. *Capital*, III, 954 (translation altered slightly). Marx probably adopted the expression "kingdom of freedom" from Hegel's *Philosophy of Right* (see below, p. 149).

ity." "In a communist society, there will no longer be any painters but, at most, people who among other things, like to paint,"[33] he says in one of his early works.

But at the end of *Capital* Marx reveals his skepticism that society will ever be able to escape the kingdom of necessity entirely: "Beyond it begins that development of human power, which is its own end, the true kingdom of freedom, which, however, can flourish only upon that kingdom of necessity as its basis. The shortening of the working day is its fundamental premise."[34] The best strategy Marx can offer is that of rationalizing, harmonizing, and increasing the productivity of labor, in order to shorten the working day and thereby increase the amount of leisure time in which human beings can enjoy themselves freely. Not only does this remain a thoroughly economic solution to what ultimately is a transeconomic problem—namely, human alienation; but also, as Jürgen Moltmann points out, "Everybody knows . . . that a man with more leisure time does not necessarily become a free man."[35]

Just this remains the crux of the dilemma for the Marxist understanding of bondage and liberation. Purely economic measures cannot overcome the alienation of labor, transform the political structure, and usher in the kingdom of freedom. In fact, it has been the advanced postindustrial societies of Western capitalism that have tried this solution and found it wanting: along with our technologically based freedoms we have reaped a new and more insidious bondage to the impersonal, alienating bureaucratic systems upon which technology depends.[36] Revision-

33. From Karl Marx and Friedrich Engels, *Die deutsche Ideologie,* pt. III; cited by Jürgen Moltmann, "The Revolution of Freedom," in *Openings for Marxist-Christian Dialogue,* ed. Thomas W. Ogletree (Nashville: Abingdon Press, 1969), p. 62, from Marx's *Frühschriften,* ed. Siegfried Landshut (Stuttgart: Alfred Kröner, 1953), p. 475. Similar statements are found in "Free Human Production," *Writings of the Young Marx,* p. 281, and in pt. I of "The German Ideology," *Writings of the Young Marx,* pp. 424–425, 468 (pts. II and III are not translated in the latter edition).
34. *Capital,* III, 954–955 (translation altered slightly).
35. *Openings for Marxist-Christian Dialogue,* p. 63.
36. Richard Goodwin points this out quite effectively in *The American Condition* (New York: Doubleday, 1974); see pp. 18–19, 227–228, 375–376. On the ambiguity in Marx's attitude toward labor and freedom, see also Arendt, *The Human Condition,* pp. 87–89, 104–105, 130–135.

ary Marxists—Ernst Bloch, Roger Garaudy, Herbert Marcuse, Eric Fromm, Milan Machoveč, Adam Schaff, and others—have wrestled with this dilemma and in the process have found themselves drawn beyond a purely Marxist framework. Marcuse, for example, advocates a new, aesthetically based sensibility, with which he begins to approximate not only Freud but also romanticism, Nietzsche, and the counter culture.[37]

3. RATIONAL-PSYCHOANALYTIC FREEDOM

A. Stoicism: Reason

Under Alexander the Great, the Hellenistic world reverted to the ancient pattern of the sacred monarchy, a pattern reinforced by new influences from the East opened by Alexander's conquests. Freedom had lost its political and legal context in the city-states. What replaced it was a world empire, which certainly permitted freedom of movement and contact, but which did not provide a coherent political context or compelling social and cultural goals. The result was a general loss of confidence and purpose, and hence a privatizing of freedom. The new philosophical schools— Hedonism, Cynicism, Skepticism, Epicureanism, and Stoicism— all took on an escapist or defeatist cast. In place of the political freedom assured by the *polis,* they sought an *inner freedom* that could be attained by the use of reason, rational self-control, psychic self-mastery. Of course, such freedom had been eloquently exampled by the conduct of Socrates; and Plato had already stressed the freedom of intellect, which restrains the lower instincts of the soul, perceives the true goal, and translates knowledge into action.[38]

If the human being is to realize his or her own possibilities, then the arena within which one really exercises power must be defined as precisely as possible. For the Stoics, it was the inner life that is within a person's power—the power of reason over will

---

37. See Marcuse's *An Essay on Liberation* (Boston: Beacon Press, 1969).
38. Muller, *Freedom in the Ancient World,* pp. 222–224, 232–234, 236–237; Pohlenz, *Freedom in Greek Life and Thought,* pp. 164–165 and the whole of chap. IV; Bultmann, "Der Gedanke der Freiheit," p. 45.

and desire. The external world is not within one's power, and if one is to be free, one must free oneself from its influence, which is expressed primarily in the form of opinion *(dogma)* and passion or emotion *(pathos).* Human beings ought to free themselves from false opinion and irrational passion, strive after self-sufficiency, cultivate renunciation and endurance. The ultimate logic of this position could lead to self-surrender and even to suicide. But suicide for the Stoic could also be interpreted as a destruction of the world rather than of self: by means of self-inflicted death, one is finally freed of the world, the non-self, over which one has no control.[39]

However Stoicism did not ordinarily pursue this nihilistic logic to its conclusion; rather it turned to pantheism. In order to free itself from the non-self, the self seeks to become pure self, pure ego, universal Logos, or God. This striving presupposes an implicit identity of finite and infinite ego, and it posits the Logos or Reason as the principle of macrocosmic and microcosmic order. To be sure, cosmic harmony is now experienced only interiorly, but ultimately the Stoic knew himself to be at home in the cosmos, whereas this was not the case with the Cynics, the Gnostics, the mystery religions. The source of a person's capacity for self-determination and freedom is the divine Logos—the principle of harmony, the ground of world unity, the power of creative potency, the spark of rationality within an irrational world. The Stoics succeeded where the earlier Greeks had failed in creating, philosophically at least, a *cosmopolis* in place of the *polis*: a universal commonwealth, a brotherhood of people, based on a natural law that embodied the principles of equality and liberty. This idea was to have an immense significance in the history of the West.[40]

---

39. Niederwimmer, *Der Begriff der Freiheit*, pp. 39, 51–52; Muller, *Freedom in the Ancient World*, p. 229; Rudolf Bultmann, *Primitive Christianity in Its Contemporary Setting*, trans. R. H. Fuller (New York: Meridian Books, 1956) , pp. 137–138; *Theological Dictionary of the New Testament*, II, 494–495.

40. Niederwimmer, *Der Begriff der Freiheit*, pp. 38–42; Bultmann, *Primitive Christianity*, pp. 135–136; and "Der Gedanke der Freiheit," p. 46; Muller, *Freedom in the Ancient World*, pp. 229–230.

Despite its importance, Stoicism had certain telling weaknesses, the chief of which was its rationalistic optimism, its assumption that a person desires and wills only what is to his or her own good, that reason shows what this is, and that the will obeys. Failure was attributed to error or to external, irrational influences over which the individual has no control. The human being, left to him- or herself, is capable of the good. But what if our interiority is not at our disposal either, and evil has roots within the heart as well as outside it? According to the Apostle Paul, who took over many of the Stoic ideas, the true duality is not between interiority and externality, but within the ego itself—the struggle of the divided will. Therefore, from the Pauline (and biblical) perspective, the retreat to interiority cannot of itself achieve liberation.[41]

B. FREUD: PSYCHOANALYTIC LIBERATION

An immense world appears to separate Freudian psychoanalysis from the Stoic apotheosis of reason. Included within it is the history of philosophical rationalism, beginning with the Neoplatonists and culminating in modernity with the turn to subjectivity inaugurated by Descartes and brought to its highest critical expression in Kant. For this tradition, thinking consciousness (the *cogito*) represents the starting point of all knowledge and the foundation of human moral and intellectual freedom. But Freud advanced a radical critique of this tradition. His topography of the psychical apparatus has the effect of dispossessing consciousness from the center of attention in favor of subconscious and supraconscious forces that dominate the psyche, and consciousness itself is disclosed to be both self-deceptive and narcissistic. At the same time, however, it is precisely by interpretive acts of consciousness that the analytic discipline is carried forward, and the final intention of Freud is to regain, at a higher, "scientific" level, "a self-

41. Bultmann, *Primitive Christianity*, p. 143; Niederwimmer, *Der Begriff der Freiheit*, pp. 44–45, 52–53.

consciousness less centered on the egoism of the ego, a self-consciousness taught by the reality principle, . . . and open to a truth free of 'illusion.' "[42]

In certain respects Freud's analysis of the psychical apparatus[43] recapitulates that of the Stoics. Just as the latter distinguished between three factors in a person's psychic makeup—passion, reason (ego, *logos*), and opinion—so did Freud—the id, the ego, and the superego. Both agreed that the task of the ego is to establish order and maintain control over the passions or instincts by a rational sublimation of them. But whereas the Stoics believed that the passions are a manifestation of the influence of the external world, from which one must free oneself, Freud saw more profoundly that the libidinal instincts, rooted in erotic desire, are internal to the very structure of the psyche (their domain is the id), and that, far from finding happiness in fleeing from them, human beings could be fully happy only in the unrepressed gratification of them, which of course is impossible under the conditions of civilized existence. Likewise with the "opinions" of the external world: Freud believed that they are introjected into the psyche and become part of its very structure, its "superego." Furthermore, he contended that the most primordial and powerful of these psychic structures is the id, the unconscious domain of the primary instincts. Under the compulsion of constraints imposed by the external world, resulting primarily from economic scarcity, part of the id gradually developed into the ego. Although the ego consists in large part of preconscious material, its most vital dimension is that of perception and consciousness, because they enable it to mediate between the id and the external world. The conscious ego organizes the id to minimize conflicts with reality,

---

42. Cf. Paul Ricoeur, *Freud and Philosophy: An Essay on Interpretation,* trans. Denis Savage (New Haven: Yale University Press, 1970), pp. 420–430, quotation from p. 428.
43. Cf. Sigmund Freud, *An Outline of Psychoanalysis,* trans. James Strachey (New York: W. W. Norton & Co., 1949), chap. I.

substituting the reality principle for the pleasure principle (unrepressed gratification).[44]

Despite the formal structural similarities with Stoicism, Freud's basic theory is quite different, for it accords ontological priority to the instinctual life of human beings rather than their rationality. Eros (the life instinct) replaces Logos (reason) as the essence of being. But Freud was a dualist, not a monist, and, beginning with *Beyond the Pleasure Principle,* he argued that Eros is locked in eternal conflict with the drive toward nonbeing, Thanatos (the death instinct). The aim of the life instinct is to establish ever greater unities, to bind together; hence Eros is often referred to as "love" as well as "life" in Freud's later writings. The aim of the death instinct is to undo connections and so to destroy things, to reduce living beings to an inorganic, inanimate state. Thanatos works silently within the psyche as a kind of inertia or resistance to change, evident in the compulsion to repeat, and also in the form of self-destructiveness or masochism. "If we are to take it as a truth that knows no exception that everything living dies for *internal* reasons—becomes inorganic once again—then we shall be compelled to say that 'the aim of all life is death.' . . ." [45]

The death instinct announces itself outwardly in the form of sadism or mutual human aggressiveness. "Men are not gentle creatures who want to be loved, and who at the most can defend themselves if they are attacked; they are, on the contrary, creatures among whose instinctual endowments is to be reckoned a powerful share of aggressiveness. . . . *Homo homini lupus.*" [46] "Man is a wolf to man." What, then, is to hinder the human race from eventually annihilating itself through internecine warfare? What

44. Ibid., pp. 37–39, 43, 109–110. On the pleasure principle and the reality principle, see Freud, *Civilization and Its Discontents,* trans. James Strachey (New York: W. W. Norton & Co., 1962), pp. 23–30. See also Herbert Marcuse, *Eros and Civilization: A Philosophical Inquiry into Freud* (Boston: Beacon Press, 1955), pp. 13–14, 29–33.
45. Sigmund Freud, *Beyond the Pleasure Principle,* trans. James Strachey (New York: W. W. Norton & Co., 1961), p. 32; cf. pp. 28–58. See Ricoeur, *Freud and Philosophy,* pp. 281–302. On the theory of the instincts, see Freud, *An Outline of Psychoanalysis,* chap. 2; *Civilization and Its Discontents,* pp. 64–68; also Marcuse, *Eros and Civilization,* pp. 22–29, 124–125.
46. Freud, *Civilization and Its Discontents,* pp. 58–60. Cf. Ricoeur, *Freud and Philosophy,* pp. 305–306.

is to prevent the ultimate victory of Thanatos over Eros, of non-being over being? In the quest for an answer, Freud was driven to his famous speculations on civilzation.

> . . . civilization is a process in the service of Eros, whose purpose
> is to combine single human individuals, and after that families,
> then races, peoples and nations, into one great unity, the unity of
> mankind. Why this has to happen, we do not know; the work of
> Eros is precisely this. . . . Man's natural instinct, the hostility of
> each against all and of all against each, opposes this programme
> of civilization. . . . The evolution of civilization . . . must present
> the struggle between Eros and Death, between the instinct of life
> and the instinct of destruction, as it works itself out in the human
> species. This struggle is what all life essentially consists of, and
> the evolution of civilization may therefore be simply described as
> the struggle for life of the human species. And it is this battle of
> the giants that our nurse-maids try to appease with their lullably
> about Heaven.[47]

Freud was not optimistic about the outcome. For one thing, in light of the global warfare of the twentieth century, Thanatos may ultimately win this "battle of the giants." [48] But more insidiously, civilization may weaken or destroy itself by its own success in sublimating aggression. In its attempt to inhibit aggressiveness, civilization causes it to be introjected back into the psyche in the form of the superego, where it expresses itself as conscience, guilt, and the need for punishment. Restrictions are imposed on the liberty of the individual and the possibilities of libidinal satisfaction; thereby Eros is weakened as well as Thanatos. "The price we pay for our advance in civilization is a loss of happiness through the heightening of the sense of guilt." Precisely this is the malaise, the "discontent" of civilization.[49] We should not be surprised at this malaise, for, as Ricoeur points out, the "supreme weapon" of civilization, according to Freud, "is to employ internalized violence against externalized violence; its supreme ruse is to make death work against death." [50] One wonders how death cannot

47. *Civilization and Its Discontents,* p. 69, cf. p. 86.
48. Cf. ibid., p. 92.
49. Ibid., pp. 70 ff., 81–86.
50. Ricoeur, *Freud and Philosophy,* pp. 307–309; cf. also Marcuse, *Eros and Civilization,* pp. 40–41, 44, 55–59, 60–64, 81–82, 108–109.

help but finally win this deadly game; and thus at the end we are left with a tragic view of life.

But as with the Stoics, the tragedy is not without relief for Freud, and at a critical juncture he resuscitates the ancient *logos* doctrine. Psychoanalysis entails the use of reason *(logos)* to achieve a therapeutic liberation of the psyche and its repressions. Pessimism at the point of culture yields to a relative optimism with respect to individual therapy.[51] The traumatic experiences of early childhood, caused by the instinctual demands from within as well as threats from the external world, cause the ego to attempt to flee its problems by repressing them, the symptoms of which show up later in the form of neuroses. The thus weakened ego may be further detached from the reality of the external world, in which case it slips down into psychosis under the influence of the internal world. Psychoanalysis is a rational-analytic hermeneutics of the unconscious, intended to strengthen or reconstitute the weakened ego in its essential function as mediator between the id and the superego. A purely libidinal freedom is an impossibility, but a partial freedom is possible so long as the ego is able to function nonpathologically. Psychoanalysis takes place by means of a dialogue between the therapist and the patient, involving a process of recollection, education, self-knowledge, interpretation, and a successful sublimation of instincts.[52]

Far from being a method for controlling human behavior by changing environmental stimuli and reinforcements, or by regulating instincts on the basis of an energetics of the psychical apparatus, psychoanalysis is an exercise of human freedom for the purpose of gaining freedom. Ricoeur regards Freudian psychoanalysis as a major contribution to hermeneutical theory—a hermeneutics of dreams (short, harmless psychoses) rather than of the cosmic myths and symbols. He points out that the medium in which psychoanalysis does its work is precisely language—the conversation between therapist and patient with regard to the text of

51. Cf. Marcuse, *Eros and Civilization*, p. 126.
52. Freud, *An Outline of Psychoanalysis*, pp. 62–63, 70–71, 75, 77–78, 83–87.

the dream account (not the dream itself). Interpretation is required because libidinal desire manifests itself in human experience through a process of symbolization, the meanings of which
must be deciphered analytically. Thereby the domain of consciousness, though chastised, is enlarged. Psychoanalysis is a
"healing through consciousness . . . by invoking the god Logos." [53]
    The latter statement suggests that for Freud psychoanalysis takes
over the functions once performed by religion. By institutional-
izing the repressions through which antisocial instincts are controlled, civilization has two vital functions: it must provide the
regulations and prohibitions by which control is established, and
it must furnish consolation for the privations thereby undergone.
These two civilizing functions have traditionally been the responsibility of religion. The archetype of the gods is the father-figure,
who on the one hand is the authority for prohibitions and is
greatly to be feared, but on the other hand is the source of protection and consolation. The gods function as lawgivers, they
exorcise the terrors of nature, they reconcile human beings to the
cruelty of fate, and they compensate for the sufferings and privations of civilization. In serving this function, religious ideas are
essentially *illusions*, fulfillments of the oldest, strongest, and most
urgent wishes of humankind, namely, the need for loving protection by one who is at the same time feared and venerated.[54]
    Although religion may have served people well enough in the
past, it is no longer adequate. It has not really succeeded in making the majority of people happy or moral or free (despite its
rhetoric of redemption and eternal blessedness). Worse than that,
it is now evident from the standpoint of scientific knowledge that

53. Ricoeur, *Freud and Philosophy*, pp. 3–8, 35, 65–67, 87–114 (quotation from
p. 35).
54. Freud, *The Future of an Illusion*, trans. W. D. Robson-Scott (New York: Anchor
Books, 1964), pp. 12, 20–27. Cf. Paul Ricoeur, "Religion, Atheism, and Faith," in
A. MacIntyre and P. Ricoeur, *The Religious Significance of Atheism* (New York:
Columbia University Press, 1969), pp. 60, 63–65, 85–86. Ricoeur points out that,
despite valid and important criticisms, Freud's treatment of religion as a whole is
reductionistic. He allows no distinction between the underlying intention of
religion and its often regressive forms; he treats it as though it remains permanently
archaic, without a history, locked into endless repetitions of the Oedipus theme;
and he avoids any serious exegesis of texts, presenting instead a psychology of the
believer based on the neurotic model. *Freud and Philosophy*, pp. 231–232, 243, 246.

religion is not merely a wish-fulfillment but a *delusion,* because its doctrines stand in stark contradiction to reality.[55] The *deception, concealment,* and *disguises* contained in religious belief are what most bother Freud. Now only the truth will set us free, and precisely this is the function of the psychoanalytic interpretation of the symbolism of dreams. "The time has probably come, as it does in an analytic treatment, for replacing the effects of repression by the results of the rational operation of the intellect." It is not that religious doctrines are totally false; it is rather that the truths they contain are "so distorted and systematically disguised that the mass of humanity cannot recognize them as truth." Just as it is better to avoid the symbolic disguisings of the truth in what we tell children (e.g., that newborn babies are brought by the stork), and not to withhold from them a knowledge of the true state of affairs commensurate with their intellectual level (for otherwise the child hears only the distorted part of what we say and feels that he or she has been deceived), so it is with humankind and the religious symbolic disguisings.[56]

Ricoeur points out that the central problem for Marx and Nietzsche as well as Freud is no longer that of the lack of correspondence between subjective ideas and objective reality (as with the critical philosophy), or even error and lying, but rather illusion and deception. What is required is a critique of *false* consciousness, and the birth of a new truth beyond deception. The hermeneutics they engage in is an "exercise of suspicion." That which is to be suspected above all else is religion, which, although it purports to be the bearer of divine revelation, is in fact a tissue of concealments and disguises.[57]

Psychoanalysis not only takes over the function of religion; it tends finally to assume the quality of a religion itself. Freud refers, at the end of *The Future of an Illusion,* to "the twin gods

55. Freud, *The Future of an Illusion,* pp. 48–63, 70–71, 80.
56. Ibid., pp 72–73.
57. Ricoeur, *Freud and Philosophy,* pp. 32–36.

Logos and *Ananke"* (reason and necessity).[58] It is his firm conviction that the scientific use of reason can, within the limits set by external reality *(Ananke)*, achieve a gradual liberation from the bondage of illusion and repression by providing an "education to reality." "Our God, *Logos*, will fulfill whichever of these wishes nature outside us allows, but he will do it very gradually, only in the unforeseeable future, and for a new generation of men. He promises no compensation for us, who suffer grievously from life."[59] As this quotation indicates, the power of *Logos* is circumscribed by that of the other god, *Ananke*—fate, necessity, external reality, nature—of which death is a figure.

> As for the great necessities of Fate, against which there is no help,
> [human beings] will learn to endure them with resignation. . . .
> By withdrawing their expectations from the other world and
> concentrating all their liberated energies into their life on earth,
> they will probably succeed in achieving a state of things in which
> life will become tolerable for everyone and civilization no longer
> oppressive to anyone.[60]

What a thoroughly Stoic vision this is! A realm of freedom may be fashioned for the individual self and perhaps even society, based on reason *(Logos)*, but only in the context of a natural-cosmic necessity *(Ananke)* that does not grant freedom but rather demands resignation and detachment.

In concluding, I shall enumerate certain questions for Freud that will prove significant later on. (1) Is such a vision really stable, and is it religiously satisfying? Can there be an inner freedom in the context of an outer bondage and an alien world? Is freedom possible without a liberating transcendence? (2) Similarly, is therapeutic optimism consistent with cultural pessimism? (3) Are life and death instincts really locked in a perpetual conflict, thus producing a tragic view of the human condition? In

58. Freud, *The Future of an Illusion*, p. 88 n. On the development of psychoanalytic therapy as an alternative religion, see Philip Rieff, *The Triumph of the Therapeutic: Uses of Faith after Freud* (New York: Harper & Row, 1966). In this matter Freud was much more restrained than some of his successors: C. G. Jung, W. Reich, D. H. Lawrence.
59. Freud, *The Future of an Illusion*, pp. 77–81, 83–92 (quotation from p. 88).
60. Ibid., p. 82.

fact, is death a natural instinct (a manifestation of one of the cosmic powers, *Anankē,* that holds sway over us) as distinguished, for example, from a "sinful" flight from life for which human beings must assume responsibility? (Here Freudianism veers toward theogony, according to which evil and death are inscribed into the very logic of being, by contrast with the biblical view of creation and fall.) (4) Is bondage to be located in the *repression* of erotic desire rather than in the false *infinitizing* of desire by the power of imagination (the sin of idolatry as distinguished from that of flight)? (5) Does Freud's criticism of religion leave no alternative but atheism? Or does the possibility exist of a faith beyond the atheistic critique of religion, a faith for which God is understood not as one who dominates and threatens men and women but as their liberator, a God who does not protect and console but rather suffers with human beings in the world?

4. TRAGIC-EXISTENTIAL FREEDOM

A. THE TRAGIC VISION

Tragedy is a mode of literary and philosophical expression that transcends cultural and historical boundaries because the tragic represents a universal and inexpungeable dimension of human experience. For this reason it is difficult to fit tragedy into our ancient-modern schema. In the ancient world, both the Greeks and the Hebrews knew this tragic dimension and gave it classic expression—the Greeks in the writings of their greatest tragedians, Aeschylus, Euripides, and Sophocles; the Hebrews in the books of Job and Ecclesiastes. A different form of tragedy found powerful expression in the drama and poetry of Elizabethan England; and according to some interpreters it reappears in the mid-nineteenth and twentieth centuries, this time especially in the genre of the novel.[61]

Tragedy raises the question of the meaning of human *existence* —the mystery of its origin, purpose, and destiny—with explosive

61. The best survey of the modes of tragic literature, and one upon which I shall draw heavily in the following pages, is by Richard B. Sewall, *The Vision of Tragedy* (New Haven: Yale University Press, 1959).

power. For this reason it is the original and perennial "existentialist" literature. It raises the question of meaning by exposing with unusual clarity the central dilemmas of human experience, yet it demands responsible action in the absence of final certainties. It exposes the mysterious interplay between freedom and destiny in human affairs, and it indicates the necessity of action together with a knowledge of inevitable guilt. Such irresolvable conflicts give rise to the tragic emotions of terror and pity. Above all, tragedy focuses on the factors of evil, suffering, and death, which appear to be ineluctable and inexplicable. The question of undeserved, unjustified, and unredemptive suffering proves to be the most difficult, although tragedy shows that the severest suffering is often not so much physical as it is the mental and spiritual anguish arising out of the awareness of ambiguity and failure.[62]

These dilemmas concerning human existence unavoidably pose the underlying question of theodicy. Classical tragedy functioned within a theistic framework, which for the most part did not question the existence of God. But his purpose, goodness, and to a lesser extent his power were subjected to intense scrutiny. The Greeks and the Hebrews seemed to agree that God or the gods are sovereign, in control of the course of affairs in nature and history (as Sewall puts it, "to the Greeks the hand of a god was in every action"). The Greeks experienced this divine sovereignty as fate, the Hebrews as holiness. The two cultures agreed that the ways of the divine are hidden and mysterious, but whereas the Greek gods were often capricious and jealous (of each other and of human beings), the Lord of Israel was more likely wrathful and harsh, but also just and merciful. The underlying goodness of God was more radically questioned in Greece than in the Old Testament, although even in the latter tragic elements were retained because of the Hebraic experience of the anteriority of evil to every human act (symbolized by the figure of the serpent), and of the problem of the suffering of the innocent: it was in Job

62. See Sewall, *The Vision of Tragedy*, pp. 4–7, 11–14, 19, 25, 27–31, 33, 45–47, 116–117; and Paul Ricoeur, *The Symbolism of Evil*, trans. Emerson Buchanan (Boston: Beacon Press, 1967), pp. 220–221.

and Qoheleth that these elements came closest to a tragic vision. In Greece, however, the terrible possibility of a satanic God who predestines men and women to evil deeds was openly explored. Partially because of the "unthinkability" of such a God, modern tragedy has tended to view the context of human action as an absurd or chaotic world from which any divine presence has long disappeared.[63]

Ricoeur argues that tragedy in its purest form requires not merely an evil God but also, in juxtaposition, free human action.

> The tragic properly so called does not appear until the theme of predestination to evil . . . comes up against the theme of *heroic greatness*; fate must first feel the resistance of freedom, rebound (so to speak) from the hardness of the hero, and finally crush him, before the pre-eminently tragic emotion—*phobos*—can be born. . . . Tragedy was the result of magnifying to the breaking point a twofold set of problems: those concerning the "wicked God" and those concerning the "hero"; the Zeus of *Prometheus Bound* and Prometheus himself are the two poles of the tragic theology and anthropology.[64]

We are introduced, thereby, to the tragic hero, through whom the theme of freedom enters the tragic vision. Human freedom expresses itself in the resistance, rebellion, indeed the pride of the hero. Such pride is preferable to the safe orthodoxies of the Greek chorus and of Job's counselors, and one might even speak of pride as a tragic virtue. But true tragedy is cautious at this point. The Greeks recognized that *hubris* represents the fatal weakness as well as the strength of the hero; and the Hebrews, even more profoundly, knew that human pride before God (or rebellion against him) is the beginning and end of sin. Perhaps this is the quintessential moment of tragedy: human beings are forced by the circumstances in which they find themselves to act defiantly, to rebel against God and the world, thereby defiling themselves in the presence of the holy, inviting the crushing rebound of fate. Thus, despite the autonomy of the hero, his free-

---

63. Sewall, *The Vision of Tragedy*, pp. 14, 19, 23, 26, 52, 69–71, 107–109, 125; Ricoeur, *The Symbolism of Evil*, pp. 212–217, 225–226, 311–322.
64. Ricoeur, *The Symbolism of Evil*, p. 218; cf. pp. 220–221, 224.

dom discloses not his nobility and greatness but his finitude and
weakness. The tragic hero is not an exalted conqueror; rather,
at the height of his straining he stands broken and defeated, and
precisely there, beauty, truth, and infinitude are disclosed—as it
were, transhumanistically. Classical tragedy is ultimately concerned to tell us something about God and the cosmos, not simply
about human nature. When the theistic framework is lost, tragedy
can veer in the direction of a romantic humanism, which does in
fact exalt the hero and make his greatness its central theme. But
an option more faithful to the original tragic vision would be that
of a sober, chastened humanism, for which human finitude and
freedom remain correlative themes in a world now devoid of
divine presence. This brings us to the subject of modern existentialism.[65]

B. HUMANISTIC EXISTENTIALISM

True tragedy has always been a rarity because of the extremity
and tensions of its vision, and it has tended to modulate into
other moods: not only romanticism, but also comedy, irony,
naturalism or realism, pathos and melodrama, the absurd.[66] All
of these moods are represented in the drama, fiction, and poetry
of the twentieth century, especially among the so-called third
generation of writers who have come to prominence within the
past twenty years. At the same time, genuinely neotragic motifs
are present in the literary and philosophical existentialism that
prevailed between the two World Wars and still exerts a powerful
influence. The writers are represented by O'Neill, Hemingway,
Fitzgerald, Faulkner, Williams, Silone, Greene, and Camus, all
of whom stand in the heritage of Dostoevsky. Philosophical existentialism finds its modern point of origin in Kierkegaard, and

65. For this paragraph, in addition to the pages cited from Ricoeur, see Sewall,
The Vision of Tragedy, pp. 10–13, 22, 27, 36, 40–41, 45, 47. On the finitude of the
tragic experience, see the excellent discussion by William F. Lynch, *Christ and
Apollo: The Dimensions of the Literary Imagination* (New York: Sheed & Ward,
1960), pp. 65–81. In contrast to Lynch, the "romantic" version of tragedy mentioned here is best represented by Joseph Wood Krutch in "The Tragic Fallacy,"
The Modern Temper (New York: Harcourt, Brace & World, 1956), pp. 79–97.
66. Sewall, *The Vision of Tragedy*, pp. 81–82.

includes such thinkers as Sartre, Marcel, Buber, Jaspers, the early Heidegger, and again Camus.

The chief characteristics of the "neotragic" vision of the twentieth century may be summarized as follows: a humanistic (i.e., nontheistic, atheistic) framework; an absurd, contingent world in which all traditional values are bankrupt; in the ensuing vacuum, an expansion of human freedom, understood as an originative, self-generating act, together with a recognition of the finitude imposed by physical and social embodiment; a preoccupation with death, but at the same time a reaffirmation of the sense of life and the rejection of nihilism; a reduction of the hero from the nobility and grandeur he enjoyed in classical tragedy to more "picaresque" proportions.[67]

Of the two thinkers I have selected to represent humanistic existentialism, both of whom are literary figures as well as philosophers, Albert Camus comes closer to exemplifying these neotragic motifs. "There is but one truly serious philosophical problem," he says, "and that is suicide. Judging whether life is or is not worth living amounts to answering the fundamental question of philosophy." Thus begins *The Myth of Sisyphus,* a book which declares (in the author's words from the Preface) "that even within the limits of nihilism it is possible to find the means to proceed beyond nihilism." It offers "a lucid invitation to live and to create, in the very midst of the desert."[68] The question as to whether life is worth living, and the nihilistic context in which the question must be decided, are engendered by the feeling of absurdity, which arises out of the juxtaposition between a sense of

67. Ibid., pp. 106–132; R. W. B. Lewis, *The Picaresque Saint* (Philadelphia: Lippincott, 1961), pp. 17–35. Not all of these characteristics are found in every existentialist thinker by any means. A theistically grounded existentialism is still a possibility, as evidenced by Kierkegaard, Buber, Marcel, and Greene, among others. I stress, however, nontheistic existentialism, not only because it is more representative, but also because it offers a serious alternative for thinkers involved in the struggle for the liberation of oppressed peoples. For example, because the question of theodicy seems irresolvable to him, the black theologian William R. Jones has turned away from Christian faith to the existentialism of Sartre and Camus. See below, Chap. VI, Sec. 3c.

68. Albert Camus, *The Myth of Sisyphus and Other Essays,* trans. Justin O'Brien (New York: Vintage Books, 1959), pp. v, 3; cf. pp. 44–47.

the world's irrationality or meaninglessness and "the wild longing for clarity whose call echoes in the human heart. The absurd depends as much on man as on the world. For the moment it is all that links them together." [69]

How is it possible to live in such a world "without appeal," i.e., without bringing in a supernatural salvation? Simply by engaging the *freedom* that is ineluctably mine *to be, to act, to revolt* against the absurd without supposing that I can overcome it. "If the absurd cancels all my chances of eternal freedom, it restores and magnifies, on the other hand, my freedom of action. That privation of hope and future means an increase in man's availability." Once I give up the illusion of a freedom from death, I become available for the present and the possibilities it holds for action; I find myself liberated from the rules and conventions contrived to achieve a promised purpose for life in some future world. "Outside of that single fatality of death, everything, joy or happiness, is liberty. A world remains of which man is the sole master. What bound him was the illusion of another world. The outcome of his thought, ceasing to be renunciatory, flowers in images." The freedom gained, of course, remains finite and limited, character-ized by the qualities of passion and intelligence, courage and rea-son, diligence and lucidity. It knows that, although death and its agents must be resisted, in the end they will prevail; the meaning and the freedom are to be found in the struggle against them.[70]

The absurd, neotragic hero, then, is the rebel, as Camus con-tends in his second major philosophical work. "Only two possible worlds can exist for the human mind: the sacred (or, to speak in Christian terms, the world of grace) and the world of rebellion." Rebellion, although apparently a negative and egoistic act, is in fact a passionate affirmation of life and a protest against all forms of death, in the name of humanity as a whole: "I rebel—therefore we exist." [71] It is the act by which human existence-in-solidary is constituted. Rebellion, however, must find the narrow and diffi-

69. Ibid., p. 16; cf. pp. 5, 13, 21–25, 38.
70. Ibid., pp. 39–44, 49, 86–87; quotations from pp. 42, 87.
71. Camus, *The Rebel: An Essay on Man in Revolt*, trans. Anthony Bower (New York: Vintage Books, 1956), pp. 16–22, 284, 304–306; quotations from pp. 21, 22.

cult way between the Scylla of resignation or acceptance (Nietzsche and the romantics) and the Charybdis of criminality, terror, and murder (the left-wing revolutionaries). Rebellion, in short, must recognize its limits and strive for the principle of moderation, without diminishing the passion of its protest.

> Man can master in himself everything that should be mastered. He should rectify in creation everything that can be rectified. And after he has done so, children will still die unjustly even in a perfect society. Even by his greatest effort man can only propose to diminish arithmetically the sufferings of the world. But the injustice and the suffering of the world will remain and, no matter how limited they are, they will not cease to be an outrage.[72]

The heroes of Camus's novels (above all, Dr. Rieux of *The Plague*) perfectly exemplify this sober, chastened humanism in a world devoid of saving grace—which is the form by which tragedy lives on in existentialist literature.

In the great chapter on freedom in *Being and Nothingness*,[73] Jean-Paul Sartre offers a richer philosophical account of freedom as the originative existential act by which human being constitutes itself. All human action, says Sartre, is intentional in character: it is able to negate both what is presently given and the causal nexus inherited from the past, in order by acts of imagination to project future possibilities. Thereby a person ceases to be a mere "in-itself," something totally coincident with itself, and becomes a being "for-itself," i.e., a conscious being who is able to distinguish possible future modes of his or her own being from the present factical situation, who is able to transcend him- or herself without a giving up of self, a being who becomes a subject by going out from and returning to itself. That which lies between the in-itself and the for-itself is the *négatité*, the nihilating power by which consciousness negates the given and projects pure possibilities. Now freedom is precisely this nihilating power by which human being constitutes itself as human. Because it literally is the "nothingness" out of which human being arises, freedom has no

72. Ibid., pp. 25, 47, 55–61, 65–80, 100–108, 279–284, 294–296, 302–306; quotation from p. 303.
73. Jean-Paul Sartre, *Being and Nothingness: An Essay on Phenomenological Ontology*, trans. Hazel E. Barnes (New York: Philosophical Library, 1956), pp. 433–566.

essence; it makes itself an act, and we attain it across the act.   It is the existential act at the foundation of all essences, or more simply put, "existence precedes essence."   Thus Sartre is able to speak of the human self as "a spontaneity determining itself to be"; our freedom is an "original freedom," and we exist by "the free up-surge of a freedom." [74]

By all of this Sartre does not intend to deny the limitation and situatedness of freedom, and here the second of the neotragic motifs, finitude, enters the picture.   To be sure, he says, our freedom is limited by the causes, motives, and capabilities deriving from our physical and social embodiment.   But, he continues, "it is our freedom itself which must first constitute the framework, the technique, and the ends in relation to which [these things] will manifest themselves as limits."   Hence he concludes that causes are really functions of free action rather than vice versa.[75]   This is certainly true in part, but on the whole Sartre's treatment of causality constitutes a radical reduction of the involuntary ele-ment in freedom, and he does not adequately analyze the complex dialectic between the voluntary and the involuntary (a matter to which I shall return in Chapter III).

There is, however, a more radical sense for Sartre in which free-dom is situated.   The freedom of the for-itself is a *choice* of its being but not the *foundation* of its being as an in-itself, the latter being a purely contingent, hence absurd, fact.

. . . we are a freedom which chooses, but we do not choose to be free.   We are condemned to freedom, . . . thrown into freedom or, as Heidegger says, "abandoned."   And we can see that this aban-donment has no other origin than the very existence of freedom. If therefore, freedom is defined as the escape from the given, from fact, then there is a *fact* of escape from fact.   This is the facticity of freedom.[76]

74. Ibid., pp. 74–79, 89–91, 435–444, 476–477, 488. See also Sartre's *Existentialism*, trans. Bernard Frechtman (New York: Philosophical Library, 1947), pp. 18–19, 59–61.
75. Sartre, *Being and Nothingness*, pp. 437–438, 445–449, 459–460, 482, 496–499; quotation from p. 482.
76. Ibid., pp. 80–84, 479, 484–486, 490–493. See also *Existentialism*, where Sartre makes more explicit the nontheistic presupposition of his humanism: God does not exist, we are alone in an absurd world, everything is possible, man is condemned to be free, and he exists purely as the ensemble of his acts (pp. 25–28, 31–33, 58–61).

Just this, however, invites the major question that must be posed to humanistic existentialism (and by indirection to the tragic vision as a whole). Somehow, freedom is spontaneously spawned in a material cosmos, which has evolved through a combination of ineluctable necessity and the sheer contingency of random variations.[77] Our subjective freedom surges up out of natural necessity, and shortly returns to it as well. In criticizing the Heideggerian *Sein-zum-Tode*, Sartre argues that death is not my peculiar possibility, not an ontological structure of the for-itself; rather it is the nihilation of nihilation, the permanent limit of my projects, hence the absurd fact that does me in.[78] This brief episode of freedom in the midst of cosmic necessity appears to be intrinsically implausible, and given the naturalistic presupposition it might appear that the behaviorists and determinists have the better of the argument. But in addition, one must wonder whether human beings can really be considered "free" under the circumstances described by Sartre. We may ask of Camus and Sartre the same question posed to Freud: Is human freedom really plausible apart from a liberating transcendence—veiled, perhaps, by natural necessity, but ultimately overcoming it?

5. ECSTATIC-VITALISTIC FREEDOM

The American counter culture, by contrast with Marxism, Freudianism, and some forms of existentialism, is not antireligious but proreligious in the sense that it is seeking to discover a transcendent basis for liberation and is highly critical of the secular, one-dimensional version of reality characteristic of the dominant cultural mentality of our time. But the religion to which the counter culture turns is not, for the most part, the historically oriented religious tradition of the West (Judaism, Christianity, Islam). It is rather more nearly parallel to the polytheistic reli-

77. Cf. Jacques Monod, *Chance and Necessity: An Essay on the Natural Philosophy of Modern Biology*, trans. Austryn Wainhouse (New York: Vintage Books, 1972). Monod's "natural philosophy" is strongly influenced by Camus and Sartre.
78. Sartre, *Being and Nothingness*, pp. 532–548.

gions of nature found everywhere in antiquity, and in much of
the modern world as a kind of underground religion. "Our
natural religion," suggests H. Richard Niebuhr, "is polytheistic.
. . . Whatever be our relation to the official monotheism of our
religious institutions, the private faith by which we live is likely
to be a multifarious thing with many objects of devotion and
worship." [79] In this respect the counter culture exhibits an overtly
primitive and pagan vitality, by contrast with what it considers to
be the exhaustion and sterility of the Christian West.

More recent antecedents also underlie the counter culture, of
course. Marxist and/or Freudian elements have been introduced
through the influence of such figures as Herbert Marcuse and
Norman O. Brown; but its more authentic heritage appears to lie
in romanticism—more nearly the romantic poets (e.g., Blake,
Goethe, Wordsworth, Shelley) than the romantic philosophers.[80]
In addition, however, the vision of Nietzsche is everywhere felt,
although rarely acknowledged. The Nietzschean doctrines of the
"will-to-power" and "eternal recurrence" engender a freedom
based on the ecstatic transcendence or "overcoming" of oneself,
through union with the vital regularities of the natural cosmos. A
full treatment of "ecstatic-vitalistic freedom" would include the
discussion of Nietzsche, but ways must be found to hold this
chapter within reasonable bounds. The counter culture appears
too important a phenomenon to omit, and its parallels with the
religions of nature are more evident.

79. H. Richard Niebuhr, *Radical Monotheism and Western Culture* (New York:
Harper & Brothers, 1960), p. 119.

80. See Theodore Roszak, *Where the Wasteland Ends: Politics and Transcendence
in Postindustrial Society* (New York: Anchor Books, 1973), pp. 255–271. Romanticism, writes Roszak, holds a "uniquely paradigmatic place in the ancestry of the
counter culture" (p. 257). On the influence of Marx and Freud (as mediated
through Marcuse and Brown), see Roszak's earlier work, *The Making of a Counter
Culture* (New York: Anchor Books, 1969), chap. III. Although rarely mentioned,
the renegade psychotherapist and self-styled Freudo-Marxist Wilhelm Reich seems
to be an authentic forerunner of the counter culture. Reich combined ecstatic and
vitalistic elements in developing a religion oriented to what he called "cosmic
orgone energy." On Reich, see Philip Rieff, *The Triumph of the Therapeutic*,
chap. VI.

A. POLYTHEISM: THE RELIGIONS OF NATURE [81]

Although any classification of religion is dangerous, Paul Tillich's distinction among three types of polytheism—universalistic, mythological, and dualistic[82]—may prove helpful. For the first of these types, writes Tillich,

> the special divine beings, like divinities of places and realms, numinous forces in things and persons, are embodiments of a universal, all-pervading sacred power (*mana*), which is hidden behind all things and at the same time is manifest through them. . . . But this unity [of *mana*] is not a real unity. It does not transcend the manifoldness into which it is split, and it cannot control its innumerable appearances. It is dispersed among these appearances and contradicts itself in them.[83]

This form of polytheism is closest to primitive animism, the belief that all things—inanimate objects as well as plants, animals, and persons—are indwelt or animated by mysterious, all-pervading, vital powers. The shaman or tribal magician communicates with these forces of nature "as if they were mindful, intentional presences, . . . [striving] to find out their ways and to move with the grain of them." [84]

The most primitive symbol of bondage for universalistic polytheism is that of defilement or contaminating stain.[85] Evil is not understood ethically or morally but rather as a "substance-force." Contamination can occur through the violation of sacred taboos

81. Evidence that the interest in polytheism is by no means dead may be found in David Miller's recently published book, *The New Polytheism: Rebirth of the Gods and Goddesses* (New York: Harper & Row, 1974). Miller himself advocates this rebirth, contending that it can be a liberating experience, for it "allows room to move meaningfully through a pluralistic universe," and "frees one to affirm the radical plurality of the self" (p. ix). Miller argues, rightly I think, that "the death of God gives rise to the rebirth of the Gods" (p. 4). See the review essay on this book by Robert S. Ellwood, "Polytheism: Establishment or Liberation Religion?", *Journal of the American Academy of Religion*, 42 (June 1974): 344–349. Ellwood notes that, despite the emphasis on pluralism, the effect of the new polytheism propounded by Miller is to enrich individualized subjectivity at the expense of social responsibility. See also the critique of polytheism by Niebuhr, in *Radical Monotheism and Western Culture*, pp. 24–37, 114–126, a critique with which Miller engages in extensive debate. Miller actually does not analyze traditional polytheism in a systematic way, so his book has not been helpful for the present section.
82. Paul Tillich, *Systematic Theology*, vol. I (Chicago: University of Chicago Press, 1951), pp. 222–232.
83. Ibid., I, 222.
84 Roszak, *The Making of a Counter Culture*, p. 244.
85. Cf. Ricoeur, *The Symbolism of Evil*, pp. 25–26.

and cultic laws, by contact with unclean things, or as a consequence
of criminal acts such as murder or incest. Sexual relations and
death are often regarded as contaminating. Liberation is accomplished by an ecstatic fusion with the sacred power of life (vitalism), a fusion achieved by a secret, visionary discipline (of which
the shaman is the expert).

In universalistic polytheism, says Tillich, "the divine beings
are not sufficiently fixed and individualized to become the subject
of stories." But precisely this happens in mythological polytheism: individual gods and goddesses, conceived as both subpersonal
and suprapersonal, become the center of the great religious
myths.[86] These include the Sumero-Akkadian theogonic myths
(especially the Babylonian epics), Greek theogony (Homeric and
Hesiodic), the Germanic myths (upon which Nietzsche drew so
heavily), and the Hellenistic mystery religions. Bondage or evil
in these mythologies usually has a theogonic basis, resulting from
the primordial struggle among the gods at the birth of the world,
leaving a permanent mark on the created order. Liberation
occurs by means of cultic participation in the life of the dying and
rising god, as with the mystery religions. Through the cycle of
death and resurrection, the original evil deed is expurgated and
being is renewed.[87]

In all religious experience, the holy is perceived as demonic as
well as divine—an ambiguity captured by Rudolf Otto's description of the numinous as a *mysterium tremendum et fascinosum.*[88]
This ambiguity is noted in the other forms of polytheism but not
conquered. But in religious dualism, divine holiness is concentrated in one realm and demonic holiness in another: the ambiguity becomes a radical split. The two realms have often been symbolized as spirit versus matter, soul versus body, heaven versus
earth, light versus dark; and the two gods as the God of good and
the God of evil (Satan, the Devil, the Demiurge). The remote-

---

86. Tillich, *Systematic Theology,* I, 222–224.
87. Cf. Ricoeur, *The Symbolism of Evil,* pp. 175–210.
88. See *The Idea of the Holy,* trans. John W. Harvey (London: Oxford University
Press, 1957), esp. pp. 31 ff. For the following paragraph, see Tillich, *Systematic
Theology,* I, 224–225.

ness of the good God from the earth means that Satan presently holds it in thrall, although for religions of redemption the true God will triumph in the end. The classic instances of dualistic polytheism are Zoroastrianism, Manichaeanism, Orphism, and above all Gnosticism. Dualistic structures appear in other religions as well, e.g., in Jewish and Christian apocalyptic and in gnosticized forms of Christianity.

Dualism takes the problem of evil more seriously than do other forms of polytheism. Bondage is the consequence of enslavement to the demonic power and alienation from the holy and the good. Imprisonment of the spirit in the flesh can occur through ignorance, or by falling into the abyss, or as a result of exile and homelessness[89]—themes that are powerfully expressed not only in the nature religions but also by modern existentialism and the counter culture. Liberation, conversely, assumes the form of release, of being set free from the bondage of the flesh, the prisonhouse of the soul.

Rudolf Bultmann points out that the radical separation between God and the world, which marked the decay of antiquity, forced a redefinition of freedom: rather than being a political or ethical ideal (as with the *polis* and the Stoics), it became purely negative, an escape or release. According to the Gnostic myth, the true self is awakened from slumber and released from its bodily imprisonment by a message or calling brought into this world by the Redeemer. Faith in the reality of this calling is the true Gnostic existence. Thus *gnosis* means *saving* rather than theoretical or rational knowledge; it is not a free spiritual act but a miraculous, fateful, natural event, over which the recipient has no control. Salvation occurs only at the end of one's earthly existence: death is the true liberation, the passage from darkness into light. Often conjoined with this eschatological release was a present libertinism. The present world is of no ultimate importance, hence the Gnostic is free in relation to it: no work, no obligation, no restraints, no responsibility. This was especially the case when

89. Cf. Ricoeur's chapter, "The Myth of the Exiled Soul and Salvation through Knowledge," *The Symbolism of Evil*, pp. 279–305.

Gnosticism became allied with the ecstasy of the fertility cults and their sensuous feeling of present participation in redemption. In other instances, Gnostic liberation could lead to an ascetic existence; but in the case of both libertinism and asceticism a radical break occurs with the present world, and freedom results from fusion with another reality.[90]

To sum up: according to the polytheistic religions of nature, the *means* of liberation is *ecstasy* or *vision* (nonrational, by contrast with Stoicism, and nonpolitical, by contrast with classical Greece); and the *end* or *goal* of liberation is a *vitalistic fusion* with the life-force (universalistic polytheism), or with the liberating god (mythological), or with the world of pure spirit, the lost paradise (dualistic). Hence the designation, "ecstatic-vitalistic freedom."

B. THE COUNTER CULTURE

Despite its amorphous character, the counter culture appears above all to represent a quest for a new consciousness, a precognitive, nonrational consciousness that breaks the bonds of objectivity and singleness of vision associated with modern science and the urban-industrial culture built upon it.[91]   Reich refers to it as "Consciousness III," "a higher, transcendent form of reason." [92] Roszak and Brown describe it as a combination of "vision" and "ecstasy." The former suggests two sources for a theory of knowledge as vision: the shamanic vision-flight, which is a root symbol for transcendent experience, and the use of imagination by the

90. See Bultmann, *Primitive Christianity in Its Contemporary Setting*, pp. 162–171; and Niederwimmer, *Der Begriff der Freiheit*, pp. 57–63. The significance of Gnosticism for the counter culture is evidenced by Roszak's reference to the "Old Gnosis" as "vision born of transcendent knowledge," which is "religion in the oldest, most universal sense." (*Where the Wasteland Ends*, pp. xv, 270, 421.) Roszak also invokes the ancient doctrine of *apocatastasis* ("restoration") : "The teaching speaks of another world that is destined to inherit from this fallen creation and which is, in fact, paradise regained. . . . In the Gnostic myth, the apocatastasis is the illumination in the abyss by which the lost soul, after much tribulation, learns to tell the divine light from its nether reflection. . . . For us, this means an awakening from 'single vision and Newton's sleep,' where we have dreamt that only matter and history are real." (Ibid., pp. 421, 422.)
91. Roszak, *The Making of a Counter Culture*, chap. VII; *Where the Wasteland Ends*, pp. xix, 379, 417.
92. Charles A. Reich, *The Greening of America* (New York: Random House, 1970), chap. IX, esp. pp. 250, 262–263; also pp. 18–19.

romantic poets. In visionary imagination, one transcends the traditional dichotomy between subject and object, experiencing instead a merger or fusion with the ultimately mysterious powers of the natural and human world. Vision thereby leads into ecstasy, a standing-outside-oneself, being grasped by or filled with (inspired by) the powers that transcend the self. True liberation occurs in a state of enthusiasm, ecstasy, inspiration, the linguistic media of which are metaphor, symbol, myth, poetry. The ecstatic experience tends to outstrip the ability of language to express; hence the fascination with the mysticism of the Eastern religions, the intoxication by music, and the experimentation with mind-expanding or hallucinogenic drugs.[93]

The *goal* of vision and ecstasy appears to be a vitalistic union (or "fusion")[94] with nature and its transcendent, sacral power. Although the notion of vitalistic union occurs repeatedly throughout Roszak's work—the communion of the shaman with the living presences of nature, the sense of the sacredness and oneness of nature on the part of the romantic poets, the notion of salvation as *apocatastasis,* the "saving return from the depths," "the way back to the source" of all things[95]—he never succeeds in describing precisely what the transcendent power of nature is, what the sacred source is, what "divinity" might be. Such descriptions, he would contend, are impossible in principle, the product of the arid rationalism of Western theism; one must experience transcendence directly and personally or not at all.[96] I have already suggested that the religious basis of the counter culture's vitalism is pantheistic, naturalistic, and explicitly anti-Christian or pagan. Only those willing to make "animistic assumptions about the world"[97]

93. See Roszak, *Counter Culture,* chaps. IV, V, VIII; *Wasteland,* pp. 261, 270, 324, 326 ff., 339; Reich, *Greening,* pp. 217, 222–224, 242–250, 258–260, 394–395; and Norman O. Brown, *Love's Body* (New York: Vintage Books, 1966) , pp. 191, 195–196, 244, 248–249, 254, 266.
94. Brown's term, *Love's Body,* pp. 253–254.
95. Roszak, *Counter Culture,* chap. VIII; *Wasteland,* pp. 339–341, 362–366, 420–427.
96. This is one of the central doctrines of Carlos Castaneda's Don Juan (Castaneda the shaman), expressed repeatedly to his overly rationalistic pupil (Castaneda the author).
97. Roszak, *Wasteland,* pp. 339–340. Roszak admits to being an alienated Catholic (pp. 353, 412) .

can understand what is meant by the power of transcendence in nature.

It is clear, however, that the counter culture represents a passionate critique of the loss of transcendence in contemporary secularized culture, even if it is not clear how transcendence is to be regained or even what it is. Roszak is at his best in showing the inability of secular humanists to mount an effective attack on the dehumanizing conditions of modern secular society.[98] What attracts one to the counter culture is its stubborn refusal to say "enough" where orthodox Marxists, Freudians, and even existentialists have reached the limit. It depicts a stretching out to something more, a sensing of the necessary transcendence of freedom—even if the representation of that transcendence entails a renovation of primitive animism (such is the depth of alienation from the Western religious tradition).

The counter culture is not so much unpolitical or antipolitical as it is *pre*political and *post*political. The prepolitical posture is evident from Reich, who speaks of a revolution in consciousness rather than in political structures, insisting that "consciousness is *prior* to structure." [99] Roszak, more than Reich, has a political program—namely, abolition of the urban-industrial "wasteland" and movement toward true postindustrialism[100]—but the means are not political in the conventional sense. He deliberately advances no concrete political program, of either a reformist or a revolutionary cast, insisting like Reich that personal transformation must come first, followed by a participative democracy in which small groups will begin working out an alternative social structure. The alternative that most attracts him is the experimentation in communitarian living styles characteristic of anarchist socialism. Out of this anarchism will somehow emerge a new "visionary commonwealth," a confederation of free communities. In this respect his position is *post*political: it seeks the realization of the authentic human community, but without going through the normal polit-

98. Ibid., pp. 412–420; see also Reich, *Greening*, pp. 18–19, 351, 354, 363–365.
99. Reich, *Greening*, pp. 4, 299–300, 334.
100. Roszak, *Wasteland*, pp. xxiv–xxvi, 380, 384, 403.

ical process; indeed, Roszak describes it at one point as a "religious politics," based on the visionary quest.[101]

One may certainly agree that the liberated human community is ultimately a postpolitical rather than a merely political reality. But the postpolitical lies only through and beyond the political, and talk about the "visionary commonwealth" is premature without a readiness to engage in the dialectics of liberation, which entails political conflict and struggles for power and policy. Nor is it the case that structures will change inevitably when consciousness changes: prepolitical as well as postpolitical naiveté must be avoided, but without losing the vision of a true realm of freedom.

One suspects that the real explanation for the counter culture's ambivalent attitude toward politics is its conviction that the self is ultimately more important than social structures. In this respect it opts for Freud against Marx. Such is the case with Roszak, who in the Introduction to *Where the Wasteland Ends* contends that "the fate of the soul is the fate of the social order," not vice versa;[102] and it is especially characteristic of Reich's *Greening of America*, which is an extended paean to the innocence, strength, and liberty of the individual self.[103] What is advocated, however, is not a rugged individualism, but rather a noncompetitive, nonaggressive sort of selfhood, which will yield authentic community and interpersonal relationships.[104] Yet the expression and fulfillment of individual selfhood remains the central goal of even the communes; they do not take on a truly "political" character. Reich contends that the real nature of contemporary servitude is not material deprivation (thereby ignoring the suffering millions of the third world) but deprivation of spirit, feeling, mind, culture, richness of experience. Hence the revolution demanded is a revolution of consciousness. The "system" can be changed basi-

101. Ibid., pp. xiv, xviii, 388–397, 400–401, 408, 420.
102. *Wasteland*, p. xvii. In *The Making of a Counter Culture*, Roszak appears to take a more neutral or dialectical posture with respect to the question he himself poses (p. 84): "Psychic reality and social reality: which is the prime mover of our lives? Which is the substance and which the shadow?"
103. See the sentimental passage on p. 225 of *Greening*, where Walt Whitman is quoted approvingly, and we are told that the first commandment is, "Thou shalt not do violence to thyself."
104. Reich, *Greening*, pp. 226–227, 230–232.

cally by individual conversions of consciousness: "When self is recovered, the power of the Corporate State will be ended, as miraculously as a kiss breaks a witch's evil enchantment." [105]

How does this differ, one might ask, from the typical Christian doctrine of salvation by conversion of the individual soul? The only difference, claims Reich, is that Christians ask people to give up power, aggression, and materialism for an imaginary other world, whereas Consciousness III proposes "the doctrine of present happiness." [106] Reich not only embraces a naive individualism, but in the final analysis also loses sight of the transcendent, eschatological dimension of true salvation, which seemed to have been one of the significant gains of the counter culture vis-à-vis the one-dimensional mentality of the dominant culture (predicated, to be sure, on a pagan rather than a Christian basis). Reich slips back into a bourgeois hedonism at just the crucial moment. He is surely correct in stressing autonomy (recovery of selfhood) as an essential structure of freedom. But without an authentic transcendence of self, and without the transformation of sociopolitical structures, autonomy remains illusory and privatistic.[107]

Reich's tendencies at this point lead one to suspect that the counter culture's quest for transcendence is in the final analysis a psychic trip for which the only certain reality remains the individual self. Philip Rieff suggests that the characteristic American type is no longer "political man," or "religious man," or "enlightened economic man," but rather "psychological man," whose "piety toward the self" stresses the virtues of autonomy, self-realization, and detachment in the context of an objectively meaningless world. In this respect, "Freud is America's great teacher." [108] In this respect, too, the counter culture remains a simulacrum of the dominant culture.

105. Ibid., pp. 287–290, 295, 305, 316, 319.
106. Ibid., p. 346.
107. Reich is more persuasive in his diagnosis than his prescriptions. For example, chap. V of The Greening of America offers a penetrating critique of the "anatomy of the Corporate State," which will prove of value for the analysis of technocracy in the next section.
108. Rieff, The Triumph of the Therapeutic, pp. 58–62.

6. PRAGMATIC-TECHNOCRATIC FREEDOM

Our final typological rival, pragmatic-technocratic freedom, differs from the others because it lacks clear parallels in antiquity, but it must be included because of its undeniable importance on the contemporary scene. The Greek term *pragma*, like *praxis* (both from the verb *prassein*, to do), referred to human activity in general, especially that of a political or historical character; while *technē* meant skill, craft, art, design—or philosophically expressed, the creative application of imagination in constructing a human world. For us, by contrast, "pragmatic" implies that the meaning of a conception is to be sought in its practical consequences, in the behavior it manifests. Behavior, in turn, is to be measured by objective scientific methods, which presuppose that all phenomena are empirically observable, quantifiable, calculable, reducible to a physical-chemical basis. "Technology" entails the application of scientific technique for the purpose of solving practical problems of behavior, management, production, governance, etc. Technique rationalizes processes, requires the most efficient means regardless of human considerations, and universalizes systems of management and control.

Among the natural sciences, the biological and behavioral sciences have posed a more direct challenge than physics and chemistry to the reality of human freedom as traditionally understood because they deal specifically with the human organism. The length and selective character of this chapter have led me to exclude any discussion of contemporary biological views of human nature. The relevance of such views for our subject is underscored by the brilliant, disturbing treatise by the Nobel prize-winning biochemist Jacques Monod, *Chance and Necessity: An Essay on the Natural Philosophy of Modern Biology.* I shall, however, examine behaviorism, not only because of its popularization through the work of B. F. Skinner,[109] but also because it combines so precisely both pragmatism and technology: it is, in the

109. I shall rely primarily on Skinner's *Beyond Freedom and Dignity* (New York: Alfred A. Knopf, 1971). For a more technical foundation, see *Contingencies of Reinforcement: A Theoretical Analysis* (New York: Appleton-Century-Crofts, 1969) .

words of Skinner, "a technology of human behavior." Skinner
proposes to move "beyond freedom" as traditionally conceived
(e.g., by all of the types hitherto considered) to a technologically
based "freedom," defined as "a person's condition when he is
behaving under nonaversive controls." [110]   Whether such a condition actually warrants the word "freedom" is the major question
before us.

A. BEHAVIORISM: BEYOND FREEDOM [111]

It seems foolish, in face of the empirical evidence, to deny that
human behavior is determined by external factors, nor is it necessary to deny this in order to defend freedom. Human beings are
not autonomous in the sense of being independent of determination by their physical and social environments. Acts of volition,
decision, self-determination, and feeling do not emerge *de novo;*
human freedom is not a creative freedom *ex nihilo.* Individuals
are born into a social world, with its languages, laws, values, cus-
toms, institutions, and cognitive consensus; and they are subject to
the fundamental necessities of their own physical condition.
Skinner is right in calling attention to the conditionedness of
human behavior, against those who seem to think of the human
being as an alien in a hostile world, who is somehow independent
of or able to escape its influences.

The question is not whether behaviorism is right about involuntary determinations, but whether it can provide an adequate
account of human experience *in its full range.* Does the involuntary necessarily expunge the voluntary? Like all theories that explain everything in terms of a single principle, Skinner's behaviorism is reductionistic. Physics, biology, and behavioral psychology
are in his view the only valid sciences; the disciplines that comprise the social sciences and the humanities are dismissed as prescientific. [112]   All the phenomena for which these disciplines have

---

110. Skinner, *Beyond Freedom and Dignity,* p. 32.
111. This section is based on a revision of material first published in my article,
"Freedom, Dignity, and Transcendence: A Response to B. F. Skinner," *Soundings,*
55 (Fall 1972): 347–358. The issues raised in this section are further discussed in
Chap. III, Secs. 2B, 3B.
112. Skinner, *Beyond Freedom and Dignity,* pp. 5, 19, 211.

developed richly variegated categories of interpretation may be explained in terms of a single principle: the contingencies of reinforcement. One is immediately suspicious of an analysis that draws all data, regardless how differentiated and complex, back to a single basic explanation. Ricoeur points to the *"monotony* of [Skinner's] conceptual apparatus and the hazardous extrapolation of one set of concepts beyond their initial sphere of validity." Behaviorism, in his judgment, fails to recognize the need for a variety of language games in speaking about human action—existential, phenomenological, structural and linguistic as well as behavioral. By insisting that it represents the only valid alternative to the now-discredited mentalistic psychology of the seventeenth and eighteenth centuries, behaviorism exhibits a hermeneutical naiveté.[113]

Moreover, Skinner is not consistent with his own principles. He acknowledges that *Beyond Freedom and Dignity* is filled with prescientific terms and that "it would be ridiculous to insist" upon the provision of scientific translations for every metaphorical and symbolic expression contained in the English language. But the rationalization he gives for the inconsistency is not persuasive: "The book could have been written for a technical reader without [mentalistic] expressions . . ., but the issues are important to the nonspecialist and need to be discussed in a nontechnical fashion."[114] The real reason, it would appear, is that the metaphorical and symbolic functions of language are inexpungeable and untranslatable into scientific terminology. They disclose an aspect of reality (volition, freedom) inaccessible to purely empirical description. "Mentalistic expressions" in fact also occur frequently in Skinner's recent work on behavioral method for "technical readers," *Contingencies of Reinforcement.* Noam Chomsky has pointed out that the ostensibly scientific terminology of behaviorism lapses back into ordinary language. And Charles Scott notes

113. Paul Ricoeur, "A Critique of B. F. Skinner's *Beyond Freedom and Dignity,*" *Philosophy Today,* 17 (Summer 1973): 166–175; see esp. pp. 167–169, 175.
114. Skinner, *Beyond Freedom and Dignity,* pp. 23–24.

the strong emotions, the passion, the concern for the future well-being of human culture expressed by the author of *Beyond Freedom and Dignity*.[115]

In describing the sorts of reinforcements appropriate to human beings, behavioral scientists actually presuppose a deciding, willing, acting, consenting subject or self.[116] By varying the character and schedule of reinforcements, behavioral technicians try in effect to persuade human beings to act in certain ways. They know that if their subjects do not "choose voluntarily" to perform the desired behavior, their influence upon them will not be effective and is likely to prove counterproductive. We can, of course, coerce or compel persons to behave according to our demands, but such controls are likely to engender revolt or escape; positive or nonaversive reinforcements are much more effective. Considerations such as the response of the subject and his or her affective relationship to the controller need not be taken into account when one is working with animals. The withholding of food until a certain type of behavior is performed is a simple form of coercion that will not work very well with human beings. On the other hand, although animals are not free, self-conscious subjects, they are sentient beings possessing a central nervous system and varying degrees of prereflective consciousness, and consequently the control of their behavior is more complex than that of other organisms.

This implicit recognition of the place of volition in human behavior may be a consequence of the shift from the old stimulus-response mechanism of the original behaviorists to Skinner's concepts of operant behavior and contingencies of reinforcement.[117] The focus has shifted from the environment as such (with its eliciting stimuli) to the human being's interaction with it, which has proven to be more complex, delicate, and less calculable than first expected.

115. Noam Chomsky, "The Case Against B. F. Skinner," *The New York Review of Books*, 17:11 (December 30, 1971) : 18–24; Charles E. Scott, "An Existential Perspective on B. F. Skinner," *Soundings*, 55 (Fall 1972) : 338–339.
116. See Skinner, *Beyond Freedom and Dignity*, chaps, 2, 4, 5.
117. See Skinner, *Contingencies of Reinforcement*, chaps. 1, 5, 8.

Another way of broaching the same point is to suggest that the practical application of behavioral science is more persuasive than its theory of human nature, and indeed that the application often belies the theory. The most successful applications have been in education (especially of younger children), management technique, and behavior modification therapy. In each of these instances, the freedom of individuals actually is not violated but rather appealed to via nonaversive reinforcements. The difficulty is that in *Beyond Freedom and Dignity* Skinner advances a general theory of human nature, of what human beings are in relation to the world, which he would like us to believe is verified by experimental data, but which in fact is merely one of several possible ways of interpreting the meaning of such data. The validity of the interpretation is a philosophical question, not an empirical one. The data of behaviorism may be valid, many of its practices successful, but its anthropology and cosmology faulty.[118]

Skinner's theoretical world does not afford a possible home for human freedom, and therefore he is obliged to dismiss as explanatory fictions the evidences of freedom and the reciprocity of the voluntary and involuntary to which his own experimental and practical work has pointed. His meta-empirical or philosophical perspective might be characterized as "physicalism" or undialectical materialism, as evidenced by his agreement with those who believe that eventually physiology will explain all there is to know about the workings of the so-called mental apparatus. He describes the human person as a "physical system" subject to the conditions under which the species evolved and the individual lives. "Man is a machine in the sense that he is a complex system behaving in lawful ways, but the complexity is extraordinary." The "self" is "a repertoire of behavior appropriate to a given set of contingencies." In place of the apotheosis of the human being discernible in the literatures of freedom and dignity, Skinner furnishes an apotheosis of the physical and cultural environment.

118. Charles Scott makes this point well, *Soundings*, 55: 337–338; also Ricoeur, *Philosophy Today*, 17: 166.

The direction of the controlling relation is reversed: a person does not act upon the world, the world acts upon him. The individual owes everything to biological evolution and social environment; even revolutionaries are almost wholly the conventional products of the systems they overthrow.[119]

The environment is constituted by a network of "contingencies of survival," which is the key to both biological and cultural evolution. In Skinner's analysis, *survival* emerges as the "transcendent" factor that determines value. "Things are good (positively reinforcing) or bad (negatively reinforcing) presumably because of the contingencies of survival under which the species evolved." According to these contingencies, those things are good that do not cause pain or harm. The ethical theory correlated with the contingencies of survival is a modified hedonism: people work to produce pleasant things (not "feelings" of pleasure) and to avoid painful things. "Epicurus was not quite right"; but for Skinner he very nearly was. Moreover, the law of survival that holds sway in biological evolution also applies to the evolution of culture, and in this sense the social environment is ultimately a function of the physical. Just as physical organisms survive and evolve because they learn how to avoid painful stimuli, so do cultures. It might be said that the contingencies of survival constitute Skinner's "uncaused cause," his "uncontrolled controller," his "god." But clearly this is an impersonal, fortuitous, nonrational, nonpurposive, morally neutral form of transcendence. Human nature will continue to change, but we cannot say in what direction, and eventually the human species will be exterminated.[120]

To be sure, Skinner also suggests that, although the individual may be controlled by his environment, it is an environment almost wholly of his or her own making. Therefore one may speak of the evolution of a culture as "a kind of gigantic exercise in self-control," and assert that "man as we know him, for better or for worse, is what man has made of man." [121] But it would be mis-

---

119. Skinner, *Beyond Freedom and Dignity*, pp. 11–12, 14–15, 123–124, 195, 199, 202, 211.
120. Ibid., pp. 26, 104, 107, 130, 132–136, 150–151, 181, 208.

leading to suppose that Skinner is hereby replacing the "autonomous inner man" with autonomous social man. For the sake of consistency, he must say that in designing an environment persons continue to be controlled; they are not acting autonomously on a collective level. Of course they are not directly controlled by what they are designing, although it may exercise counter-controls in the process; the point is rather that they must remain subject to the contingencies of survival and engage in the design of cultures with survival value because they are positively reinforced by such actions. Thus in Skinner's theoretical world no room for freedom is to be found, and the talk about man being what man has made of man is misleading. Man is a maker, even a maker of men, but he is not free, nor does he gain freedom, in the process. We are in fact "beyond freedom."

B. TECHNOLOGICAL BONDAGE AND LIBERATION [122]

"Technocratic"—the other term by which we are designating the final type of freedom—refers to the condition of being "governed by technique." "Technocracy" describes a form of governance in which most economic and social functions are controlled by technologically based bureaucratic systems, operated by corporate managers and technical experts on behalf of either private interests or the state. The paradox is that technology provides the means for attaining freedom from poverty and physical need, from drudgery and inhuman labor, from disease and ignorance, from geographic isolation and bondage to nature, but only at the expense of new and more subtle forms of oppression and alienation.

121. Ibid., pp. 205–208.
122. Major critical analyses of the impact of technology on society include Thorstein Veblen, *The Engineers and the Price System* (1921), Oswald Spengler, *Man and Technics* (1932), Lewis Mumford, *Technics and Civilization* (1934), and *The Myth of the Machine* (1967–1970), Jacques Ellul, *The Technological Society* (1964), and John K. Galbraith, *The New Industrial State* (1967). The recent and more popular literature on technology is enormous: one good example of it is Emmanuel G. Mesthene's *Technological Change: Its Impact on Man and Society* (1970). These and other sources are presupposed by the less technical or specialized writings oriented to the American scene upon which I shall rely: Richard Goodwin, *The American Condition* (1974), Charles Reich, *The Greening of America* (1970), Theodore Roszak, *Where the Wasteland Ends* (1973), and Gibson Winter, *Being Free: Reflections on America's Cultural Revolution* (1970).

It was not so long ago that Harvey Cox published his famous book, *The Secular City* (1965), intended as "a celebration of its liberties and an invitation to its discipline." The "liberties" Cox proposed to celebrate were based on such features of the secular city ("technopolis") as anonymity, mobility, pragmatism, and profanity or this-worldliness. The book was written at the height of the "secularization theology," which saw secularization itself as a liberating process—the "disenchantment of nature," the "desacralization of politics," and the "deconsecration of values," as Cox put it.[123] Although the cultural and theological mood has shifted sharply since the mid-sixties, and the optimism of Cox and others now seems premature in light of the intervening urban, ecological, and political crises, an important insight is stated here that must not be lost with our new awareness of the destructive potential of technocracy. Gibson Winter expresses it this way:

> Liberation is inextricably bound up with high technology. Our massive populations cannot survive without mass-production systems. Our enlarged humanity depends upon media and complex systems of transportation to realize its possibilities. Thus, groups who would destroy these systems in their search for liberation only court disaster. Technical rationality is not demonic in itself. . . . But its creative power . . . has become a destructive principle.[124]

This warning must be kept in mind as we review the criticisms of technocracy advanced by Reich, Roszak, Goodwin, and others. Although they do not propose to destroy technology, they do not show how to reform it, and they tend to lose perspective on what is essential in it.

The technocracies of America and Western Europe are clearly benevolent rather than totalitarian or vulgar in character.[125] They permit a wide latitude of dissent, of experimentation in life-styles, of personal privacy, of exotic entertainment; they assure relative

123. Harvey Cox, *The Secular City: Secularization and Urbanization in Theological Perspective* (New York: Macmillan, 1965), pp. 21–37. The statement quoted above appears on the cover of the book but not in the title.
124. Winter, *Being Free*, p. 7.
125. See Roszak's distinction between suave, vulgar, and teratoid technocracies, *Wasteland*, pp. 38–44.

Rival Freedoms   97

economic security for all but the bottom twenty percent (a surd
that begins to cloud the picture of benevolence); they exercise
their controls by behavior modification and opinion persuasion
rather than by totalitarian political methods. But still they are
benevolent *despotisms*, in which rule is exercised not so much by
the people (*demo*cracy) as by the technological structure itself
(*techno*cracy). They do not respond to the will of the people but
rather create and manage it. Government and politics have become functions of the economic and social realities, and the true
province of politics is in the administration of existing interests.
Hence *genuine* political alternatives are with rare exceptions not
realistic possibilities, and this fact is reflected in a general public
cynicism about the political process.[126]

Technology not only increases productive capacity and rationalizes organizational procedures (although whether it actually increases *efficiency* is doubtful because of its proliferation of bureaucratic red tape). More significantly, it tends to concentrate power
in a critical mass and at a level where very few individuals are
engaged in making significant decisions. The amalgamation and
integration of power have occurred in two ways: the combination
of public and private functions in a single "corporate state," with
an easy reciprocity between governmental agencies and private
industry; and horizontal corporate mergers, whereby a single
gigantic corporation controls the manufacture of many different
types of products, very often on an international scale. The result is the destruction of the system of checks and balances between
the public and private sectors, the reduction of real competition,
the control of products on the market, the elimination of true
differences and options. Beneath the carnival-like variety, everything is monotonously the same.[127]

But who actually controls all this power? Clearly it is not
subject to the democratic process, to public opinion, or to controls

126. Ibid., pp. 39–41, 63–64; Goodwin, *The American Condition*, pp. 312–317,
321–322, 338–343; Winter, "The Question of Liberty in a Technologized World,"
Anglican Theological Review, Supplementary Series, no. 1 (July 1973), p. 86.
127. Reich, *Greening*, pp. 91–97; Roszak, *Wasteland*, pp. 39–41; Goodwin, *The
American Condition*, pp. 216–217, 234, 286–287, 291; Winter, *Being Free*, p. 70, and
"The Question of Liberty in a Technologized World," p. 81.

of the market since producers largely create their own demand for products. The legal owners of "public" corporations are the stockholders, but they have no claim on the value of a corporation and are virtually powerless to control or even influence its policies. Control would appear, then, to pass to the professional experts, corporate managers, and governmental administrators who "operate" the system. But as Reich points out, "the bureaucracy is so powerful that no executive, not even the President of the United States, can do much to budge it from its course. Top executives are profoundly limited by lack of knowledge. . . . The man in the chic office turns out to be a broker, a decider between limited alternatives, a mediator and arbitrator, a chairman, but not an originator." [128]   In effect, the corporation owns itself, and the bureaucratic system runs itself. In Goodwin's words, "the true sovereign does not wear a human face." This, he suggests, is the ultimate alienation, beyond what even Marx was able to envision: "Alienated labor is not owned by a single man or even a single class. To a very large extent, it is owned by a system, a process, which rules everyone and belongs to no one" [129]—a system that has become its own end and whose exigencies are not those of human freedom.

As a lawyer, Reich is especially sensitive to the ways in which the functions of the law have been subverted by the corporate state. Law becomes an instrument of oppression and control instead of justice. Indeed, the nature of law itself undergoes a change. A bureaucratically controlled, technocratic system needs a vast number of rules, regulations, and procedures as the very substance of its organizational structure. The law ceases to be a definition of traditional values and prohibitions, becoming instead the value-free medium by which the corporate state functions.

> As the nation has become a legalistic society, law has increasingly become the medium in which private maneuver for power, status, and financial gain could take place. . . . The game of law is

128. Reich, *Greening*, pp. 101–107.
129. Goodwin, *The American Condition*, pp. 218–220, 225, 246, 258, 282–285, 288, 340.

played with all of the legal powers of government to provide benefits, subsidies, allocate resources and franchises, and grant special
exceptions and favors. . . . Lawyers are the professional strate-
gists for this game and vast amounts of energy and activity are
poured into playing it. The legal game board builds up into
structures that embody, *in the law itself,* almost every inequity,
injustice, and irrationality that has become accepted in our society.

The inequity and injustice are felt most severely by powerless and
minority groups, who know that the law is both constructed against
them and enforced against them in special ways.[130]

Gibson Winter points to the paradox that the material web of
interdependence provided by technocratic society creates the conditions for participation, communication, and unification far
beyond anything imaginable in earlier cultures, yet at the same
time it provokes a heightened sense of estrangement, alienation,
and powerlessness on the part of individuals. Technology
estranges as it unites because its functions are objective and
impersonal.

The power of technology depends upon extending the horizon
of calculability. The alienating character of technology is precisely this reduction of the world to the calculable. Yet men
and cultures resist being reduced to calculable entities. Thus in
creating interdependence, the techno-society also alienates and
estranges. . . . Technological society creates a participatory web
with one hand, while tearing the fabric of common humanity with
the other. Thus the participatory world moves inexorably toward deepening estrangement.[131]

Another significant social effect of technocracy is that it requires
institutions that will serve to "disburden" the individual of his or
her sense of alienation and objective powerlessness—safety valves
as it were, permitting the release of dangerous pressures, thus in-
suring the stability of the technological society. Institutions and
activities such as churches, communes, encounter groups, civic
clubs, sporting events, entertainment, recreational and vacation

130. Reich, *Greening,* pp. 117–128; quotation from pp. 121–122.
131. Winter, *Being Free,* pp. 37–40; quotation from p. 38. See also "The Question
of Liberty in a Technologized World," pp. 84–86; and Roszak, *Wasteland,* pp.
19–20.

areas, serve this function—in the process of which their own intended purposes may be subverted.

I suggested at the outset that technical rationality is not itself demonic, nor is the society produced by technology intrinsically evil. It is rather the *use* to which technological power is put, and the *image* that men and women create of themselves and their world through its use, that become demonic and destructive. Essentially this image is one of self-creation, unlimited power and knowledge, narcissistic delight in the products of one's own making, arrogant exploitation of anything that stands in the way of personal autonomy or group mastery, reduction of reality to a complex of energies to be analyzed, controlled, and consumed. The Greeks called it *hubris*—"the overweening pride of the doomed." [132] The Bible called it *sin*—the idolatrous veneration of oneself in place of God, the prideful confusion of one's own finite creative powers with the infinite creativity of God, and the consequent rape of the earth.

The danger with technology is that it makes this self-deification so terribly plausible. It creates the illusion that human beings are indeed their own maker and savior, that they can know, do, desire, and have without limit. The will-to-power, aroused and enhanced by technical rationality, has expressed itself not only in technocracy and exploitation of the environment, but also in the enslavement and oppression of blacks and other minorities, in military adventures such as Vietnam, and in political scandals such as Watergate. Racism and war may be seen as logical extensions of techno-man. The environmental crisis, the exploitation of human beings, the use of military force and subversive activities to impose our policies throughout the world, and the abuse of political office, all represent "over-extensions" of American will-to-power that are now bringing a "transcendent judgment" to bear against the American system itself.[133]

Viewed this way, technocracy represents a religious crisis, a crisis

132. Roszak, *Wasteland*, p. 18; cf. pp. 10, 16–18.
133. So argues Winter in *Being Free*, pp. 113–132; and "The Question of Liberty in a Technologized World," pp. 81–83.

of soul and spirit. The resolution of the crisis must likewise be religious, for technology cannot cure itself. Salvation from a religious perspective would entail the recovery of a transcendence that *limits* human beings but does not *oppress* them—a liberating transcendence that delimits human autonomy without destroying it, that engenders a true community without alienation and depersonalization; a transcendence that sets men and women free as finite, intrinsically communal beings in a world not of their own making, but in which they can dwell humanely. The counter culture offers its own version of salvation from the bondage of the dominant technological culture, and we have examined its strengths and weaknesses. Insofar as it turns to nature as transcendent, saving power, the liberation it offers appears illusory—for the Earth-Mother is both the womb that nurtures human beings and the unfeeling deity that consumes them. The saving, liberating god is not nature but "nature's God."

7. CHRISTIAN FREEDOM: ANTICIPATIONS

A. HUMAN FREEDOM, ATHEISM, AND FAITH

It is not without significance that the contemporary representatives of our parallel types may be aligned with major challenges to belief in God in the Western religious tradition. The question of the reality of human freedom poses also the question of the reality of God in a fundamental, inescapable way. In the case of Marxism, Freudianism, and existentialism, atheism is rooted in the conviction that these two realities—that of human freedom and of God—cannot coexist, for the God of religious belief is perceived as an accuser, dominator, and destroyer of human freedom rather than as a liberator. For Marx and Freud, religious beliefs are viewed as *illusions* that serve to sanction certain social, cultural, and psychological oppressions and prohibitions. Camus and Sartre start with the assumption that persons find themselves in an absurd, godless world, devoid of values and purpose, in which, nonetheless, human freedom is able to constitute itself out of nothingness by a sheer, self-generating act.

This "atheism of human freedom" [134] is represented in its purest form by Nietzsche, who was persuaded that the will-to-freedom (or will-to-power) of the "overman" must put to death all belief in God and the gods. In *Thus Spoke Zarathustra,* Nietzsche wrote:

> Whatever in me has feeling, suffers and is in prison; but my will always comes to me as my liberator and joy-bringer. Willing liberates: that is the true teaching of will and liberty—thus Zarathustra teaches it. . . . Away from God and gods this will has lured me; what could one create if gods existed? But my fervent will to create impels me over again toward man. . . .[135]

The implicit atheism of modern technology also belongs to this type, for it encourages the apotheosis of human autonomy and will-to-power—but in a way and for reasons quite different from any that Nietzsche would have acknowledged.

The atheism of natural science, by contrast, questions not only the reality of God but also the reality of human freedom: *both* are rejected, as in the philosophical biology of Monod and the behaviorism of Skinner. The human being is rather understood to be fully determined by his or her natural and cultural environments, and what science must seek to do is to rationalize and modify the environmental controls for human good insofar as possible. These scientists may start with the same philosophical assumptions regarding the absurdity of the cosmos as the existentialists do, but they draw different conclusions about the possibility of human freedom in such a world.

Finally, as we have observed, the counter culture does not share the atheism of modern science, technology, and philosophy; but its quest for a transcendent, sacred basis of human freedom has for the most part led it to embrace the religions of nature rather than the historically oriented religious tradition of the West. Its liber-

134. Cf. Wolfhart Pannenberg, "Types of Atheism and Their Theological Significance," in *Basic Questions in Theology,* vol. II, trans. George H. Kehm (Philadelphia: Fortress Press, 1971) , p. 192.
135. Friedrich Nietzsche, *Thus Spoke Zarathustra,* 2:2 *(The Portable Nietzsche,* trans. Walter Kaufmann [New York: Viking Press, 1954], p. 199); see 1:22, 4:13. See also *The Gay Science,* Aphorisms 125, 341 *(The Portable Nietzsche,* pp. 95–96, 101–102. On the equation of the will-to-power and the will-to-freedom, see Kaufmann, *Nietzsche: Philosopher, Psychologist, Antichrist* (Princeton: Princeton University Press, 1950) , p. 215.

ating deity is the Earth Goddess, not the God of Moses, the prophets, and Jesus.

To meet the challenges of modern atheism and paganism, biblical faith must undertake to show that the freedom of human beings and the freedom of God are co-constitutive and interdependent themes. This proposal may assume two basic forms. First, starting from a phenomenological description of human freedom, it may be argued that such freedom is structurally open to and has its foundation in the ultimate reality of God. Dependence upon and openness to the infinite God do not cancel human subjectivity but rather constitute it within embodied limits; the reality of God as absolute or perfect freedom belongs to the essence of human being as finite freedom. This argument was formulated by Schleiermacher and especially Hegel in classic form and has been revived by a number of contemporary theologians.[136] My own version of this argument is presented in Chapter III of the present work.

Second, starting from a hermeneutic of the symbols of faith, it may be argued that the reality of God is to be defined by reference to his activity as one who suffers with human beings and sets them free, rather than as one who protects, dominates, and accuses, which is the way the gods have traditionally functioned for religious belief. This form of the argument has been explored by Paul Ricoeur in his attempt to move through and beyond the atheistic critiques of religion to a new basis for faith.[137] Chapters V–VII of the present work contain an extended elaboration of this argument.

According to biblical tradition, the co-constituted freedom of God and humankind takes place across a *history,* a *drama,* a

---

136. See Friedrich Schleiermacher, *The Christian Faith,* ed. H. R. Mackintosh and J. S. Stewart (Edinburgh: T. & T. Clark, 1928), § 4; and G. W. F. Hegel, *Encyclopedia of the Philosophical Sciences,* §§ 382–386; and *Philosophy of Right,* trans. T. M. Knox (Oxford: The Clarendon Press, 1952), § 22. Among contemporary theologians, see especially Wolfhart Pannenberg, *The Idea of God and Human Freedom,* trans. R. A. Wilson (Philadelphia: Westminster Press, 1973), chaps. 3, 5. Others include Karl Rahner, Henri Duméry, and Paul Tillich.
137. Paul Ricoeur, "Religion, Atheism, and Faith," in *The Religious Significance of Atheism,* pp. 59–98.

story.[138]   It is not a static, timeless phenomenon, patterned after
the cyclical regularities of nature or the metaphysical categories of
Greek thought.   Rather it entails novelty, disruption, new birth,
and a telos or eschaton.   Who God is, and what human beings are,
only gradually take shape as the story is told, retold, and lived out.
This entire story is a "theodicy"—a justification of God in light of
the experienced realities of bondage and liberation in the world;
as such it provides the basis for a response to the atheistic critiques
and pagan alternatives.   The story begins with an affirmation that
freedom constitutes the essence of human existence, because men
and women were created in the "image" of the free God.   This
essence was faulted by a self-imposed bondage of the will, which
infected not only individual persons but also social and institutional structures.   God acted to liberate his creatures, not by a
supernatural rescue, but by subjecting himself to the consequence
of their loss of freedom: according to Christian faith, he took on
the form of one who was oppressed in the figure of Jesus of
Nazareth, who lived, died, and is now raised from the dead as the
agent of God's liberating power in history.   The goal of this story
is to transfigure freedom and inscribe it afresh upon the structures
of the human and natural worlds, so that "the creation itself will
be set free from its bondage to decay and obtain the glorious freedom of the children of God."   In order to suggest the centrality of
freedom to this story, and to penetrate the meaning of these old
categories—creation, fall, redemption, consummation—I offer the
following formulations in their place: *essential freedom, bound
freedom, liberated freedom, final freedom.*   Together these motifs
constitute the story of Christian freedom; they provide its distinctive structure, which sets it off from the rival meanings of freedom
considered in this chapter, however much it also overlaps them
and incorporates their concerns.   The structure of the Christian
story is clearly comic or tragicomic rather than tragic.   Like all

138. The narrative or "story" form of the biblical tradition in general and of Christian faith in particular has been stressed in much recent discussion.   For a summary
of it, see Sallie McFague TeSelle, *Speaking in Parables: A Study of Metaphor and
Theology* (Philadelphia: Fortress Press, 1975), pp. 35–38, 119–144.

comedy, it encompasses tragic motifs but reverses or transfigures their meaning. Therefore, God no longer functions as the dominating Father-figure, as in the Oedipal story, but as the One who suffers with human beings and liberates them through the life, death, and resurrection ("new birth") of his Son.[139]

This work is intended as a project in *Christian* theology. Although in many important respects Jewish and Christian views of freedom are closely related if not identical, especially by comparison with the rival types, and although Christianity is inconceivable apart from its foundation in the faith of Israel, it is not appropriate to continue speaking indeterminately of "biblical faith" or "biblical freedom." The integrity of both Judaism and Christianity must be respected, for each resists being assimilated into the other. The Christian "story" is born out of the Jewish story but carries it forward in ways that set it apart and give it a distinctive structure. In choosing to elaborate the determinate features of the Christian story, which is my own, I intend also to acknowledge and honor the determinacy of the Jewish story.

B. ELEMENTS OF THE CHRISTIAN STORY

(1) Essential Freedom

I shall begin with a phenomenological description of freedom as the essence of humankind created in the image of God, prior to and apart from the "fall" by which freedom was lost and the "new birth" by which it is liberated from bondage. The human essence is *created freedom*—a freedom limited by and reciprocal with the body (individual and collective, organic and social), an incarnate, finite, embodied freedom, yet still a freedom. The behaviorists correctly insist that individuals are determined by both the physical and the social involuntary, but I shall dispute the claim that the voluntary is thereby expunged.

---

139. See Dan O. Via, Jr., *Kerygma and Comedy in the New Testament: A Structuralist Approach to Hermeneutic* (Philadelphia: Fortress Press, 1975), chap. II, esp. pp. 45–49, and pp. 97–101.

The essential structures of freedom are not one but three: autonomy (subjective freedom), community (intersubjective and objective freedom), and openness (transsubjective freedom). This triadic structure means that freedom cannot be understood simply as autonomy (self-determination, self-mastery, self-fulfillment), as in the classical Greek, Stoic, Freudian, and existentialist views. Nor is it simply a community of free human production, based upon non-alienating economic structures, as Marxism claims. Nor, finally, are subjective, intersubjective, and objective modes of human freedom ultimately viable apart from a liberating transcendence to which humankind is structurally open—a gracious rather than a hostile or indifferent "environment," which engenders freedom rather than destroys it, and offers the possibility of reconciling the inherent conflict between autonomy and community. Here I shall enter into controversy with Marx, Freud, and the existentialists, who want to have human freedom without transcendence, and with behaviorism and natural science, which more consistently question the reality of freedom as such because of the absence of transcendence. The question as to whether there exists *in fact* a transcendent liberating power to which human beings are structurally open must remain bracketed at this stage of the investigation. Here the analysis focuses on the phenomenon of human *openness* as implied in and required by the dynamics of consent in the context of necessity. That *to which* human beings are open is dependent upon bringing in the symbols of a determinate religious tradition.

(2) Bound Freedom

Bondage is perceived by Jews and Christians alike to be a dimension of human freedom itself, not something imposed by alien, nonhuman powers (paganism), not a flaw inscribed upon the logic of being (theogony), not the work of an evil god (tragedy). This is a freedom that enslaves itself by an interior act of self-deception, engendering a false, aberrant pursuit of life that not only issues in revolt against God (idolatry, pride), but also constitutes a way that leads to death (flight, sloth). Against Freud I shall contend that human bondage results neither from a tragic conflict between life and death instincts, nor from the repression of libidinal desire, but from the false infinitizing of desire by the power of imagination. Moreover, the interior act of bondage (sin) is objectified and demonically reinforced by the oppressive powers and alienating structures of culture, society, politics, and ultimately of death itself, the final form of bondage. These objectifications may be symbolized by the Pauline categories of law, death, and the worldly powers.

Because of this internal-external dialectic, liberation cannot be accomplished simply by a removal of the objective conditions of estrangement, or by a revolution in economic and political structures, as Marxism claims. For the powers that enslave persons are in the first instance internal to the psyche rather than external to it. On the other hand, liberation cannot be accomplished simply by an inner liberation of the psyche, as Stoicism, Freudianism, and existentialism claim. For bondage is demonically reinforced and intensified by the process of institutionalization; it will not simply disappear when consciousness changes or the psyche is liberated. As behaviorism and technology make clear, consciousness does not merely precede structures but is shaped and controlled by them. In the third place, because deception deceives and forgets itself in the act of deceit, and thus cannot rescue itself from its self-imposed bondage, liberation is not possible by knowledge alone—whether it be the old *gnosis* of saving knowledge brought into this world by the Redeemer, or the new *gnosis* of vision and ecstasy (the counter culture), or the rational self-control of the Stoic and the psychoanalytic rationality of Freud, or even the disciplined intelligence of the existentialist hero. Education, to be sure, is a critical factor in the struggle for liberation, especially on the part of oppressed peoples. It must be neither downplayed nor elevated to an idol. According to Christian faith, *saving* knowledge is not a human achievement but a divine gift, a revelation, which occurs, however, precisely in the midst of the human struggle for knowledge and freedom.

(3) Liberated Freedom

Jesus of Nazareth brought freedom to speech in a quite radical, unprecedented fashion, but he lacked a specific word for it. He was the radically free person, and he proclaimed and enacted a gospel of liberation. He embodied the essence of human freedom in terms of his sonship or openness to God, his communion with downtrodden people, and his radical selfhood or sense of personal identity and authority. The central image of his ministry was that of the kingdom of God or the kingdom of freedom, whose imminent coming he proclaimed. The salvation accomplished by the life and death of Jesus was understood as "liberation" by Paul and John, although in different ways (for Paul, as redemption and love, for John, as unconcealment and life). Both Paul and John supplied the vocabulary of "freedom," borrowed from the Greek world, lacking in Jesus.

Jesus not only proclaimed the nearness of the kingdom but also struggled to liberate his brothers and sisters from the bondage of disease, poverty, personal guilt and sin, patriarchal structures of authority, religious and ethical legalism, sociopolitical injustice, and ultimately from death, which is foreshadowed by these other oppressions. The kingdom of freedom, therefore, is not only an eschatological but also a political and historical symbol.

"Liberation" may be defined as "the actualization of freedom." When we ask how the freedom first engendered by Jesus is to be actualized, the answer must be framed in terms of the dialectics of the historical process, which includes socioeconomic and political as well as personal and psychic dimensions. Hence at this point I shall affirm the Marxist insistence on an objective basis for human liberation, although I do not share the Marxist doctrine that freedom can be achieved merely by an alteration in production-relations. Against Marx's materialism and economic determinism, I shall advocate a return to the Aristotelian (and Hegelian) vision of the *polis* as a "community of the free." Such a community, by transforming structures, must eventuate in the transformation and renewal of individuals.

The question of actualization will be addressed on two levels, one being a general theory of the historical-political-psychological process of liberation, the other representing an explicitly theological interpretation. I shall argue that freedom is actualized *both* as a goal to be accomplished by the human struggle for emancipation in the arenas of consciousness and politics, *and* as the advent of redemptive power, the inbreaking of the new over which human beings have no control. The possibilities for freedom immanent in history become the bearers of a new birth of freedom as the liberating power of the future. According to Christian faith, the latter is understood to be the power *of God,* mediated in history through the agency of the *crucified and risen Jesus.* For Christians, the resurrection of Jesus from the dead is the energizing force in the dialectics of emancipation and redemption by which liberation occurs historically. The coming of the kingdom of freedom, which entails a deliverance of the self from sin and death and of sociopolitical structures from law and the powers, is the work of the risen Jesus, who is now the agent of what he once proclaimed.

(4) Final Freedom

The last element of the story concerns the *meaning* of the freedom actualized through the life, death, and resurrection of Jesus. By contrast with the timelessness of the Greek world view, freedom for Christian faith means *openness to the future.* The Stoic believed it possible to escape from time. He concentrated exclusively on his Logos-being, thus rising superior to all future obligations, freeing himself *from* the future, focusing entirely on the present. The Greek image of "eternal presence" is reflected also in Freud's fascination with the return to Nirvana, the Nietzschean doctrine of eternal recurrence, and the preoccupation of the counter culture with present happiness or ecstatic fusion with the vital powers. All of these views lose the temporal-eschatological tension of Christian faith, according to which the present moment assumes the form of a decision *for* a future which is ever new, *out of* an unalterable, unrepeatable past. Human beings exist toward the future, they are always in process of becoming what they might be. Yet the sinful person is bound to the past and is not free to decide in response to the call of the future. Thus freedom is experienced as the *gift* of the future, liberating from the past—a future that stands in sharp antithesis to and judgment upon the past, calling humankind forward into a new world out of the old (here the apocalyptic contrast between two aeons is appropriate); yet a future that is not distant but is now breaking in with its transforming power, *a future whose advent engenders a new birth of freedom.*

On the basis of the symbols, images, and events of Christian experience, we may construct a "symbolics" in which the essential structures of freedom undergo a reversal of priorities and a transformation of meanings. The articulation of this symbolics entails a transition from Christology to Pneumatology, for it is the Spirit that is both the source and the norm of the new life-in-freedom. The symbolics of freedom takes its initial orientation, no longer to power, self-determination, *autonomy* (as in all humanistic views —Greek, Stoic, Freudian, existentialist), nor to *society* (as with Marxism and behaviorism), but to *openness*—openness to future liberating power, which, on the basis of the symbols of Christian experience, may now be identified with *God* as the One whose essential being *is* freedom. In place of the neutral phenomenological category of openness, I shall introduce the biblical symbol of *faith*—a symbol based on the Hebraic experience of God, yet one whose meaning was transfigured by the person of Jesus. (The counter culture's quest for transcendence may be viewed as in sympathy with this reversal of priorities, but its identification of transcendence with the vital powers of nature must be rejected.)

From the perspective of what is now the basic horizon of freedom, the other two structures may be redefined as *love* (non-separated, non-alienated community), and *life* (non-privatistic, non-autonomous subjectivity). Finally, the three symbolic structures coalesce in an encompassing image, that of the *kingdom of freedom* as a liberated communion of free subjects founded upon the power of God's free grace. The advent of this kingdom remains fragmentary and incomplete under the conditions of history, and therefore the liberated community represents an eschatological, *postpolitical* vision, a vision that should infuse political action but not be confused with it. Our proper relation to the kingdom is one of *hope* rather than of scientific calculation or political utopianism.

To sum up: Christian freedom acknowledged and transformed the rival concepts of freedom at stake in the ancient world, but in its essential character it derived from none of them. The same could be said of the modern possibilities and their relation to Christian faith. Christianity acknowledges the necessity of the struggle for political and economic liberation, and its gospel of the kingdom is a political gospel; but the freedom of which Christianity speaks has its ultimate source neither in politics nor in economics but in the word of God which liberates men and women by calling them forward into true communion with God and with each other—a realm of freedom in which each finds his or her own fulfillment in the fulfillment of the other.

Christianity acknowledges that freedom entails an inner psychic liberation—a liberation from the binding forces of sin (infinitized desire), law (the regulations and norms of culture), and death (not a natural instinct but the consequence of a false pursuit of life), a liberation that leads to the recovery of authentic selfhood. But it does not agree that people on their own can achieve such a liberation by rational or psychoanalytic means, or by nihilating the given and rebelling against cosmic absurdity, or by achieving a new *gnosis.* Nor does it agree that a revolution in consciousness is all that is required to bring about a change in structures.

Christianity acknowledges that freedom means a new life, a new vitality—a life of love, unity, peace, play, marked by the qualities of ecstasy, vision, and communion with the vital powers of life that transcend ordinary experience. But it rejects the libertinism, eroticism, and nihilism that often accompany such ecstasy, replacing them by a *nova oboedientia*, an obedience to the God of the Exodus and the Prophets, of the Cross and the Resurrection. This is a God who is not to be confused with the mysteries of nature or the hidden infinity of the human species; nor is he to be confused with the traditional gods of "religion." He is a God who liberates rather than dominates and accuses, a God who suffers with men and women in history rather than protects and shelters from harm.

In each respect, the "qualifier" by which Christianity acknowledges and transforms is the figure of Jesus of Nazareth, the radically free person who called his brothers and sisters to enter into God's kingdom, the proclaimer and bringer of a new birth of freedom.

PART TWO
ESSENTIAL FREEDOM

Chapter III

Structures of Freedom

1. FOUNDATIONAL AND SYMBOLIC THEOLOGY

A. PHENOMENOLOGICAL FOUNDATIONS

That phase of theological investigation antecedent to the interpretation and conceptual articulation of the symbols of a determinate faith community has been known traditionally as "natural theology" or "fundamental theology." To avoid misleading nuances of the terms "natural" and "fundamental," I prefer to speak instead of "foundational theology," for which the following working definition is proposed: a phenomenological description of basic structures of the human being's experienced existence in the world, which may provide—in their essential, disrupted, and redeemable manifestations—a foundation for the experience of revelation and language about God. Thus defined, foundational theology is neither a deductive argument (or "proof") for the existence of God nor an alternative to "revealed" theology. Description does not *prove* anything but rather *lets us see* the structural situation in which revelation and faith are real possibilities in the humanly experienced world. The *actuality* of revelation, and the truths it may disclose about the human condition in relationship to God, are another matter, the explication of which requires a transition from foundational to revealed or symbolic theology.

The method of foundational theology is *phenomenological.* "Phenomenology" is a study *(logos)* of the way in which the contents of experience present themselves or appear as phenomena (from *phainesthai,* "to appear") to human consciousness. It deliberately looks away from or suspends the "objectifying standpoint" of the empirical sciences, which conceives objects as discrete entities existing "out there." Rather it views experience as it presents itself in our everyday "life-world" in the form of an intentional unity of subject and object. Following Edmund Husserl, this suspension of the objectifying standpoint is often referred to as "phenomenological bracketing." "By imposing the phenomenological brackets we transform the contents of experience from a physical world of objects into a world of *phenomena,* that is, objects as meanings presenting themselves to a consciousness. It is this radically human world which then becomes the proper subject for philosophy as phenomeno-logy."[1] Such a phenomenology is *structural* or *existential* in the sense that it intends to describe the universal, foundational structures (or "existentials") of human being-in-the-world.[2] Structural phenomenology as a whole is carried out within phenomenological brackets as described above.

Following the suggestion of Paul Ricoeur, three levels of structural phenomenological description may be distinguished.

(1) *Essential Structures.* Humankind's *essential* structures or fundamental *possibilities* may be described prior to and apart from the special characteristics (faulted or redeemed) of *actual existence.* These are structures that apply universally to the human life-world as such, since in any determinate social world existence has already been shaped and modified by the fault (and perhaps also by redemption). Essential human structures are brought into view by imposing a second set of brackets within the phenomenological brackets, namely, "eidetic brackets" (from *eidos,* "essence" or "idea"). An eidetics of the will discloses a fundamental reciprocity of the voluntary and the involuntary, which constitutes the human being as an embodied, finite freedom in both subjective

---

1. Erazim V. Kohák, "Translator's Introduction" to Paul Ricoeur, *Freedom and Nature: The Voluntary and the Involuntary,* trans. E. Kohák (Evanston: Northwestern University Press, 1966), pp. xiii–xiv. Husserl's critique of scientific objectivism and the foundations of his own transcendental phenomenology are presented in *The Crisis of the European Sciences and Transcendental Phenomenology,* trans. David Carr (Evanston: Northwestern University Press, 1970). For a recent introduction to phenomenological method, see Richard M. Zaner, *The Way of Phenomenology* (New York: Pegasus, 1970).
2. See Ricoeur, *Freedom and Nature,* p. 3; Ricoeur, "From Existentialism to the Philosophy of Language," *Philosophy Today,* 17 (Summer 1973): 89–90; and Don Ihde, *Hermeneutic Phenomenology: The Philosophy of Paul Ricoeur* (Evanston: Northwestern University Press, 1971), chaps. 2, 4. The term "existentials" is used in this sense by Martin Heidegger in *Being and Time,* trans. John Macquarrie and Edward Robinson (New York: Harper & Brothers, 1962).

and intersubjective dimensions. The subjective structure of free-dom may be defined as *autonomy;* its intersubjective structure, as *community.*[3]

(2) *Fallibility.* The second level of phenomenological descrip-tion moves from an eidetics of the will to an "empirics," for its concern is no longer with fundamental possibilities but with the human being as he or she *in fact exists (empeiros)* in the world—i.e., as finite, fallible, faulted, guilty. The *possibility* of faulted existence is human *fallibility,* which belongs to a person's ontolog-ical constitution and must be described as such. Nevertheless, because the fault flaws and distorts the relation between freedom and nature, casting human beings into a self-imposed bondage, and can only be conceived as an accident or interruption, falli-bility should not be considered one of the "horizons" or "struc-tures" of freedom. It does not add anything essential to the definition of freedom but constitutes a weakness adhering to each of the three horizons of freedom to be elaborated in this chapter. The actual passage from fallibility to fault, from the possibility to the actuality of evil, is not accessible to structural phenomenology, but requires instead a *hermeneutic* phenomenology of the symbols and myths of evil. Such a hermeneutics is the first task of theo-logical symbolics.[4]

3. This first level corresponds to the first volume of Ricoeur's *Philosophy of the Will,* namely, *Freedom and Nature: The Voluntary and the Involuntary.* However, in this volume Ricoeur does not consider the *intersubjective* structure of freedom. Other variations from Ricoeur's model will be noted in due course.

4. Ricoeur treats fallibility and fault, and the passage between them, in the second phase of his *Philosophy of the Will* under the motif, "empirics of the will." "Em-pirics" includes a "phenomenology of fallibility" (*Fallible Man,* trans. Charles Kelbley [Chicago: Henry Regnery Co., 1967]), a hermeneutic phenomenology of the symbols of evil (*The Symbolism of Evil,* trans. Emerson Buchanan [Boston: Beacon Press, 1968]), and a projected philosophy of fault. (See *Freedom and Nature,* pp. xvi–xvii, xxix–xxxi; *Fallible Man,* pp. xiii, xix; and *The Symbolism of Evil,* pp. 3–18.) The transition from a structural to a hermeneutic phenomenology, de-manded by the *Symbolism of Evil,* occasioned an extended series of investigations on hermeneutics, language, and texts, and Ricoeur has not yet completed the third volume of empirics or taken up the projected third part of his main work, the "poetics of the will." He has indicated his intention, however, to complete the entire project. What he proposes to treat under the rubric of hermeneutic phenomenology—namely, the symbolics of evil and transcendence—lies beyond the province of foundational theology and properly belongs to symbolic theology. Likewise, the projected *philosophies* of fault and of transcendence would correspond to the *doctrinal* component of theological symbolics.

(3) *Redeemability*. Just as the human structure is fallible, so also is it redeemable; and this redeemability can likewise be described phenomenologically, although it requires a shift in method from eidetics and empirics (with their focus upon the structures of human subjectivity and intersubjectivity) to a "poetics of the will." Poetry, says Ricoeur, "is the art of conjuring up the world as created" *(poieisis)*. Hence the poetics of the will should understand the human subject in relation to a gift, a power, a transcendence independent of itself—a transsubjective source of its creation and of its liberation (understood as a new birth, a re-creation).[5] Human redeemability first comes into view phenomenologically in the form of *consent*—consent to the experienced necessities of life. Consent and necessity can be analyzed at the eidetic level of phenomenological description in terms of the reciprocity of the voluntary and the involuntary, but a movement from consent to *openness* is engendered by the interior dynamic of consent itself. This further move from consent to openness is presumably what Ricoeur intends by a poetics of the will, although it is a move he himself has not yet executed. It might be characterized as a poetic "phenomenology of redeemability," for which the key category is "openness." [6] Openness *does* constitute one of the structures or horizons of freedom, without which the definition of human freedom would be incomplete, in a way that fallibility does not. For it is precisely a person's openness to liberating transcendence that reveals the fault to be a distortion rather than an essential feature of our being.[7] Thus openness, together with autonomy and community, make up three horizons of freedom—subjective, intersubjective, transsubjective—although

---

5. Ricoeur, *Freedom and Nature*, pp. 29–30, 471–472.

6. It is not clear whether Ricoeur himself would assent to this formulation. The proposal for a *structural phenomenology* at the level of *poetics* (in addition to eidetics and empirics) represents the most crucial as well as problematic aspect of the present chapter (see esp. Sec. 5c). It should be clear, however, that I am assuming that a poetics of the will can be constructed on a model analogous to the empirics of the will, and that therefore it will include a phenomenology of redeemability, a symbolics of redemption or liberation, and a philosophy (or theology) of freedom. The term "openness" is not used in this sense in *Freedom and Nature;* it rather is of Heideggerian provenance.

7. Ricoeur, *Freedom and Nature*, pp. xvii, xxxi, 30–33.

openness comes into view at a different level of phenomenological description from the other two.

By contrast with openness as redeem*ability*, the *actuality* of redemption and a redeemer are matters that lie beyond the competence of a structural phenomenology, requiring instead a symbolics of liberation. However, it is doubtful whether it would make real sense to speak of human redeemability in the absence of the actuality of redemption: if redemption is not in fact available, then redeemability would be a tragic deception. In this respect the *phenomenology* and the *symbolics* of liberation are dialectically interrelated. I shall return to this matter at the end of the chapter.

B. FROM FOUNDATIONS TO SYMBOLICS

The passage from foundational to symbolic theology occurs with the move beyond the phenomenological description of fallibility and redeemability to two great clusters of religious symbols corresponding to fallibility and redeemability: the symbols of bondage (or of evil, fault, alienation), and the symbols of liberation (or of redemption, reconciliation). Every religion seems to have such symbol-clusters, and the Christian religion is no exception. In the present work, this passage occurs in Chapter IV at the point of transition from the fragility of freedom to the act of sin.

Symbolic theology, in my view, has two interrelated functions: an *interpretation* of the *symbols* of a determinate faith community, which requires a "hermeneutic phenomenology"; and a *reformulation* or *translation* of the symbols in the form of theological and ethical *concepts* (or *doctrines*), which represents the constructive work of the systematic theologian and ethicist. These two functions, while distinguishable, are not actually separable in practice. Theological symbolics as a whole is a hermeneutic discipline, engaging in the thought to which the symbols give rise,[8] thinking back, critically and imaginatively, to the experience primordially expressed in the symbols, but also rethinking their meaning,

8. Cf. Ricoeur, *The Symbolism of Evil*, pp. 349 ff.

theoretically and practically, in light of present-day experience and the anticipated future.

Hermeneutics (or "interpretation") is required with the transition from foundations to symbolics because the experience of bondage and liberation cannot be expressed straightforwardly, as is the case with foundational human structures, but only indirectly by means of symbolic, metaphorical language, which must be deciphered or interpreted. Moreover, these symbols occur only as imbedded in intricate textual structures, which tell the story of how evil began or how redemption occurs. Texts exhibit an objectivity vis-à-vis the subjective intention of the author and the existence of the reader. They fixate meaning in literary structures and refer to a world beyond the limits of ostensive reference, namely, a world in which human beings might dwell and project their own possibilities. To read symbols and to enter into the objectivity of a text and its world, interpretation is required.[9]

Two basic forms of religious texts may be distinguished. On the one hand, the symbols that express the experience of evil, sin, guilt, and bondage are more typically embedded in mythical texts, which explain the origin of evil in terms of universally representative actions on the part of gods and goddesses, men and women, with no fixed locus in space and time.[10] On the other hand, the symbols that express the event of redemption or liberation are more likely—at least in the Bible—to be found in *narrative* texts or history-like accounts which tell a story of the new work of redemption, a unique, unrepeatable story that occurs in the everyday world and has spatio-temporal specificity.[11] Although the distinc-

9. Ricoeur's discovery of the necessity of a hermeneutics of symbols and texts began with *The Symbolism of Evil;* expanded with *Freud and Philosophy: An Essay on Interpretation,* trans. Denis Savage (New Haven: Yale University Press, 1970) ; and has been brought to its present stage through his assimilation of structuralism, Heideggerian hermeneutics, and ordinary language philosophy. See the following recent essays, all published in *Philosophy Today:* "Structure—Word—Event," 12 (1968): 114–129; "From Existentialism to the Philosophy of Language," 17 (1973): 88–96; "Creativity in Language: Word, Polysemy, Metaphor," 17: 97–111; "The Task of Hermeneutics," 17: 112–128; "The Hermeneutical Function of Distanciation," 17: 129–141; also "Philosophy and Religious Language," *Journal of Religion,* 54 (1974) : 71–85; and "The Model of the Text," *New Literary History,* 5 (1973): 91–117.
10. Cf. Ricoeur, *The Symbolism of Evil,* pp. 5, 18.
11. Cf. Hans W. Frei, *The Eclipse of Biblical Narrative* (New Haven: Yale University Press, 1974), chap. I. Whether the history-*like* narratives reflect actual *history* is another question, which can be settled only by critical exegesis.

tion is not hard and fast, myths tend to be concerned with the past and with origins, narratives with the present and with future destiny. The creation stories in Genesis 1–3 are clearly mythical, whereas the stories about Jesus in the Gospels (as well as the stories or parables told by Jesus) are good examples of narrative texts embodying the symbols of liberation.

The several traditional loci of systematic theology may be derived from a hermeneutic of the biblical symbols of bondage and liberation. The following schema, which also illustrates the transition from foundations to symbolics, shows such a derivation. In this respect, a theology of freedom encompasses all of the theo-

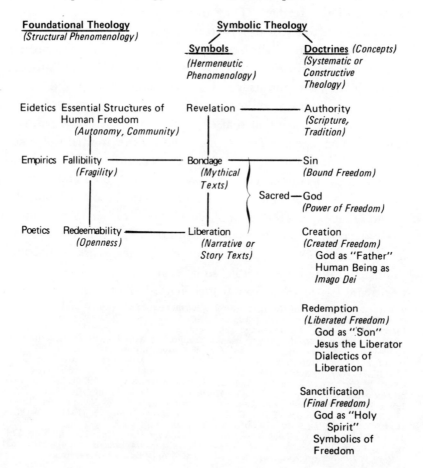

Foundational Theology
(Structural Phenomenology)

Symbolic Theology

Symbols
*(Hermeneutic
Phenomenology)*

Doctrines *(Concepts)*
*(Systematic or
Constructive
Theology)*

Eidetics Essential Structures of
Human Freedom
(Autonomy, Community)

Revelation ———— Authority
*(Scripture,
Tradition)*

Empirics Fallibility ———————— Bondage ———————Sin
(Fragility)   *(Mythical   (Bound Freedom)*
                                     Texts)*
                                               Sacred—God
                                               (Power of Freedom)

Poetics Redeemability ———— Liberation
(Openness)   *(Narrative or
                              Story Texts)*

Creation
(Created Freedom)
    God as "Father"
    Human Being as
    Imago Dei

Redemption
(Liberated Freedom)
    God as "Son"
    Jesus the Liberator
    Dialectics of
    Liberation

Sanctification
(Final Freedom)
    God as "Holy
      Spirit"
    Symbolics of
    Freedom

logical doctrines and offers a way of approaching the work of systematic theology for today. The whole meaning of Christian faith can be expressed in terms of the "story" of human freedom in the world and before God: essential or created freedom, bound freedom, liberated freedom, final freedom.

Several observations may be made on the basis of this schema. The first concerns the parallel between anthropological structures, as disclosed phenomenologically, the biblical "story" of bondage and liberation, and the doctrines or concepts of symbolic theology. If the parallel is valid, it should indicate that theological doctrines are not simply random, arbitrarily selected topics, but rather correspond to something essential in human being and experience. In this respect, foundational anthropology functions as a systematizing principle for theological reflection. At the same time it must be acknowledged that the determinate way in which bondage and liberation have been experienced in the Western religious tradition has exerted a reciprocal influence on our description of essential human structures, especially at the point of understanding fallibility and redeemability. Such reciprocity seems unavoidable and not damaging to the project of a foundational anthropology. The relativity of descriptive categories, and the necessity of making interpretive decisions that may reflect a philosophical or religious "wager," does not mean that the phenomenological attempt to reach the level at which universal or essential structures of being can be described must be abandoned.

In the second place, it should be noted that on the model here proposed the general concept of "God" derives from the symbols of the sacred, which in turn arise from the experience of *both* bondage and liberation. The sacred *first* comes into view when human beings become conscious of having violated their relationship to it; only later are its salvific qualities thematized. On the other hand, the Christian doctrine of the Trinity arises from a determinate way of experiencing liberation—namely, as the creative work of the "Father," the redemptive work of the "Son," and the sanctifying work of the "Spirit." Trinitarian theology does not negate the general concept of God; rather it builds upon it, giving it greater specificity.

Thirdly, the theological doctrine of man and woman as created in the image of God both anticipates and reduplicates, in light of the biblical story of creation, the phenomenological description of essential structures of human freedom. Created freedom and essential freedom are correlative approaches to the same foundational human reality, prior to and apart from the fault and redemption. In the present work, created freedom is limited to a brief discussion in the next section, as an introduction to our foundational anthropology.

Finally, it might be noted that Friedrich Schleiermacher proposed that Christian religious consciousness is determined by the antithesis between sin (bondage) and redemption (liberation). It was this antithesis that helped to define the systematic structure of the Second Part of his Christian dogmatics, *The Christian Faith.* Moreover, in the Introduction and First Part of his work, Schleiermacher offered a phenomenological description of religious experience formally similar to what we are proposing under the rubric of foundational theology. Thus our conception of theological method and of the structure of symbolic theology bears some striking similarities to Schleiermacher. However, for reasons that cannot be elaborated here, Schleiermacher chose to thematize not the "feeling of freedom" but the "feeling of absolute dependence" as the quintessential element of religious piety.

2. CREATED FREEDOM AS THE ESSENCE OF THE HUMAN BEING

A. Homo Liber as Imago Dei

"Man," wrote Herder, is "the first liberated being in creation." [12] That which decisively distinguishes the human being

---

12. J. G. Herder, *Ideen zur Philosophie der Geschichte der Menschheit,* in *Sprachphilosophische Schriften,* ed. Erich Heintel (2d ed., Hamburg: Felix Meiner, 1964), p. 164. In his *Abhandlung über den Ursprung der Sprache,* Herder associated this liberation with the origin of language (cf. *Sprachphilosophische Schriften,* pp. 19–30).

from all other living creatures is not simply reason or intelligence but language and freedom. The higher animals are endowed with greater or lesser degrees of intelligence, but they lack the ability to speak and are not free in relation to the natural environment, even though certain prototypes of human language and freedom are discernible in their sign-like communication and their playfulness. Hence it would be appropriate to designate humankind, not only as *Homo sapiens,* but also as *Homo liber.*

Such at least appears to be the emphasis in the mythic accounts of creation found in the first two chapters of Genesis. In the Priestly story (1:26–27), we read: "Then God said, 'Let us make humankind *('adham)* in our image, after our likeness; and let them have dominion over the fish of the sea, and over the birds of the air, and over the cattle, and over all the earth, and over every creeping thing that creeps upon the earth.' So God created humankind in his own image, in the image of God he created him; male *(zakar)* and female *(neqebhah)* he created them." In commenting on this account Bonhoeffer notes that, prior to the creation of man and woman,

> The work does not resemble the Creator, it is not his image. . . . Even in its aliveness the work is dead, . . . because, while it comes out of freedom, it is itself not free but determined. Only that which is itself free is not dead, is not strange. . . . Only in something that is itself free can the One who is free, the Creator, see himself. But how can the creation be free? The creation is fixed, bound in law, determined and not free. If the Creator wills to create his own image, he must create it in freedom; and only this image in freedom would fully praise him and fully proclaim the honour of its Creator.[13]

In the Genesis passage, human freedom is defined in terms of certain constitutive *relationships:* the relationship to God, in whose image (as the Free One) we are created; the relation to the earth and its living creatures, over which *'adham* is to have dominion; and the relationship between man and woman as the primordial

13. Dietrich Bonhoeffer, *Creation and Fall: A Theological Interpretation of Genesis 1–3,* trans. John C. Fletcher (London: SCM Press, 1959), pp. 33–34.

community in which human beings can be free "for the other."
Freedom is not an individualistic but a communal, relational concept for the Old Testament. Autonomy does not come into view,
except insofar as it is implied by the "dominion" that human
beings are to exercise over nature, and by the fact that a true relationship presupposes free subjects.

Of great significance is the fact that according to Gen. 1:27 the
image of God in creation is not man alone, nor the male alone,
but man and woman together, who are free only insofar as they
belong to each other, sharing in the being of the other, finding
fulfillment through the other. All free human relationships,
whether bisexual or not, reflect this archetypal community, in
which the two partners are equal. The Yahwist's account of creation (Gen. 2:4 ff.) stresses the equality of the woman with the
man. Both are created from raw materials (dust for the man, a
rib for the woman), solely by a divine act in which the man plays
no role (2:7, 21). The woman is the "counterpart" or "helper"
equal to man (2:18), by contrast with the animals who are inferior
helpers and God who is the helper superior to man. The man
"names" the animals (2:20), thus reflecting his power and authority over them, but he does not "name" the woman—not until after
the fall (3:20). Although the man is created first, the woman is
created last, thus completing a ring composition (2:4–25) whereby
the two creatures are designated free and equal, the crown of
creation.[14]

Human beings are free primarily in virtue of their capacity to
speak: language is the road to freedom. This is already reflected
in the Adamic myth: the Lord communicates with Adam by means
of *spoken commands;* the man is given the capacity of *naming* the
animals; and the man and the woman *speak* to each other. In all
these respects human beings stand in quite a different category

14. See Phyllis Trible, "Depatriarchalizing in Biblical Interpretation," *Journal of
the American Academy of Religion,* 41 (March 1973): 35–39. Trible points out
that the Hebrew word *'adham* is a generic term for humankind. Until the specific
differentiation of "male" and "female" in Gen. 1:27 (P) and 2:21–23 (J), *'adham*
is basically androgynous, incorporating the two sexes, and as such images the one,
androgynous God.

from the other creatures. This ancient insight is confirmed by modern anthropological and linguistic studies, according to which language in some sense marks the "threshold crossing" between the higher primates and *Homo liber*. What Susanne Langer wrote over thirty years ago is still valid:

> Language is, without a doubt, the most momentous and at the same time the most mysterious product of the human mind. Between the clearest animal call of love or warning or anger, and a man's least, trivial *word*, there lies a whole day of Creation—or in modern phrase, a whole chapter of evolution. In language we have the free, accomplished use of symbolism, the record of articulate thinking; without language, there seems to be nothing like explicit thought whatever. All races of men—even the scattered, primitive denizens of the deep jungle, and brutish cannibals who have lived for centuries on world-removed islands—have their complete and articulate language. . . . Animals, on the other hand, are one and all without speech. They communicate, of course; but not by any method that can be likened to speaking.[15]

How this threshold crossing actually came about, or to put it another way, how and why human beings learned to speak, remains an abiding scientific and philosophical mystery. It surely has something to do with the mental capacity to transform experience symbolically (words being by far the most supple symbols for interpreting reality), the tendency to play with sound (speech may very likely have originated in the form of song), and the impulse of the human species to converge upon itself and communicate (for which purpose language is essential).[16] In any case, language liberates because speech is the indispensable factor in the constitution of the relational structures—subjective, intersubjective, and transsubjective—by which human existence transpires

15. Susanne K. Langer, *Philosophy in a New Key: A Study in the Symbolism of Reason, Rite, and Art* (New York: Mentor Books, 1948), pp. 94–95. A similar statement is made by George Steiner in *Language and Silence: Essays on Language, Literature, and the Inhuman* (New York: Atheneum, 1972), p. 36.
16. For these speculations, see not only Langer but also Wilbur Marshall Urban, *Language and Reality* (London: George Allen & Unwin, 1939); Ernst Cassirer, *An Essay on Man* (New York: Anchor Books, 1944); Edward Sapir, *Language: An Introduction to the Study of Speech* (New York: Harcourt, Brace & Co., 1921); Pierre Teilhard de Chardin, *The Phenomenon of Man*, trans. Bernard Wall (New York: Harper & Row, 1965); and Eugen Rosenstock-Huessy, *Speech and Reality* (Norwich, Vt.: Argo Books, 1970).

in the world.   I shall examine the role of language at appropriate
points in the ensuing analysis of these structures of freedom.

B. THE RECIPROCITY OF THE VOLUNTARY AND THE INVOLUNTARY

Before turning directly to this subject, however, we should note
that human freedom is not an infinite, disembodied, purely voluntary freedom.   If it were so, it would mean that humankind is
not merely created in the "image of God" *(imago Dei),* but in fact
is "like God" *(sicut Deus),* as the serpent insinuated (Gen. 3:5).
But such an insinuation is the quintessence of sin, of prideful
rebellion against God; for, as the Yahwistic account makes unmistakably clear, *'adham* was formed out of dust (Gen. 2:7), and
therefore his bond with the earth belongs to his essential being
as much as does his freedom in God's image.[17]   Or expressed philosophically, human freedom is experienced only in the reciprocity
of the voluntary and the involuntary.   The essence of the human
being is *created, embodied freedom*—a freedom limited by and
reciprocal with the body (both individual and collective, organic
and social), an incarnate, contingent, finite freedom, *yet still a
freedom.*

Again, *speech* is the clue to this embodied freedom of humankind.   In virtue of its quality as physical sound, speech is the
mediation of body and mind, of involuntary and voluntary:
speech grants freedom, yet rivets it to the finitude of bodily existence in the world.   Speech is a physical, organic act by means of
which a person escapes the limits of the physical and is able to
create a distinctively human world, a world whose law is freedom
rather than necessity, yet a world that exists in profound reciprocity with the world of physical necessity.   Moreover, what we
say and how we say it are limited by the possibilities intrinsic to
the language out of which we speak, which in turn is the product
of a given social world.   Hence speech/language functions as the
mediating link between freedom and the social as well as the
physical involuntary.

17. See Bonhoeffer, *Creation and Fall,* pp. 44–45, 71.

The description of human experience in terms of the reciprocity of the voluntary and the involuntary is one of the major contributions of Paul Ricoeur. According to Ricoeur, the involuntary functions

> acquire a complete significance only in relation to a will which they solicit, dispose, and generally affect, and which in turn determines their significance, that is, determines them by its choice, moves them by its effort, and adopts them by its consent. The involuntary has no meaning of its own. Only the relation of the voluntary and the involuntary is intelligible.[18]

Moreover, it is the experience of the voluntary that comes first for humanity. I understand myself in the first place as one who says, "I will." The involuntary has meaning only with reference to the voluntary, as that which gives it its motives and capacities, its determinate social world, its organic foundations and limits. Ricoeur refers to this reversal of perspective as the first Copernican revolution in philosophy—the turn to the subject of which Descartes remains the great symbol.[19] A common subjectivity is the basis for the homogeneity of voluntary and involuntary structures.

Hence it is an abstraction when the body is studied *merely* as an empirical object by the experimental sciences (biology and behavioral psychology). This rupture of living experience destroys the humanity of the body and discarnates the will, engendering on the one hand the loss of personal agency for behaviorism, and on the other the illusion of absolute human autonomy for some forms of existentialism. Against these two extremes, Ricoeur contends that the body must be understood as "personal body" or "subject body."[20] Yet the bond between body and will is a fragile one, full of potential conflict. Existence tends to break itself up, and a reconciliation must be sought which restores the unity at a higher level. The fragility of the voluntary synthesis, and the potential conflict between autonomy and community,

18. Ricoeur, *Freedom and Nature*, pp. 4–5.
19. Ibid., pp. 5, 29–31.
20. Ibid., pp. 9–10, 85–87.

together constitute a person's fallibility, his or her susceptibility
to failure or fault.[21]

In order to defend human agency in the context of the voluntary
synthesis, it is not necessary to ascribe it to supernatural, indwelling, personal or quasi-personal powers. B. F. Skinner, for example, tends to take a mythological conception of personhood as
normative for the so-called literatures of freedom and dignity.[22]
But the notion of a substantial soul or "mental person" indwelling
the body has been abandoned by theology and philosophy. The
human being as a psychosomatic unity *is* a personal agent; he or
she is not indwelled *by* personal agents. Consciousness (will,
volition, freedom) emerges out of nature (according to Hegel it is
the telos of nature),[23] is intimately sustained by it, and enters into
dialectical relation with it, thus constituting a human world, both
individual and social.

C. STRUCTURES OF FREEDOM

Three fundamental structures of freedom may be distinguished:
autonomy (subjective freedom), community (intersubjective and
objective freedom), openness (transsubjective freedom). Within
each, a correlation of voluntary and involuntary functions occurs.
As noted earlier, in the case of the first two structures, the reciprocity of the voluntary and the involuntary is mediated by speech
or language. Although autonomy is the more accessible and
readily acknowledged structure of freedom, I shall argue that
openness is the most fundamental, sustaining the other two in
their potentially conflictual relation. It should be noted, however,
that openness comes into view only at the point of a "poetics" of
the will, although it arises out of an involuntary-voluntary correlation (necessity-consent) that can be described eidetically. The

21. Ibid., pp. 67, 71, 78, 84.
22. B. F. Skinner, *Beyond Freedom and Dignity* (New York: Alfred A. Knopf, 1971),
pp. 7–8, 200–202.
23. G. W. F. Hegel, *Encyclopedia of the Philosophical Sciences*, §§ 376, 387–388.
This work has been translated in three volumes: *The Logic of Hegel*, trans. William
Wallace (London: Oxford University Press, 1892), §§ 1–244; *Hegel's Philosophy of
Nature*, trans. A. V. Miller (Oxford: The Clarendon Press, 1970), §§ 245–376; and
Hegel's Philosophy of Mind, trans. William Wallace and A. V. Miller (Oxford: The
Clarendon Press, 1971), §§ 377–577.

second structure, community, incorporates both an intersubjective and an objective element. Intersubjectively, freedom means "communion" between free subjects, based on the involuntary substratum of a social world. But communal freedom must also be actualized *objectively* in the transformation of socioeconomic and political structures, i.e., in the constitution of an objective "realm of freedom." At this point, the voluntary-involuntary correlation is no longer relevant, for the social world itself is to become freedom actualized; and the eidetic phenomenology of human subjectivity and intersubjectivity must be supplemented by a social and political phenomenology.

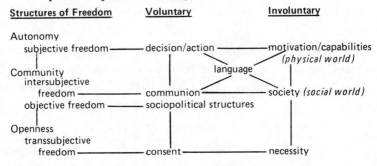

Although Ricoeur does not use the terms "autonomy" and "openness," the analysis presented here of the voluntary-involuntary synthesis under the first and the third of these structures is heavily influenced by his procedure in *Freedom and Nature*. Not so with the second structure. Not only does Ricoeur neglect what I am calling objective freedom; he also believes that intersubjectivity (the relation of a will to a will) cannot be brought within the purview of an eidetics of consciousness but already presupposes a relationship to transcendence that can be described only poetically.[24] It is certainly true that intersubjective freedom

24. Ricoeur, *Freedom and Nature*, pp. 31–32. In this work Ricoeur actually develops the analysis in terms of a triadic structure of the will—decision, action (or voluntary motion), and consent—to which are correlated the involuntary functions of motivation, capabilities, and necessity. I have linked decision and action under the category of autonomy, since they appear to be distinguishable phases of the same subjective volitional process, joined together by the intention of the agent. To this I have added the category of community with its voluntary/involuntary correlates, namely, communion and social world, and its objective actualization in sociopolitical structures. Moreover, in *Freedom and Nature* Ricoeur does not make the move from consent to openness that is central to my own project.

requires fulfillment in a transsubjective relationship if human community is to overcome its separatism and alienation. But the same is true of subjective freedom if it is not to remain privatistic and autonomous. It would seem that both subjective and intersubjective freedom *can* and *must* be described eidetically prior to the relationship to transcendence, in order to have a foundation in consciousness for that relationship. But the analysis in *Freedom and Nature* is largely restricted to individual acts of will, and freedom is abstracted from its corporate matrix. In more recent writings, Ricoeur has begun to concern himself with both intersubjective and objective structures, but he has not yet shown how these materials relate to the overall project of a philosophy of freedom.

An approximate correlation exists between the structures of freedom here proposed and the rival concepts of freedom and the spiral of liberation discussed in Chapter II. This correlation can be exhibited most clearly by means of another schema.

Structures of Freedom	Rival Freedoms	Spiral of Liberation
	Political-Economic	Economic
Objective Freedom	Freedom	Liberation
	Pragmatic-Technocratic	Political
	Freedom	Liberation
	Rational-Psychoanalytic	Psychic
Subjective Freedom	Freedom	Liberation
	Tragic-Existential	Personal
Intersubjective	Freedom	Liberation
Freedom		Cultural
	Ecstatic-Vitalistic	Liberation
Transsubjective	Freedom	Religious
Freedom	Biblical Freedom	Liberation

Political-economic and pragmatic-technocratic freedom both provide a basis for the liberation of objective social conditions, but with quite different strategies and results; the latter in particular threatens the integrity of the very freedom it engenders. Rational-psychoanalytic and tragic-existential freedom are primarily subjective in orientation, but at the same time they evidence a concern for intersubjective relations and are not purely individualistic (e.g., the interest in culture on the part of the tragedians and Freud, and the analysis of intersubjectivity on the part of at least some existentialists). Ecstatic-vitalistic freedom has a pagan religious vision as its basis, but it also advocates a cultural rebirth (the "counter" culture) and a new (inter)subjectivity. Finally, although the biblical religions (Judaism and Christianity) are oriented in the first instance to transsubjective freedom (the relationship to the God of freedom), they evidence a profound interest in the other structures as well. If valid, this correlation indicates that the ways in which freedom has been understood in Western culture are not simply arbitrary or contingent but correspond in some measure to different structures of the phenomenon itself. The schema also suggests that, while autonomy is the first structure of freedom to come into view phenomenologically, from the point of view of historical experience and the struggle for liberation objective freedom is the first exigency to be experienced and is foundational for the others.

3. AUTONOMY: SUBJECTIVE FREEDOM

A. Decision/Action

According to a widespread consensus in modern philosophical anthropology (including idealism, existentialism, phenomenology, process philosophy), the minimal condition of being human is to be a *subject,* a *self,* the principles of whose actions are self-determined *(auto-nomos).* Subjectivity may be defined as a temporal integration of conscious experience by means of language, which gathers the modes of time into a living, meaningful, presence.[25] Language integrates human temporality by providing the sym-

25. The philosophical basis for this formulation, which cannot be further elaborated here, is found in Martin Heidegger, *Being and Time,* esp. §§ 5, 65, 68, 74. My own appropriation and interpretation of Heidegger on this matter is contained in *Jesus—Word and Presence: An Essay in Christology* (Philadelphia: Fortress Press, 1971), pp. 83–92, 104–110. On the temporal integration of conscious experience, see also Edmund Husserl, *The Phenomenology of Internal Time-Consciousness,* ed. Martin Heidegger, trans. James Churchill (Bloomington: Indiana University Press, 1964); and Alfred Schutz, *The Phenomenology of the Social World,* trans. George Walsh and Frederick Lehnert (Evanston: Northwestern University Press, 1967), chap. II.

bolic tools for an intentional projection of future action, based on the heritage and causal nexus of the past, lending coherence and direction to the present moment. (Later I shall argue that this intentional projection of the future is based upon an availability or advent of the future, which precedes all decisions, calling us forward into new possiblities, liberating from the bondage of the past. In this sense "openness" will be understood to found "autonomy.") Without temporal integration human life would disintegrate into an irredeemable past, an unachievable future, and a meaningless present. Such disintegration is the essence of schizophrenia—the loss of the center. Thus subjectivity can be described as *presence to oneself,* and such presence to oneself is the first horizon of freedom. Hegel writes: "The being of subjective spirit is to be present to itself, i.e., free [*bei sich, d.i. frei zu sein*]." [26]

When we think of ourselves as free, we ordinarily mean that we are able to *decide upon* or *determine for ourselves* a course of action, in the context, of course, of external determining influences, but without our decision actually being *caused* or *coerced* by these nonvolitional factors. Decision appears to lie at the heart of freedom: I posit myself by my decisions, I am who I am because *I* decide. Yet as Ricoeur points out, a peculiarity of decision is its *intentional* character, which in the first instance at least entails a turning away from the self. "To decide is to turn myself towards the project, to forget myself in the project, to be outside myself in the project, without taking time to observe myself willing." [27] A decision signifies a future action in which the project of the action is realized, and it implies possession of the power or capacity of movement that could realize the project. The latter distinguishes an authentic decision from a wish or command, the execution of which is not in my power. A decision

26. Hegel, *Encyclopedia,* § 385 (translation altered), cf. § 160. See also Karl Rahner, who refers many times to the *Bei-sich-sein* of human being: *Hörer des Wortes: Zur Grundlegung einer Religionsphilosophie,* 2d ed., ed. J. B. Metz (Munich: Kösel-Verlag, 1963), chap. 3; *Theological Investigations,* vol. I, trans. Cornelius Ernst (Baltimore: Helicon Press, 1961), pp. 168–170; vol. V, trans. K.-H. Kruger (Baltimore: Helicon Press, 1966), pp. 200–201, 205, 207–209, 211.
27. Ricoeur, *Freedom and Nature,* pp. 42–43.

is an intention to act in which the decider himself is momentarily forgotten and attention is directed to the future project. Thus decision and action are joined together in the actual process of willing, although they may be distinguished for analytical purposes and usually do not occur simultaneously. Indeed, the characteristic trait of a project is its reference to the future. The project is pro-jected; I decide for a time to come. Human purposiveness organizes time ahead of the present, and in that fashion a temporal integration is achieved, which is the minimal condition of sanity.[28]

Almost as a byproduct of intentionality, *self-imputation* also occurs in the act of deciding, from which emerges *self-consciousness* and therefore subjective freedom in the full sense. Precisely in projects directed toward objects and/or other persons, and not apart from such projects, there occurs an imputation or implication of the self, which in the first instance is prereflexive. I catch hold of myself in the process of deciding on a course of action; I find myself implicated in such projects by the interrogation of another—"Who did that?" This prereflexive self-imputation is reflexively articulated in the judgment (and response), "It is I who . . ."; and thereby the consciousness of being an "I," subject to an internal regulation or determination ("autonomy"), comes about. Such self-consciousness and autonomy do not mean that the self constitutes itself *ex nihilo;* it does not will itself in a void but in its projects. In this respect, intersubjective relations and existence in a social world are already essential elements in the constitution of subjectivity.[29]

Above all it was Hegel who first described the dialectical process by means of which the freedom of human subjectivity is constituted. At the first stage there is no reflective separation of subject and object; rather consciousness appears to have a direct apprehension of its objects, and the ego is reflected back to itself in pure immediacy and indeterminacy. But already at the level of consciousness of an object, self-consciousness is involved. For

28. Ibid., pp. 40–41, 48–49, 51.
29. Ibid., pp. 55–66.

I am aware of the object as mine, and thus in it I am aware of myself. This is an abstract freedom, however, because there is really no distinction between consciousness and its objects. Self-consciousness proper emerges when the object becomes *another person*. "In that other as ego I behold myself, and yet also an immediately existing object, another ego absolutely independent of me and opposed to me. . . . This contradiction gives either self-consciousness the impulse to *show* itself as a free self, and to exist as such for the other—the process of *recognition*." After working through the process of conflict and recognition, consciousness arrives at what Hegel calls "universal self-consciousness," which is "the affirmative awareness of self in an other self: each self as a free individuality has his own 'absolute' independence, yet . . . without distinguishing itself from that other. . . . Each has 'real' universality in the shape of reciprocity, so far as each knows itself recognized in the other freeman, and is aware of this insofar as it recognizes the other and knows him to be free." [30] As this brief summary indicates, according to Hegel true subjectivity already includes an intersubjective relationship to other persons as essential to its own constitution—a matter to be examined in greater detail in the next section.

Ricoeur points out that Hegel inherited the problem of subjectivity from Kant, who had thought through the concept of freedom and led it "to its most radical conditions of possibility, . . . conditions . . . not denied but incorporated into the Hegelian endeavor." [31] Kant demonstrated that subjective freedom or "autonomy" is not to be thought of as sheer indeterminacy, spontaneity, or equilibrium of choice. All decision has its motives, its maxims or principles, its determinations. The question is whether such determinations are also *self*-determinations. Kant proposed

30. Hegel, *Encyclopedia*, §§ 413–439 (quotations from §§ 430, 436); *The Phenomenology of Mind*, trans. J. B. Baillie (2d ed. revised, London: George Allen & Unwin, 1949), chaps. I-V; *Philosophy of Right*, trans. T. M. Knox (Oxford: The Clarendon Press, 1952) , §§ 5–7. I shall return to the Hegelian dialectic of self-consciousness, and in particular the relationship between master and slave, in greater detail in Chap. VI, Sec. 2B.
31. Ricoeur, "A Critique of B. F. Skinner's *Beyond Freedom and Dignity*," *Philosophy Today*, 17 (Summer 1973): 173, 174.

that freedom is not lawless but rather a law unto itself *(autonomos)*. He argued that the law to which freedom is linked is not a natural or empirical law (although human action is *also* subject to natural laws) but a law of moral obligation, self-imposed yet universally valid. "Autonomy of the will is that property of the will by which it gives a law to itself." The principle of autonomy is identical with the categorical imperative, which accordingly is the law of freedom: "Act only on that maxim which will enable you at the same time to will that it be a universal law." The alternative to autonomy of the will is heteronomy ("the source of all spurious principles of morality"), which means to seek the principles of one's action in the objects of volition or in the sensible desires that impose themselves upon the will.

> The *will* is a kind of causality of living beings insofar as they are rational. *Freedom* then would be that property of such causality by which it can become operative without being dependent on foreign causes *determining* it; whereas *physical necessity* is the property of the causality of all non-rational beings to be determined to activity by the influence of foreign causes. . . . Freedom . . . is not therefore without its positive laws. It must, on the contrary, be a causality following immutable laws, but be of a very special kind [namely, having the legislative form of the categorical imperative].[32]

Freedom thus defined, according to Kant, is a postulate of practical reason. In other words, it is a necessary presupposition of the moral law (the categorical imperative), which we know as rational beings once pure reason is applied practically. Pure reason applied theoretically can show that freedom is *possible* but not necessarily *real*. The *reality* of freedom is an a priori deduction from the principle of morality; it cannot be based on experience, which discloses only empirical dependence. Although the *reality* of freedom (and of a supersensible, intelligible world) can be established on the basis of what is needed for us to act morally,

32. Immanuel Kant, *The Fundamental Principles of the Metaphysic of Ethics,* trans. Otto Manthey-Zorn (New York: Appleton-Century-Crofts, 1938), pp. 38, 59–60, 65–66, 78 (quotation from p. 65). See also *Critique of Practical Reason,* trans. Lewis White Beck (New York: Liberal Arts Press, 1956), pp. 28, 30, 33–34.

no *explanation* is thereby attained of *how* freedom is possible, nor strictly speaking do we have any *knowledge* of *what* freedom is; it is rather an object of "rational faith." [33]

Although these Kantian formulations may leave something to be desired, they make an important contribution to the proper understanding of freedom. As a *practical* concept, freedom is not an object that "exists" in the sense of an "observable" to either internal or external perception. It belongs to a different "language game" than that of behavioral science and can be brought into view only phenomenologically. It cannot be made the object of either an empirical or a speculative investigation; rather it is a task to be achieved—in the process of deciding and entering upon a course of action. Moreover, Kant rightly insisted that freedom and norms must be thought together. This link, says Ricoeur, "denies as much the dream of a freedom without laws as the idea of a law which would not be from the beginning a law of freedom." [34] These two matters will be pursued further in the next subsection.

B. MOTIVATION/CAPABILITIES

We have noted that subjective freedom is not a matter of sheer spontaneity; it is determined by inner moral principles and is contingent upon intersubjective relations and existence in a social world. But it is also related to the physical involuntary—i.e., to the body, whose instinctual needs present motives for decision, and whose physical capabilities are the means by which decisions are carried forward into actions. "There are no decisions without motives," writes Ricoeur. "In this initial relation the body enters into the voluntary synthesis even as it presents itself as an organ to moving and as invincible necessity to consent." Motives, in the sense of reasons for an action, can be said to *solicit, influence,* or *determine* decisions, but they do not *cause* or *coerce* them on the model of the cause-effect nexus that holds sway between phys-

33. Kant, *Critique of Practical Reason,* pp. 3–4, 6, 47–49, 137–140; *Fundamental Principles,* pp. 68, 76, 80.
34. Both these points are directly indebted to Ricoeur, "A Critique of B. F. Skinner's *Beyond Freedom and Dignity,*" p. 173.

ical objects. The distinction in nuance between *determination* (the act of setting limits, bounding, defining—*de-terminus*) and *causality* (production of an effect on the basis of invariant laws of nature—physical, chemical, biological, psychic) should not be lost. The motive, Ricoeur points out, is not an independent factor apart from the decision that invokes and shapes it in the process of being shaped by it. Once it is brought into the voluntary synthesis it ceases to be a static extrinsic magnitude. The motive determines the will only as the will determines itself; *motives incline without compelling.* Determination by motives and self-determination are linked together in decision in such a way as to indicate the liaison of *activity* and *receptivity* at the heart of deciding.[35] In other words, motivational factors $a, b, c, \ldots x$, do not add up to or "produce" an action apart from the free decision that invokes them. We cannot describe an action simply by enumerating its motives; something novel, qualitatively different, occurs with the action itself.

The same point is made by Sartre. The motive, he says, does not cause the act but is an integral part of it. "The motive, the act, and the end are all constituted in a single upsurge. . . . It is the act which decides its ends and its motives, and the act is the expression of freedom." He points out that a physical obstacle to an action, such as a craggy peak, reveals itself as such only in the context of a human project, in this case the decision to climb the peak; apart from such a project the crag is no obstacle at all. "Although brute things . . . can from the start limit our freedom of action, it is our freedom itself which must first constitute the framework, the technique, and the ends in relation to which they will manifest themselves as limits."[36] The same would appear to be as true of physical motives as it is of physical limits.

But does this language of "motivation" really refer to the same thing that behaviorists such as Skinner have in mind when they refer to biological and environmental "controls," operant condi-

35. Ricoeur, *Freedom and Nature,* pp. 66 (quotation from this page), 67, 71, 78, 84.
36. Jean-Paul Sartre, *Being and Nothingness,* trans. Hazel Barnes (New York: Philosophical Library, 1956) , pp. 437–438, 482; cf. pp. 443, 445–449, 488–489.

tioning, and contingencies of reinforcement, all under the general rubric of a "technology of behavior"? [37] No, it does not. Here we confront a basic distinction between the discourse of phenomenology, which refers to "motives" in the sense of "reasons for" an action, and the discourse of the natural sciences, with its concern for "controls" (Skinner's favorite expression) and "causes" in the sense of relations between observable facts. It is a question of distinguishable "language games" for speaking about human activity.[38] The science of behavior seeks to observe a *causal link* between conditioning factors and patterns of behavior. From a purely empirical point of view, limited to the observation of external connections, such a link undoubtedly appears to exist. But phenomenological description—together with the psychoanalytic interpretation of dreams—uncovers an essential intermediary process between various "causative" factors (e.g., the needs and primitive instincts of the body, social and environmental stimuli, controls, and reinforcements) and observable human behavior. This intermediary process consists in the production of *motives,* in the sense of "reasons for" a particular decision and action, out of the underlying biological and environmental causative factors. The *causes* of human behavior enter the voluntary synthesis only in the form of *motives.*

When we ask *how* motives are produced, we are directed to the activity of *imagination*—the "symbolic transformation of experience" (Susanne Langer) by means of which raw data gain meaning and signification for human beings. For example, it is by means of imagination that the finite *needs* (or instincts) of the body are raised to the level of infinite, intrinsically unfulfillable *desires* (or motives). What Freud described as "libido" already represents the transforming and infinitizing of animal instincts by imagination. The instrument of imagination, as a process of symbolization, is of course *language* or *speech,* the unique capability of human beings. Speech, itself an indivisibly psychosomatic

37. See the discussion of Skinner in Chap. II, Sec. 6A.
38. Cf. Ricoeur, *Freud and Philosophy: An Essay on Interpretation,* pp. 360, 363; and "A Critique of B. F. Skinner's *Beyond Freedom and Dignity,*" p. 167.

act, stands at the point of mediation between body and mind, nature and freedom, the involuntary and the voluntary. Speech grants freedom, yet rivets it to the motivations arising from our bodily existence in the world. It is not surprising, therefore, that the analysis of human speech represents a key point of theoretical disagreement between behaviorism and phenomenology. Skinner wants to understand speech itself merely as the product of an environment of verbal contingencies,[39] in which case it can scarcely function as the means by which we transcend environment and incorporate its "causes" into the voluntary synthesis. But Skinner's theory of language learning has been severely criticized from the point of view of the science of linguistics, above all by Noam Chomsky.[40] The possible convergence of linguistics and phenomenology on the question of the origin and nature of language is a matter that cannot be further pursued here.

Imagination not only infuses experience with meaning; it also charms and seduces. The images of speech have a deceptive power by which they fascinate consciousness, producing desire without measure—the "bad infinity" of desire that far outstrips biological needs. Thus the imagination, while functioning as the essential factor in the voluntary-involuntary synthesis, is at the same time "a privileged point of entry" of the fault. It is the key to human fallibility or fragility, an aspect of human behavior that nowhere comes into view on the behaviorist model.[41]

Just as decision is determined by the needs of the body, which enter into the voluntary synthesis in the form of motives by means of the imagination and its distortions, so also the action intended by decision is contingent upon the capabilities of the body. Action "traverses" the body, which is not its object but its organ or medium. What is enacted is an alteration of environment, human and physical. Action stretches between the "I" as willing and the world as a field of action. That upon which it stretches is the

39. Cf. his *Verbal Behavior* (New York: Appleton-Century-Crofts, 1957) ; also *Beyond Freedom and Dignity*, pp. 185–193.
40. See his review of Skinner's *Verbal Behavior* in *Language*, 35 (1959): 26–58.
41. On this point, see Ricoeur, *Freedom and Nature*, pp. 94–103. I return to the question of fragility in Chap. IV, Sec. 1.

body as organ, which both facilitates and inexorably delimits the sorts of action one can take in the world.[42]

Bodily capabilities include sheer physical power, the refinement of that power by skill and habit, the emotions, the senses (seeing, hearing, tasting, smelling, touching)—all of which are subjected to a thorough analysis by Ricoeur in *Freedom and Nature*.[43] Perhaps the highest of all the human capabilities—yet one not considered by Ricoeur in this context—is that of *speech*, which is the body's organic mediation par excellence between self and world. Speech is the *organic* means by which *I* act intentionally in the *world*. Speech utilizes many tools as its extensions (alphabet, pen, typewriter, print, electronics), but in itself, as symbolically articulated sound, it is indivisibly mental-organic. By means of speech the body becomes personal body or subject body. Speech is limited, not only by physiological capabilities and our skill at utilizing them, but also by the grammatical structure and vocabulary of the language out of which we speak, which is a "given" of the social world in which we find ourselves. Most of us can speak and understand only one or two of the thousands of tongues found among the human family, despite structural similarities that relate all these languages. Thus speech is reciprocal with both the physical and the social involuntary. The means by which we gain subjective freedom vis-à-vis nature and culture is not infinite; rather it is a finite, fragile, fallible instrument, itself a product of nature and culture.

4. COMMUNITY: INTERSUBJECTIVE AND OBJECTIVE FREEDOM

The second structure of freedom—community—is comprised of two elements or aspects: *(a) A voluntary communion between free subjects* on the basis of an involuntary, pregiven "social world." The term "intersubjectivity" has been used to designate both the voluntary and the involuntary components of this reciprocity; hence it does not appear inappropriate to refer to an "intersubjec-

42. Ibid., pp. 210–214.
43. Ibid., pp. 201–337.

tive freedom." Methodologically, I shall focus primarily on an eidetic phenomenology that discloses intersubjectivity to be an essential element in the constitution of human consciousness. But to describe the objectivation and institutionalization of the intersubjective social world, elements of a sociology of knowledge will also be required. *(b) An objective "realm of freedom"* comprised of socioeconomic and political structures. It is not enough that the social world should function merely as the involuntary substratum for free encounters between individual persons. Rather the true destiny of the social world itself is to become freedom actualized; apart from liberating institutional arrangements, neither subjective nor intersubjective freedom can flourish. Here it is necessary to move beyond both an eidetics of consciousness and neutral sociological description to a phenomenology of objective freedom.

A. INTERSUBJECTIVE FREEDOM: COMMUNION AND SOCIAL WORLD

Just as decision is intentional in character, so communion is *co-intentional*. In the reciprocal co-intentionality of communion, we intend each other neither as idols, nor as enemies, nor as mere means of self-gratification; rather we intend each other for the sake of each other, putting ourselves at the other's disposal, yet knowing that we will not thereby be lost or destroyed but rather fulfilled. The intentions and needs of the other become the motives for my own action and vice versa. Because our streams of consciousness are synchronized and intermeshed, the other enters integrally into the constitution of my own lived experience, and I enter into his or hers.[44] The sense of being fulfilled by and with the other, and thus of being free to share oneself, is suggested by the Latin roots of the word *communion: com* (with) + *munus* (a service, gift, present), from *munire* (to build, to fortify). A "communion" is a building for mutual service, a sharing, a mutual

44. Cf. Alfred Schutz's description of interaction in the "face-to-face" situation, *Social World*, pp. 162–173. Strictly speaking, what Schutz is describing here is a universal structure of the social world which makes concrete reciprocities possible. But it is the structure or region closest to living communion itself.

participation, a freedom for-and-with-the-other, an upbuilding through love.

Both Hegel and Marx associated the reciprocal co-intentionality of communion with the concept of freedom. Earlier in this chapter I noted that Hegel regards the dialectic by which subjectivity is constituted as culminating in a stage of "universal self-consciousness," which he describes also as a

> *free* self-consciousness for which the other self-consciousness confronting it is no longer . . . unfree but is likewise independent. In this stage, therefore, the mutually related self-conscious subjects, by setting aside their unequal particular individuality, have risen to the consciousness of their real universality, of the freedom belonging to all, and hence to the intuition of their specific identity with each other. . . . In this state of universal freedom, in being reflected into myself, I am immediately reflected into the other person, and, conversely, in relating myself to the other I am immediately *self*-related.[45]

Hegel goes on to note that this *intersubjective* universal freedom forms the "substance" of "ethical life," namely, freedom actualized *objectively* in the family, civil society, and the state.

Karl Marx adopted a similar vision in his description, in one of the early manuscripts, of a true society based on "free human production," in which the fulfillment of the needs of each becomes the responsibility of all, and in which each individual mediates between the other person and the human social whole.[46] The problem with Marx, as suggested by our earlier discussion (Chap. II, Sec. 2b), is that he believed it would be possible to inaugurate true human communion merely by a restructuring of the social involuntary, e.g., by abolishing private property and altering production relations. Thus he tended to reduce the voluntary to the involuntary and the subjective/intersubjective to the

45. Hegel, *Encyclopedia*, § 436 A. (The abbreviation "A" following the citation of some sections from the *Encyclopedia* and *The Philosophy of Right* refers to the "Additions" or *Zusätze* added by the original German editors, containing materials from student notes of Hegel's lectures.)
46. "Excerpt-Notes of 1844," in *Writings of the Young Marx on Philosophy and Society*, trans. Loyd Easton and Kurt Guddat (New York: Anchor Books, 1967), p. 281. This passage is quoted and discussed more fully above, pp. 58–59.

objective. In the final analysis Marx's historical dialectic is controlled by its materialistic basis.

Communion, in the sense of actual interpersonal relations, can occur only in the context of a social world (or life-world) that is pregiven and functions as the involuntary substratum for communal freedom. This social world is comprised of various strata or regions: temporal and spatial arrangements in terms of which the world is constituted as world; intersubjectivity as an essential structural component of human consciousness; social relationships with consociates, contemporaries, predecessors, and successors; and the objectivation and institutionalization of these relationships.[47] The relation between communion and social world is analogous to that between decision/action and motivation/capabilities. The social involuntary does not *cause* or *coerce* interpersonal relationships, but it *determines* them in the sense of providing the structural framework that both permits and delimits or defines them. These social structures enter into the voluntary synthesis, are accessible only there, and are constantly reshaped and modified as human beings interact. The relation between the voluntary and the involuntary is as reciprocal or dialectical at the intersubjective level as it is at the subjective. This is especially evident from the analyses by Alfred Schutz of the life-world and the social world.

Above all it was Edmund Husserl who brought the concept of "intersubjectivity" into phenomenological discussion.[48] According to Edward Farley,[49] Husserl turned to intersubjectivity in order to overcome the problem of solipsism, i.e., of being isolated in the sphere of one's own transcendental consciousness, cut off

47. Cf. Alfred Schutz, *Social World*, chap. IV; and Alfred Schutz and Thomas Luckmann, *The Structures of the Life-World*, trans. Richard M. Zaner and H. Tristam Engelhardt (Evanston: Northwestern University Press, 1973), chap. II; also Peter L. Berger and Thomas Luckmann, *The Social Construction of Reality: A Treatise in the Sociology of Knowledge* (New York: Anchor Books, 1967), chaps. I, II.
48. Perhaps the clearest, although still exceptionally technical, discussion is found in Husserl's *The Crisis of European Sciences and Transcendental Phenomenology*, part III, A, esp. §§ 49–54. See also Schutz, *Social World*, chap. III.
49. Edward Farley, *Ecclesial Man: A Social Phenomenology of Faith and Reality* (Philadelphia: Fortress Press, 1975), chaps. II, IV. The first part of this book contains the most thorough and lucid discussion available in English of Husserl's later philosophy and its significance for theological construction.

from the objective reality of the world and other persons. His proposal was that human beings constitute *each other as persons* at the same prereflective levels of consciousness at which they constitute themselves and external objects in nature. *Self*-constitution means the constitution of the sphere of "my own" and therefore a body that is not just a space-time entity which I perceive as a spectator but a personal body which is the locus of my receptivities and is at my disposal in ways that other bodies are not. To view the *other* as a person like myself involves intending the other as a sphere of "my own" centered in a personal body, by means of an imaginative, empathetic projection based on my own inner experience. Intersubjectivity in this technical sense does not mean the actual dialogue or interpersonal relationships that occur between two or more persons. It refers to an interpersonal structure that exists prereflectively and is already given prior to any actual relationship or dialogue as its condition. It is the pregiven, socially structured consciousness presupposed by concrete communion between persons. In this sense, intersubjectivity is the involuntary substratum of freedom-in-communion, enabling and delimiting it in determinate ways.

Schutz has argued persuasively that the structures of intersubjectivity vary depending upon whether we are directly related to other persons as "consociates" in a "face-to-face" situation, or whether we are indirectly related to contemporaries, predecessors, and successors. The face-to-face situation permits a "We-relationship," in which each partner is able to participate sympathetically in the lived experience of the other. Schutz notes that the pure We-relationship, as a formal, universal, involuntary structure of the social world, is a limiting concept, yet it is that structure closest to actual voluntary communion. "The directly experienced social relationship of *real* life is the pure We-relationship concretized and actualized to a greater or lesser degree and filled with content." [50]

With the transition to *indirect* social experience, the We-rela-

50. Schutz, *Social World*, p. 164 (italics mine); cf. pp. 139–144, 163–176. See also Schutz and Luckmann, *Life-World*, pp. 59–68.

tionship becomes a *They*-relationship (cf. Heidegger's *das Man*). The other person becomes a "contemporary" rather than a "consociate" (or in Ricoeur's terms, a *socius* rather than a neighbor).[51] My relationship to contemporaries is mediated by social institutions, roles, and anonymous typifications; I am no longer oriented to the subjectivity of a concrete, individual Thou, but to an anonymous person who functions in relation to me according to certain typified social expectations (e.g., a postman, an airplane pilot, a store clerk).[52] Such anonymity is of course essential for much of our social intercourse and permits a kind of freedom— a freedom from debilitating, exhausting, or even destructive face-to-face relationships. We simply cannot become involved with every other human being as a Thou; such involvement would disrupt the social fabric upon which all of us depend. At the same time, as Ricoeur points out, it is not impossible for a kind of liberating communion to occur even between persons related anonymously and typically—a momentary recognition of the dignity and value of the other person, an appreciation for his or her faithful execution of a given social role, a humanizing exchange in the context of an essentially abstract relationship. It is not enough to exercise charity only toward the neighbor and not also the *socius*, because of course every human being is both a neighbor and a *socius*, both a consociate and a contemporary.[53]

The *institutional* stratum of the social world serves to objectify, integrate, and thereby order human relationships, which left to themselves are potentially chaotic and anarchic. What is objectified and integrated are not the concrete reciprocities of specific human beings but the intersubjective structures that fund these reciprocities. As a result of becoming institutionalized, intersubjectivity gains a legitimation and perpetuation over time that strengthens its power and authority vis-à-vis individual subjects.

51. Ricoeur, "The *Socius* and the Neighbor," in *History and Truth*, trans. C. A. Kelbley (Evanston: Northwestern University Press, 1965), pp. 98–109.
52. Schutz, *Social World*, pp. 177–205; Schutz and Luckmann, *Life-World*, pp. 68–87.
53. Ricoeur, *History and Truth*, pp. 103–109. On the relationships to predecessors and successors, which need not concern us here, see Schutz, *Social World*, pp. 207–214; and Schutz and Luckmann, *Life-World*, pp. 87–92.

The elements of objectification and institutionalization include language, the social stock of knowledge, typifications and structures of relevance, symbols, rituals and traditions, the cognitive and valuative consensus, and legal, cultural, religious, socioeconomic and political structures.[54] Since it is self-evident that these institutions function as an involuntary in relation to free communion, it seems unnecessary to elaborate the process of institutionalization more fully here.

It should be evident from the discussion thus far that *subjective* and *intersubjective* freedom are dialectically interrelated.[55] To preserve this dialectic, I have treated intersubjectivity under a separate structure of freedom, namely, "community." Intersubjectivity is not reducible merely to a moment in the constitution of the subject, nor subjectivity to a disappearing element in the social process. The dialectic between these two nonreducible "poles" may be illustrated as follows: (a) The social world functions as an involuntary for decision/action as well as for communion. This is evident from the fact that individual decisions and actions are based on knowledge mediated *socially*, as Schutz's analyses of the social stock of knowledge, structures of typification, and motivational relevance have demonstrated. Motives, in the sense of reasons for an action, are generated not only by physical needs and desires but also by social values and conventions, which must be assimilated and perhaps modified by the individual. (b) Conversely, bodily motives and capabilities function as an involuntary for communion as well as for decision/action. Human communion not only arises quite frequently out of physical attraction or erotic desire. It also is mediated organically or bodily, especially in the face-to-face situation; it involves the use of speech, vision, gestures, and sometimes physical contact or touch. (c) The individual, as Hegel makes clear, has full access to him- or herself

54. Cf. Farley, *Ecclesial Man*, chap. IV. An excellent discussion of institutionalization is found in Berger and Luckmann, *The Social Construction of Reality*, chap. II. The foundations of a sociology of knowledge are laid by Schutz and Luckmann in *Life-World*, chaps. III–IV.
55. On the dialectical relation between the individual and society, see Berger and Luckmann, *The Social Construction of Reality*, pp. 60–61, 129–130, 180–183.

only by means of a circuit through the otherness of the world, by means of which he or she is constituted as an object in the world for another person, recognizing his or her own subjectivity as reflected in that of the other. It takes at least two to make a human being: intersubjectivity is a precondition of subjectivity. (d) Conversely, subjectivity is a precondition of intersubjectivity. What is at stake is precisely inter*subjective* relationships. A community is made up of a reciprocity of self-determining subjects, who are self-constituting as well as being constituted by the other.

Even though subjectivity and intersubjectivity are mutually necessary, the relation between them is inherently conflictual. Each alone has the tendency to subjugate the other, either by absolutizing autonomy at the expense of community, or by absolutizing community at the expense of the integrity of individuals. (Today one senses a dangerous oscillation between two extremes: doing one's own private thing versus fusion into a mystical totality.) Similarly, resistance and conflict are constituent elements within intersubjectivity itself, insofar as people attempt to live and work with each other while at the same time retaining their own self-determination. In Chap. IV, Sec. 1, I shall observe that such conflicts are the consequence of a certain "fragility" or structural instability of the finite human being, who exists at the point of intersection between freedom and nature, consciousness and body, the individual and the social. These conflicts or tensions are not in themselves sinful, but they can readily "fall" into actual situations of *alienation*.[56] Alienation becomes rooted and demonically intensified in the social involuntary, by which it "surrounds" the individual, rendering unfaulted human existence impossible, even though sin has its root in an interior act of the will. In this respect social alienation is formally parallel to the infinitizing of bodily needs and desires by the imagination in subjective freedom. In each instance the involuntary becomes the "seat" of sin, although sin itself is a voluntary act. Every determinate social

---

56. See Farley, *Ecclesial Man,* chap. VI; and "God as Dominator and Image-Giver: Divine Sovereignty and the New Anthropology," *Journal of Ecumenical Studies,* 6 (1969) : 365–368.

world has been infected by idolatry, flight, and guilt, providing the means by which these originally individual acts are institutionalized and intersubjectively reinforced.

Out of this alienation arises the exigency for an objective actualization of freedom. It is not enough for the social world to function as a "neutral," involuntary substratum of communion, for its neutrality is soon subverted by institutionalized alienation. Freedom *itself* must be embodied institutionally.

B. THE OBJECTIVE ACTUALIZATION OF FREEDOM IN SOCIOPOLITICAL STRUCTURES

In the *Phenomenology of Mind,* Hegel argues that the "unhappy consciousness" of Stoicism and Skepticism reflects the awareness that the self "cannot possess its freedom and truth independently of the conditions of the world." [57] Therefore spirit must move beyond both subjectivity and intersubjectivity (or "self-consciousness" and "reason" in Hegelian terms) to true objectivity, i.e., to the objective actualization of freedom in social and political structures. [58]

Among modern philosophers, none addressed himself to this task more resolutely than Hegel, and it is to him that we must turn for an as yet unsurpassed treatment of the subject, despite the fragmentation of his system in the traumas of the twentieth century. We are still confronted by Hegelian problems, even if his solutions no longer satisfy us. According to Hegel, freedom is actualized by "generating a world as our own creation," as distinguished from "finding a world presupposed before us," which is the condition of subjective spirit as it emerges out of nature. [59] The world created by us is to be a truly human world, structured according to the principles of freedom rather than the necessities of nature. Only such a world, the world of culture and politics, offers an adequate environment for the nurture of human spirit. Human

---

57. Hegel, *Phenomenology of Mind,* pp. 241–267. The quotation is from Wolfhart Pannenberg's description of Hegel's position in *The Idea of God and Human Freedom,* trans. R. A. Wilson (Philadelphia: Westminster Press, 1973), p. 149.

58. Cf. Hegel, *Philosophy of Right,* § 27; *Encyclopedia,* §§ 385 A, 482, 484.

59. Hegel, *Encyclopedia,* § 386.

beings cannot dwell in the "kingdom of nature" alone; they must create a "kingdom of freedom" as their true home in the world. "The system of right is *the kingdom of freedom actualized,* the world of spirit brought forth out of itself like a second nature." [60] The Hegelian "kingdom of freedom" is reminiscent, not only of the "kingdom of God" proclaimed by Jesus, of which it is a secularized translation,[61] but also of Aristotle's definition of the *polis* as the "community of the free" *(koinōnia tōn eleutherōn).*

But what in fact is this realm of "objective spirit," this "kingdom of freedom"? Despite the prevailing interpretation, for which Hegel's own language is at least partly responsible, it does not appear that Hegel intends it as a super-person or super-subject identifiable with nations, races, or peoples.   Nor on the other hand is it simply a collection of individuals or of intersubjective intentionalities.   It seems rather to be the substantial actualization of the principle of subjective human spirit, namely, freedom, in the structures or "system" of the sociopolitical world.   In it *subject* becomes *substance*[62] and vice versa; i.e., the principle of subjectivity, freedom, takes on sociopolitical substance, and the sociopolitical substance ought to be the actualization of the principle of subjective spirit (freedom) rather than of nature (necessity).[63] In being "substantialized," however, freedom takes on a *higher* necessity by which the contingency or caprice of merely subjective (and intersubjective) freedom is overcome: "Freedom, shaped into the actuality of a world, receives the form of necessity, the deeper

60. Hegel, *Philosophy of Right,* § 4 (translation altered; italics mine). In German the italicized phrase reads, *das Reich der verwirklichten Freiheit.* As far as I can determine, Hegel is the original source of this expression, Marx having probably adopted it from him (see above, p. 59).

61. The connections between the kingdom of God, freedom, and love are drawn elsewhere in the Hegelian corpus, e.g., "The Spirit of Christianity and Its Fate," in *Early Theological Writings,* trans. T. M. Knox (New York: Harper & Brothers, 1961), pp. 277–279; and *Vorlesungen über die Philosophie der Religion,* ed. Georg Lasson (Hamburg: Verlag von Felix Meiner, 1966), II/2, 143–155, 178–179, 201. On Jesus' proclamation of a "kingdom of freedom," see Chap. V, Sec. 3A.

62. The dialectic of "subject" and "substance," which recurs throughout Hegel's philosophy, is first introduced in the Preface to the *Phenomenology of Mind,* p. 80.

63. For this reason Hegel resists *organicist* metaphors in describing the objective realm of freedom. He does not refer to it, e.g., as a "body politic," as Hobbes does. This is often overlooked by critics who see Hegel as a forerunner of totalitarian politics.

substantial nexus of which is the system . . . of the principles of freedom." [64]

These abstruse Hegelian insights are clarified in the work of Hannah Arendt, who has reflected more profoundly than any other contemporary thinker on the philosophical significance of politics. She argues that there are only two distinctively *political* activities: action and speech, *praxis* and *lexis, exousia* and *parrēsia,* which means "not only that most political action, insofar as it remains outside the sphere of violence, is indeed transacted in words, but more fundamentally that finding the right words at the right moment . . . is action." Action and speech constitute an *intersubjective* "in-between" that takes on *objective* reality in the world, functioning as "the 'web' of human relationships," within which human beings are able to disclose themselves to each other as distinct and unique persons. The *polis*—the political realm, the realm of freedom—is precisely this "web of human relationships." In essence it was neither a place nor an institutional structure, although it depended upon both. In the Greek view, the *walls* and the *laws* of the city-state secured the *space* and the *structure* within which political actions could take place. "Not Athens, but the Athenians, were the *polis*"—although there could be no *polis* without a physical, legal, and institutional setting. "The *polis* . . . is the organization of the people as it arises out of acting and speaking together, and its true space lies between people living together for this purpose, no matter where they happen to be. . . . It is the space of appearance . . . , the space where I appear to others as others appear to me, where men exist not merely like other living or inanimate things but make their appearance explicitly." [65] These statements suggest how freedom actualized in the political realm can and must be both an (inter)-subjective and an objective, "substantial" reality.

Hegel's "objective spirit" *is* the "space of appearance" and "web of human relationships" described by Arendt. As such it

64. Hegel, *Encyclopedia,* § 484; cf. *Philosophy of Right,* §§ 28, 145, 149.
65. Hannah Arendt, *The Human Condition* (Chicago: University of Chicago Press, 1958), pp. 13, 22, 25–27, 176–184, 194–195, 198–199 (quotations from pp. 26, 182–183, 195, 198–199).

arises out of and consists in the words and deeds that transpire between persons, but it must be secured by legal, ethical, socio-economic, and political (or constitutional) structures. Accordingly, therefore, the objective realm of freedom, or "the system of the principles of freedom," is actualized in three stages:[66] abstract or formal right (law), morality of conscience, and ethical life or the sociopolitical structure *(Sittlichkeit)*. The latter is the unity and truth of the first two moments, "the idea of the good . . . so realized both in the will reflected into itself and in the external world that freedom exists as *substance*, as actuality and necessity, no less than as *subjective* will." Ethical life, in turn, is comprised of three elements: the family, civil society (in which individuals relate to each other, not according to family ties, but through reciprocal social and economic needs—the so-called system of needs), and the state.

Hegel's treatment of the latter as the highest form of objective freedom is of great interest for our purposes. He describes it in a highly idealized, utopian form:

> The state is the actuality of concrete freedom. But concrete freedom consists in this, that personal individuality and its particular interests not only achieve their complete development and gain explicit recognition for their right . . . but, for one thing, they also pass over of their own accord into the interest of the universal, and, for another thing, they know and will the universal; they even recognize it as their own substantive mind; they take it as their end and aim and are active in its pursuit. The result is that the universal does not prevail or achieve completion except along with particular interests and through the co-operation of particular knowing and willing; and individuals likewise do not live as private persons for their own ends alone, but in the very act of willing these they will the universal in the light of the universal, and their activity is consciously aimed at none but the universal end. The principle of modern states has prodigious strength and depth because it allows the principle of subjectivity to progress to its culmination in the extreme of self-subsistent personal particularity, and yet at the same time brings it back to the substantive unity and so maintains this unity in the principle of subjectivity itself.[67]

66. See Hegel, *Philosophy of Right,* § 33; *Encyclopedia,* § 487.
67. Hegel, *Philosophy of Right,* § 260; cf. §§ 257–271.

What is portrayed here is obviously not the modern state in any empirical sense but an eschatological/utopian vision of a "kingdom of freedom" in which the freedom and fulfillment of each is simultaneously the freedom and fulfillment of all—a liberated community of free subjects. This utopianism renders more intelligible Hegel's tendency to divinize or absolutize the state,[68] but it also increases the mystery as to why he apparently believed this ideal human community to have been embodied in constitutional principles patterned after the German constitutional monarchy of his time! [69] One may discern in Hegel the danger of an over-politicization of biblical images and of a de-eschatologization of religion. With Hegel's description of the ideal state, we have in fact already arrived at the perspective of "absolute spirit" or "transsubjective freedom," for the kingdom of freedom is not an immanent human, historical possibility; it transcends as the infinite goal and depth of history.

5. OPENNESS: TRANSSUBJECTIVE FREEDOM

A. The Transition to the Third Structure of Freedom

The dialectic between subjective and intersubjective freedom, and the exigency for an objective actualization of freedom that arises out of the alienation into which the social world falls, are readily understandable matters and indeed common themes of phenomenology, sociology, and political philosophy. But why should it be necessary that the first two structures of freedom—autonomy and community—be superseded by or founded in a *third* structure, that of "openness" or "transsubjective freedom"? [70]

68. The state, we are told, "is [divine] spirit standing in the world," "the march of God in the world," "the divine will . . . unfolding itself to be the actual shape and organization of a world." Ibid., §§ 258 A, 270.
69. Ibid., §§ 272 ff.
70. The expression "transsubjective freedom" is not entirely adequate; for it is a question not merely of moving beyond subjectivity and intersubjectivity to a trans*subjective* structure, but also of moving beyond the objective actualization of freedom to a trans*objective* structure, one that founds and transcends sociopolitical freedom. But it is simply too awkward to refer constantly to "transsubjective and transobjective freedom"; and the move from consent-necessity to openness described in the last two subsections of Sec. 5 is in fact based on an analysis of the structural openness intrinsic to every human *subject*. Since the major thrust of my argument is on trans*subjectivity*, I shall continue using that term.

Is it not the case, as the Marxists have contended, that the kingdom of freedom can be actualized out of purely immanent, historico-economic possibilities, i.e., that human beings can liberate themselves from the bondage of self and society? [71] Or, dismissing this Marxist expectation as an illusion, is it not the case, as Skinner suggests, that human beings remain permanently bound to the necessities of the physical and social environments, and that one day the species will perish or destroy itself?

The answer to these questions may take two directions—the first starting from the fact that freedom cannot be actualized objectively other than in ambiguous form, the second from the reciprocity of the voluntary and the involuntary in subjective and intersubjective experience.

The first direction is the one taken by Hegel himself, although he does not use the specific term "ambiguity." In the *Phenomenology of Spirit,* he develops two reasons for the necessary advance from objective to absolute spirit (or from "spirit" to "religion," in the terminology of that work). First, objective spirit falls into a situation of alienation in human culture; the inability of the individual to achieve a true mediation between him- or herself and the universal spiritual whole results finally in a reign of terror such as occurred during the French Revolution.[72] Second, the morality of conscience (one of the forms of objective spirit) tends to cut itself off from the concrete substance of actual society and to cultivate goodness in solitary isolation—the "beautiful soul" of pietism and romanticism.[73] In both cases it is the failure to achieve a true, non-alienating mediation between subjective and objective freedom that drives consciousness on to the absolute, which is the ground of ultimate reconciliation—a reconciliation manifested in works of art, in religion, and in the absolute knowledge of philosophy.

71. I noted in Chapter II that Marx himself remained ambiguous about this possibility: while proposing an economic solution to the problem of alienation, at the same time he believed that the kingdom of freedom must lie beyond the necessity of labor entirely—a possibility about which he grew increasingly skeptical (see above, pp. 59–60).
72. Hegel, *Phenomenology of Mind,* pp. 507–610, esp. pp. 507–508, 510–512, 599–610.
73. Ibid., pp. 611–679, esp. pp. 613–614, 642–643, 751–753.

In the *Philosophy of Right* and the *Encyclopedia*, the finite, limited, determinate nature of the ethical reality of the state is seen as the basis for the necessity of religion.   Although the divine spirit is present in the true state, the various empirical states are limited by factors of geography, climate, ethnic heritage, and cultural circumstances.   Each of the various national spirits *(Volkgeister)* must be seen as a moment in the advancement toward the universal or world spirit *(Weltgeist)*—a romantic term for divinity.[74]   Hence religion, whose essence lies in the consciousness of absolute truth and the revelation of absolute spirit in and for itself, is the "substance of the ethical life and the state," the "groundwork which includes the ethical realm . . . and the state's fundamental nature—the divine will." [75]   Without religion there can be no finally valid social and political emancipation, for the ultimate source and power of this emancipation would be lacking.[76]

These Hegelian arguments could be supplemented by an analysis of the *ambiguous* character of the actualization of freedom in sociopolitical structures.[77]   Such ambiguity means that we are confronted not merely by social *alienation* (which is already evident from the dialectic of subjectivity and intersubjectivity) but also by institutionalized *oppression* (the classic symbol of which is the master-slave relation).   All empirical human communities are ambiguous mixtures of communion and estrangement, freedom and oppression.   This situation creates the exigency for *an openness to a transcendence* that would give both the image and the reality of a liberated communion of free subjects—a "kingdom of freedom" that is the gift of God and the true destiny of humankind.   Such a kingdom would liberate from the false infinity of subjective imagination, the alienation of intersubjective social structures, and objectively institutionalized oppression.   I return

74. Hegel, *Philosophy of Right,* §§ 33, 341–360; *Encyclopedia,* §§ 548–549.
75. Hegel, *Encyclopedia,* § 552; *Philosophy of Right,* § 270.
76. Cf. Pannenberg, *The Idea of God and Human Freedom,* pp. 145–146, 155–157.
77. On the ambiguity of all human achievements in the realms of morality, culture, politics, religion, and history, see especially Paul Tillich, *Systematic Theology,* vol. III (Chicago: University of Chicago Press, 1963).

to these themes—from the point of view of a hermeneutic of the symbols of the Christian tradition—in Chapters VI and VII.

The *second* answer to the question concerning the reasons for the transition to a third structure of freedom starts from the experience of the reciprocity of the voluntary and the involuntary. I have argued that a phenomenological description of human consciousness (both subjective and intersubjective) brings voluntary decisions, actions, and relationships into view alongside involuntary determinants. The question now is how these evidences of freedom are to be accounted for. What prevents the voluntary from being absorbed into the involuntary? How is it possible to have determination—through motives, physical needs and capacities, the social system—without compulsion and coercion? What prevents the imagination from enslaving the will totally? What enables communion to survive in the midst of an alienating and oppressive social world? How are the conflicting interests of autonomy and community to be reconciled? In short, if the will is finite, contingent, non-self-positing, by what power can it sustain itself against the seemingly crushing force of the physical and social environment? The quest for an answer drives us beyond subjective, intersubjective, and objective freedom to look for the possibility of a transsubjective freedom.

The answer, briefly formulated, is this: finite, embodied, created freedom remains a viable possibility in the context of the organic and social necessities of life only if persons are open to a liberating power that transcends all their physical and social environments. It is a peculiarity of the human being that he or she remains open into the beyond, the infinite. No other organism demonstrates that characteristic. Human needs and instincts, like those of other animals, are not in themselves infinite; it is only when they are traversed by language that they become desires, quests, passions, intrinsically unfulfillable. No matter how frequently we are positively reinforced, we remain unsatisfied, unfulfilled, unable to attain a final happiness. St. Augustine perceived the infinitude of human openness when he wrote, "The heart is restless until it finds its rest in Thee." This answer will be elaborated in the next two subsections. I shall begin with an eidetic description of the reciprocity between consent and the "absolute" involuntary, then move to a "poetic" phenomenology of openness to transcendence by showing that such a move is required if consent is not to revert to either refusal of the involuntary or surrender to it.

B. NECESSITY AND CONSENT

Openness first comes into view phenomenologically in the form of consent. The greatest contribution of Ricoeur's study of the voluntary and the involuntary is his analysis of consent. Consent as the highest form of freedom occurs in relation to the *absolute* involuntary, namely, the experienced necessities that comprise the conditions of human life itself. Hence, paradoxically, the discovery of openness requires penetration into the depths of the involuntary, where liberating transcendence first appears in veiled form. Only in this fashion do we discover that freedom is neither a self-creation nor a product of social dialectic, but a gift of transcendence that is reducible neither to nature nor to finite spirit. By absolutizing the involuntary, the voluntary is also "absolutized"; freedom becomes a more-than-human possibility; its gratuitous quality is disclosed.

The necessity that constitutes "the human condition" [78] as such lies at the basis of both the physical and the social involuntary. This is the necessity to which I yield by the fact that I have not chosen to exist—namely, the conditions of character, the unconscious, life (birth, growth, structure), and death (or mortality). [79] Necessity is ambiguous, for what grounds me also destroys me, what supports me abandons me. Therefore my condition includes a negative aspect, which can become enslaving, as well as something positive, to which I must consent. [80]

Among the forms of necessity, death is the most ambiguous. Ricoeur correctly points out that death differs from the other

---

78. Cf. Arendt, *The Human Condition*, pp. 7–21, 83–84, 121.
79. For Ricoeur's exhaustive analysis of all but the last of these necessities, see *Freedom and Nature*, pp. 355–443.
80. Ibid., p. 354.

contingencies of life because we have no inner experience of it and no means of anticipating the actual event of dying. It is an externally learned idea, of which the child only gradually becomes aware. "Death remains an accident with respect to the design of life." [81] Yet the accident of death is an inescapable, universal necessity, and it would be wrong to conclude from its seemingly "accidental" character that we are not essentially mortal. Mortality *is* an essential component of the finite, embodied human condition. What is not essential is that physical mortality attain a kind of binding, deadly power vis-à-vis freedom. When that happens, mortality becomes "death" (*thanatos* in the Pauline sense), and mortality-as-death is a form of bondage or sin.[82] Mortality as such is not sinful or evil, but it can become an occasion for sin when persons regard themselves solely from the perspective of their transient existence, living by its criteria, seeking to gain their lives from it, or denying and defying it in a bid for immortality. "Death" is what lies in wait as the consequence of a false and aberrant pursuit of life. Thus bondage becomes rooted in the absolute involuntary in the form of death, analogous to its rootage in the alienated social world at the intersubjective level, and in the bad infinity of desire at the subjective level. As already observed, the involuntary becomes the "seat" of sin, although sin itself is a voluntary act. Mortality converted into death is the absolute form of bondage, and hence death is the final enemy of humankind—an enemy that ought to be refused rather than consented to.

The refusal of death and other forms of bondage is proper and necessary. Ricoeur argues that freedom is born in refusal, which is the transcendental origin of human existence. Yet the tendency of refusal is to carry itself too far, to turn against the necessities themselves, which constitute authentic human finitude, rather than against bondage to them. Refusal thus issues in the "faulty infinite" of freedom: an assertion of sovereignty against the con-

81. Ibid., pp. 456–462.
82. I return to this matter in greater detail in Chap. IV, Sec. 3B.

striction of character, of *absolute* consciousness against the unconscious, of self-creation against birth and growth, of immortality against mortality. Refusal thereby turns to defiance, rebellion, idolatry; and defiance is the fault par excellence.[83]

The alternative at the other extreme from refusal is surrender or flight: a giving of oneself up to the necessities of life and the other forms of the involuntary. Surrender is described by Ricoeur as hyperbolic consent, which he says is the soul of Orphism and Stoicism, of the modern lyric tradition, of the final philosophies of Goethe and Nietzsche. Here the temptation is to lose one's subjectivity and to sink into the great metamorphoses of nature—a nature worship in which the unique status of freedom evaporates.[84]

Authentic consent stands between refusal and surrender, preserving both finitude (which is denied when refusal turns to defiance) and freedom (which is lost in surrender). But consent implies that, in spite of appearances, the world is a possible home of freedom; it is not merely a network of contingencies of survival, but the cipher of a liberating transcendence which is present in veiled form in the involuntary aspects of human existence and in the voluntary acts that emerge from the involuntary.[85] The involuntary as we experience it—in the form of motivation, bodily needs and capabilities, social world, the necessities of life—is neither a demonic, enslaving power turned against us, nor sheer, meaningless contingency, but the hidden form of transcendence, more perfectly unveiled elsewhere. That is what consent perceives about the world, and thereby it gains freedom from and in relation to the absolute involuntary. Consent has not yet turned away from nature to transcendence, although its appreciation of nature is distinguishable from veneration of it or surrender to it. It is a form of freedom—the highest freedom—in the context of natural necessity.

83. Ricoeur, *Freedom and Nature*, pp. 29, 354, 444–446, 463, 477.
84. Ibid., pp. 473–476.
85. Ibid., pp. 346–347, 467–469, 471–472, 476–478.

C. From Consent to Openness

Yet consent alone is insufficient.

> . . . the way of consent does not lead only through admiration of marvelous nature focused in the absolute involuntary, but through hope which awaits *something else*. Here the Transcendence implied in the act of consent assumes an altogether new form: admiration is possible because the world is an analogy of Transcendence; hope is necessary because the world is quite other than Transcendence. . . . Admiration says, the world is good, it is the *possible* home of freedom; I can consent. Hope says: the world is not the *final* home of freedom; I consent as much as possible, but hope to be delivered of the terrible and at the end of time to enjoy a new body and a new nature granted to freedom.[86]

For hope the transcendence hidden in natural necessity manifests itself openly.

Hope is oriented to the future in radical openness. The most distinctive and essential structure of human existence can be defined as *openness to the future,* with futurity understood as the temporal mode in which transcendence manifests itself. The category of "openness" has its provenance in the existential phenomenologies of Martin Heidegger and Max Scheler. Heidegger, in analyzing the existential constitution of human being-in-the-world, argues that Dasein is open to the *world* in the form of "disposition" or "mood" *(Befindlichkeit),* to its own *future possibilities of being* in the mode of "understanding" *(Verstehen),* and to other persons in the mode of "discourse" *(Rede),* which includes hearing as well as speaking.[87] In virtue of its structural openness, Dasein ex-sists (stands outside itself) as finite transcendence. Later Heidegger will name that *toward which* Dasein transcends or is open, as itself "Openness" or "the Open" *(das Offene),* which is one of the many names for "Being" *(Sein).*[88]

According to Scheler, "the essential characteristic of the [hu-

---

86. Ibid., p. 480.
87. Heidegger, *Being and Time,* pp. 176, 183, 206.
88. Cf. Heidegger, "The Origin of the Work of Art," in *Poetry, Language. Thought,* trans. Albert Hofstadter (New York: Harper & Row, 1971), pp. 61 ff.; *Über den Humanismus* (Frankfurt: Vittorio Klostermann, 1947), p. 35; and *Discourse on Thinking,* trans. John M. Anderson and E. Hans Freund (New York: Harper & Row, 1966), pp. 68 ff. Another of the Heideggerian names for Being is "the Free" *(das Freie)* (see Chap. VII, Sec. 2) .

man] spiritual being . . . is its existential liberation from the organic world." This liberation is defined as "openness to the world," which is based on the human ability to transform the things of the environment into "objects" of a humanly constituted world.

> The animal has no "object." It lives, as it were, ecstatically immersed in its environment which it carries along as a snail carries its shell. It cannot transform the environment into an object. It cannot perform the peculiar act of detachment and distance by which man transforms an "environment" into the "world," or into a symbol of the world.[89]

But in addition, argues Scheler, human beings are not merely open *to* the world; they are also open *through* and *beyond* the world to something else. This "something else" is first confronted as the possibility of absolute nothingness, the discovery of which drives us to ask, "Why is there a world as such, and why and how do I exist?" The quest for an answer to this question gives rise to what Scheler calls the *formal* consciousness of an absolute Being (or "God"), or what I am calling "openness to transcendence." This formal consciousness of, or openness to, that which in some sense lies beyond and is the foundation of the world forms "an inseparable structural unity" with consciousness of the world and of the self; in other words, it is one of the essential structures of free human existence.[90]

These phenomenological analyses of human openness have been brought into theological anthropology by Karl Rahner and Wolfhart Pannenberg. Rahner, who has been more directly influenced by Heidegger than by Scheler, argues that the so-called natural existential of the human being includes within itself a transcendental openness to and capacity for communication with the infinite ground of Being, an openness which he also describes as the *"potentia oboedientialis* for a possible free revelation." "Man," according to Rahner's inclusive definition of the human

---

89. Max Scheler, *Man's Place in Nature*, trans. Hans Meyerhoff (New York: Noonday Press, 1971), pp. 37–40 (quotation from p. 39).
90. Ibid., pp. 88–90.

being as a "hearer of the word," "is the being of receptive spirituality opened for history, who stands in and as freedom before the free God of a possible revelation, which, if it comes, occurs in his history—as its highest actualization—'in word.' " [91] This statement shows how, in Rahner's view, the openness of persons to the world (or history) is *at the same time* an openness to God, since the revelation of the latter is mediated precisely through those words and events by which human history is most fully actualized. To find God, one must turn to the world; to know the world *as* world, one must be open to a horizon beyond the world.[92]

Pannenberg follows Scheler's argument that human beings are open not only to the world but also through and beyond it. If the latter were not the case, then the world would be for men and women what the environment is for animals—gigantic and very complicated, to be sure, but still an environment. "Rather, openness to the world must mean that man is completely directed into the 'open.' He is always open further, beyond every experience and beyond every given situation. . . . Such openness beyond the world is even the condition for man's experience of the world." [93] Against Sartre, Pannenberg argues that this openness cannot be the expression merely of a human lack or need that manifests itself in creative drives, for even the lack presupposes the possibility of a totality that is lacking. Consequently, there must be a "supporting ground" for the experience of openness that can lie neither in the human being himself nor in the extant world. "This reality is . . . not simply 'hypostatized' as tran-

91. Rahner, *Hörer des Wortes*, pp. 47–88, 141, 199–200 (quotation from p. 200). This theme occurs many times in Rahner's *Theological Investigations*, e.g., vol. I, pp. 162, 171, 183–184, 315; vol. II, trans. K.-H. Kruger (Baltimore: Helicon Press, 1963), pp. 235–240, 246–247, 272; vol. IV, trans. Kevin Smyth (Baltimore: Helicon Press) , pp. 108–110, 117.
92. Cf. Rahner, *Hörer des Wortes*, pp. 71–88, 173–174. This principle is based on Thomistic epistemology, which Rahner attempted to reinterpret in the light of idealism and existential phenomenology.
93. Wolfhart Pannenberg, *What Is Man? Contemporary Anthropology in Theological Perspective*, trans. Duane A. Priebe (Philadelphia: Fortress Press, 1970) , pp. 1–13 (quotation from p. 8). Pannenberg acknowledges the influence not only of Scheler but also of Adolf Portmann, Arnold Gehlen, Helmuth Plessner, Michael Landmann, Ernst Bloch, and Jean-Paul Sartre.

scendence beyond the world, nor is it only the 'ideal' that man projects in his desire for self-realization, since he is instead already dependent for all self-realization upon that supporting reality, which is antecedent to all such projections as the ground of their possibility." [94]   Human desires appear to be infinite, intrinsically unfulfillable, driving beyond every finite object into the open beyond. What constitutes this infinite ground or power of reality cannot be brought into view by foundational anthropology. Pannenberg believes, however, that it can be shown phenomenologically that it is experienced as the *power of the future*.[95]   That to which above all else persons are open, as temporal-historical beings, is the open, incalculable future. Again, what actually constitutes the power of the future lies beyond the range of phenomenological investigation.   But it can be argued that it is experienced as redemptive, because it is precisely the open future that frees persons from the inexorability of the past and the bondage and alienation of the present by bringing new possibilities for being onto the horizon.

If human beings are open to transcendence, then they are open to the possibility of redemption; in other words, they are *redeemable*.   Redeemability, I argued earlier, can be brought into view by means of a "poetic" phenomenology, i.e., a phenomenology that understands the human subject in relation to a gift, a creativity *(poieisis)*, a transcendence independent of itself.[96]   At the outset, at least, this ought to remain a phenomenologically neutral poetics, which leaves open the question as to the nature and source of the creative-redemptive event.   That *some such* event is experienced, however, can be argued phenomenologically from the

94. Pannenberg, "The Question of God," in *Basic Questions in Theology*, vol. II, trans. George Kehm (Philadelphia: Fortress Press, 1971), pp. 216–217, 221–226 (quotation from p. 222).
95. See Pannenberg, *What Is Man?*, chap. IV; and *Theology and the Kingdom of God* (Philadelphia: Westminster Press, 1969), chap. I.
96. See Ricoeur, *Freedom and Nature*, pp. 29–30, 471–472; also *Freud and Philosophy*, pp. 524–525: a poetics of the will "concerns the radical origin of the *I will* . . . [in] a call, a kerygma, a word addressed to me."   Heidegger in his later essays on poetry and language has articulated a "poetic" mode of thinking in which the relation between language and the human being, as traditionally understood, is inverted. See especially ". . . Poetically Man Dwells . . ." in *Poetry, Language, Thought*, p. 216.

dynamics of consent. Consent, if it is to remain *consent* and not revert to either *defiance* of the involuntary or *surrender* to it, *must* issue in an openness to a creative transcendence independent of both self and world; for the very heart of consent is its perception that the world as a cipher of transcendence is not *identical* with transcendence and thereby points beyond itself. Thus human beings appear to be structurally open to a liberating power that is reducible neither to themselves nor to the natural or cultural world; they appear to be redeem*able,* capable of being set free. This much can be concluded from the phenomenological observation that persons *do* in fact consent, make decisions, carry out intended acts, and enjoy communion.

But the question remains as to whether these acts are the mere *semblance* of freedom or freedom *in fact*. Are redemption and liberating power *realities* as opposed to mere possibilities? Are human beings not simply redeemable but in fact redeemed? These are questions that cannot be settled by an analysis of essential human possibilities. They require turning to a determinate community of faith with its symbols of bondage and liberation. However, in the final analysis even redeem*ability* in some sense presupposes the actuality of redemption: if redemption is not in fact available, then redeemability would be a tragic deception, and it would appear senseless even to speak of it. A *poetic* phenomenology requires bringing in the symbols of liberation, because poetics understands the human being *already* in relation to an *event* of creation/redemption. Thus the relation between redeemability and redemption is a thoroughly dialectical one. This does not mean, however, that redeemability is simply reduced to redemption, or that the project of a poetic phenomenology is a chimera. For the fact that human beings really do consent, hope, play, and love implies that the event of liberation has inscribed itself upon the very structural possibilities of human existence and is discernible there *prior to and apart from* a hermeneutic of the symbols of faith. This has important ramifications for a foundational theology. But the inscription remains ambiguous and obscure, subject to varying symbolic interpretations. *Some* sort of liberation has occurred (or is in the process of occurring), but *what* sort is another matter. There are, after all, humanistic and pagan poets as well as Jewish and Christian ones.

Within the limits of a structural phenomenology, perhaps one further argument is possible—although admittedly this argument pushes the limits to their breaking point and may in fact cross over into a wager of faith. That to which men and women are open beyond all controlling environments, biological and cultural, is the final home of freedom, or to use the image coined by Hegel, a "kingdom of freedom," which will reconcile the voluntary and the involuntary, furnish the utopian/eschatological image of a liberated communion of free subjects, and set human beings free from the self-imposed bondage into which they have fallen and from which they cannot rescue themselves. Such a kingdom can be neither the kingdom of our own making, nor the kingdom of nature or of the void.

Might it be the kingdom of humankind, the realm in which the hidden human essence (the species-essence, the *homo absconditus*) is concealed, toward the realization of which men and women are slowly and painfully moving through the struggles of history (Marx, E. Bloch)? In this case, liberation is a self-assigned task, and we appear to be back with "autonomous man," whether individual or social. Does not this position contradict all that has been said about the determinants of the physical and social environment, the conflictual relation between the voluntary and the involuntary, the fallibility of human beings and their self-imposed bondage, the fact that human freedom is not self-creative and self-redemptive?

Might it be the kingdom of nature—that inner physiological structure and outward environing womb that nurtures human life yet ultimately consumes it (Freud, Skinner, Roszak, Rubenstein, and many others)? But then we are in fact "beyond freedom," as Skinner rightly recognizes, for we are prone to forget that the necessity of nature is at best a cipher of transcendence, not transcendence itself. The gods of nature are false gods.

Finally, might it be the kingdom of the void, of the abyss, of nothingness—that empty space upon which the human being projects him- or herself and by which he or she is "thrown" into existence (Sartre, Camus, the early Heidegger)? If this is the case, it is difficult to avoid a tragic conception of the human condition. For nothingness has no power to create or to liberate, and ultimately it destroys all life. Death is sovereign. The hoped-for reconciliation of the voluntary and involuntary remains permanently beyond reach. The world is not a possible stage for freedom.

Thus the kingdom of freedom, if the image has any significance at all, cannot be either the hidden human essence or nature or the void. Of course hope for such a kingdom might be a sheer illusion (a wish projection), and liberating consent a folly, in which case the only viable alternatives would remain refusal or surrender, existential despair or scientific controls. The fact that human beings do consent without surrendering—that they hope for a new birth of freedom which is anticipated as a gift and is presently experienced in a life of liberating obedience, that they know how to play in the face of the sheer necessities of existence, that they experience a fleeting reconciliation of freedom and nature in contest, art, dance, music, poetry, and love—provides a phenomenological warrant for saying that men and women live *as though* the kingdom of freedom were the kingdom *of God*. But which God? Is "he" one or many, known or unknown, named or nameless, present or absent?

PART THREE
BOUND FREEDOM

Chapter IV

Forms of Bondage

1. THE FRAGILITY OF FREEDOM

Thus far we have examined the structures of embodied human freedom apart from the fault that disrupts and distorts these structures. It was necessary to do so in order to be in the position now of understanding the fault (or "sin") as a *self-imposed bondage of the will*. Human beings inflict a *bondage* upon themselves, which must be distinguished from the *necessity* of the involuntary; subsequently, this bondage becomes objectified in the physical and social involuntary, taking on the aspect of inevitability or fate, but still distinguishable from the involuntary as such. The essential point is that freedom precedes bondage and is its origin, rather than vice versa. According to the biblical story of creation, human beings were not born into a situation of objective bondage or evil (as the theogonic myth claims, for example), from which they must struggle to deliver themselves by their own efforts, with the help of the gods. Rather they were born into freedom, and because this freedom deceives itself in the process of self-enslavement, deliverance is not something that humankind can manage on its own. Freedom is the more fundamental category; bondage is an accident that befalls freedom.

Before turning to the fact of bondage, we must analyze its possibility in terms of essential structures. Just as a person is redeemable, so also is he or she fallible. Fallibility is not a structure of freedom in the sense that redeemability or openness is. Rather fallibility is the susceptibility of all the structures of freedom to failure. This susceptibility to failure, this weakness of men and women, may be described as the *fragility* of freedom—a fragility inherent in the very language that makes embodied freedom possible. Fragility does not *cause* sin; rather it is its precondition or occasion. The transition from fallibility to fault (like that from redeemability to redemption) is not a logically necessary one but rather entails a "leap" from essential structures to religious symbols, from essence to existence, from "creation" to "fall."

According to Paul Ricoeur, the fragility of finite freedom is rooted in the human being's "disproportion." That which is disproportionate, non-coincident, conflictual is precisely the polarity within persons of the finite and the infinite, of nature and freedom, of the involuntary and the voluntary, which makes up the essential human structure. The human being is not just a finite system of bodily instincts; he or she is rather a mysterious mediation of finitude and infinitude, of body and "spirit." It is not our finitude as such, but the disproportion or non-coincidence of finitude and infinitude, that constitutes our peculiar limitation and makes that limitation synonymous with fallibility.[1] Of course every created thing is limited, but the limitation of finitude per se is not fallibility. It would be inappropriate to say that animals or plants can "fail" in the sense that persons fail, unless one believes that finite nature or matter is intrinsically evil. Rather the limitation synonymous with fallibility is peculiar to human beings alone and has to do with the fact that their freedom, their capacity for self-transcendence, outstrips or is not coincident with their bodily nature.

The fragility of human freedom is most evident precisely in the use of *language*. Language, as we have observed, is the means by which the relational structures of freedom are constituted; but, situated as it is at the point of non-coincident polarity between body and spirit, it remains contingent, fragile, susceptible to failure and abuse. It is the fragile vessel of human power, readily subject to demonic perversion. The fragility of language (or more precisely, of human speech), is rooted in the disproportion between what Ricoeur calls the finitude of perspective and the

1. Paul Ricoeur, *Fallible Man*, trans. Charles Kelbley (Chicago: Henry Regnery Co., 1967) , pp. xx, 6–7, 204–205, 208.

infinitude of speech. Every perception of an object is limited by a point of view or perspective, but through speech we are able to transcend perspectives and represent objects in terms of their non-perceived sides as well. "I say more than I see when I signify." Therein lies the possibility, not only of transcending one's physical environment, but also of falling into error or deception, for it is quite possible to make absurd significations, which in principle have no referent in seeing. The peculiar infinity of language is rooted in its verbs: by the act of predication, verbs can posit the existence or nonexistence of anything the speaker chooses; false statements can be made with the same grammatical and logical precision as true ones. The possibility of error, deception, and falsehood is the price paid for the symbolic transformation of experience. Linguistic imagination can express truths hidden from sense experience and open up new worlds of non-ostensive reference; but it can also charm and seduce, luring consciousness to forget its rootedness in finitude and the involuntary.[2]

Ricoeur's analysis of disproportion as the clue to human fallibility is similar to Paul Tillich's portrayal of the "tension" that characterizes the ontological polarities of finite or essential being, a tension that generates "ontological anxiety" as the precondition of sin.[3] This form of anxiety has been analyzed by Reinhold Niebuhr in an especially illuminating way in *The Nature and Destiny of Man*.[4] Niebuhr actually distinguishes two preconditions of sin, one internal, the other external.

Anxiety is identified with the *internal precondition*. Kierkegaard is the classic source of this identification. "Anxiety [*Angst*]," he writes,

> is the dizziness of freedom which occurs when the spirit would posit the synthesis [of soul and body], and freedom then gazes down into its own possibility, grasping at finiteness to sustain itself. In this dizziness freedom succumbs. Further than this psy-

2. Cf. ibid., pp. 29–57.
3. Paul Tillich, *Systematic Theology*, vol. I (Chicago: University of Chicago Press, 1951), pp. 198–201; vol. II (Chicago: University of Chicago Press, 1957), pp. 31–36.
4. Reinhold Niebuhr, *The Nature and Destiny of Man* (2 vols.; New York: Charles Scribner's Sons, 1941, 1943), vol. I, chaps. 6, 7.

chology cannot go and will not. That very instant everything is changed, and when freedom rises again it sees that it is guilty. Between these two instants lies the leap, which no science has explained or can explain. . . . Anxiety is the last psychological state out of which sin breaks forth with the qualitative leap.[5]

Anxiety is near to sin, yet it is not sin, nor is it the "explanation" for sin. It is not sin itself because it is an intrinsic concomitant of fragile or disproportionate human nature. Tillich traces it to the tension that exists in finite being between the ontological polarities of individualization and participation, dynamics and form, freedom and destiny. Tension occurs the moment that finite freedom becomes aware of itself, aware, that is, of both its finitude (which means that it is non-coincident with its destiny) and its infinite desires. Similarly Niebuhr writes: "Anxiety is the inevitable concomitant of the paradox of freedom and finiteness in which man is involved. Anxiety is the internal precondition of sin. It is the inevitable spiritual state of man, standing in the paradoxical situation of freedom and finiteness." [6]

The *external precondition* of sin is *temptation*.[7] The situation of tension, anxiety, or disproportion becomes the occasion for sin only when it is *falsely interpreted,* which is not purely the product of human imagination but is suggested by a principle or force of evil antecedent to any individual human action. This is the function of the serpent in the story of the fall; indeed, temptation as the external precondition of sin cannot be explicated apart from the act of sin itself, which requires the telling of a story. Hence we shall have to return to it when examining the actual passage from fallibility to fault. The point now is that false interpretation or *deception* is the key to temptation. But this deception is already a product of sin, an objectification of the internal acts of idolatry and flight. That is why we can catch this precondition

5. Søren Kierkegaard, *The Concept of Dread,* trans. Walter Lowrie (Princeton: Princeton University Press, 1946), pp. 55, 83. The key term *Angst* is better translated as "anxiety" than as "dread."
6. Niebuhr, *The Nature and Destiny of Man,* I, 182.
7. Ibid., pp. 179–181.

only, as it were, in motion, in the telling of a story.   In this sense, Kierkegaard is right: sin "posits" or "presupposes" itself.[8]

The internal and external preconditions (anxiety, temptation) provide the *occasion* for sin but do not *cause* it.   Sin remains a free act for which the individual must accept at least partial responsibility.   In a famous statement Niebuhr says that sin is "inevitable though not necessary."[9]   "Inevitable" may be a bad choice of terms; by it he means "always in fact happens" or "universal."[10]   "Not necessary" means that sin cannot be identified with either the involuntary as such or with the essential human condition.   In fact, it represents a flawing of that condition for which each individual remains responsible, although a bias toward sin already exists in the linguistic and social environment ("temptation").

In view of the "inevitability" or "universality" of sin, it is possible to agree with Tillich that *creation* and *fall* coincide as far as human beings are concerned, since there is no point in time and space at which created goodness was actualized in unfaulted form.   "Actualized creation and estranged existence are identical."   The transition from essence to existence is not necessary, but once the transition occurs, existence is "inevitably" estranged.   But estrangement is not an intrinsic necessity of creation; quite to the contrary, it is a distortion and disruption of what is essentially good.   Therefore the *possibility* of nonestranged existence is not excluded; and in fact according to Christian faith there is at least one instance of such, namely, the power of New Being in Jesus as the Christ.   Here the disruptions of existence are conquered in a life which (to use Tillich's terms) is unambiguous but still

8. Kierkegaard, *The Concept of Dread*, pp. 29–31, 99–100. Tillich defines temptation as follows: "The state of dreaming innocence drives beyond itself. The possibility of the transition to existence is experienced as temptation" (*Systematic Theology*, II, 34). But because *anxiety* is what drives dreaming innocence beyond itself, temptation is in effect reduced to anxiety.   Tillich is more helpful in discussing what he calls "the tragic element, the element of destiny, in man's predicament," understood as the totality of the biological, psychological, and sociological powers by which human beings are determined (ibid., pp. 41–42).   It is this destiny that "tempts" us, insofar as sin has already become rooted there.
9. Niebuhr, *The Nature and Destiny of Man*, I, 150.
10. Ibid., p. 242.

fragmentary, and still subject to ontological anxiety and historical temptation.[11]

In concluding the discussion of fragility, one cannot avoid asking why God should have created human beings with this peculiar susceptibility for sin. Has not theogony been ruled out only at the price of introducing tragedy—i.e., the doctrine of the evil God? There can be no finally satisfying answer to this question, in part because the Judeo-Christian tradition, by internalizing the tragic dimension, acknowledges its power. Our tradition includes Job and Ecclesiastes as well as the cross. The "logical" answer to the question is that if God wished to create free beings distinct from himself (i.e., finite), then the disproportion between freedom and finitude was endemic to that very project, the human project. This answer is logically correct but, like all theodicies, religiously unsatisfying, as Job eloquently attests. The only religiously satisfying answer would be that of a God who takes upon himself, internalizes as it were, the human tragedy, thereby completing and suppressing it. This is the meaning of the vicarious and redemptive suffering of Jesus Christ, a suffering undergone by God himself.[12]

2. THE INTERIOR ACT OF SIN: THE SERVILE WILL

A. The Origin of Sin: Deception

According to the Jewish and Christian heritage, human bondage originates in an interior act of self-deception, which issues in two archetypal modes of sin corresponding to the fragile polarity of human nature itself: the sin of idolatry (or of pride, rebellion, infinitude), and the sin of flight (or of sloth, failure, finitude). The consequence of both idolatry and flight is an inward and an outward binding of sinful human beings. The inward binding may be understood as guilt, whereas bondage is outwardly objec-

11. Tillich, *Systematic Theology*, II, 44, 125–135; III (Chicago: University of Chicago Press, 1963), 144–149.
12. Cf. Paul Ricoeur, *The Symbolism of Evil*, trans. Emerson Buchanan (Boston: Beacon Press, 1969), pp. 327–328.

tified in forms of estrangement and oppression such as those described by the Apostle Paul: law, death, and the worldly powers. The outward objectifications correspond to the interior structure of the servile will. Law, for example, understood as the institutions, structures, and norms of social existence, may be considered an objectification of guilt; death is an objective consequence of the sinful flight from life; while the "powers" are objectifications of the idolatry or pride that constitutes sin as an act of rebellion against God. These relations may be represented diagrammatically as follows:

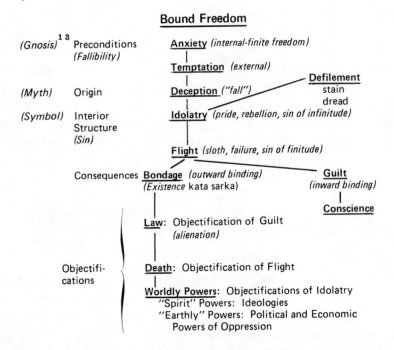

Bound Freedom

(Gnosis)[13] Preconditions <u>Anxiety</u> *(internal-finite freedom)*
                (Fallibility) |
                               <u>Temptation</u> *(external)*
                                              | — <u>Defilement</u>
(Myth)   Origin   <u>Deception</u> *("fall")* ——————   stain
                                              | dread
(Symbol)   Interior   <u>Idolatry</u> *(pride, rebellion, sin of infinitude)*
              Structure |
              (Sin)
                               <u>Flight</u> *(sloth, failure, sin of finitude)*
                                    /
          Consequences <u>Bondage</u> *(outward binding)*   <u>Guilt</u>
                        (Existence kata sarka)   *(inward binding)*
                                              | |
                                              | <u>Conscience</u>
                               <u>Law</u>: Objectification of Guilt
                                              | *(alienation)*
              Objectifi- |
              cations   <u>Death</u>: Objectification of Flight
                                              |
                               <u>Worldly Powers</u>: Objectifications of Idolatry
                                   "Spirit" Powers: Ideologies
                                   "Earthly" Powers: Political and Economic
                                       Powers of Oppression

13. The terms "gnosis," "myth," and "symbol" refer to different levels of reflection at which the experience of sin is brought to expression. The most primitive level is that of symbol, which is found imbedded in confessions of sin. The primary symbols of evil are defilement (stain and dread), sin (idolatry and flight), bondage and guilt. Reflection on the origin of sin takes place in the form of myth. Finally, speculation about *why* evil or sin should have first occurred leads to the formation of explanatory doctrines or theories (or "gnosis"). See Ricoeur, *The Symbolism of Evil*, pp. 3–10. Hence our order of procedure in this chapter—moving from the preconditions of sin in the preceding section, to its origin, and finally to its inward and outward structure—is *inverse* to the genesis of consciousness of sin. This is appropriate because we are moving from a structural to a hermeneutic phenomenology.

Several consequences follow from this understanding of the matter. First, salvation or liberation cannot be gained *simply* by a removal of the objective conditions of estrangement and oppression, as Marxism claims, or by an alteration in environment, as behavioral and technocratic views of freedom tend to advocate. For the powers that enslave human beings are not in the first instance external to* the psyche but internal to it. Self-enslavement follows from the rupturing of certain basic, life-sustaining relationships, a rupturing that has its roots in a fundamental and continuing act of deceit or falsehood. The servile will is founded in self-deception and therefore cannot free itself. But in the second place, the outward objectifications of bondage demonically reinforce and intensify the interior act. Not only are the pretensions and pride of a collective or social self more excessive than those of the individual ego, but also, by becoming a social and political phenomenon, bondage precedes the individual and ensnares him or her, despite one's own innocence and good intentions.[14] Hence genuine liberation cannot be attained merely by a retreat into inwardness that leaves these objectifications untouched, as proposed by the Stoics, Freudian psychoanalysis, existentialism, and much of the counter culture. Although Marx and Freud have each grasped important dimensions of the total phenomenon, the dynamics of bondage and oppression are such as to preclude either a purely Marxist or a purely Freudian strategy for liberation.[15]

The transition from fallibility to fault, and the paradox of a servile or captive free will, resist rational explanation. The Bible offers no philosophical speculations about either the transition or the paradox. Instead, it tells a story—the story of the temptation and "fall" of the first man and the first woman (Gen. 3:1–24), the "Adamic myth," as Ricoeur calls it.[16]

14. Cf. Niebuhr, *The Nature and Destiny of Man*, I, 208–219.
15. This is a way of responding to Theodore Roszak's query, "Psychic reality and social reality: which is the prime mover of our lives? Which is the substance and which the shadow?" *The Making of a Counter Culture* (New York: Anchor Books, 1969) , p. 84.
16. *The Symbolism of Evil*, pt. II, chap. 3.

On the basis of this story it can be argued that the "originative" act of sin is one of *deception* or *falsehood*.[17] At least this is the way Paul interprets the story in 2 Cor. 11:3: "I am afraid that as the serpent deceived Eve by his cunning, your thoughts will be led astray from a sincere and pure devotion to Christ."[18] At the outset of the story we are told explicitly "the serpent was more cunning [*ʿārûm*] than any other wild creature that Yahweh had made" (Gen. 3:1); and after the transgression the woman complains, "The Serpent tricked [*hiššîʾanî*] me, and I ate" (3:13). The deception takes two forms, both of which are entirely *verbal* or *linguistic* (a significant point to which I shall return shortly). The first is a question that cunningly exaggerates Yahweh's command: "Did God say, 'You shall not eat of *any* tree of the garden'?" (3:1).[19] The woman rightly responds that only the fruit of the tree in the middle of the garden is forbidden, on penalty of death. But, as Ricoeur notes:

> the question makes the limit suddenly appear as an interdiction. Dizziness begins with alienation from the commandment. . . . At the same time as the meaning of the ethical limit becomes hazy, the meaning of finiteness is obscured. A "desire" has sprung up, the desire for infinity. . . . The soul of the serpent's question is the "evil infinite," which simultaneously perverts the meaning of the limit by which freedom was oriented and the meaning of the finiteness of the freedom thus oriented by the limit.[20]

Thus the woman is ripe for the second deception, which comes in the form of a quite plausible yet idolatrous assertion: "You will

17. Most interpretations of sin have not focused on this point; but cf. Dietrich Bonhoeffer, *Ethics*, trans. Neville Horton Smith (1st ed.; New York: Macmillan, 1955), pp. 326–334; *Creation and Fall; A Theological Interpretation of Genesis 1–3*, trans. John C. Fletcher (London: SCM Press, 1959), pp. 68–71; and Karl Barth, *Church Dogmatics*, vol. IV/3:1, trans. G. W. Bromiley (Edinburgh: T. & T. Clark, 1961), § 70, "The Falsehood and Condemnation of Man."

18. The verb *exapataō* occurs several more times in the Pauline and deutero-Pauline epistles: Rom. 7:11; 16:18; 1 Cor. 3:18; 2 Thess. 2:3; 1 Tim. 2:14 (in the latter passage the woman is explicitly blamed for the transgression). Similar terms occur in Jn. 8:44; Rom. 1:25; 3:13; Col. 2:8; 3:9; Eph. 5:6; Heb. 3:13; Rev. 2:2; 21:8, 27; 22:15. This demonstrates that the definition of sin as deception or lying, often with an implicit or explicit reference to Genesis 3, is fairly common in the New Testament. For the Old Testament, see esp. Jer. 17:9.

19. Bonhoeffer refers to this as the "religious question" and therefore to the serpent as *die fromme Schlange*. *Creation and Fall*, p. 67.

20. Ricoeur, *The Symbolism of Evil*, p. 253. "Dizziness" is of course the term used by Kierkegaard to describe anxiety in *The Concept of Dread*.

not die. For God knows that when you eat of it your eyes will be opened, and you will be like God [Vulg., *sicut Deus*], knowing good and evil" (3:4–5). As it turns out, the assertion is partially true: the penalty for disobedience is not death but a life of pain, toil, and estrangement. The reason for the serpent's "accuracy" in this instance is not the one given, namely, that men and women will in fact become omniscient gods and live forever; nor is it because the original commandment was false, but rather because Yahweh is merciful and chooses not to execute his full judgment.

But what does this cunning serpent, who is at once pious and idolatrous, really represent? The whole point of the Adamic myth, by contrast with theogonic and tragic accounts of the origin of evil, is to make it impossible for human beings to avoid *their own responsibility for sin before God* (see especially 3:8–13, where precisely this attempt is made and fails). In the Yahwist's account, since the serpent is "the only monster who survived from the theogonic myths," his retention must serve a special function—namely, to symbolize the human experience of *self*-deception as a seduction *from without.* "The serpent, then, would be a part of ourselves which we do not recognize; he would be the seduction of ourselves by ourselves, projected into the seductive object." [21] Ricoeur points out that this interpretation is already invoked by the Epistle of James: "Let no one say when he is tempted, 'I am tempted by God'; for God cannot be tempted with evil and he himself tempts no one; but each person is tempted when he is lured and enticed by his own desire" (1:13–14). Just as sin posits itself, so *deception deceives itself.* Therefore we do not recognize it as our own doing when it happens, experiencing it rather as a temptation from without. The originative act of sin keeps disappearing from view; it has a peculiarly self-concealing quality.

But, continues Ricoeur,

> the serpent is also "outside" in a more radical fashion. . . . In the historical experience of man, every individual finds evil *already there;* nobody begins it absolutely. . . . Evil is part of the interhuman relationship, like language, tools, institutions. . . .

21. Ricoeur, *The Symbolism of Evil*, pp. 255, 256.

There is thus an anteriority of evil to itself, as if evil were that
which always precedes itself, that which each man finds and continues while beginning it, but beginning it in his turn. . . . This
. . . explains why the chthonic animal resisted the demythologization of theogony; he represents the aspect of evil that could not
be absorbed into the responsible freedom of man. . . . Man is
not the absolute evil one, but the evil one of second rank, the
evil one through seduction; . . . he makes himself wicked by a
sort of counter-participation, counter-imitation, by consenting to
a source of evil that the naive author of the Biblical tale depicts
as animal cunning. To sin is to yield.[22]

Pursued too consistently, this theme would lead back to tragedy
and/or theogony. Within the context of the Adamic myth, an
interest in Satan can never become direct and controlling; the
figure of Satan (represented here by the serpent) is already im-
plicitly demythologized. Such demythologization becomes explicit in Jn. 8:44, when Jesus says of the Devil, "When he lies, he
speaks according to his own nature, for he is a liar and the father
of lies." In other words, the Devil is a personification of the
power of the lie. That to which human beings yield is ultimately
their own cunning, the falsehood of their own speech, hidden
even from themselves. The evil that we find already present in
the world is also of our own making: it is our own deceitfulness
objectified, universalized, demonically intensified by the institutions and structures of social existence. It seems to get out of
control, becoming more absolute than any individual act of sin.
The "animal cunning" "naively" depicted by the biblical author
is a distinctive quality of human existence.

But *why* do human beings yield to the deceptions of their own
making? It is misleading, as most commentators have done, to
designate the role of the woman, Eve, in the story as symbolizing
human *weakness* (the "eternal feminine") in the presence of
seduction and deceit.[23] Phyllis Trible points out that the narrative does not in any sense represent the woman as "weaker" or
more vulnerable than the man. To the contrary, "throughout the

22. Ibid., pp. 257–259.
23. Cf. ibid., pp. 254–255.

myth she is the more intelligent one, the more aggressive one, and the one with greater sensibilities." She is the one who engages in verbal dialectics with the serpent, interprets the commands of Yahweh, perceives the possibilities afforded by the tree, and makes the fateful decision to taste of its fruits—some of which she also fed to her husband, who passively ate (Gen. 3:2–6).[24]

It is not at the point of human weakness, but rather of *strength,* that sin enters in. Humankind's greatest strength lies in the power of language, imagination, and intelligence (and it is these with which the woman is richly endowed). But, as I have pointed out, the strength or power of language is highly *fragile* or *delicate.* It is better, therefore, to speak of human fragility than of human weakness, a fragility-in-strength. The proper and fundamental purpose of language is to speak the *truth,* to unconceal or open up reality. But in fact language is more often used to distort, conceal, and deceive than it is to clarify, open, and tell the truth. Language and deception are frequently associated in the New Testament.

> You brood of vipers! how can you speak good, when you are evil? For out of the abundance of the heart the mouth speaks. The good man out of his good treasure brings forth good, and the evil man out of his evil treasure brings forth evil. I tell you, on the day of judgment men will render account for every careless word they utter; for by your words you will be justified, and by your words you will be condemned.
>
> —Matt. 12:34–37

Paul says that the throat of unrighteous persons "is an open grave, they use their tongues to deceive. The venom of asps is under their lips. Their mouth is full of curses and bitterness" (Rom. 3:13–14, quoting Pss. 5:9; 140:3; 10:7). Liars are sometimes catalogued with other types of sinners and regarded as the worst sort, and the Devil is "the father of lies" (Col. 3:8–9; Rev. 2:2; 21:8, 27; 22:15; Jn. 8:44).

In brief, it can be argued that deception is the "original" form

24. Phyllis Trible, "Depatriarchalizing in Biblical Interpretation," *Journal of the American Academy of Religion,* 41 (March 1973): 39–41.

of sin because it is a corruption of people's most vital and unique capacity, their linguisticality. Language does not die out; rather it spoils and decays.[25] The decay of language lies about us in great abundance: the trivialization of words in advertising and mass media, the contrived falsehoods of politics, the pedantry of scholarship, the trite gossip and idle talk of everyday encounters. The world of language is a massive deception. The profoundest impact of the Pentagon, Watergate, and CIA disclosures has been the discovery that the American public has been systematically lied to for many years by the highest officials of government, who succeeded of course in deceiving themselves in the process of inventing coverups and falsehoods.

B. The Structure of Sin: Idolatry, Flight, Bondage, Guilt

Ricoeur argues that the most primitive symbol of evil in all cultures is that of *defilement,* which is never simply abolished but retained and transformed at higher levels of consciousness. It entails the sense of being contaminated by something *like* a stain (a symbolic, not a real, stain), which invades from without and gains control over one's psychic and corporeal existence, and which gives rise to a sense of dread at having violated a sacred inderdict.[26] When defilement occurs "before God" (*coram Deo,* as Luther put it), it becomes *sin* proper.

> It is already the personal relation to a god that determines the spiritual space where sin is distinguished from defilement. . . . The category that dominates the notion of sin is the category of "before" God. . . . It is . . . the prior establishment of the bond of the Covenant that is important for the consciousness of sin; it is this that makes sin a violation of the Covenant.[27]

Existence in relationship to God is what raises defilement to the explicit consciousness of sinful rebellion and bondage—rebellion

---

25. Cf. Gerhard Ebeling, *God and Word,* trans. James W. Leitch (Philadelphia: Fortress Press, 1967) , chap. 1.
26. Ricoeur, *The Symbolism of Evil,* pp. 25–46.
27. Ibid., pp. 48–51. Rudolf Bultmann makes the same point in *Theology of the New Testament,* trans. Kendrick Grobel (2 vols.; New York: Charles Scribner's Sons, 1954–55), I, 228.

against the Creator, bondage to the created world and oneself. A primitive awareness of this relationship may already have been expressed by the feeling of dread that accompanies defilement. But at this level, what it is that constitutes the term of the relationship has not yet come to consciousness, and instead there prevails a vague sense of ineluctability, of the ambiguity involved in the drive toward life.

Already the story of the temptation and fall suggests that two basic structures of sin may be distinguished: on the one hand, the *idolatrous rebellion* against the commandment of Yahweh and the striving to become *sicut Deus* (Gen. 3:1–7); on the other, the *flight* from responsibility before Yahweh and the passing of the blame (3:8–13).

Of these two structures, one active and the other passive, the more fundamental is undoubtedly the first, namely, the sin of *idolatry* or *pride*—a rebellious rupturing of the life-giving relationship with God by setting onself up *as* a god, thereby defying and denying the finitude of the human condition. The several Hebrew words for "sin" express this rupturing of a relationship: *chattat* (missing the target), *'awon* (a tortuous road), *pesha'* (revolt, stiff-neckedness, cf. Greek *hubris*), *shagah* (going astray, dereliction, alienation).[28] Paul uses similar concepts to express the idea of sin as rebellion against the covenant relationship with God: *epithumia* (covetous desire, a life of self-reliant pursuit of one's own ends [Rom. 1:24; 7:7–8; 13:9, 14, etc.]), *merimnan* (anxiety about worldly affairs [1 Cor. 7:32 ff.]), and above all *kauchasthai* (boasting, which is characteristic both of the Jew, who boasts of God and the Torah [Rom. 2:17, 23], and of the Greek, who boasts of wisdom [1 Cor. 1:19–31]).[29]

Idolatry can be described as the sin of infinitude, the apotheosis or "faulty infinite" of freedom. In Chapter III, I noted that the *refusal* of death and other forms of bondage can readily turn into a *defiance* of finitude and of the necessities of the human condi-

---

28. See Ricoeur, *The Symbolism of Evil*, pp. 70–73.
29. Bultmann, *Theology of the New Testament*, I, 224–225, 241–242.

tion.   Such defiance, or radical autonomy, is profoundly sinful.
Thus understood, idolatry is one of the forms of sin corresponding
to human fallibility or disproportion, the unstable polarity within
us of finite and infinite.   In the case of idolatry, our infinitude or
transcendental openness outstrips its finite basis; the quests of
the human heart issue in a passional madness.

The sin of infinitude has been known traditionally as the sin of
pride.   Reinhold Niebuhr is at his best in setting forth a typology
of human pride: pride of power (the lack of realization of finitude,
as well as a darkly conscious awareness of insecurity); pride of
knowledge (ignorance of the finitude of the mind); pride of virtue
or moral pride; spiritual pride or rebellion against God; and collective pride issuing in social injustice (the pretensions of a collective self, which exceed those of the individual ego).[30]   Niebuhr
attempts to distinguish from this first form of sin a second, which
he calls the sin of sensuality.   Following St. Thomas's understanding of sin as concupiscence,[31] Niebuhr defines sensuality as "the
inordinate love for all creaturely and mutable values which results
from the primal love of self, rather than love of God." [32]   It seems
clear, however, that sensuality or concupiscence is not the dialectical opposite of the sin of idolatry but the final manifestation of
it.   Tillich makes this clear by defining concupiscence as "the
unlimited desire to draw the whole of reality into one's self." [33]
Concupiscence is what Paul means by *epithumia* (covetous desire),
and indeed the *locus classicus* cited by St. Thomas is Rom. 7:8.
Despite the great importance of this theme, a tendency exists in
the entire discussion of concupiscence, from Paul through Augustine and Thomas to Niebuhr, not to distinguish sharply enough
between the authentic quests or desires which constitute the
human being (having, power, and worth, Ricoeur calls them),[34]
and their passional perversions (in the form of greed, exploitation,

30. Niebuhr, *The Nature and Destiny of Man*, I, 186–203, 208–219. On the latter, see also *Moral Man and Immoral Society* (New York: Charles Scribner's Sons, 1932) . See Tillich's discussion of *hubris* in *Systematic Theology*, II, 49–51.
31. *Summa Theologica*, IaIIae, Q. 77, a. 4.
32. Niebuhr, *The Nature and Destiny of Man*, I, 228–240; quotation from p. 232.
33. Tillich, *Systematic Theology*, II, 52.
34. Ricoeur, *Fallible Man*, pp. 161–191.

and pride); hence the unfortunate Christian tendency to regard sexuality and other bodily desires as inherently sinful.

The true dialectical opposite to the sin of idolatry is not sensuality but *flight* or *sloth.*[35] Rather than the denial of finitude, flight is the embrace of it and the denial of life and freedom instead, a sinking down into the certainties of the flesh. This nuance of meaning is evident in the Hebraic terms for sin mentioned earlier. Sin is a false, aberrant pursuit of life that not only issues in revolt against God but also constitutes a way leading unto death. If human beings go astray or miss the target, the result is the opposite of life, namely, death.[36] Similarly, covetousness, anxiety, and boasting are not only false concerns about worldly affairs, hence perversions of the covenantal relationship; they represent also a debilitating fear of death and finitude that robs life of wholeness and power.[37] Thus the dialectical opposites, idolatry and flight, the sins of infinitude and finitude, are at the same time closely related and feed into each other.

Sin in the form of flight or sloth bears similarities to the Freudian theory of repression (whereas idolatry issues in aggression). According to Freud, the id must be repressed because the primary instincts, life and death, Eros and Thanatos, are conflictual, and because of the scarcity of the external world, which precludes unrepressed gratification. With repression emerges the instrumentalities of civilization, but the results are paradoxical. The perpetual repression of Eros weakens the life instinct and strengthens its opposite, Thanatos; thus civilization seems to be moving toward its own annihilation.[38] Of course the Freudian interpretation of repression differs from the biblical understanding of flight. For the latter, life and death instincts are not locked in eternal combat. Rather the disproportion between bodily nature and freedom constitutes a fragility that leaves the human being open

35. The latter term is Karl Barth's; see *Church Dogmatics*, vol. IV/2, trans. G. W. Bromiley (Edinburgh: T. & T. Clark, 1958), pp. 403 ff.
36. Cf. Bultmann, *Theology of the New Testament*, I, 246.
37. Cf. Jesus' sayings about men of "little faith" and about anxiety, fear, doubt: Matt. 6:30–31; Lk. 12:28–29; Matt. 8:26; 13:22; 14:31; 17:20.
38. See Chap. II, Sec. 3B.

to the temptation to abandon freedom and to sink down into the securities of flesh, especially when the failures of freedom become evident. For the Bible, death is not a natural instinct at all but a form of bondage—an objectification of precisely the sin of flight.[39]

Both of the primary forms of sin—idolatry and flight—issue in *bondage*, which is experienced as a hypersubjective reality or power. Idolatry engenders a bondage to the flesh, living according to its criteria and idolizing its qualities, while flight is an escape from freedom into the embrace of death. In the Bible sin is frequently characterized as a quasi-personal power that possesses human beings. According to Paul in the Epistle to the Romans, sin "came into the world" (5:12) and "reigned in death" (5:21); human beings are enslaved to it (6:6, 17 ff.), sold under it (7:14); or they place themselves at its disposal (6:13), and it pays them wages (6:23). The experience of the objective power of sin makes it possible to reinstitute the symbolism of defilement at a higher level. It is no longer merely contamination but a binding power, to which persons have fallen victim and against which they are helpless. "The personification of these powers expresses the fact that man has lost to them the capacity to be the subject of his own actions." [40]

Paul characteristically employs the concept of existence "according to the flesh" *(kata sarka)* to symbolize the bondage into which human sin inevitably falls. "Flesh" *(sarx)* is not just animal flesh, but flesh that serves as the body of a human self. Thus, like *psychē* and *pneuma, sarx* can be used by Paul to designate the whole person or human nature as such, emphasizing the fact that the human being is embodied, finite, a creature belonging to the

39. See below, Sec. 3B. Erich Fromm has criticized the Freudian theory of a death instinct, arguing that the attraction to death, or "necrophilia" as he calls it, is not a natural, biological instinct, but rather a *pathological perversion* of the life instinct ("biophilia"). *The Anatomy of Human Destructiveness* (New York: Holt, Rinehart and Winston, 1973), pp. 364–366, 439–478. Fromm's criticism of Freud is based not on a theological perspective, which views the bondage of death as the manifestation of primordial human sin, but rather on his conviction that necrophilia is rooted primarily in social and environmental factors which human beings themselves are capable of rectifying.
40. Bultmann, *Theology of the New Testament*, I, 244–245; Ricoeur, *The Symbolism of Evil*, pp. 81–90, 92–93; Kurt Niederwimmer, *Der Begriff der Freiheit im Neuen Testament* (Berlin: Verlag Alfred Töpelmann, 1966), pp. 113–116.

corporeal world, sharing its fragility and transitoriness, but also its basic thrust toward life.[41] Obviously, then, *sarx* (the embodied human self) is not sinful or evil; it is good and it wills the good—life. But, according to the Bible, the "life" that characterizes the world of *sarx* is not self-derived and self-sustained; it is the gift of the Creator. The life toward which all flesh thrusts is not some sort of organic core of the cosmos but the being of God, who *is* life. At this point Judaism and Christianity divide from Freud and all forms of naturalism, no matter how refined. Finite matter and erotic desire are not ultimate. The human attempt to derive life from this source and to maintain it according to this standard and by this power is a self-delusion.

> Thus says Yahweh:
> "Cursed is the man who trusts in *man*
>   and makes *flesh* his arm,
>   whose heart turns away from Yahweh.
> He is like a *shrub in the desert*,
>   and shall not see any good come.
> He shall dwell in the parched places of the wilderness,
>   in an uninhabited salt land.
> Blessed is the man who trusts in *Yahweh*,
>   whose trust *is* Yahweh.
> He is like a *tree planted by water*,
>   that sends out its roots by the stream. . . .
> The heart is *deceitful* above all things,
>   and desperately corrupt;
>   who can understand it?"
>
> —Jer. 17:5–9

Before God, existence *according to* the flesh is a sinful deception because it constitutes a denial that Yahweh, not "man" or "flesh" (note the parallel), is the giver of life (for which Jeremiah's symbol is water). It leads not only to rebellion against God and a life of self-reliant boasting (idolatry), but also to a retreat into the securities of fleshly existence (flight). In both respects it issues finally in *bondage*—a bondage to precisely that which persons think they can control and according to which they live, "flesh." Thus Paul commonly speaks of "flesh" (just as he does of sin) as a quasi-

41. Bultmann, *Theology of the New Testament*, I, 233–234, 246.

personal being which exercises demonic power over people, to which they lose the capacity to be the subject of their own actions (hence the problem of the divided will).[42]   But the mythological language is already demythologized in the Pauline context. "Flesh" is not an alien cosmic power, as in Gnosticism, nor is it sensual lust; rather when people live "according to" it, it rises up and ensnares them, becoming a deadly idol.   Living *kata sarka* converts *sarx* from *erōs* to *thanatos,* resulting in a bondage to the flesh.

The final stage in the dialectical structure of sin is *guilt.* Guilt, according to Ricoeur, is "the achieved internality of sin," the subjective awareness of individual responsibility for a situation that nonetheless transcends and captures the individual.   Guilt in the form of "conscience" is an inward binding, corresponding to the outward binding symbolized by "flesh" (both the inward and the outward binding become objectified, as we shall see, in law, death, and the worldly powers).   Thus guilt expresses the paradox that lies at the heart of the biblical understanding of sin, the paradox, in Ricoeur's words,

> of a man who is responsible *and* captive, or rather a man who is responsible for being captive—in short, the concept of the *servile will.* . . . The paradox of a captive free will . . . is insupportable for thought.   That freedom must be delivered and this deliverance is deliverance from self-enslavement cannot be said directly; yet it is the central theme of "salvation." [43]

42. Rom. 1:24 ff.; 6:19; 7:5, 25; 8:3–10, 12–15; Gal. 5:13, 17, 19.   Bultmann, *Theology of the New Testament,* I, 236–246.
43. Ricoeur, *The Symbolism of Evil,* pp. 100–106, 151–157; quotation from pp. 101, 152.   I am aware that a distinction must be drawn between nonpathological and pathological forms of bondage, and that sin as described in this section falls under the category of the nonpathological.   The paradox of responsibility and captivity, intrinsic to sin, is not applicable in cases of psychopathology, for serious mental disorders, whatever their cause, subvert and disrupt essential structures of human being-in-the-world to such an extent that individuals can no longer be considered responsible for the bondage into which they have fallen (and which they may inflict on others).   Although the distinction between sin and psychopathology is clear in principle, they may both be inseparably present in concrete cases.   My understanding of this distinction is indebted to an unpublished paper by Edward Farley, "Psychopathology and Evil: Toward a Theory of Differentiation," presented at a meeting of the Society for Phenomenology and Existential Philosophy, October 31, 1974.   Erich Fromm's distinction, in *The Anatomy of Human Destructiveness,*

3. OBJECTIFICATIONS OF SIN:
ESTRANGEMENT, EXPLOITATION, AND OPPRESSION

A. LAW: THE OBJECTIFICATION OF GUILT—THE INSTITUTIONS, STRUCTURES, AND NORMS OF ALIENATED SOCIAL EXISTENCE

For the Greek world law was the indispensable *precondition* of freedom in the city-states. The principles of "freedom under law" and "equal justice under law" are indispensable to any constitutional democracy, for they delimit political power, deny arbitrary or capricious rule to an individual, small group, or the masses, and insure that all citizens will be judged equitably, regardless of social or political status. For the Old Testament the law was the consequence of an initial *loss* of freedom. Because humankind misses the good toward which it is striving, the latter takes on the character of demand. God's demand encounters us in the Torah, the purpose of which is to lead to the good life that has been lost (Rom. 7:10, 12, etc.). For Paul the law has become an occasion of sin and therefore a *form of bondage*. Thus we encounter a progressive theological radicalization of the concept of law: first it is a source of freedom; then it becomes a substitute for freedom; finally it emerges as a threat to freedom.

For the liberation-Exodus and prophetic traditions of Israel, the purpose of the law is *mišpaṭ*, "the defense of the weak, the liberation of the oppressed, doing justice to the poor." [44] As such, it is the only true revelation of the will of Yahweh, who demands a

---

between "benign" and "malignant" aggression is helpful. As described by him, malignant aggression, which takes the forms of malicious cruelty, sadistic destructiveness, and "necrophilia" (an "incestuous attraction to death"), is clearly pathological and is to be distinguished from the prideful aggression and slothful flight of sin. (Fromm himself does not make the latter distinction, and for him the category of "sin" has no place between benign and malignant aggression.) Similarly, one might postulate a condition of "psychotic repression," to be distinguished from the sinful, guilty conscience which internalizes responsibility and accuses itself. This entire matter is both complex and important, and requires further investigation by persons competent in psychology and philosophical anthropology. Suffice it to say for now, with Farley, that whereas sin requires salvation (or redemption), pathological bondage requires therapy, and that the two, while related, are not to be confused.

44. José Miranda, *Marx and the Bible: A Critique of the Philosophy of Oppression*, trans. John Eagleson (Maryknoll, N.Y.: Orbis Books, 1974), pp. 137 ff.

rectification of social injustice. This original intent of the law is preserved in sayings of Jesus, where the whole of "the law and the prophets" is embodied in an unconditional love of neighbor, including the love of God in the neighbor (Matt. 7:12; 22:37–40; Lk. 10:25–37).[45] For later, postexilic Judaism, the law no longer functions as a demand for social justice but becomes a religious way of life through minute and detailed practice. This is true of the entire epoch between Ezra and the compilers of the Talmud, during which the Pharisees play a crucial role. The "delicate and scrupulous conscience" (as Ricoeur describes Pharisaism) lives according to the law. The law is to be fulfilled, not by clinging to the Scriptures, but by making it an actual, living divine teaching through an ongoing process of oral interpretation and supplementation. Through the law the consciousness of guilt is objectified, rationalized, codified, and sublimated in a life of thoroughgoing obedience. This is a radically heteronomous mode of existence in which subjectivity and autonomy are sacrificed for the sake of righteousness.[46]

Paul shares both the prophetic and the Pharisaic views of the law, up to a point. He agrees that the law is the revelation of the will of God (in this sense "holy and just and good," Rom. 7:12), and that its purpose is both to achieve justice in the world [47] and to serve as a measure of right conduct. But he does not agree that it is possible for sinful persons to satisfy the demand of the law or to achieve justice through it.[48] Therefore, the law cannot be a means to salvation (Gal. 2:16; Rom. 3:20); and all that remains is its exposure of sin and the sacrifice of freedom to heteronomy. By this means the law itself becomes one of the primary forms of bondage, a "law of sin and death" (Rom. 8:2). In Galatians, circumcision is the symbol of the law's objective bondage (Gal. 2:4;

45. Ibid., pp. 70, 159.
46. Ricoeur, *The Symbolism of Evil*, pp. 118–139; Bultmann, *Theology of the New Testament*, I, 259–260, 262–263.
47. Miranda writes: "Paul's revolutionary and absolutely central message, that justice has been achieved without the law, would lack all force if this were not precisely the same justice that the law hoped to realize; this is the revolutionary and unprecedented core of his message." *Marx and the Bible*, p. 152.
48. Ibid., pp. 184–185, 187.

3:13; 4:21–31; 5:1, 13). In Romans 7, Paul develops the theme that through the law comes knowledge of sin (meaning "practical knowledge," learning how to sin, says Bultmann).[49]

> What then shall we say? That the law is sin? By no means! Yet, if it had not been for the law, I should not have known sin. I should not have known what it is to covet if the law had not said, "You shall not covet." But sin, finding opportunity in the commandment, wrought in me all kinds of covetousness. Apart from the law sin lies dead. I was once alive apart from the law, but when the comandment came, sin revived and I died; the very commandment which promises life proved to be death to me. For sin, finding opportunity in the commandment, deceived me and by it killed me.
>
> —Rom. 7:7–11

The concept of law thus understood could be taken as a symbol designating the political, social, and psychological structures by which human consciousness of guilt is objectified and rationally sublimated. Freud's interpretation of "civilization" as an institutional network for the repression of aggressive and erotic instincts, and for the sublimation of this repression, exemplifies such an understanding. The superego—the consciousness of guilt instilled by parental and cultural sanctions—has the function of "law" in the psyche.[50] José Miranda, noting that "law is the most symptomatic and concentrated expression of a culture and of a social system," advances a theological version of this analysis:

> Sin, although it entered the world because of the guilt of one man, . . . has become structured into human civilization itself, whose most characteristic and quintessential expression is the law. It seems to me that this is the only way we can understand how sin is a current within human history, a manifestly supraindividual force which gains control over peoples as such and increases its own power, even when men, trying to be conscientious observers of the law, believe they are struggling against sin.[51]

49. On the Pauline understanding of law as bondage and as objectification of guilt, see Bultmann, *Theology of the New Testament*, I, 259–269; Ricoeur, *The Symbolism of Evil*, pp. 139–150; and Niederwimmer, *Der Begriff der Freiheit im Neuen Testament*, pp. 120–129.
50. See especially Freud's *Civilization and Its Discontents*, trans. James Strachey (New York: W. W. Norton & Co., 1962) ; also our discussion of Freud in Chap. II, Sec. 3B.
51. Miranda, *Marx and the Bible*, pp. 182–183, 185, 187 (quotation from p. 182). See the whole of chap. 4, "Law and Civilization."

Civilization, he notes, is equivalent to what Paul referred to as "this world" or "the present age" (Rom. 11:12, 15; 1 Cor. 11:32; 2 Cor. 5:19; Gal. 1:4), which stands condemned by the law but cannot be saved through it.

Recent analyses of the "corporate state" or bureaucratic-technological society have pointed out that the social world in which we live is highly legalistic; however, law serves no longer primarily as an instrument of justice and delimitation of power but as the value-free medium which permits the bureaucratic system to function smoothly and to maintain a high degree of institutional control. Laws are enacted primarily to satisfy the exigencies of administration rather than to protect the rights of individuals.[52] Because of its external, impersonal, and often dehumanizing effect, law has a profoundly alienating impact on millions of citizens. For oppressed peoples everywhere in the world, law is experienced not merely as alienating but also as oppressive. The poor and powerless know that the law is both constructed against them and enforced against them. The role of the law first in legitimating the institution of slavery, then in enforcing patterns of segregation and discrimination, is a shameful episode in the history of American jurisprudence. Racist societies tend to be highly legalistic (e.g., the antebellum slave-holding states and present-day South Africa), because law provides a means both of social repression and of sublimating guilt feelings for the injustices perpetrated. At the same time, new legislation, law suits, and judicial review can prove one of the most effective means for social reform. The profound ambiguity of law is that, while indispensable to civilized existence, and even a weapon in the struggle for liberation, it readily converts into a form of bondage from which humankind must *be* liberated.

B. DEATH: THE OBJECTION OF FLIGHT

Death is the ultimate form of human bondage, infusing all the

52. Cf. Charles Reich, *The Greening of America* (New York: Random House, 1970), pp. 117–124, 126–128; also Richard N. Goodwin, *The American Condition* (New York: Doubleday, 1974); and above, Chap. II, Sec. 6B.

others. As Freud noted, death works in silence:[53] it is the deadly power masked behind fear and anxiety, the guilty conscience, the repressions of civilization, and the aggression and destructiveness of the human species. But according to biblical religion, death itself, in the sense of mortality, is not binding, nor ought humankind to fear death.[54] Death is an oppressive, anxiety-producing event only when it becomes the occasion for the objectification of flight from life and freedom; it is that which lies in wait as the consequence of a false and aberrant pursuit of life, the result of "going astray" or "missing the target."

An important (though fluid and unsystematic) distinction may be detected in the Pauline epistles between *thanatos* ("death" as binding power) and *thnētos* (physical mortality). *Thanatos* presupposes *thnētos* but adds a dimension of "deadliness" to it. *Thanatos is* physical mortality *as* binding, "deadly." It does not refer to a "spiritual" death in contrast to physical death, as spurious interpretations of the Apostle have sometimes argued. Paul says that *thanatos* came into the world through Adam (1 Cor. 15: 22), through Adam's sin (Rom. 5:12, 17–18). *Thnētos* he associates with *sarx* or *sōma* (2 Cor. 4:11; Rom. 6:12; 8:11). It refers to a person's transient, impermanent, perishable nature, which of itself is not evil or sinful but which can become an occasion for sin when the individual regards him- or herself solely from the perspective of *sarx*, living by its criteria, seeking to gain life from it rather than from the source of all life (the Spirit of God, Rom. 8:2), or denying and defying it in a bid for immortality.[55] When that happens *thnētos* becomes *thanatos*, mortality becomes death.

53. Freud, *Civilization and Its Discontents*, p. 66; cf. Paul Ricoeur, *Freud and Philosophy: An Essay on Interpretation*, trans. Denis Savage (New Haven: Yale University Press, 1970), p. 294.
54. Gerhard von Rad notes that for ancient Israel "death is seen, it is true, as something extremely lamentable, but it is nevertheless taken simply for granted as something against which one does not revolt." "Life and Death in the Old Testament," in *Bible Key Words*, vol. V/2 (New York: Harper & Row, 1965), p. 8. Nor did Jesus regard death as an obstacle to faith in God or as the crucial dimension of human existence that must be overcome: so Leander Keck, "New Testament Views of Death," in *Perspectives on Death*, ed. Liston O. Mills (Nashville: Abingdon Press, 1969), p. 42.
55. Bultmann, "Death in the New Testament," *Bible Key Words*, V/2, 87–90, 101–102.

Humankind makes its mortality, its perishable nature, into an event of death. Only the human being does that: no other animal undergoes dying as "death" in the uniquely human sense.

Paul links death to sin in two different (not entirely reconcilable) ways. First, death is the *punishment* for sin: "the wages of sin is death" (Rom. 6:23); "the sting of death is sin" (1 Cor. 15:56). Here he perpetuates the juridical concept of death already prevalent in Judaism.[56] The second argument is more characteristically Pauline, namely, that death is a *fruit* growing organically out of sin. Bultmann writes:

> If . . . sin is man's false pursuit of life, and if this consists in leading one's life "after the flesh,"—i.e., living out of the created, the earthly-natural and transitory—*then sin leads with inner necessity into death:* "If you live according to the flesh you will die" (Rom. 8:13). He who derives life out of the transitory must, himself, perish with the perishing of the transitory. "He who sows to his own flesh will from the flesh reap corruption" (Gal. 6:8). . . . Thus, death grows out of flesh-ly life like a fruit—organically, as it were: "While we were living in the flesh, our sinful passions, aroused by the law, were at work in our members to bear fruit for death" (Rom. 7:5). . . . The perversion of human striving that pursues life and yet only garners death is described at length in Rom. 7:7–25. . . .[57]

When mortality becomes the occasion for sin and "death" *(thanatos),* then it is also the ultimate form of human *bondage* (cf. Rom. 6:20–22; 8:2, 21).

The transience, impermanence, perishability of nature should not be considered as "death." Nature does not die; living things after a time return to the earth but only after having freshly engendered the cycle of life. "Death" is an anthropomorphism imposed upon nature. In nature, there is only a constant, myriad metamorphosis. We speak more appropriately of the "death" of animals, for animals exhibit a greater or lesser degree of consciousness, they experience pain, and they do prey upon each other under the exigency of survival. For humankind, mortality be-

56. See also Rom. 1:32; 6:16; 8:13; Gal. 6:8; 1 Cor. 7:31.
57. Bultmann, *Theology of the New Testament,* I, 246–247 (italics his). See also 1 Cor. 7:31; 2 Cor. 7:10; Rom. 6:21.

comes a serious problem when it is believed that each person is an irreplaceable, unsubstitutable individual. Then mortality as such appears to become the enemy ("death") because it cuts the individual off from the life-sustaining covenantal relationship with God. But mortality is in fact the enemy only if it is *not* the case that God remains faithful to his covenantal promise and therefore is himself the victor over mortal death,[58] preserving every individual in his life-giving presence (perhaps by taking him or her up into a higher unity). *Not* to believe that God is the victor is to live according to the flesh, to venerate the flesh (or mortality) as god. In that case, mortality becomes a binding power, "death" proper, *thanatos*, which is a form of sin.

There are really only two serious alternatives to the biblical-Pauline understanding of death, namely, the theogonic and the tragic. The theogonic view is represented by Martin Heidegger's famous analysis of death as an existential structure of Dasein.[59] Because of its essential finitude, Dasein's own distinctive being-toward-an-end must be understood as a being-toward-death *(Sein zum Tode)*. The theogonic basis of this analysis becomes clearer in later writings of Heidegger, where death is understood as the disruptive, violating power of Being itself, the negativity and concealment of Being. "Death as the shrine of Non-being is the mountain stronghold [*Gebirg*] of Being." [60] If death is inscribed into the logic of Being as its negative element, its *Gebirg*, then it scarcely could be otherwise than that authentic human existence

58. "It was above all the question of Yahweh's justice and thus of the ultimate realisation of his covenant promises which pressed [the Hebrew people] towards a solution beyond death." Von Rad, "Life and Death in the Old Testament," pp. 12–14. See also his *Old Testament Theology*, vol. I, trans. D. M. G. Stalker (Edinburgh: Oliver and Boyd, 1962), pp. 388–389. Keck notes that the central question for the New Testament is not immortality as such but the justice and goodness of God ("New Testament Views of Death," pp. 97–98). The question as to *whether* God in fact remains faithful to his promise, and whether therefore redemption from death is a reality that can be counted on, must remain bracketed at this point. I return to it in Chap. VI, Sec. 4B (1), in the context of a theology of the resurrection.
59. Martin Heidegger, *Being and Time*, trans. John Macquarrie and Edward Robinson (New York: Harper & Brothers, 1962), §§ 46–53.
60. See William J. Richardson, *Heidegger: Through Phenomenology to Thought* (The Hague: Martinus Nijhoff, 1963), pp. 276–277, 573–574. The quotation is from *Vorträge und Aufsätze* (Pfullingen: Neske, 1954), p. 177.

would require the *acceptance* of death as the only authentic mode of finite freedom: freedom for Dasein must be a *Freiheit zum Tode.*[61] Yet the theogonic motif, which prevails in Heidegger's middle period, may actually fade in the latest writings, where the emphasis is no longer on the concealment and negativity of Being but rather on its granting, clearing, freeing power. For example, in "Building Dwelling Thinking," Heidegger says that, although mortals dwell in the fourfold as the beings capable of death, yet "to initiate mortals into the nature of death in no way means to make death, as empty Nothing, the goal." [62] But the matter remains obscure and unresolved in these last essays by Heidegger.

Jean-Paul Sartre sharply criticizes Heidegger's view, contending that because "death is never that which gives life its meaning" but rather "removes all meaning from life," a being-toward-death would be an absurd, self-destructive project. Sartre's alternative to theogony is tragedy: death is an aspect of the absurd facticity of existence. "It is absurd that we are born; it is absurd that we die." Death is a permanent, radical alienation of the for-itself, which cannot be nihilated; but as such it remains exterior to my projects, even though it limits all of them.[63] Freud's view of death as a biological instinct locked in eternal combat with the instinct for life, and his dark suspicion that Thanatos is more likely to prevail over Eros than vice versa, may also be viewed as tragic, although it also bears analogy to the dualistic mythologies which attribute the origin of death to the Demiurge.[64] Against both theogony and tragedy, Ricoeur rightly contends that "death remains an accident with respect to the design of life," [65] although as I argued earlier,[66] what is "accidental" is not physical mortality as such, but rather that it should attain its binding, deadly power vis-à-vis human freedom. The accident, in other words, is precisely "sin."

61. Heidegger, *Being and Time,* p. 311.
62. Martin Heidegger, *Poetry, Language, Thought,* trans. Albert Hofstadter (New York: Harper & Row, 1971), pp. 150–151.
63. Jean-Paul Sartre, *Being and Nothingness,* trans. Hazel E. Barnes (New York: Philosophical Library, 1956) , pp. 531–548.
64. See above, pp. 65–66.
65. Paul Ricoeur, *Freedom and Nature,* trans. Erazim Kohák (Evanston: Northwestern University Press, 1966), p. 457.
66. See above, p. 157.

Prideful idolatry, objectified in socioeconomic and political structures of oppression, and in ideologies of racial, class, or sexual superiority, is the characteristic sin of oppressors. By contrast, flight into death, slothful acceptance of the degrading security of the flesh in lieu of freedom, is the form that sin often assumes for poor and oppressed peoples. In *Children of Freedom*, I suggested that for black slaves in America, "sin" might be understood as the acquiescence in enslavement that was the ultimate objective of the institution of slavery.[67] This insight was expressed in the nineteenth century by the black pastor Henry Highland Garnet, who warned his hearers that the goal of oppression is to make slaves slavish in nature. *"To such degradation it is sinful in the extreme for you to make voluntary submission. . . .* God will not receive slavery, nor ignorance, nor any other state of mind, for love and obedience to him." [68] Likewise, according to James Cone, "sin" for black people is the acceptance of an alien identity, the attempt to understand and accept the oppressor on his own terms.[69] The bitter paradox is that under certain conditions flight has been a necessity for survival. Thus one saves one's life only to lose it, and individuals find themselves enmeshed in a bondage not of their own making. Still, acquiescence draws the net all the tighter and encourages the oppressor all the more. In this sense the slave becomes an "accomplice" in the objectification of bondage, and his or her life becomes a living death.

C. WORLDLY POWERS: OBJECTIFICATIONS OF IDOLATRY

(1) *"Spirit" Powers: Ideologies—Racism and Sexism*

For biblical understanding the term "world" *(kosmos)* can refer to the total world of creation, including both "heaven" *(ouranos)* and "earth" *(gē)* (cf. 1 Cor. 8:4–5, where "in the world" is equivalent to "in heaven or on earth"). But for Paul in particular, the category "world" (more characteristically, "this world") contains

67. Peter C. Hodgson, *Children of Freedom: Black Liberation in Christian Perspective* (Philadelphia: Fortress Press, 1974), pp. 31–33.
68. "An Address to the Slaves of the United States" (1843), quoted in Herbert Aptheker, ed., *A Documentary History of the Negro People in the United States* (2 vols.; New York: Citadel Press, 1951), I, 229.
69. James Cone, *A Black Theology of Liberation* (Philadelphia: Lippincott, 1970), pp. 100, 196.

a theological judgment: *kosmos* designates the sphere of human possibilities and conditions in enmity toward God and in bondage to the "powers"; it intends human civilization as the "structuraliza-tion of oppression." [70]

"Heaven" is not an other-worldly place, somehow locatable "above" this world. Rather it is an integral *part* of the *kosmos*, that sphere or dimension of the world where the so-called spirit powers have their domain, by contrast with "earth" as the sphere where mortals have their domain. Paul refers to these "spirit powers" in various ways: "angels," "principalities," "powers" (Rom. 8:38; 1 Cor. 15:24), "elemental spirits of the *kosmos*" (Gal. 4:3, 9). To be sure, this is mythological language, but the *logos* of myth has already been broken. The "spirit powers" do not belong to a satanic world of darkness as the Gnostics believed, but to God's creation (Rom. 8:39). They are powers by which God exercises his dominion in the world, but they have been perverted into enemy powers by human defiance. In this sense the powers really exist as demonic only "for us," and our situation is an enslavement to powers for whose demonic dominion we ourselves are responsible. The "spirit powers" symbolize the fact that "the reality in which man finds himself is already one full of conflicts and struggles, a reality which threatens and tempts." [71]

Is there a contemporary, nonmythological equivalent to what Paul meant by the spirit powers? I believe there is if we can point to a parapsychological, parapolitical structure of reality that holds humankind in thralldom. What Marx and Engels referred to as "ideology" would be a good example of such a parapolitical struc-ture.[72] Ideologies are the rationalization of a practice by uncritical beliefs, doctrines, or "ideas" that often have a deeply emotional basis and reflect the political and socioeconomic interests of the one holding the belief. They are a form of false consciousness, of what Paulo Freire describes as the mythicizing of reality.[73]

70. Bultmann, *Theology of the New Testament*, I, 254–256; Miranda, *Marx and the Bible*, pp. 186–187, 250–252.
71. Bultmann, *Theology of the New Testament*, I, 257–259.
72. Cf. Karl Marx and Friedrich Engels, *The German Ideology*, in *Writings of the Young Marx on Philosophy and Society*, ed. and trans. Loyd Easton and Kurt Guddat (New York: Anchor Books, 1967), pp. 414–415.
73. Cf. Paulo Freire, *Pedagogy of the Oppressed*, trans. Myra Bergman Ramos (New York: Herder and Herder, 1972), pp. 21, 168.

In *Children of Freedom* I proposed that racism is a prime instance of an ideology. It is the rationalization of economic and political exploitation by a theory asserting the inherent biological inferiority of races other than one's own (notably of black-, red-, and brown-skinned peoples). It represents a primal manifestation of idolatry, for it entails the apotheosis of one's own race and the negation of others: its logic is genocide, although its practice is usually segregation.[74] It demonstrates the inherent deceptiveness of all sin, because "race" is actually a mythological concept that calls attention to merely superficial differences between ethnic groups. It is an extraordinarily resistant ideology because it is so deeply rooted in the archaic consciousness of light-skinned people, namely, the association of darkness with defiling, contaminating stain. It generally cannot be overcome by intellectual argument, requiring rather something like "conversion" by means of a disclosure situation in which the whole deceptive structure is brought into the harsh light of reality and dissipated. Thus racism is a "demon," a "spirit power," which appears to hold us in its grip but is in fact an objectification of the primordial sin of idolatry.[75]

The same is true of sexism,[76] which is the oldest and most universal form of domination known to history, even if it has not proved as degrading and destructive of life as racism. Rosemary Ruether locates sexual domination in a fundamental alienation that occurs in primitive societies with the emergence of a self-conscious, individualized ego. For reasons so remote they remain

74. Cf. George D. Kelsey, *Racism and the Christian Understanding of Man* (New York: Scribner's, 1965), p. 32.
75. Hodgson, *Children of Freedom*, pp. 19–20, 23–30. In addition to the books cited there, for an excellent discussion of the origins of white racism in America, see Winthrop D. Jordan, *White Over Black: American Attitudes Toward the Negro, 1550–1812* (Baltimore: Penguin Books, 1969), esp. pt. One. Also see above, Chap. I, Sec. 2ʙ (3).
76. In the North American experience especially, sexism and racism have been closely interrelated. For a brief but excellent study of this phenomenon, see Rosemary Ruether, "Crisis in Sex and Race: Black Theology vs. Feminist Theology," *Christianity and Crisis*, 34 (April 15, 1974) : 67–73. Her thesis is that racism and sexism "have been interstructural elements of oppression within the overarching system of domination by white males." (See above, Chap. I, Sec. 2ʙ[4].) The interlacing of racism and sexism was also experienced in Latin America. Enrique Dussel writes: ". . . the colonizer was usually male and his victim in our case was the Indian woman. . . . The male conquistador . . . sexually oppressed and alienated the Indian, the mestizo or the poor woman." "Domination—Liberation: A New Approach," in *The Mystical and Political Dimension of the Christian Faith*, ed. C. Geffré and G. Gutiérrez (*Concilium*, vol. 96; New York: Herder and Herder, 1974), p. 37.

obscure, the male psyche becomes identified with this dominating, objectifying, controlling ego, while the feminine principle was associated with the submissive body. In classical Greek civilization, the male-female dualism was correlated with a soul-body dualism: the male is the rational principle, the *logos*, the soul, whereas the female is the irrational, contumacious body, into which spiritual man falls in consequence of sin or ignorance.[77] Whether or not one is willing to accept this interpretation, it seems indubitably clear that throughout history and in almost all cultures women have been treated as "instrumental" to men. "Their relationship is not the 'I-Thou' of two persons equal in worth and dignity, but of subject-object, dominant-subordinate, stronger-weaker, superior-inferior. The relationship is *sexist* rather than human." [78] Sexism, then, is a form of male idolatry.

Moreover, sexism exhibits the same inherent deceptiveness as racism. Elizabeth Janeway argues that the oppression of women has generated two fundamental and widespread but nonetheless illusory myths, which in turn reinforce the oppressive situation: the myth of female weakness and the myth of female power. "The latter goes deeper, was born earlier and is universal. Male or female, we have all grown up in the shadow of the powerful mother. The myth of female weakness appears to be a reaction to this frightening figure; whether by origin or simply by present need, it holds the myth of female power at bay." [79] The "power" of woman—power over the child, the private power of the home— is really weakness (at least in terms of worldly power relations); and the "weakness" of woman—her alleged submission to the desires and physical strength of man—is the secret of her power, for

77. Rosemary Ruether, *Liberation Theology* (New York; Paulist Press, 1972), pp. 122, 99–100, 106; "Women's Liberation in Historical and Theological Perspective," *Soundings*, 53 (Winter 1970): 364–366.
78. Donald McDonald, "The Liberation of Women," *The Center Magazine*, 5 (May/June 1972): 31.
79. Elizabeth Janeway, *Man's World, Woman's Place: A Study in Social Mythology* (New York: Dell Publishing Co., 1971), p. 279. Much of this book is a study of the interplay of these two myths, which tend to merge into each other. If we are correct in arguing that the serpent tempts Eve because she is the *stronger* partner of the primordial pair, might it be because the story of the fall reflects the myth of female power? Ruether argues that "sexism cannot be understood, historically or psychologically, unless it is recognized that it rests not on female weakness but on the suppression of female power." "Crisis in Sex and Race," p. 72.

he is dependent upon her for proof of his manhood. Hence the dissipation of one of these myths—and it is feminine "weakness" that is most under attack today—should cause the other to dissolve as well. Women are neither stronger nor weaker than men; the differences between the sexes cannot be calculated by such a measure.

(2) *Political and Economic Oppressive Powers*

Paul did not pay so much attention to the "earthly" powers of bondage, which are socioeconomic and political in character, as he did to the "spirit" powers. It is true that he tended to treat worldly, institutionalized bondage under the category of "law" instead, but this category did not permit him to confront the political form of oppression. He does mention "the rulers of this age," but merely says of them that they do not understand the "secret and hidden wisdom of God" and are "doomed to pass away" (1 Cor. 2:6, 8).

Among the most significant political and social facts of his day were the hegemony of Rome, the institution of slavery, and the subordination of women. With regard to the first, he counsels subjection to the governing authorities (the notorious Chapter 13 of Romans).[80] To be sure, the early Christian communities were

80. Paul Lehmann argues that the "submission" advocated by Rom. 13:1 does not entail a "legitimization of legitimacy" but is a way of "exposing the disestablishment of the establishment," which is already moving toward its own destruction. Moreover, such submission, together with obedience to the higher law of mutual love (13:8), serve as safeguards that protect the revolution, which is much closer than the established authorities to what God is doing in the world, from devouring itself. Finally, "submission becomes the moment—not of obedient surrender but of obedient waiting." *The Transfiguration of Politics* (New York: Harper & Row, 1975), pp. 35–48. Lehmann relies heavily on Karl Barth's interpretation of this passage in *The Epistle to the Romans*, trans. from the 6th ed. by Edwyn C. Hoskyns (London: Oxford University Press, 1933), pp. 475–502. Despite the appeal of this interpretation, a number of questions occur; for example, "Waiting for what?" For Paul it is clearly a matter of waiting for God's eschatological salvation, which is near at hand (13:11–14). It is not a matter of waiting for the right moment to challenge or reform the "governing authorities" on political grounds; hence there would never appear to be an appropriate moment for political revolution in the Pauline scheme. Is Paul really concerned, then, with the problem of safeguarding revolution in this chapter? Moreover, is "revolution" the only alternative to "submission" that might have occurred to Paul (or other early Christians)? There is certainly the possibility of strategies for political reform through nonrevolutionary means, or at the very least, of passive resistance and civil disobedience. (In this chapter, of course, Paul mentions no alternative political options to submission at all, whether revolutionary or reformist.) However, my chief difficulty with Paul's "political theology" and Lehmann's defense of it is that it led the Apostle to downplay the realities of structuralized oppression (see the next paragraph).

in no objective condition to launch a revolution against Rome, which later persecuted them severely; and Paul anticipated the imminent eschatological salvation of God, which would overthrow all authorities. Yet, as Ricoeur points out, for Israel "Egypt" became the cipher of objective captivity, from which Yahweh is the liberator: "I am Yahweh your God, who brought you out of the land of Egypt, out of the house of bondage" (Ex. 20:2). "Henceforth," says Ricoeur, "the fundamental problem of existence will be less than that of liberty . . . than that of liberation. . . . All our ideas of salvation, of redemption . . . proceed from this initial cipher."[81] How could Paul have forgotten this cipher with reference to Rome? Certainly the author of the book of Revelation did not forget it, for there Rome is symbolized as Babylon, "the mother of harlots and of earth's abominations" (Rev. 17:5 ff.), and the Apocalypse is a manual for political liberation in disguise.[82] Nor did Jesus forget it, in view of the way that he called all of the established structures (including the Roman domination of Palestine) radically into question by his proclamation of God's near kingdom of freedom.[83]

The problem with Paul's position is that by urging "submission" to the governing authorities (Rom. 13:1), and by not recognizing various possible modes of political change (revolutionary or nonrevolutionary), he also tended to overlook the structuralized or systemic forms of oppression, which require a structural solution. The only "structural" solution Paul allows is that of the eschatological act of God, which has the effect of defusing all sociopolitical projects. This is underscored by his suggestion that obligation to the neighbor is higher than any political obligations (13:8). The difficulty is that neighbor-love can be construed on a purely interpersonal level, leaving systemic oppressions untouched (e.g., a master can love his slave as a person while doing nothing to change the institution of slavery).

81. Ricoeur, *The Symbolism of Evil*, p. 93.
82. Cf. Ernst Käsemann, *Jesus Means Freedom*, trans. Frank Clarke (Philadelphia: Fortress Press, 1969), chap. 6.
83. See below, Chap. V. Sec. 3c.

Neighbor-love is profoundly important, but it alone does not go far enough.

Paul certainly did not condone the institution of slavery. A veiled attack on it seems to occur in Gal. 4:21–5:1 (". . . brethren, we are not children of the slave [Hagar] but of the free woman [Sarah]"). Yet for the most part Paul seems only to be saying that the social distinctions between free man and slave, male and female, Jew and Greek, have lost their significance in Christ (Gal. 3:28; 1 Cor. 12:13). This is true and important, but it does not constitute an attack upon an institutionalized form of bondage. And Paul is able to counsel that "everyone should remain in the state in which he was called," developing the Stoic-like paradox that the slave is a freedman of the Lord, and the free man a slave of Christ (1 Cor. 7:20–24; 9:19). A similar attitude characterizes his stance toward women. While affirming the liberation and full equality of women in the community of faith, he tends to postpone the abolition of sexual distinctions to the eschatological age (Gal. 3:28); he is not willing to challenge social structures such as marriage that perpetuate the present subordination of women, although he calls for equality within the structure for believing couples (1 Cor. 7); and when disorder threatens, he defends the custom requiring women to be veiled in public worship as a symbol of their subordination to men (1 Cor. 11:2–16).[84]

The reason for Paul's hesitation on all these issues, and for his relative indifference to concrete social and political oppression, was his sense of the imminent end of this "present age" in which all such issues matter. But as Pagels points out, the "eschatological reservation" did not prevent Paul from putting into practice something that concerned him deeply, namely, the new equality of Jew and Gentile "in Christ," and freedom from ceremonial and cultic laws (see especially Galatians 2–5). This leads one to suspect

---

84. I am not fully persuaded by Robin Scrogg's "defense" of Paul in his article, "Paul and the Eschatological Woman," *Journal of the American Academy of Religion,* 40 (1972) : 283–303; and find the careful response by Elaine H. Pagels, "Paul and Women: A Response to Recent Discussion," *Journal of the American Academy of Religion,* 42 (1974): 538–549, more balanced and convincing. Additional literature on the subject is cited in the two articles.

that although Paul "desires liberty, he fears and distrusts the diversity potentially involved in genuine liberty," and "finds the possibility of social disorder extremely disturbing." [85]   Paul was indeed the "apostle of freedom," and he more than any other New Testament author was responsible for interpreting the saving event of Jesus in terms of "liberation";[86] but his own theological vision should serve as a critical canon for testing the adequacy of his practice on specific matters.

Modern racial slavery is of course a major instance of an "earthly" power of oppression by which idolatry is objectified. In the ancient world, foreigners taken in battle and debtors were enslaved primarily to perform personal services but were not utilized as an economic resource to produce wealth. But beginning in the fifteenth century slavery became a major factor in the production of income by an exploitation of human and natural resources without parallel in earlier history. The expansion of trade during the period of the Commercial Revolution, the colonization of frontier lands, and the large-scale cultivation of cash crops, created a situation in which a highly competitive and unrestrained capitalism began to flourish. Above all, it was the exigencies of capitalism that produced the most inhuman slave system known to history. To maximize profits it demanded perpetual servitude, utter disregard for the personality, family, education, and religion of the slave, and elimination of virtually all legal protections; the slave was, both by law and in fact, property or chattel over which the master exercised complete control. Even after the abolition of slavery and abandonment of the plantation system, economic exigencies (now reinforced by racial prejudice) caused the continued exploitation of blacks by means of legal and extra-legal segregation, political disenfranchisement, and rigorous patterns of discrimination.[87]

85. Pagels, "Paul and Women," pp. 545, 547–548.
86. See below, Chap. V, Sec. 5A.
87. I have discussed these matters more fully in *Children of Freedom*, pp. 20–23. Stanley Elkins has described the unique brutality of North American slavery in *Slavery: A Problem in American Institutional and Intellectual Life* (2d ed.; Chicago: University of Chicago Press, 1968), esp. chap. II.

Although slavery was not so dehumanizing and widespread in the Spanish and Portuguese colonies of Latin America,[88] it issued nonetheless in a system of economic and political exploitation that today holds peasants and industrial workers in a brutal servitude, reinforced by the economic interests of the industrial nations of the West. Gustavo Gutiérrez contends that the key factors in the exploitation of Latin America and other third world areas are domination, dependence, and underdevelopment, which are systematically interrelated:

> The underdevelopment of the poor countries . . . appears in its true light: as the historical by-product of the development of other countries. The dynamics of the capitalist economy leads to the establishment of a center and a periphery, simultaneously generating progress and growing wealth for the few and social imbalances, political tensions, and poverty for the many.[89]

José Miranda argues passionately that because capitalism generates an unjust distribution of income, wealth, and property, it represents the most demonic structuralization of oppression in the history of civilization. "The capitalism denounced by Marx is the consistent development of human civilization and oppression. It is the culture of injustice and of the crushing of men carried to extreme perfection and systematic refinement." [90] Policies of "developmentalism," promoted especially by the United States and other capitalist countries, only tend, according to Gutiérrez and others, to consolidate economic and social injustices, to cover over deep-seated ills with superficial reforms, and to lock Latin America into the fate of the industrialized West and international capitalism. Hence what is demanded is not development but liberation, not reform but social revolution.[91]

The slavery and exploitation being considered here are objec-

88. Elkins, *Slavery,* pp. 63–80.
89. Gustavo Gutiérrez, *A Theology of Liberation,* trans. Sister Caridad Inda and John Eagleson (Maryknoll, N.Y.: Orbis Books, 1973), pp. 84–85.
90. Miranda, *Marx and the Bible,* pp. 1–27, 250–254 (quotation from latter page).
91. Gutiérrez, *A Theology of Liberation,* pp. 22–27, 82–83, 88, 90–91, 111–112. See also the discussion of these issues in Louis M. Colonnese, ed., *Conscientization for Liberation* (Washington, D.C.: United States Catholic Conference, 1971); Freire, *Pedagogy of the Oppressed,* chap. I; and special issues of *Christianity and Crisis,* 33 (September 17 and October 15, 1973) .

tifications of the interior act of idolatry in the sense that they are the consequence of the struggle among human beings for power and mutual recognition. It has been our historical experience and fate that when the human self first becomes aware of itself in the other person, it strives to reduce the other to a function of its own self-relatedness. The individual thus becomes an idol to him- or herself, and each person tries to lord it over others. According to Hegel, the struggle issues first in a battle unto death, then in a one-sided or unequal resolution of the conflict, in which the slave surrenders his or her claim to recognition and the master destroys the true other through whom he might gain access to himself.[92] The master-slave relation, whether or not it assumes the literal form of chattel slavery, may be taken as a symbol representing the structuralization of inequality and oppression in human civilization. The structuralization reinforces and intensifies the genetic idolatry through a whole system of alienating practices—such as monetary exchange, private capital, division of labor, classes, mass production, technocratic bureaucracy—upon which all of us rely and which seem self-evidently necessary, but which could in fact be changed if they did not captivate and enthrall us.

The "logic" of the system demands the inner enslavement of the oppressed, or as Freire puts it, a "housing" of the oppressor in the oppressed.[93] But as both Hegel and Marx pointed out, the oppressed are in a dialectically advantageous position to break the chains of the system and to emancipate not only themselves but also their oppressors. Not only are they free for the risk of a new future because they have nothing to lose but their chains; but also, because of their involuntary servitude, they are free of the idolatry that engenders oppression, and they learn skills that will eventually lead to their emancipation.[94]

92. G. W. F. Hegel, *The Phenomenology of Mind*, trans. J. B. Baillie (2d ed.; New York: Macmillan, 1949), pp. 228–240. Cf. Frantz Fanon on "The Negro and Hegel," in *Black Skin, White Masks*, trans. Charles Lam Markmann (New York: Grove Press, 1967), pp. 216–222.
93. Freire, *Pedagogy of the Oppressed*, pp. 30, 32–33, 169.
94. Cf. G. W. F. Hegel, *Encyclopedia of the Philosophical Sciences*, §§ 435–436 (for full bibliographical information, see above, Chapter III, n. 23); and Rubem A. Alves, *A Theology of Human Hope* (Washington: Corpus Books, 1969), pp. 114–115. I return to this matter in Chap. VI, Sec. 2B.

(3) *The Exploitation of Nature*

A third way in which the sin of idolatry has been objectified lacks a specifically Pauline category because it was not clearly perceived as an issue until the time of the industrial and technological revolutions—namely, the exploitation of nature. For most of history, human beings have had to struggle against nature in order to survive, but now the question of survival has taken a new and more ominous form, linked to the question of the survival of nature itself in unravaged, undefiled, "unfallen" form.

Hints of this issue do appear, however, in the Bible. Although humankind, according to the Priestly account, was "blessed" by God and commanded to "be fruitful and multiply, and fill the earth and subdue it," and to "have dominion . . . over every living thing that moves upon the earth" (Gen. 1:28), this blessing cannot be taken as a sanction for exploitation, greed, and overextension (although it was sometimes misused in this fashion), but rather as an exhortation to care for the earth, to be responsible for it, and also to live from it. When, however, human behavior issued in the former rather than the latter, the blessing became a curse: "Cursed is the ground because of you; in toil you shall eat of it all the days of your life" (Gen. 3:17).[95]

On the basis of this statement, the theological tradition has argued for a "fall" of nature coincident with the fall of man and woman.[96] If this tradition makes any sense, it can only mean, not that nature itself has rebelled against the Creator, but rather that *human* rebellion has set askew the relationship of the whole of the created order to God, and in addition has set the natural and human worlds at enmity against each other. The necessities of nature, for example, are no longer perceived by human beings as veiled manifestations of transcendence but have become occasions for bondage; and conversely, nature now suffers human abuse and exploitation, thus requiring "redemption" along with human beings, perhaps *from* them. It is conceivable that Paul had some-

95. See Bonhoeffer's exegesis of these two passages in *Creation and Fall*, pp. 39, 85–89.
96. Cf. ibid., p. 77; and Tillich, *Systematic Theology*, II, 40–41, 43.

thing like this in mind when he wrote, in the context of describing redemption through Christ from the law of sin and death: "The created universe waits with eager expectation for God's sons to be revealed. It was made the victim of frustration, not by its own choice, but because of him who made it so; yet always there was hope, because the universe itself is to be freed from the shackles of mortality and enter upon the liberty and splendour of the children of God" (Rom. 8:19–21, NEB). The redemption of creation as a whole is contingent upon a reestablished relationship of liberating obedience to God on the part of his human creatures.

That the exploitation of nature is a manifestation of the primordial sin of *idolatry* (rather than of flight or guilt) is already evident from the Pauline and Genesis accounts. This has become overwhelmingly obvious in the modern environmental crisis, which is a consequence of the overextension of humankind's creative, controlling, and consumptive capacities. We have acted as though we were the unlimited lords of nature, subject to no constraints, forgetting that our "dominion" over nature was to remain under the Lordship of the one God (Gen. 1:26–31). Theodore Roszak refers to this "earth-rape" specifically as "*hubris*—the overweening pride of the doomed." He notes that it is rooted in the illusion of infinite power and knowledge, which is blind to the consequences of its own arrogance.[97] Thus the objectifications of idolatry disrupt all the relationships—to transcendence, to the human community, to nature—by which human life is sustained in health and wholeness.

PART FOUR

LIBERATED FREEDOM

Chapter V

Jesus the Liberator

1. JESUS THE LIBERATOR: BLACK CONSCIOUSNESS AND NEW TESTAMENT FOUNDATIONS

For Christian faith, human liberation has its focus in the figure of Jesus of Nazareth. The event of liberation radiates out from him and is shaped by his model and agency, although it is by no means restricted to those who confess his name or act on his behalf. It is he who gives the symbols for liberation in the Christian tradition their determinacy and authority. If Jesus does not "mean freedom," [1] then neither does Christianity, and a Christian theology of freedom would be an empty project.

"Liberator" is not a christological title to which we are accustomed (although we often speak of Jesus Christ as the "Redeemer" without reflecting on the meaning of that term). One of the great contributions of black theology—as well as of third world and Marxist liberation theologies[2]—has been to articulate not only a new christological title but also an entire hermeneutical framework for interpreting the biblical and theological tradition afresh. The interpretation has arisen out of a determinate condition of oppression and the felt need for liberation, but it is relevant to the human condition as such, which is one of bondage to sin and its objectifications. Although the title "Jesus the Liberator" has been explicitly formulated by black theology in recent years,[3] it

1. Cf. the English title of the book by Ernst Käsemann, *Jesus Means Freedom*, trans. Frank Clarke (Philadelphia: Fortress Press, 1970).
2. Cf. Leonardo Boff, *Jesus Cristo libertador: ensaio de cristologia crítica para o nosso tempo* (Petrópolis, Brazil, 1972). A brief description of the contents of this book is found in Francis P. Fiorenza, "Latin American Liberation Theology," *Interpretation*, 28 (October 1974): 451–452. For a recent Marxist interpretation of Jesus in terms of both personal and social transformation, see Milan Machoveč, *Jesus für Atheisten* (Stuttgart: Kreuz Verlag, 1972).
3. It first appeared in a Theological Statement of the National Committee of Black Churchmen, June 1969: "Black Theology is a theology of black liberation. . . . The message of liberation is the revelation of God as revealed in the incarnation of Jesus Christ. Freedom is the gospel. Jesus is the Liberator!" Quoted in Gayraud S. Wilmore, *Black Religion and Black Radicalism* (New York: Anchor Books, 1973),

has its roots deep within black history and consciousness. Oppressed black slaves in America experienced Jesus as the Liberator —not primarily as a historical datum but as a present, living reality. Theologically speaking, the slave spirituals, which abound in christological language, were oriented to the risen Christ rather than to the historical Jesus. Jesus was now at work to comfort the afflicted, to provide companionship for those who find themselves on a "lonesome journey," to feed and clothe the oppressed, to help slaves survive and escape, to work for the ultimate destruction of slavery, and to prepare the way for entrance into the promised land, where the freedom of body, voice, and movement could be celebrated. To fill out the details of this "resurrection theology," the spirituals of necessity turned to the Gospel stories about the earthly Jesus (richly supplemented, of course, by Old Testament accounts of God's liberating activity).[4]

How successfully can a Christology of liberation be supported on the basis of a critical evaluation of the New Testament portrayals of Jesus? Leander Keck rightly points to the danger of an ideological misuse of the New Testament by both "the upper- and middle-class pietistic right" and the radical left, the symptom of which in both cases is proof-texting.[5] Evidences of proof-texting —or at least of an uncritical use of sources—are present in black liberation theology. For example, Cone writes that "Jesus himself defines the nature of his ministry" in the words found in the Lukan story of his rejection at Nazareth ("He has sent me to proclaim release to the captives . . ." Lk. 4:18–19),[6] whereas it is clear to critical scholarship that these words are the construction of the

p. 293. James H. Cone, who had a hand in drafting this Statement, has developed the title in his books, *Black Theology and Black Power* (New York: Seabury Press, 1969), pp. 35–42; and *A Black Theology of Liberation* (Philadelphia: Lippincott, 1970), p. 213 (and the whole of chap. VI). See also Joseph A. Johnson, "Jesus, The Liberator," in *Quest for a Black Theology*, ed. James J. Gardiner and J. Deotis Roberts (Philadelphia: Pilgrim Press, 1971), pp. 97–111.
4. See James H. Cone, *The Spirituals and the Blues: An Interpretation* (New York: Seabury Press, 1972), pp. 47–57. I have discussed this matter at greater length in *Children of Freedom: Black Liberation in Christian Perspective* (Philadelphia: Fortress Press, 1974), pp. 57–62.
5. Leander E. Keck, "The Church, the New Testament, and Violence," *Pastoral Psychology*, 22 (October 1971): 7–8.
6. Cone, *Black Theology and Black Power*, p. 35.

Evangelist as part of his effort to provide proofs from prophecy that Jesus is the Messiah. And in one of his recent articles, Cone works through some of the thematic highlights of the Gospel story (birth, baptism, temptation, rejection at Nazareth, response to the disciples of John the Baptist, exorcisms, etc.), without really attempting to distinguish the theological interpretations of the Evangelists from what may be authentic sayings or actions of Jesus.[7]

The point of this criticism is not to suggest that these texts do not support Cone's constructive theological argument: in a very profound way they do. But failure to work critically provides an opening for neutralizing black theology on the part not only of "the upper- and middle-class pietistic right" but also of the liberal theological establishment. Moreover, I think a *stronger* case can be made for interpreting Jesus as "the Liberator" by establishing a certain critical distance between the New Testament writers (who, after all, were concerned to present Christianity on good terms to the Roman Empire and who had therefore ideological interests of their own) and the historical Jesus. Cone, to be sure, has discussed these critical issues briefly,[8] but his conclusion is simply that "there is no radical distinction between the Jesus of history and the Christ of faith." I should not want to disagree with this if the "radical" is stressed and the precise meaning of the statement is unpacked, but the effect of the conclusion for Cone is to allow him to proceed as though there was no distinction at all. I am persuaded that liberation theology simply must work more critically with biblical texts than heretofore has been the case.[9]

7. Cone, "Biblical Revelation and Social Existence," *Interpretation,* 28 (October 1974): 431–438. He still appears to represent Lk. 4:18–19 as an actual saying of Jesus.
8. In Cone, *A Black Theology of Liberation,* pp. 199–203; and "Biblical Revelation and Social Existence," p. 432 n.
9. A notable exception is José Miranda's *Marx and the Bible: A Critique of the Philosophy of Oppression,* trans. John Eagleson (Maryknoll, N.Y.: Orbis Books, 1974). Miranda concentrates on Old Testament exegesis, on Paul, and to a lesser extent on the theology of the Evangelists, but he nowhere attempts a critical assessment of the historical Jesus.

It would be illusory to suppose that the historical-critical method will necessarily protect from ideological deception, as Keck sometimes implies.[10] It can readily become a tool of the establishment, generating a fascination with arcane (and politically harmless) minutiae instead of praxis-oriented interpretation or resulting in a curiously neutral "both . . . and" or "neither . . . nor" mode of theologizing. We are left with such observations as that Jesus attracted *both* Zealots *and* tax collectors, or that he was *neither* a social revolutionary *nor* a defender of the status quo, in which case it is not clear *where* he stood on anything, and one can only assume that he was above all such partisan issues—a conclusion that has the effect, of course, of reinforcing the status quo. What makes this method especially insidious is that it reflects the hermeneutical abuse of a partially correct evaluation of the historical evidence (a point to which I shall return later). In other words, the more serious danger of ideology comes not from black theology or from poor and oppressed minorities, but from the theological establishment.[11]

Under the impact of redaction criticism, New Testament research has focused recently on the creative theological role of the Evangelists in constructing the story of Jesus.[12] Not only has this focus borne important critical results (providing, for example, a better basis for evaluating the way in which the Evangelists modified traditional materials and thus for reconstructing the earlier tradition), but also it has helped to highlight the distinctive structure of the Gospel form and to underscore the centrality of story or narrative as the characteristic literary genre of Christian the-

10. Keck, "The Church, the New Testament, and Violence," p. 8.
11. This point is made by Frederick Herzog in a forceful though obscure article, "Liberation Hermeneutic as Ideology Critique?", *Interpretation*, 28 (October 1974): 387–403. On the susceptibility of historical criticism to ideological perversion, see Dorothee Soelle, *Political Theology*, trans. John Shelley (Philadelphia: Fortress Press, 1974), chaps. 1–2; and Walter Wink, *The Bible in Human Transformation* (Philadelphia: Fortress Press, 1973). For Cone's response to the charge of ideology, see "Schwarze Theologie und Ideologie. Eine Antwort an meine Gesprächspartner," *Evangelische Theologie*, 34 (January–February 1974): 80–95.
12. See Norman Perrin, *A Modern Pilgrimage in New Testament Christology* (Philadelphia: Fortress Press, 1974), chaps. VIII, IX.

ology.[13] At the same time Christians believe the story of Jesus to
be a "true story" in the sense of "having actually happened."
Hence it continues to be important to press the question of the
"historical Jesus" (i.e., the Jesus who can be reconstructed on the
basis of the earliest strata of the Synoptic tradition) in the context
of redaction criticism, indeed on the basis of its more sophisticated
methods. It is necessary to make new moves, but we are not at a
methodological impasse.

One of the new moves will be to free ourselves from what
Leander Keck has called the "tyranny" of the negative criterion,
according to which material is regarded as more likely to be from
Jesus if it is "dissimilar to characteristic emphases both of ancient
Judaism and of the early Church." [14] Although indubitably the
negative criterion is the critical canon with which serious scholarship must start, an overly consistent or exclusive application of it
leads to the isolation of Jesus from his social and historical environment (first-century Judaism, divided against itself under the
yoke of Roman tyranny), and to the erection of something like an
absolute barrier between Jesus and early Christian proclamation
of him as "the Christ," in which case such proclamation was a
religious and historical fraud. Therefore we must press on from
the negative criterion to what Norman Perrin calls the criteria of
coherence and multiple attestation, by which the hard-core data

13. The latter point has been emphasized in quite a different way by structuralism.
See Dan O. Via, *Kerygma and Comedy in the New Testament: A Structuralist Approach to Hermeneutic* (Philadelphia: Fortress Press, 1975), chaps. I, III, IV.
Because of the novelty of its application to New Testament study and my lack of
competence in its methods, I have not attempted to make use of sructuralist exegesis in this chapter. In view of its emphasis upon the total literary structure of
the Gospels and its opposition to historical modes of criticism, one would not ex-
pect structuralism to contribute directly to the so-called quest of the historical Jesus.
However, by focusing upon the *transformational impact* of the memory of the figure
of Jesus upon the genre, structure, or *Gattung* from which a particular text has
been generated, it might be possible to begin delineating certain distinctive features
of that figure. But I do not know of any New Testament structuralist critics who
have taken this line or even raised the question of the historical Jesus so far.
Analyses of the narrative or story form of the Gospel from non-structuralist perspectives have been developed by such scholars as Stephen Crites, Hans Frei, Sallie
McFague TeSelle, and Amos Wilder.
14. Leander Keck, *A Future for the Historical Jesus* (Nashville: Abingdon Press,
1971), pp. 33–35. The definition is from Norman Perrin, *Rediscovering the Teaching of Jesus* (New York: Harper & Row, 1967), p. 39.

can be "surrounded by a penumbra of 'softer' materials that must not be ignored." [15]

In addition to these refinements in method, our interpretative efforts can be assisted by a hermeneutical key that will permit the "construction" of the figure of Jesus in such a way as on the one hand to expose both the similarities and differences among him, his environment, and the kerygma, and on the other hand to make him available to the sociocultural situation of today in a relevant and responsible fashion. Any such construction represents a *theological* or *christological* proposal rather than a strictly historico-critical one. On the basis of form-critical and redactional analyses of the earliest strata of Christian tradition, New Testament scholars are able to construct a hypothetical picture of the pattern, shape, or "career" of the public activity of Jesus, which can lay reasonable claim to historical validity, although it always retains the character of a projection based on secondary evidence. The christological construction I am proposing must be funded at every point by this historico-critical representation of Jesus, but it also goes beyond it because it introduces hermeneutical categories in an effort to elicit the coherence and meaning of the figure of Jesus Christ for human existence today. And it does so in a more explicit, holistic fashion than a strictly historical sketch of what we can know about the public activity of Jesus will permit.[16] The theological construction relies not only on what can be learned from historical study, but also on the experience of the Christian faith community in its ongoing encounter with Jesus, and it seeks to be faithful to the intention of early Christian kerygma in proclaiming Jesus to be the Messiah of God. To be sure, the distinction between historico-critical and theological construction is a

---

15. Perrin, *Rediscovering the Teaching of Jesus*, pp. 43–47. The quotation is from Keck, *A Future for the Historical Jesus*, p. 34.

16. A similar distinction between hermeneutical and historico-critical approaches to the figure of Jesus is made by Leonardo Boff, "Salvation in Jesus Christ and the Process of Liberation," in Claude Geffré and Gustavo Gutiérrez, eds., *The Mystical and Political Dimension of the Christian Faith* (*Concilium*, vol. 96; New York: Herder and Herder, 1974), pp. 79–80. I do not, however, agree with Boff that a hermeneutic reconstruction oriented to the theme of liberation permits a putative *ipsissima intentio Jesu* to emerge.

fluid one: the latter presupposes the former; and if the former is
to achieve the coherence in the figure of Jesus that it seeks, it will
issue finally in the latter.[17]

One such hermeneutical key for a theological construction of
Jesus is provided by the theme of *liberation*. Not only does this
key permit an understanding of Jesus relevant to the struggles for
human liberation in the modern world; it also provides a way of
specifying the relation of Jesus to his social environment and to
the apostolic Christian witness. On the one hand, the Jewish
people of first-century Palestine urgently needed a "Liberator"
from Roman oppression; on the other hand, Jesus was proclaimed
as the "Liberator" or "Redeemer" from sin, law, death, and the
powers by primitive Christian faith. Although he was closely
related to both, Jesus himself fitted neither of these molds precisely. In the remainder of this chapter, I shall attempt a constructive theological portrayal of Jesus as "the Liberator," located
between the environment and the kerygma, identical with neither,
yet shaped by the one and shaping the other. This portrayal will
unfold in four major steps, as follows: *(a)* Jesus lived a life of
radical personal freedom in liberating openness to God, in communion with his sisters and brothers, and manifesting a unique
sense of personal identity and authority (Sec. 2); *(b)* he announced
and enacted a gospel of liberation from law and piety, from social
and political domination, and from death and the powers of death
(Sec. 3); *(c)* he was executed because he was perceived to be a
blasphemer against the God of Israel and an agitator against the
Pax Romana, and he died raising questions about the liberating
power of God (Sec. 4); *(d)* on the basis of a belief in his resurrection from the dead, by which God vindicated him, Paul and John
developed Christologies of salvation-as-liberation, thereby introducing the vocabulary of freedom into Christian faith (Sec. 5).

17. My reflections in this paragraph have been influenced by discussions with W.
R. Farmer, R. H. Fuller, V. A. Harvey, L. E. Keck, and S. M. Ogden during a
Consultation on Christology and the Historical Jesus at the Perkins School of
Theology, March 6–9, 1975. I am indebted to these colleagues for their criticisms
and suggestions; not all of them, I recognize, will agree with what is said here.

Before addressing these major themes, it is worth noting that the New Testament uses several words that carry the general meaning of "freedom," "redemption," or "liberation." The most common of these is the classical Greek term *eleutheria,* which occurs forty-one times (including derivative forms). Twenty-six of these occurrences are found in the Pauline corpus. The term occurs only once in the Synoptic Gospels (Matt. 17:26), and in John four times in the section 8:30–36. The remaining occurrences are in Ephesians and Colossians, the Pastoral Epistles, and Revelation.

The term *lutrōsis* and derivatives, meaning "ransom," "release," "redemption," occurs nine times, but only once on the lips of Jesus (Mk. 10:45 = Matt. 20:28), in a saying that is clearly the product of Markan theology ("For the Son of Man also came not to be served but to serve, and to give his life as a ransom for many"). *Apolutrōsis* (with the same meaning) occurs once in the Synoptics (in the Lukan apocalypse, 21:28) and is used by Paul in Rom. 3:24; 8:23; 1 Cor. 1:30. Paul also uses *(ex)agorazein,* in which the image of a financial transaction is more clearly present—hence meaning "to purchase or buy back one's freedom"—in 1 Cor. 6:20; 7:23; Gal. 3:13; 4:5. But the characteristic Pauline term for freedom is *eleutheria,* where the imagery of purchasing one's freedom from slavery is not present. The words found in Lk. 4:18, "He has sent me to proclaim release *(aphesis)* to the captives, . . . to set at liberty *(apostellein)* those who are oppressed," do not ordinarily mean "freedom" in Greek (their more natural sense is "dismissal," "send away"), and they are used in the Septuagint translation of Is. 61:1; 58:6. They cannot be considered authentic words of Jesus but a Lukan proof from prophecy, which need not detract from the significance of this passage as an interpretation of Jesus.

Thus in all likelihood Jesus himself did not speak explicitly of "freedom." Although he was the radically free person, and brought freedom to speech and praxis in a quite unprecedented way, he lacked a specific word for it. This is not surprising in view of the fact that the terminology of freedom is for the most part lacking in

Hebrew and Aramaic,[18] and considering the way that freedom was defined in the Greek world (a point to which I shall return momentarily). "Freedom" is a distinctively Greek concept, and it was above all Paul who took this concept and transfigured its meaning in light of what had happened in and through Jesus.[19] Thus in order to defend the hypothesis that Jesus was portrayed as and in fact was "the Liberator," one cannot look for a specific vocabulary but rather one can attempt to understand the basic meaning of his personal identity, his proclamation and action, and his death in terms of liberation.[20]

2. THE RADICAL FREEDOM OF JESUS

The paucity of the term *eleutheria* in the Synoptic Gospels is not without significance when the predominant meaning of freedom in the Greek world is recalled. *Eleutheria,* I have pointed out,[21] designated those who belong to an ascendant people or are citizens, by contrast with oppressed subjects or slaves. Thus freedom meant autonomy, self-determination, power over oneself, membership in a privileged community (the *polis*) that excluded slaves, women, foreigners, manual laborers. The Greeks were never able to attain a viable understanding of an open community, including all, or of a transcendence that grants freedom rather than threatens it (as with the tragic vision). Nor did they arrive at the insight that evil is a bondage humankind imposes on itself. They believed that a personal, private, individual freedom was achievable, despite the irrational passions of the external world (Stoicism), or the flawed character of reality itself (theogony), or the antagonism of the gods (tragedy).

All this is unmistakably changed when one turns to Jesus, the New Testament, and the Hebraic tradition. Freedom is defined

18. According to Martin Hengel, "the term 'liberty' or 'freedom' (*ḥērût*) appears for the first time on the coins issued during the Jewish revolt A.D. 66–67." *Victory Over Violence: Jesus and the Revolutionists* (Philadelphia: Fortress Press, 1973), p. 33.
19. See Gerhard Ebeling, *Frei aus Glauben* (SgV no. 250; Tübingen: J. C. B. Mohr, 1968), p. 10.
20. Keck makes this point in "The Son Who Creates Freedom," in *Jesus Christ and Human Freedom (Concilium,* vol. 93; New York: Herder and Herder, 1974), pp. 72, 77; also Rudolf Pesch in "Jesus, a Free Man," *Concilium,* 93: 56–70.
21. See above, pp. 8, 50.

primarily with reference, not to the first of the structures of freedom (autonomy), but to the second (community) and especially the third (openness). What has taken place is a reversal of priorities and a transfiguration of meanings. That which is most important for the Greeks—autonomy—is, relatively speaking, least important for Jesus. Its meaning is changed, but its importance is not *lost*. Far from advocating the dissolution of subjectivity in surrender to a transcendent, unapproachable Lawgiver, Jesus spoke instead of the "nearness" of the God of the kingdom, whom men and women ought to address as *Abba*, "Father." Subjectivity is de-privatized and removed from its autonomous basis by being taken up into a community of the liberated, a kingdom of God's children. Similarly, the alienation, elitism, and caste-like character of human communities is quite radically transformed, and that to which human beings are "structurally open" no longer remains obscure and threatening but is named and identified as the God of freedom, the God who *is freedom* and who *sets free*.

On the basis of the New Testament's portrayal of Jesus, the phenomenological categories of *autonomy, community,* and *openness* may be translated into more personal equivalents—*selfhood, brotherhood/sisterhood,* and *sonship*. With reference to these terms, we may speak of the "radical freedom" of Jesus. "Radical" is taken in its etymological sense, deriving from *radix*, "root," meaning that which pertains to or proceeds from the ultimate source, foundation, reality, or truth of human experience. "Radical freedom" designates a freedom that has its source in openness to the free God, manifests itself in acts of liberation and reconciliation in the world, and issues in a fulfilled subjectivity.[22] On the basis of the personal freedom of Jesus, we may construct a symbolics of freedom—a description of human freedom as portrayed by the symbols of Christian faith.[23]

22. See my book, *Jesus—Word and Presence: An Essay in Christology* (Philadelphia: Fortress Press, 1971), p. 192. The whole of Sec. 2 represents a revision, with some significant modifications, of materials presented on pp. 188-202 of the earlier work, which provides a more technical and detailed foundation for the present discussion. See also Pesch, "Jesus, a Free Man," pp. 63–70.

23. I turn to this task in the concluding chapter, Chapter VII. See especially the schema relating the structures of freedom, Jesus' radical freedom, and the symbolics of freedom, on p. 325.

A. SONSHIP: OPENNESS TO GOD

The definitive horizon of Jesus' life was his relationship to God, yet this relationship cannot be grasped directly and is visible for the most part only in the communal and personal structures of his existence. Although he apparently awakened messianic expectations on the part of both friend and foe, he advanced no direct messianic claims, he did not refer to himself as "Christ," "Son of God," or "Lord," he customarily spoke *about* God with a parabolic indirectness, and he did not claim to speak *on behalf of* God after the fashion of the prophets of Israel. There are only a few instances in the Synoptic tradition where Jesus' relationship to God comes to the surface in *his own words:* his distinctive reference to God as "Father" with the child's familiar term, *Abba;* the use of the formula, "Truly (or 'faithfully') I say to you" *(amēn legō humin),* a strong and unique expression that suggests a correspondence between the sayings of Jesus and the word of God; a similar formula, "But I say to you" *(egō de legō humin),* used in the antitheses of the Sermon on the Mount, which pits the authority of Jesus against that of Moses and the Torah, thereby implying a messianic role; and the saying in Matt. 12:28, "If it is by the Spirit of God that I cast out demons . . .," which, if authentic, suggests that Jesus regarded himself as inspired, the instrument of the Spirit of God.[24] In addition to these sayings, there are certain actions that imply a divinely given authority and a life lived in immediate openness to God: the exorcisms and other acts of healing, the conflicts with the authorities of Israel, and of course the journey to Jerusalem and Jesus' struggle with his impending destiny, in the context of which his relationship to God comes to an ambiguous climax.

Despite (or perhaps because of) all this, the New Testament and Christian tradition concluded that Jesus was a uniquely God-

24. See *Jesus—Word and Presence,* pp. 137–138, 166–168. On the probable, or at least possible, authenticity of these sayings, see Ernst Käsemann, "The Problem of the Historical Jesus," in *Essays on New Testament Themes,* trans. W. J. Montague (London: SCM Press, 1964), pp. 37–42. See also Gerhard Ebeling, "Jesus and Faith," in *Word and Faith,* trans. James W. Leitch (Philadelphia: Fortress Press, 1963), pp. 236–238.

filled man. They expressed this by the idea of "sonship": Jesus was the "Son of God," the "Son of Man." Clearly, Jesus did not refer to himself as "Son of God." The provenance of this title was possibly the Jewish Davidic Messianology of the earliest church, the Palestinian Jewish-Christian community, but it came into its own with the emergence of an incarnational Christology in the Hellenistic-Gentile milieu, since it proved readily transferable from Jewish to Greek and Roman soil.[25]

The title "Son of Man" frequently occurs on the lips of Jesus in all the Gospels, but recent scholarship has made it seem increasingly unlikely that Jesus himself used the title in any significant sense, either as a self-reference or to designate a future, heavenly figure distinct from himself. After a decade of research on this question, Norman Perrin concludes that the use of Son of Man in the New Testament arose in connection with an interpretation of the resurrection of Jesus by the use of Dan. 7:13 in a manner akin to pesher exegesis, and that the Gospel of Mark used the title to give content to the idea of Jesus as Son of God—namely, by specifying his authority on earth, his necessary suffering, and his authority in judgment. Perrin allows one logion (Lk. 7:34 par.) in which Jesus may have used the Aramaic *bar nash* ("son of man") as an idiomatic self-designation, and another (Lk. 12:8 f. par.) where the tradition has added "Son of Man" to an authentic saying of Jesus in which he makes the future destiny of his hearers before God contingent upon their present acknowledgment of him.[26]

Despite the secondary origin of these titles in primitive Christian faith, "sonship" is not an invalid way of symbolizing Jesus' relationship to God in the light of the community's memory of his words and deeds. When we reflect upon the meaning of the con-

25. See Reginald H. Fuller, *The Foundations of New Testament Christology* (New York: Scribner's, 1965), pp. 114–115, 164–167, 187–188, 192–197, 231–232. Also Ferdinand Hahn, *Christologische Hoheitstitel* (3d ed., Göttingen: Vandenhoeck & Ruprecht, 1966), pp. 280–333. In the Synoptic tradition there are no instances where "Son of God" appears on the lips of Jesus as a self-reference. The title is attributed to Jesus *by others* (the Devil, Peter, the High Priest, etc.). In Matt. 11:27 par. Jesus speaks of "the Son," presumably in the sense of the "Son of God," but this saying must be attributed to the tradition.
26. Perrin, *A Modern Pilgrimage in New Testament Christology*, chaps. V, VI, VIII; and *Rediscovering the Teaching of Jesus*, pp. 119–121, 185–191.

cept "Son of God," especially as it functions in the theology of
Paul and the Gospel stories, it is evident that it need not be taken
to refer to a preexistent divine "person," which enters into hypo-
static union with the human nature of Jesus (this is the product
of later christological speculation based on Greek metaphysics).
Rather it refers to the humanity of Jesus as it was completed in
obedience and self-surrender to the Father and the assumption of
responsibility for the world. Jesus' life was one of radical *openness* or *obedience* to God, an obedience unto death (as Paul thematically formulated it, Phil. 2:8; Rom. 5:18–19), whereby all
people might be set free from bondage to sin, law, and death.[27]
The course of events that led to Jesus' execution reflected on his
part not a mere consent to necessity but an openness to the will of
the Father (thematized by the Evangelists in the prayer at Gethsemane, ". . . nevertheless not my will, but thine, be done," Lk.
22:42 par.)—this despite the fact that Jesus also struggled against
his fate and cried out in protest to God upon the cross (Mk. 15:34
par.). The cry of God-forsakenness indicates Jesus' recognition
that death is the final enemy, not a road to freedom, and it suggests that for him the very God whose nearness he had proclaimed
was on trial.[28] Thus the openness or obedience maintained by
Jesus was not, in the final analysis, his own accomplishment but
itself the gift of God.

The last point may be underscored by suggesting that the term
"faith" best characterizes the qualities of openness and obedience
to God. Jesus, who spoke about faith in a new and distinctive
fashion, was himself the truly *faithful* one. Both from what he
said about faith, and from his exemplification of it, it is clear that
faith is not a human virtue, product, or psychological state.
Rather faith enjoys a peculiar objectivity vis-à-vis the believer: it
is the power of God within him or her, making life whole, healing
the fractures of physical and social existence, opening the believer

27. See Hodgson, *Jesus—Word and Presence,* pp. 200–202. This interpretation has
been formulated in various ways by Wolfhart Pannenberg, Emanuel Hirsch, Friedrich Gogarten, and Karl Rahner (references in ibid.).
28. See below, Sec. 4B.

to participation in God's rule upon the earth (the near kingdom of freedom).[29] Moreover, faith in the *one* God clears the world of finite, idolatrous deities (nation, race, cult, ideology, party), which compete for our loyalties and frequently enthrall us. That is what Käsemann means when he writes that the first commandment ("You shall have no other gods before me") "becomes the basis of human freedom and the sum of all theology and real piety." [30] Jesus lived out the first commandment by his faithful sonship to God; therefore he was the radically free person.[31]

The reference to Jesus' "sonship" calls attention to his maleness. Although the personal God is beyond sexual distinctions, human persons are ineluctably male or female. That God should have designated a male, an obscure Jew of first-century Palestine, as the Liberator of all people—female as well as male, Gentiles as well as Jews—is part of the scandal of particularity with which Christian faith must come to terms. Given the social realities of that religious and cultural milieu, perhaps only a male could have attained even the relative freedom and following that Jesus did in carrying forward a ministry of liberation. What is more scandalous is that these realities have changed so very little in the intervening centuries. Jesus enjoyed a special and open relationship with women, whom he welcomed as equals and treated as unique individuals instead of in terms of cultural stereotypes.[32] He himself manifested qualities of love, compassion, healing, and deep sensitivity often associated culturally with women. But more importantly, for him the biological distinction between men and

---

29. See *Jesus—Word and Presence*, pp. 155–188.
30. Käsemann, *Jesus Means Freedom*, p. 32.
31. I return to "faith" as the first of the symbols of Christian freedom in Chap. VII, Sec. 2.
32. See especially the following texts in Mark and Luke: Mk. 3:35 par.; 7:24–30 par.; 12:41–44 par.; 14:3–9; 15:40–41; Lk. 7:36–50; 8:1–3; 10:38–42; 13:10–17; 23:55–24:11 par. Clearly the setting and form of many of these sayings are products of the tradition. But Bultmann regards Mk. 3:35 as an original saying of Jesus, and suggests that an authentic core may lie behind Mk. 7:24–30; 14:3–9; Lk. 7:36–50; 13:10–17. (Rudolf Bultmann, *The History of the Synoptic Tradition*, trans. John Marsh [New York: Harper & Row, 1968], pp. 12, 21, 29, 33, 37–38.) Jesus does seem to be remembered by the Synoptic tradition and the Evangelists (especially Luke) to have taken a special interest in the healing of women and to have called attention to their service, generosity, and compassion. The same is true of the Gospel of John: cf. 4:7–30; 11:1–44; 12:1–3; 19:25–27; 20:1–18.

women faded into insignificance.[33]   He lived already as though
there were "neither male nor female," to use Paul's designation
(Gal. 3:28) of an eschatological possibility.   Thus women as well
as men should be able to affirm his "sonship," meaning thereby
not that he was the male offspring of a male deity, but that he was
the radically free person because he lived in liberating openness
to the God of freedom.

B.   Brotherhood/Sisterhood: Existence for Others

Jesus' responsibility for human liberation in the world is the
positive form that his sonship to God assumes, by contrast with
the self-negating character of obedience and sacrifice.   Jesus is
obedient *to* God *on behalf of* the world: his mission to the world
is the primary place where his open relationship to God becomes
concrete and visible.   The directness of his relationship to his
brothers and sisters is the converse of the indirectness of his speech
about God.   Openness to God and responsibility for the world
are co-constitutive structures of freedom.[34]   Responsibility entails
the emancipation of men and women from the dehumanizing,
alienating bonds of the established order—"this world" as Paul
describes it.

In similar fashion, Jesus' *subjectivity* or self-relatedness becomes
visible primarily in the form of *intersubjectivity,* his relationship
to others.   Karl Barth has pointed out that the Gospels show no
interest in Jesus' private or personal life; his was a totally "public"
existence.[35]   One suspects this is the case not merely because of the
kerygmatic function of the Gospels, but also because Jesus was
remembered as one who called little attention to himself, whose
identity was his ministry, whose being was for others, whose humanity was cohumanity.   The Gospels do in fact report the "com-

---

33. On this matter, see Letty M. Russell, *Human Liberation in a Feminist Perspective—A Theology* (Philadelphia: Westminster Press, 1974), pp. 137–139.
34. Cf. Dietrich Bonhoeffer, *Letters and Papers from Prison,* rev. ed.; ed. Eberhard
Bethge; trans. R. H. Fuller, F. Clarke, et al. (New York: Macmillan, 1967), p. 202.
35. Karl Barth, *Church Dogmatics,* ed. G. W. Bromiley and T. F. Torrance, vol.
III/2 (Edinburgh: T. & T. Clark, 1960), pp. 203–222; vol. IV/2 (Edinburgh: T.
& T. Clark, 1958), pp. 180–192.

passionate" character of Jesus' relationship to those whom he healed (Mk. 1:41; Lk. 7:13; Matt. 20:34) and to "the crowds" (Mk. 6:34 par.; 8:2 par.; Matt. 14:14). The term "compassion" *(splagchnizesthai)*, used by Jesus himself in certain parables to characterize the Good Samaritan, the father of the prodigal son, and the king of the unforgiving servant (Lk. 10:33; 15:20; Matt. 18:27), is a strong one that goes beyond the sense of "sympathy." Insofar as it is intended by the Evangelists to refer to Jesus, it means that he took the misery and suffering that surrounded him literally into himself (into his viscera, *splagchna*), so that now it was more his misery than those who suffered it. As such it is strikingly similar to the concept of "communion" that I introduced as the intersubjective structure of freedom—namely, an intending the other for the sake of the other, putting ourselves at the other's disposal, finding self-fulfillment by and with the other, hence the freedom to share oneself, a freedom for-and-with-the-other.

The community that gathered about Jesus was a *non-separated, non-alienated* community. It was open to all, without regard to piety, status, class, sex, or familial relationships. Jesus included in his table fellowship[36] not only "tax collectors and sinners" (Matt. 11:19; 8:11), but also liberation fighters (Zealots), day-laborers (fishermen), women (a social outclass), foreigners (Samaritans), the poor and diseased. It was indeed a new brotherhood/ sisterhood, which challenged the patriarchal, androcentric, and familial structures of society.[37] For example, in Mk. 3:31–35 par.,[38] Jesus responds to his own question, "Who are my mother and my brothers?" by saying, with reference to his hearers, "Here are my mother and my brothers! Whoever does the will of God is my brother, and sister, and mother." And in Matt. 23:8–9,[39] he

---

36. Perrin, *Rediscovering the Teaching of Jesus*, pp. 102–108.
37. Cf. Soelle, *Political Theology*, pp. 65–66.
38. Bultmann regards vss. 31–34 as secondary and vs. 35 as original (*Synoptic Tradition*, pp. 29–30).
39. Bultmann says this could be a genuine dominical saying, but it might also be the product of the church or of Jewish tradition (*Synoptic Tradition*, p. 144).

challenges the authority of teachers and fathers because God is the one father and teacher.

Perhaps the best word for describing freedom at the intersubjective or communal level is *love,* in the strong sense of compassion. In the Synoptic materials, Jesus speaks of love *(agapē)* relatively infrequently but with great significance.[40] In Matt. 5:43–46 par., he radicalizes the command of Lev. 19:18 to love one's neighbor by insisting that it must include the love of enemies as well. Thereby the whole legalistic "friend-enemy" schema of conventional morality is transformed in principle. In Mk. 12:29–31 par., Jesus links the love of God (Deut. 6:5) and love of neighbor (Lev. 19:18), thus bringing together the two fundamental commandments of the Torah. The suggestion that these two co-imply each other is strengthened by his judgment in Lk. 11:42 that the Pharisees "neglect justice and the love of God." In other words, to do justice—to one's neighbor, one's brothers and sisters—*is* to love God; God is known and loved (only?) in the neighbor.[41] The "only" might be supported by the fact that, in Matt. 19:16–19, when Jesus is asked what one must do to have eternal life, he responds only in terms of the *second* table of the Decalogue (in which there is no explicit reference to God), to which he adds, "You shall love your neighbor as yourself." Similarly, we are told in Matt. 6:24 par. that if one loves God one must hate "mammon," which is the opposite of social justice. This language about love, which has its genesis on the lips of Jesus, is expanded by Paul in his attempt to explain what Christian freedom means in a positive sense: we are set free *from* bondage to sin, law, and death, *for* a life of self-giving love, a life whose "law" is love rather than hatred, fear, subjugation, or sheer libertinism. Such love "upbuilds," constituting a liberated community.[42]

40. The authenticity, in one form or another, of most of the passages to be considered here has been defended critically. See the relevant discussions in Bultmann, *Synoptic Tradition,* and Perrin, *Rediscovering. Agapē* is predicated *of* Jesus only once, Mk. 10:21.
41. According to José Miranda, this is one of the central principles of the prophetic understanding of God. (*Marx and the Bible,* pp. 44 ff.)
42. I return to the Pauline theology of love in Sec. 5A, and to "love" as the second of the symbols of Christian freedom in Chap. VII, Sec. 3.

C. SELFHOOD: PERSONAL IDENTITY AND AUTHORITY

On the basis of the critical evidence,[43] there seems little doubt that Jesus exercised a remarkable *authority (exousia)*—an authority that marked the central mystery of his person, for it was the manifestation of his unique self-identity or subjectivity, a self-identity founded in openness to God and expressed in the directness of his relationships with other persons. Yet this authority is not something Jesus laid claim to; it showed itself rather in the quality of his speech and actions. His hearers (both friends and enemies) *recognized* it; it was a quality *predicated of* him by the Evangelists (twenty-nine times); but he himself did not *claim* it (the term is found on Jesus' lips as a self-reference only four times—Matt. 9:6 par.; 21:24; 21:27 par.; 28:18—all of which are doubtless products of the tradition), nor did he suggest that it could be legitimated by some future event, such as his resurrection from the dead.[44] Thus the authority that was the mark of Jesus' radical selfhood already points away from itself: it is not a self-constituting (autonomous) or self-referential quality. His authority is really the authority *of God, on behalf of* the kingdom he proclaimed. Because his word —which is not his alone—is authoritative, so also is he.

The term *exousia* does not mean "authority" in the sense of an authoritarian tradition or law, inherited privilege, physical coercion, or power. Rather it means "freedom" in the sense of "freedom to act" or "original freedom," a freedom exercised not by physical power *(dunamis)* or legal authority but by word.[45] Such "original freedom" is usually found in conflict with "tradition," which replaces originality with the question of legitimation. Thus it is no accident that Jesus' *exousia* was expressed in

---

43. See Günther Bornkamm, *Jesus of Nazareth,* trans. Irene and Fraser McLusky, with James M. Robinson (New York: Harper & Row, 1960), pp. 60–61; Käsemann, "The Problem of the Historical Jesus," *Essays on New Testament Themes,* pp. 37 ff.; and Hans von Campenhausen, *Kirchliches Amt und geistliche Vollmacht in den ersten drei Jahrhunderten* (2d ed.; Tübingen: J. C. B. Mohr, 1963), chap. I, esp. p. 4.

44. Here I disagree with Wolfhart Pannenberg, *Jesus—God and Man,* trans. Lewis L. Wilkins and Duane A. Priebe (Philadelphia: Westminster Press, 1968), pp. 53–66.

45. See Kurt Niederwimmer, *Der Begriff der Freiheit im Neuen Testament* (Berlin: Verlag Alfred Töpelmann, 1966), pp. 4, 165–166. Gerhard Ebeling makes the same point in unpublished lectures on Christology.

his conflict with the legal and cultic tradition of Israel. He came
forward as a teacher with disciples, occasionally argued in rabbinic
fashion, and allowed himself to be addressed as "rabbi." Yet he
was independent of the scribes, belonged to no school, and founded
none.[46] The Evangelists express this as follows: "And when Jesus
finished these sayings, the crowds were astonished at his teaching,
for he taught them as one who had *exousia,* and not as their
scribes" (Matt. 7:28–29; cf. Mk. 1:21–22; Lk. 4:31–32). He introduced a new mode of speaking and teaching—original, not derived,
internally authoritative rather than dependent upon external
tradition.

Jesus' conflict with the tradition is most clearly seen in the opposition of his own teaching to that of Moses and the Torah—especially in the "but I say to you" *(egō de legō humin)* of the antitheses found in the Sermon on the Mount. This formula occurs
six times in the Gospels (Matt. 5:22, 28, 32, 34, 39, 44; cf. Lk.
6:27), and according to Käsemann was one of Jesus' most authentic
and characteristic expressions, reflecting his sense of inspiration or
consciousness of special mission, perhaps even of messianic authority.[47] The same dialectical opposition to the law (the substitution
of a higher authority in pursuit of the deeper meaning of the law)
may be observed from the conflict over the laws of purification
(Matt. 15:1–20 par.), and from Jesus' attitude toward the sabbath
commandments (Mk. 2:23–28).

Other than *exousia,* whose English translation, "authority,"
carries an unfavorable connotation with many, it is difficult to
specify a single biblical symbol for this third structure of freedom,
selfhood. Perhaps the Johannine category of *life* is the best can-
didate. Unlike authority, but like faith and love, life is available
to every human being, and indeed is the *sine qua non* of subjective
freedom. In the first instance life is a radically particular, individualized phenomenon, although it may also be used in a generic
sense to describe that which all "living" beings have in common.

46. Ibid., pp. 166–168.
47. Käsemann, "The Problem of the Historical Jesus," pp. 37–38; *Jesus Means Freedom,* pp. 24–25. See also Niederwimmer, *Der Begriff der Freiheit,* pp. 151, 153–158.

The dialectic between the particular and the universal, the personal and the non-privatistic, is characteristic of the Fourth Gospel. "Life," for human beings, suggests an integrated, self-conscious subjectivity, based upon a personal body, issuing in joy, celebration, play. Hence the celebrative and sensual quality of Jesus' life ("The Son of Man has come eating and drinking; and you say, 'Behold a glutton and drunkard, a friend of tax collectors and sinners!' " Lk. 7:34 par.) [48] ought not to be overlooked in the context of a discussion of his subjective freedom.[49]

3. THE GOSPEL OF LIBERATION

A. THE KINGDOM OF FREEDOM

The central symbol of Jesus' proclamation is the *kingdom of God (basileia tou theou)*. The Gospel of Mark summarizes this proclamation as follows: "Jesus came into Galilee, preaching the gospel of God, and saying, 'The time is fulfilled, and the kingdom of God is at hand; repent, and believe in the gospel' " (Mk. 1:14–15 par.). But what is the meaning of this "kingdom"? Jesus does not tell us directly; in fact, according to the Gospels, he refused to give "signs" by which its coming could be observed (Lk. 17:20).[50] On this basis, Norman Perrin suggests that "kingdom of God" is not a sign or "steno-symbol" but a true, "tensive" symbol, whose meaning is not obvious but is hidden and built up by means of metaphorical tension. As a true symbol, it has a second or double intentionality, hidden beneath the first or literal meaning.[51]

48. As noted earlier, this is one of the few Son of Man sayings whose authenticity is allowed by Perrin, *A Modern Pilgrimage in New Testament Christology*, p. 70.
49. I return to these matters more fully in discussing "life" as the third of the symbols of Christian freedom in Chap. VII, Sec. 4. See also the analysis of the Johannine theology of freedom in Sec. 5B of this chapter.
50. On the probable authenticity of this saying, see Perrin, *Rediscovering the Teaching of Jesus*, pp. 68–74; also Bultmann, *Synoptic Tradition*, p. 25. Jesus' refusal to give signs is reflected elsewhere in the tradition: Matt. 12:38–39; 16:1–4; Mk. 8:11–12; Lk. 11:29.
51. Norman Perrin, "Eschatology and Hermeneutics: Reflections on Method in the Interpretation of the New Testament," *Journal of Biblical Literature*, 93 (March 1974): 3–14, esp. 10–13; also *A Modern Pilgrimage in New Testament Christology*, pp. 37–39. The distinction between steno-symbol and tensive symbol is from Philip Wheelwright, *Metaphor and Reality* (Bloomington: Indiana University Press, 1962), chaps. III, V, esp. pp. 92–96; and the theory of the double intentionality of symbols is based on Paul Ricoeur, *The Symbolism of Evil*, trans. Emerson Buchanan (Boston: Beacon Press, 1969), pp. 15–16.

Actually, a symbol such as "kingdom of God" is plurisignificative, evoking different meanings in different historical and cultural contexts. The new "realm" *(basileia)* constituted by God's rule, power, or word is a realm of faith, love, joy, peace, unity, life. It is also *a realm of freedom*—a liberated communion of free subjects, founded on the power of God's grace. God's kingdom is a kingdom of freedom, a "place" where freedom prevails as the defining relationship among human beings instead of the bondage and alienation that ordinarily characterize human affairs. In light of the consciousness of and struggles for liberation in the contemporary world, "freedom" appears—for the time being—to be the most helpful concept for articulating the tensive, metaphorical intentionality of the kingdom symbolism.[52]

Because the "kingdom of God" is a symbol, Jesus for the most part spoke of it *parabolically,* i.e., metaphorically, indirectly, nonconceptually. That Jesus spoke and taught in parables, and that it is possible to approximate the original form and situation of at least some parables, is now widely accepted by New Testament scholarship (with many debates over details, of course). Jesus' parables are stories that depict the kingdom of God as a kingdom of freedom. This is not to suggest that freedom is the only theme in the parables by any means, but it is a central one. In fact, the parables themselves are *events of freedom.* They open up human

52. The expression "kingdom (or realm) of freedom" has its provenance in Hegel's doctrine of "objective spirit" in the *Philosophy of Right,* trans. T. M. Knox (London: Oxford University Press, 1952), § 4 (see above, p. 149); it was taken over and modified by Marx in the third volume of *Capital* (above, p. 59). Karl Barth links the two concepts by suggesting that the revolutionary freedom of Jesus was the "freedom of the kingdom of God" *(Church Dogmatics,* vol. IV/2, pp. 172, 175). The expression is also found in recent essays by Jürgen Moltmann, notably, "The Revolution of Freedom: The Christian and Marxist Struggle," in *Openings for Marxist-Christian Dialogue,* ed. Thomas W. Ogletree (Nashville: Abingdon Press, 1969), pp. 66–71. A reference to God's "Kingdom of freedom" appears in the 1969 "Message to the Churches from Oakland" of the National Committee of Black Churchmen (quoted in Wilmore, *Black Religion and Black Radicalism,* p. 306). Finally, the symbol "kingdom of freedom" is the central theme of Hans-Joachim Kraus's *Reich Gottes: Reich der Freiheit. Grundriss systematischer Theologie* (Neukirchen-Vluyn: Neukirchener Verlag, 1975). This important work was published and became available after the manuscript for this book had been completed and was in the press, and it has been possible to add only two or three references to it. Kraus covers many of the same themes that I do, but from a rather different perspective. His method is essentially that of "biblical theology," with a special concern for the theological significance of the Old Testament and a dialogue with Judaism.

reality, setting it free from the constraints of established structures and everyday experience, often in terms of their surprising endings or by means of the "imaginative shock" produced by the juxtaposition of the familiar and the unfamiliar; they also demand a free response on the part of their hearers (ancient and modern) if their meaning is to be apprehended, since they provide no "application" of their own (although the Evangelists have frequently appended applications to the original parables).[53]

Because of the absence of the term *eleutheria* from the Synoptic tradition, freedom is not explicitly thematized in any of the parables.[54]   But it belongs to the hidden meaning or metaphorical intentionality of many of them, especially when we consider them as holistic literary units engendering a new vision of reality.   For example, the Parable of the Good Samaritan (Lk. 10:30–37) is concerned not only with the "goodness" of the Samaritan but also with his freedom from more urgent or worthy causes, which makes him available to respond compassionately to immediate human needs.   The Priest and the Levite are also "good" men—indeed the very best of their time—but they are in bondage to the accepted patterns of behavior of their socioreligious world and therefore cannot stop to help.   Because of his freedom and availability, the Samaritan represents an aspect of the hidden reality of the kingdom, which transcends all established structures.   Moreover, the

---

53. See especially Robert W. Funk, *Language, Hermeneutic, and Word of God* (New York: Harper & Row, 1966), chap. 5; also Dan O. Via, *The Parables: Their Literary and Existential Dimension* (Philadelphia: Fortress Press, 1967), chaps. 1–3.
54. A possible exception is Matt. 17:25b–26, the only occurrence of *eleutheria* in the Synoptic Gospels: " 'What do you think, Simon?   From whom do kings of the earth take toll or tribute?   From their sons or from others?'   And when [Simon] said, 'From others,' Jesus said to him, 'Then the sons are free' [*eleutheroi eisin hoi huioi*]." It is conceivable that this is a fragment of a lost parable or saying about the kingdom, associated by Matthew with two other units of tradition (the question about the temple tax, vss. 24–25a, and the miracle of the shekel in the fish's mouth, vs. 27) clearly alien to its original setting.   (See Bultmann, *Synoptic Tradition*, pp. 34–25.)   If indeed it was part of a parable or saying about the kingdom, it could have meant that, just as the sons of earthly kings are free, so also are the sons of the heavenly king, the sons of God, free: God's kingdom as a kingdom of sons is a kingdom of freedom.   By appropriating the traditional association of sonship and freedom, Jesus exploded its limits.   The sonship of which he speaks is not based on blood, sex, race, inheritance, or property.   It is founded solely on the gratuity of God.   Because God's grace is universal, all human beings without exception may become God's sons and daughters; there are no slaves, no outsiders, no excluded class from God's kingdom.   On the possible relation of this passage to Jn. 8:35–36, see n. 116.

Samaritan pays in advance the cost of the victimized man's lodging and promises to reimburse the innkeeper for any additional costs as well, so that the man will not be indentured for debt. In other words, the parable also shows a concern for preserving and enhancing the social reality of freedom.[55]

I wish to look at the Parable of the Great Supper (Lk. 14:12–24; Matt. 22:1–10) in greater detail,[56] as a way of epitomizing an interpretation of the parables as a whole in terms of freedom. This parable is intended as a parable of the kingdom of God (Matt. 22:2; Lk. 14:15): it describes a new realm of freedom constituted by God's saving presence and liberating power. It is concerned with a transformation of "worlds"—i.e., of the entire sociopolitical nexus of human life—not just with the conversion of the individual heart. As such it provides a warrant for Dorothee Soelle's statement that today theological hermeneutics must hold open "an horizon of interpretation in which politics is understood as the comprehensive and decisive sphere in which Christian truth should become praxis." [57] This is especially clear in the *parables* of the kingdom, by contrast with Jesus' *sayings* about the kingdom, for the parables are stories of human beings interacting in social, political, and economic settings—banquets, wedding feasts, farms and farm workers, vineyards, royal households, merchants and stewards, noblemen and servants, public highways, law courts, the temple—indeed, almost every aspect of public and social existence in Jesus' time.

Equally as important as this public and therefore political setting is the fact that the parables portray a radical alteration of conventional social and institutional structures, an alteration in the direction of liberation. All of the established orders—family, economics, politics, law, cult—are shaken to the foundation by Jesus' proclamation of the nearness of the kingdom.[58] The "logic"

55. I am indebted to my colleagues Daniel Patte and John Donahue respectively for these two observations.
56. In much of what follows I am indebted indirectly to Funk's masterful exegesis of this parable in *Language, Hermeneutic, and Word of God*, chaps. 6–7. See also Perrin, *Rediscovering the Teaching of Jesus*, pp. 110–114.
57. Soelle, *Political Theology*, p. 59.
58. Cf. Barth, *Church Dogmatics*, IV/2, 175–179.

that prevails in the everyday world is both challenged and replaced by a new logic, the logic of grace and freedom. The contents that make up the old world remain the same, but relations, values, behavior, consequences have been set strangely askew; a new, unsettling world is juxtaposed with an old, familiar one. Precisely this juxtaposition and reversal of values such as one finds in the Great Supper is the way that liberation impinges upon the world. The opposition between rich and poor, powerful and powerless, healthy and sick, privileged and disinherited, and the invitation of the latter together with the eventual exclusion of the former, is by no means an arbitrary illustration of some apolitical allegory about the history of salvation (such as the rejection by Israel and the mission to Gentiles). From what we know of his ministry and teaching as a whole, Jesus condemned social injustice, religious arrogance, and political exploitation, and identified himself with the poor, the powerless, the sick, the disinherited. Indeed it was a special practice of his to have a table fellowship with people such as these—as a kind of continuing enactment of the Parable of the Great Supper.

Despite the political setting and significance of the parables, it must be stressed that the kingdom of God portrayed therein is not only a political but also a *post*political or eschatological symbol. "Postpolitical" is a helpful expression because it reminds us that what we are speaking of is post*political,* not apolitical or unworldly. When we describe an idea or cultural epoch as *post-,* we usually mean that the preceding reality (in this case, "politics") does not cease to exist but furnishes the foundation for a further development and thus is included in a new framework. It no longer functions as a wholly appropriate metaphor for characterizing the new age, *but we have not yet found what that new metaphor might be,* and so we continue to use the old one in a qualified way. We do not know how to describe concretely what lies "beyond politics," but we do know that political aspirations and struggles will be fulfilled in a new and unexpected way.

Why does the symbol of the kingdom of God envision something new and unexpected? Because in the first place it refers explicitly to the action *of God,* although human action is by no means excluded; indeed, it serves as the vehicle of divine action in the parables. But the term "kingdom" is a way of describing *God's* rule or kingship, by which he will visit and liberate his people, not transporting them to another world but setting them free in this one. In the second place, what the kingdom of God envisions is not a purely political possibility. Rather it is a kingdom *of freedom,* a true communion of free subjects in which the alienation and power struggles characteristic of politics are overcome, a communion in which the conflict between individuals and society is resolved. True or final freedom is an eschatological, not a political, possibility; and it requires a "poetics" (or a "parabolics"), not a "politics," to describe. We might say that *emancipation* is the goal of politics, but that *redemption* is the gift of God, and that *liberation* encompasses both elements—the human and the divine, the immanent and the transcendent—of this dialectic.[59]

Because Jesus was not a political revolutionary but a proclaimer of freedom, his parables and teachings cannot be taken as a blueprint for social reform—that was the mistake of the Social Gospel movement, although in other respects it was close to the truth. As Soelle says, "there are no specifically Christian solutions to world problems."[60] The parables make this point in their own distinctive way. They are filled with surprises, exaggerations, hyperboles, paradoxes, which give them a strangely surrealistic quality. Surrealism does not mean the rejection of realism but its intensification to the point where reality begins to break apart and point beyond itself. The surrealism of the Great Supper is unmistakable. Every single one of the invited guests refuses to come

59. Cf. Jürgen Moltmann, "Die Revolution der Freiheit," *Perspektiven der Theologie: Gesammelte Aufsätze* (Munich: Chr. Kaiser Verlag, 1968), p. 207. The distinction between *Emanzipation* and *Erlösung* is obscured by the translation of this essay in the work cited in n. 52. I return to this distinction in Chap. VI, Sec. 2.
60. Soelle, *Political Theology,* p. 59.

without any credible explanation. Then the hall is filled with a great horde of people swept off the streets: now the invitation seems to have no limits (to say nothing of the host's supply of food and drink!). The sedate dinner party has become a joyous eschatological feast: it truly is a "great supper," as the King James Version quaintly puts it.

But we are not limited to the parables of the kingdom. *Jesus himself*—all that he said and did—*is a parable,* a parable of the kingdom he proclaimed.[61] He enacted the kingdom *parabolically,* which is the only way that an eschatological, postpolitical reality can be actualized in the realities of the political present. Jesus' action may be characterized as a liberating activity of parabolic significance. He proclaimed and enacted a freedom from law and religious piety, from social and political bondage, from death and the powers of death.

B. FREEDOM FROM LAW AND PIETY

We have already considered Jesus' freedom in relation to the law as an expression of his unique authority (Sec. 2c). His conflict with the Torah may be broadened to include conflicts with religious piety in general. Most of the conflict pericopes are concerned with some aspect of religious life and practice: the law of purification (Mk. 7:1–23 par.); the temple tax (Matt. 17:24–27); alms, prayer, and fasting as the three chief practices of piety (Matt. 6:1–18); conflicts over conduct on the sabbath (Mk. 2:23–28 par.; 3:1–6 par.; Lk. 13:10–16; 14:1–6; Jn. 5:1–17; 9:1–41). Many of these conflict stories are stamped by the situation of the early church, and some are pure products of the tradition (e.g., the temple tax pericope), but they surely reflect an aspect of Jesus' conduct which left its mark on Christianity.[62] In these conflict situations, Jesus exercised primarily a freedom of word, to be sure, but it entailed a call to the practice of freedom in the sphere of religion that was quite unprecedented, a freedom epitomized by

61. Cf. Leander Keck, *A Future for the Historical Jesus,* pp. 243–249.
62. See Niederwimmer, *Begriff der Freiheit,* pp. 158–163; Bultmann, *Synoptic Tradition,* pp. 12, 16–18, 34–35, 133.

the saying in Mk. 2:27: "The sabbath was made for man, not man for the sabbath." [63] Moreover, as Käsemann notes, "the pious people of the time were deeply incensed by Jesus' association with sinners, tax-collectors, and prostitutes." By these associations Jesus "infringed not only a social and political taboo . . . [but also] repeatedly violated what was regarded as God's will, and in so doing seemed to attack God the Father himself." [64]

The freedom from law and religious piety proclaimed by Jesus was concretely actualized by his cleansing of the temple (Mk. 11: 15–19 par.). This was a religious action with overtly political ramifications. Jesus' purpose does not appear to have been to challenge the authority of the sacerdotal aristocracy in Jerusalem,[65] or to perform an eschatological sign,[66] but rather to break up the *all-too-religious* temple trading system, namely, the exchange of coins for the Passover tax and the selling of sacrificial animals. It is not that the temple traders and worshipers were insufficiently religious; rather they were *too* religious, and therefore they defiled the real meaning of worship, which is to serve God and humankind—the direct antithesis of "robbery" (cf. Mk. 11:17). It is also likely that profits from the trading system were enriching the coffers of the priestly aristocracy, while the poor were made to

63. It is worth noting that this saying is omitted in the Matthean and Lukan parallels (Matt. 12:8; Lk. 6:5). This reflects an effort of the community to soften the harshness of a saying of Jesus, denying the freedom for all men and women (not just the Son of Man) that Jesus claimed for them. See Käsemann, *Essays on New Testament Themes*, pp. 38–39. Even if there are rabbinic parallels for this statement, as Bultmann claims, *Synoptic Tradition*, pp. 75, 108, the fact is that religion in practice, including Christianity as well as Judaism, always tends to absolutize cultic conventions. Jesus' challenge to this convention falls into the context of a questioning of "religiousness" per se, which goes beyond rabbinic wisdom.
64. Käsemann, *Jesus Means Freedom*, p. 28. See also Jürgen Moltmann, *The Crucified God: The Cross of Christ as the Foundation and Criticism of Christian Theology*, trans. R. A. Wilson and John Bowden (New York: Harper & Row, 1974), pp. 128–129. Moltmann argues that Jesus' freedom from the law reaches its highest point in his forgiveness of sin, a presumption of authority for which he was accused of "blasphemy" (cf. Mk. 2:1–12 par.). I return to this point in Sec. 4A.
65. As S. G. F. Brandon claims, *Jesus and the Zealots* (New York: Scribner's, 1967), pp. 331–338. Brandon's argument that the cleansing was a revolutionary act closely associated with a Zealot insurrection in the city at the time simply cannot be defended critically. On the other hand, Brandon correctly perceives the close association between religious and political authority in Jerusalem, so that what began as a religious act unavoidably had political consequences as well.
66. As Oscar Cullmann claims, *Jesus and the Revolutionaries*, trans. Gareth Putnam (New York: Harper & Row, 1970), pp. 20–21. Cullmann interprets the cleansing as a prophetic sign of God's coming judgment on all worldly institutions.

pay for cultic procedures irrelevant to true worship. Hence it is not surprising that the Sadducees, who were in charge of the temple, should interpret the "cleansing" as a challenge to their authority—and indirectly to that of the Romans, by whom the chief priests were expected to maintain a religiously stable situation—for they feared that Jesus' activity might lead to an outbreak of public disturbances. Consequently, the Sadducees, not the Pharisees, took the lead in arresting Jesus, as Mk. 11:18 makes clear: "The chief priests and the scribes heard it and sought a way to destroy him; for they feared him, because all the multitude was astonished at his teaching." [67] But their fears were not merely political. Like the Pharisees, they were disturbed by Jesus' sabbath healings and his parables (Mk. 3:6 par.; 12:12 par.), and they understood his challenge to the religious institutions of Israel all too well, although their direct action may have been triggered by their political interest in keeping peace during the Passover festival.

C. Social and Political Freedom

Jesus did not attack the "social injustice" of his time in the sense of *defining* it as such and proposing a political program for the reform of unjust institutional structures. Such definitions and actions presuppose a form of consciousness and conditions for the possibility of change that are distinctly modern. Rather many of the sayings and actions of Jesus about which we can be reasonably certain—e.g., his deep distrust of wealth, his self-identification with the poor and outcasts, his ministry of healing, his relation to the Zealots, his challenges to the established authorities of Jerusalem and Rome—reflect a response to a cultural situation that *we* would describe as socially unjust. Jesus called this situation radically into question by proclaiming the immediate inbreaking of God's kingdom, which would judge and transform all arrangements of power and authority in this world.

67. Cf. William R. Wilson, *The Execution of Jesus* (New York: Scribner's, 1970), pp. 97–103, 109.

One aspect of social injustice that is reflected with special clarity in the sayings of Jesus took the form of wealth or riches. Jesus does not suggest that money *per se* is evil, and he does not advocate an ascetic, world-denying attitude. Rather the fact of having money *in abundance in the context of widespread poverty* reflects a situation of social injustice, of fundamental inequities achieved by violence and spoliation. This is what is suggested by the Lukan version of the Beatitudes and Woes—"Blessed are you poor. . . . But woe to you that are rich, . . ." "Blessed are you that hunger now, . . . Woe to you that are full now" (Lk. 6:20, 24, 21, 25)—and by the parables about the difficulties faced by the rich in entering the kingdom of God (Mk. 10:17–31 par.; Lk. 12:16–21; 16:19–31). The relation between wealth and injustice is more explicit in the expression *mamōna tēs adikias* in Lk. 16:9, 11, customarily translated "unrighteous mammon," but more meaningfully rendered, according to José Miranda, as "money of injustice." Miranda notes that St. Jerome commented on this expression as follows:

> And he [Jesus] very rightly said, "money of injustice," for *all riches come from injustice.* Unless one person has lost, another cannot find. Therefore I believe that the popular proverb is very true: "The rich person is either an unjust person or the heir of one." [68]

If the connection between wealth ("mammon") and injustice is valid (the reasons for which are more complex than the one adduced by Jerome),[69] then when Jesus says, "You cannot serve God and mammon" (Lk. 16:13), the meaning is not only that wealth functions as a rival object of devotion, upon which one

---

68. Miranda, *Marx and the Bible*, p. 15. The quotation of Jerome is from "Carta 120," *PL*, 22: 984 (italics Miranda's).
69. In the modern world, at least, it is not a matter of a fixed or limited quantity of money and other capital resources, as Jerome suggests. Rather it is because in most economic systems great wealth is acquired by means of either a direct or an indirect, "structural" exploitation of the poor. It is not that capital is unavailable; rather it tends to concentrate in the hands of wealthy individuals and corporations. Miranda argues for a correspondence between the biblical critique of wealth and the Marxist critique of capitalism: injustice of ownership (privately held capital) is based on injustice of income (achieved by exploitive, coercive means). Ibid., chap. I.

comes to rely for salvation, but also that it represents the direct antithesis to serving or loving God, because as we have seen (Sec. 2B) the love of God entails precisely doing *justice* to the neighbor.

Jesus' mission in relation to the fact of social injustice is expressed thematically by Luke with the words from Is. 61:1–2 and 58:6 in the story of the rejection at Nazareth:

> The Spirit of the Lord is upon me,
> because he has anointed me to preach good news
>   to the poor.
> He has sent me to proclaim release to the captives
> and recovering of sight to the blind,
> to set at liberty those who are oppressed,
> to proclaim the acceptable year of the Lord.
>
> —Lk. 4:18–19

Although this is a characteristically Lukan proof from prophecy, it reflects an authentic dimension of Jesus' ministry. A similar enumeration of prophetic signs is found in Jesus' reply to the disciples of John the Baptist, which may reflect an originally independent dominical saying:[70] "Go and tell John what you hear and see; the blind receive their sight and the lame walk, lepers are cleansed and the deaf hear, and the dead are raised up, and the poor have good news preached to them." In reflecting on the fact that so many of these eschatological signs of the kingdom have to do with the curing of physical disease—to say nothing of Jesus' ministry of healing—one should not forget the close association among disease, poverty, and social injustice.

Despite the abundance of this evidence, many interpreters have attempted to portray Jesus in an essentially neutral stance, or as displaying a "double attitude" toward the conditions of the world, as Cullmann puts it.

> This judgment of the present social order is as such revolutionary. But it is not so in the sense that Jesus called for the overthrow of this order itself. . . . These norms [of the coming kingdom] are not components of a *revolutionary reform program of the existing institutions.* Soon God will pass sentence on the unjust order. But man *on an individual level* is to be already radically changed

70. Bultmann, *Synoptic Tradition,* p. 23.

by the law of love. He is as such an object of the call of repentance.[71]

Similarly, Barth portrays Jesus as both a passive conservative and a
radical revolutionary (each somehow canceling out the other);
Bultmann stresses the individualistic, non-world–reforming character of Jesus' ethic; and Hengel opts finally for a purely inward,
nonviolent freedom.[72]

To be sure, there is an element of truth in what these theologians are saying. The kingdom of God may not be identified with
any of the social orders, and its freedom transcends that of all
liberation movements. Nevertheless, precisely the *nearness* of the
kingdom, as Jesus proclaimed it, does not permit a stance of
neutrality with respect to the religious, social, and political issues
at stake in the world. Rather it demands a form of partisanship[73]
—a *critical partisanship* within and for movements of liberation
rather than against them. A *critical* partisanship is one that is
iconoclastic: it challenges and seeks to break the idolatry, ideology,
alienation, and propaganda that accompany most political movements, whether to the left or the right. It has a passion for telling
the truth in politics, for uncovering deception, for raising the level
of public consciousness rather than anesthetizing it. It seeks to
introduce an element of celebration and play to counteract the

71. Cullmann, *Jesus and the Revolutionaries*, pp. 25–26 (italics his); cf. pp. 12–13,
55–56.
72. Barth, *Church Dogmatics*, IV/2, 173–179; Rudolf Bultmann, *Theology of the
New Testament*, vol. I, trans. Kendrick Grobel (New York: Scribner's, 1954), p. 19,
cf. pp. 9–22; Hengel, *Victory Over Violence*, pp. 45–59.
73. On the idea of partisanship, see Jürgen Moltmann, "Political Theology,"
Theology Today, 28 (April 1971): 20–21; and "God in Revolution," *Religion,
Revolution, and the Future*, trans. M. Douglas Meeks (New York: Scribner's, 1969),
pp. 140–143. Moltmann describes this as "the dialectic of siding with the humiliated," for the sake of effecting the liberation of all—an insight that he learned
from Marx, Camus, and Martin Luther King. God's partisanship on the side of
the oppressed is a central theme of black theology. To share in God's liberating
work today, one must "become black," meaning thereby the renunciation not of
white skin color but of white racism, experiencing what it means to be oppressed
by white power structures, seeking to transform those structures, thereby liberating
whites as well as blacks. See Cone, *A Black Theology of Liberation*, pp. 120–138.
Similarly, Gustavo Gutiérrez, in the context of the Latin American situation, insists
that the church must achieve an identification with the oppressed classes and a
solidarity with the poor, precisely in order to overcome the class structure of society
and poverty. See *A Theology of Liberation*, trans. Caridad Inda and John Eagleson (Maryknoll, N.Y.: Orbis Books, 1973), pp. 273–275, 287–302. The dangers in
the idea of partisanship will be considered in Chap. VI, Sec. 4B (2).

legalism and potential violence of political conflict. It perceives the difference between the human struggle for liberation and God's kingdom, and it refuses to absolutize relative political achievements. Its goal is not simply to invert the relation between oppressors and oppressed but rather to achieve the liberation of all.

Yet it is still a *partisanship,* for the nearness of the kingdom requires not merely a change of heart but also a reordering of social and institutional structures. This is the significance of the fact that the "signs" of the kingdom are concerned with a transformation of the objective social and physical conditions of life: the blind receive sight, the lame walk, lepers are cleansed, the deaf hear, the poor have good news preached to them, the captives are released, the oppressed are set at liberty. To be sure, these signs were used by the Evangelists as prophetic proof that Jesus was the bringer of the messianic kingdom. But Jesus was remembered to have done such deeds, and neither he nor Jewish tradition understood the kingdom of God to entail merely an inner conversion of the heart nor an escape from this earth into a transcendent sphere. Rather the kingdom of God meant a *transfigured earth.* It is naive to suppose, as Cullmann and many others do, "that the social question would actually be solved already in this age if every individual would become as radically converted as Jesus demands." [74] Such a statement overlooks the social and institutional forms of bondage examined in the preceding chapter under the categories of "law" and the "powers." Repentance of the individual will not cause the demonic objectifications of bondage to vanish.

Jesus himself exemplified such a critical partisanship (although of course he did not *conceptualize* his role in these modern terms). The sayings mentioned earlier indicate that he identified himself with the poor, the oppressed, the diseased, the sinners, the disinherited of the earth, designating them as the special objects of God's saving and liberating grace. His opposition to the rich, the

---

74. Cullmann, *Jesus and the Revolutionaries,* p. 28. See Käsemann's remarks on the limits of the existentialist interpretation in *Jesus Means Freedom,* pp. 132–133.

pious, the religious and political "establishment" was for the purpose not of destroying the latter but rather of achieving their salvation as well.   Oppressors must be liberated from acts of oppression, just as the oppressed must be set free from the effects of these
acts.   All hierarchial and oppressive structures are fundamentally
incompatible with God's kingdom.

But the question remains, Did Jesus also understand himself as
a revolutionary political leader—indeed, as a political Messiah who
would lead his people in a violent struggle against the Roman
occupying power in order to reestablish the Davidic throne in
Israel?   There was in fact a revolutionary group in Jesus' time with
just this aim—the Zealots.   Was Jesus himself a Zealot leader, or at
least a member of the Zealot party?   This question has been examined at length by Eisler, Hengel, Brandon, Cullmann, and
others.   The issue is very complex, and impressive evidence can be
marshaled on both sides.[75]   Jesus must have sympathized profoundly with the Zealots' sense of outrage toward the Romans and
the Jewish aristocracy, included Zealots or former Zealots among
his disciples, made critical statements about the Roman authorities, occasioned religious and political unrest by his proclamation
of the nearness of God's kingdom and his association with the
enemies of both religion and state, engaged in provocative actions
in Jerusalem, and was crucified with two Zealots on a charge of
sedition.   Despite all these factors, however, I think we have to
conclude that Jesus himself was not a Zealot leader and did not
become an *uncritical* partisan of any political group.   The counter-
vailing evidence—his insistence on nonviolence and love of enemies, his rejection of the friend-enemy schema, his unrevolution-
ary joyousness, his radical antilegalism, his resistance of any
messianic role—is simply too strong to classify him as a Zealot
revolutionary.   Indeed, he may have been peculiarly sensitive to

75. On this matter, see especially Martin Hengel, *Was Jesus a Revolutionist?*, trans.
William Klassen (Philadelphia: Fortress Press, 1971), pp. 14–35; *Victory Over
Violence*, pp. 45–59; Brandon, *Jesus and the Zealots*, pp. 322–358; Cullmann, *Jesus
and the Revolutionaries*, pp. 1–15, 31–50; Moltmann, *The Crucified God*, pp. 138–
144; and D. F. Strauss, *The Life of Jesus Critically Examined*, trans. G. Eliot, ed.
P. C. Hodgson (Philadelphia: Fortress Press, 1972), §§ 65–66.

the trap that the Zealots could fall into. Matt. 5:43–48 might be interpreted this way, as a word of warning to Zealots: It isn't enough for you to love your friends and hate your enemies. For if you love those who love you, what reward have you? Don't even the tax collectors—the collaborators with Rome—do the same? If you salute only your brethren, what more are you doing than others? Don't even the Gentiles—the Romans—do the same? Therefore I say to you, love your enemies and pray for those who persecute you.

Cullmann may be right that Jesus viewed the political conception of messiahship as his special temptation. "One is tempted only by those things which are close to him." [76] This could account for that element in the temptation story in which the Devil proposes a political role for Jesus (Matt. 4:8–10 par.). It might also explain Jesus' rejection of Peter's identification of him as the Messiah at Caesarea Philippi (Mk. 8:30 par.), his refusal to kindle a revolt at Gethsemane (Matt. 26:52 par.), his avoidance of Pilate's question as to his identity (Mk. 15:2 par.). Unless all these texts are constructions of the Evangelists—and that seems unlikely in view of the embarrassment the church faced as a result of Jesus' not having claimed messiahship—then there are good grounds for believing that Jesus avoided the role of political messiahship, which was the only way the messianic role could be understood at the time, but perhaps at the price of inner struggle and temptation. The latter, however, can only be a conjecture, for we have no way of knowing the inner intentions and thoughts of Jesus.

On the basis of what we do know, we may say that Jesus' liberating activity did not take the form of a call to political revolt and was more fundamental than a castigation of the temple trading system. It had to do with the way that he called all of the established orders of domination and control—familial, cultic, legal, economic, political—into question by contrasting them with the radical freedom of the kingdom of God, of which his own freedom was a notable foretaste. Dorothee Soelle argues that Jesus did not

76. Cullmann, *Jesus and the Revolutionaries*, pp. 39–42.

criticize "the structural conditions under which tax collectors became tax collectors and prostitutes became prostitutes," because, to put it in Marxist fashion, "the means of production had not developed to the point where the restructuring of society was technically possible." But, she adds, this should not blind us to the fact that

> in an indirect sense, the manner in which Jesus thought and acted *de facto* broke open and transformed the social structures of the world in which he lived. . . . In Jesus' proclamation there begins an exodus from familiar and traditional structures of authority based on knowledge and achievement—a proclamation to which those who throughout the history of Christendom have stood in need of an exodus constantly appealed. "You know that in the world, rulers lord it over their subjects, and their great men make them feel the weight of authority; but it shall not be so with you" (Matt. 20:25–26, NEB).[77]

Soelle calls this a "cipher of liberation" that demands of us not a literal imitation but a relevant response in our social and political situation.

Had social conditions been transformable in the first century in a way similar to what is now possible through appropriate technological and socioeconomic policies, Jesus would most likely have demanded such a transformation and acted to bring it about. But the issue is more basic than that. Gustavo Gutiérrez makes the point as well as anyone I know:

> For Jesus, oppression and injustice were not limited to a specific historical situation; their causes go deeper and cannot be truly eliminated without going to the very roots of the problem: the disintegration of brotherhood and communion among men. . . . Jesus is opposed to all politico-religious messianism which does not respect either the depth of the religious realm or the autonomy of political action. . . . The liberation which Jesus offers is universal and integral; it transcends national boundaries, attacks the foundation of injustice and exploitation, and eliminates politico-religious confusions, without therefore being limited to a

77. Soelle, *Political Theology*, pp. 64–66.

purely "spiritual" plane. . . . Jesus' posture precludes all over-simplification. To close one's eyes to this complexity amounts to letting the richness of his testimony on this score escape.[78]

These words are written by a theologian who believes that only a social revolution can transform conditions in Latin America today, and that Christians are called in the name of Jesus Christ to participation in such a revolution. But their participation will remain critical and nonideological so long as they remember that the liberation accomplished by Jesus is more fundamental than that of any particular liberation movement, although the political implications of the gospel derive, as Gutiérrez says, not from various peripheral elements but "from the very nucleus of its message." [79] Such a perspective should enable Christians to be realistic about what can actually be accomplished by political means, and to risk failure in political conflicts, without losing their utopian vision of a liberated kingdom which is at once the gift of God and the goal of humankind's historical project.

D. FREEDOM FROM DEATH AND THE POWERS OF DEATH

Käsemann points out that for the Gospel of Mark in particular Jesus is viewed as the cosmic victor over death and the demonic powers. Mark gives less attention to the sayings of Jesus than do the other Gospels, concentrating instead on his actions, especially his acts of healing. Jesus' cures of demoniacs, by which the evil powers are exorcised, and his healings of physical diseases and infirmities, by which the power of death is broken, constitute one of the central themes of this Gospel. "Whatever else Mark tells

78. Gutiérrez, *A Theology of Liberation*, pp. 227–228; cf. pp. 225–239. The intriguing study of Jesus by the Czech Marxist philosopher Milan Machoveč downplays the social-revolutionary aspects of Jesus' proclamation and action (without denying the latter) because of the author's conviction that contemporary Marxists have understood all too well the structural elements of liberation but have lost sight of one's personal responsibility for humanizing action in the context of specific needs and suffering. Therefore Machoveč stresses Jesus' call for radical personal transformation and response to the claim of the inbreaking future, from which will follow a revolutionary transformation of the sociopolitical order. See *Jesus für Atheisten*, pp. 18–22, 261–269, 287–290, and the whole of chap. IV, "Jesu Botschaft." In the American context, just the opposite emphasis is necessary in order to arrive dialectically at the same total understanding of the liberating significance of Jesus.
79. Gutiérrez, *A Theology of Liberation*, p. 231.

us about Jesus fits in with this.   The fact that the power of death, which is another manifestation of satanic rule, is broken is constantly being proclaimed in healing miracles.   The strength that radiates from Jesus helps the sufferers to new life, to health, to an anticipation of eternal salvation." [80]

Although the Evangelists' accounts of the miracles were fashioned to serve apologetic purposes, the fact of the healings was undoubtedly an authentic aspect of Jesus' ministry: he was remembered to have cured people who were possessed and to have made well those who were broken in body and spirit.   *How* he did so is not terribly important.   It seems apparent from the Synoptic tradition as a whole that he was not an ordinary miracle worker who healed by magical means such as touch, esoteric medicines, or secret incantations; he was not a tribal shaman.   Rather the extraordinary power of his personal presence and the authority of his words seemed to have had a transforming effect upon the sick, evoking in them a restorative, saving faith.   The theme of faith is associated with about half of the healing narratives.   Typically, Jesus says to those who have been cured, "Your faith has made you well."   Perhaps for this reason the tradition stresses Jesus' healing of demoniacs, because the instrument of his exorcisms is precisely his verbal command to the possessing demon: "What is this word? For with authority and power he commands the unclean spirits, and they come out" (Lk. 4:36 par.); ". . . he cast out the spirits with a word, and healed all who were sick" (Matt. 8:16 par.).[81]

According to the world view of the first century, demons were personifications of the power of death; sickness and disease were foretastes of the onslaught of death, which will destroy the body. Lepers in particular were living symbols of death and accordingly were excluded from any social contact.[82]   Thus in his healing ministry Jesus came face to face with the ultimate enemy, the final bondage of sin—death itself.   Jesus was victorious over these

80. Käsemann, *Jesus Means Freedom*, pp. 55–58; quotation from p. 57.
81. Cf. Hodgson, *Jesus—Word and Presence*, pp. 174–180.
82. Hengel, *Victory Over Violence*, p. 53.   Jesus' ministry to lepers has an important thematic place at the beginning of Mark's Gospel, 1:40–45 par.; cf. Lk. 17:11–19.

anticipations of death. But he had still to face his own death. His acts of liberation from death and the powers of death would have little meaning if his own death should prove to be an ultimate and inescapable bondage. Thus the whole of Jesus' "gospel of liberation" in a sense hung in the balance, dependent upon the outcome of his own death.

4. THE DEATH OF JESUS AND THE QUESTION OF FREEDOM[83]

The death of Jesus is related to the question of freedom in at least two ways. First, his death resulted from the revolutionary freedom with which he questioned and opposed the established orders, both religious and political: he was accused of "blasphemy" by the chief priests and of "agitation" or "sedition" before the political authorities. Second, the manner of his death—the cry of God-forsakenness—discloses that death itself is not a road to freedom and therefore poses in an ultimate way the question about God: either God's credibility is destroyed by death and death itself becomes the real God, or else God liberates from the bondage of death by his own death-destroying power. God and death are ultimate antitheses; one or the other must finally prevail.

A. JESUS AS "BLASPHEMER" AND AS "AGITATOR"

According to the Markan account of the trial of Jesus before the Sanhedrin, he was condemned on a charge of "blasphemy" (Mk. 14:64), specifically the blasphemy of claiming to be the Messiah of God. Quite apart from the question of the historicity of this account (to which I return shortly), it is possible that Jesus comported himself in such a way as to have led pious Jews to conclude that he was a "blasphemer," having committed sacrilege not only against Israel's God but also against her cultic and legal traditions.

We have already observed that Jesus apparently found himself

83. For this section as a whole I am indebted to Jürgen Moltmann's discussion of "Jesus' Way to the Cross," under the rubrics of "The Blasphemer," "The Agitator" (*Aufrührer*), and "The Godforsaken," in *The Crucified God*, pp. 126–159. My translation of the second of these terms differs from that of the English edition.

in continual conflict with the scribes and Pharisees over the *meaning* of the law—not the law itself, which he came not to "abolish" but to "fulfill" (Matt. 5:17–18). He not only challenged the authority of Moses and the Torah; he also claimed the *authority to forgive sins,* which was viewed as *blasphemy* against God by the pious. After Jesus healed a paralytic in Capernaum, the scribes asked: "Why does this man speak thus? It is blasphemy! Who can forgive sins but God alone?" (Mk. 2:7 par.).[84] Jesus occasioned a "revolution in the concept of God" by portraying God as one who is free from the constraints of law and cult, who does not take revenge upon sinners but forgives them instead, and whose dominant mode of action is not judgment but grace.[85]

This suggests that there existed an opposition to Jesus on religious grounds, traces of which are found in the Gospels. After Jesus healed on the sabbath, we are told that "the Pharisees went out and took counsel against him, how to destroy him" (Matt. 12:14 par.). His telling of the Parable of the Wicked Tenants in Jerusalem evoked the following response, according to the tradition: "The scribes and chief priests tried to lay hands on him at that very hour, but they feared the people; for they perceived that he had told this parable against them" (Lk. 20:19 par.). The specific occasion for the arrest of Jesus was very likely the cleansing of the temple (Mk. 11:15–19 par.; see Sec. 3B above). He was probably seized by agents of the temple priests, as the Synoptists report (Mk. 14:43 par.), rather than by a Roman cohort (Jn. 18:3).[86]

84. The authenticity of this story is under dispute. Bultmann regards vss. 5b–10 as a secondary interpolation in the healing pericope, a construction of the church because it wanted to trace back to Jesus its own right to forgive sins. (*Synoptic Tradition,* pp. 15–16.) Perrin, on the other hand, argues that the eschatological forgiveness of sins was a major aspect of Jesus' proclamation of the kingdom; and he regards the account of the controversy this practice engendered with the scribes, together with the accusation of blasphemy, as essentially corresponding to an aspect of the historical ministry of Jesus, although what Mark gives us is an "ideal" or "typical" scene. (*Rediscovering the Teaching of Jesus,* pp. 139–140.)
85. Moltmann, *The Crucified God,* pp. 128–130, 141–142.
86. So Wilson, *The Execution of Jesus,* pp. 107–110. On the basis of the Johannine account, Cullmann argues that Jesus was a prisoner of the Romans from the beginning, but the evidence appears dubious. See *Jesus and the Revolutionaries,* pp. 33–34.

It is quite clear that a nocturnal trial of Jesus before the San-hedrin, as elaborately reported by Mark (14:53–72), never took place. Modern scholarship has demonstrated that this story is a construction of the Evangelist for theological and political pur-poses. Theologically, it enabled Mark to bring to a climax the themes that run throughout his Gospel: opposition to Jesus, the messianic secret, and the christological titles (Messiah, Son of God, Son of Man) to which Jesus now admits (14:61–62).[87] Politically, it enabled Mark and the Gentile church as a whole to shift the responsibility for Jesus' death away from Pilate and the Romans to the Jewish leaders, and by implication to the Jewish people (cf. Matt. 27:25).[88] This may have been a useful strategy as far as the church's survival in the Roman world was concerned, but at the same time it unleashed the tragic history of Christian anti-Semitism. Historically, what is likely to have happened is that the high priests held a brief informal inquiry for the purpose of preparing an indictment against Jesus to be presented to the Roman governor. We may be fairly confident that the charges were of a political character, since these are the only sort that would have interested the Romans, and because the temple priests were moved to act as much by their own political fears as by Jesus' sacrilegious attitude toward the law, the temple, and religious authority.[89] Perhaps it would be more accurate to say that in the Roman and Jewish worlds of that time religion and politics were inseparably intertwined. A religious "disturbance" such as that occasioned by Jesus could not help but have political conse-quences, and vice versa.[90] Thus it is that the religious freedom proclaimed by Jesus came to be perceived as a threat to the *Pax Romana*.

According to Lk. 23:5, Jesus was accused before Pilate of having "stirred up" the people throughout all Judea. Indeed, he did not

87. The most recent and conclusive study is by John R. Donahue, *Are You the Christ? The Trial Narrative in the Gospel of Mark* (Missoula, Mont.: Society of Biblical Literature, 1973) ; see pp. 99–102, 135–138, 181–186, 236–239.
88. Wilson, *The Execution of Jesus*, pp. 75–84, 117; Brandon, *Jesus and the Zealots*, pp. 221–282, 303–304.
89. Wilson, *The Execution of Jesus*, pp. 125–128.
90. Moltmann, *The Crucified God*, pp. 136, 143–144.

die the death prescribed in Jewish law for blasphemy, namely,
stoning. Rather he died the death prescribed in Roman law for
political agitators against the Roman government, crucifixion.
Crucifixion, the most agonizing of deaths, was a punishment reserved for runaway slaves and for political criminals; it was not
used for general criminal justice. Jesus' execution on Golgotha,
outside the walls of Jerusalem, meant that he died "outside the
camp" (Heb. 13:12–13) and "was reckoned with transgressors"
(Lk. 22:37).[91]

The fact that Pilate was equally if not more threatened by a
non-Zealot disturber of the peace (Jesus) than by an anti-Roman
Zealot leader (Barabbas) indicates, suggests Moltmann, that his
condemnation of Jesus as an "agitator" against the *Pax Romana*
was not based just on a "misunderstanding" of Jesus, as Bultmann
has claimed.[92] Jesus' freedom and his proclamation of the grace
of God challenged not only Pharisees and Zealots but also the
religious-cultic and religious-political foundations of the Roman
Empire; it called into question the primitive notion of justice
shared by all parties, namely, justice based on retribution, revenge,
punishment, divine sanctions and prohibitions. Pilate did mis-
understand Jesus in the immediate sense of assuming that he was
a Zealot agitator who would stir up the people. But in the deeper
sense of Jesus' calling into question the *Pax Romana* with its gods
and laws, Pilate understood him correctly. The allegiance to a
"crucified God" on the part of the early Christians contained an
overt political meaning. Their denial of emperor worship in the
name of the God who was crucified at the hands of the authorities
made them martyrs in a political as well as a religious sense; it
made them agitators against the gods in heaven as well as against
the political gods on earth. Jesus had the effect of breaking up the
religious-political "game"—the game of using divine judgment as a

91. Cf. ibid., p. 136; Moltmann, "Political Theology," *Theology Today*, 28: 15–16.
92. Rudolf Bultmann, "The Primitive Christian Kerygma and the Historical Jesus,"
in *The Historical Jesus and the Kerygmatic Christ*, ed. and trans. Carl Braaten and
Roy Harrisville (Nashville: Abingdon Press, 1964), p. 24.

legitimation of political force—and therefore he "had to be" done away with.[93]

Hence Pilate sentenced Jesus to death because he was quite prepared to believe him actually guilty of the political crimes of which he was accused by the Sanhedrin: "We found this man perverting our nation, and forbidding us to give tribute to Caesar, saying that he himself is Christ a king" (Lk. 23:2). Nor were these charges entirely false. The "perverting" of the people could reflect Jesus' challenge to the authority of the Torah, his forgiveness of sins, and his cleansing of the temple; while the prohibition against paying taxes to Caesar is a valid way of interpreting the saying, "Render to Caesar the things that are Caesar's, and to God the things that are God's" (Mk. 12:17 par.).[94] Finally, it is quite possible that both friends and enemies of Jesus *believed* him to be the Messiah—on the basis of the authority of his teaching, his charismatic power, his challenge to the tradition of Moses and the Torah, and his actions in Jerusalem—without his ever having claimed or acknowledged a messianic role. That Pilate believed him to be guilty of political crimes—above all, the seditious claim to Jewish kingship—tends to be confirmed by the title on the cross, which stated the charge against him, "Jesus of Nazareth, King of the Jews" *(INRI)*, as reported in all the Gospels (Mk. 15:26 par.; Jn. 19:19).[95] Some scholars have argued that the title is a creation of the Evangelists to support Christian belief in Jesus' messiahship;[96] but this seems unlikely because of the politically damaging character of the inscription, and because such an addition would

93. Moltmann, *The Crucified God*, pp. 137, 143–144.
94. Brandon suggests that this saying is not to be taken as advocating the payment of tribute money but just the opposite. For it was presupposed that the land of Israel and its resources (including its wealth) belong to God, not Caesar. Hence only those engaged in making profit with Caesar's money—i.e., the Jewish aristocracy—owe him tribute. See *Jesus and the Zealots*, pp. 345–348.
95. Cf. Wilson, *The Execution of Jesus*, pp. 130–136 (I do not accept Wilson's argument, however, that Jesus claimed a messianic role before the Sanhedrin and Pilate); Brandon, *Jesus and the Zealots*, p. 382; Moltmann, *The Crucified God*, p. 137.
96. So Herbert Braun, *Jesus* (Stuttgart: Kreuz-Verlag, 1969), pp. 50–51; Hans Conzelmann, "Historie und Theologie in den synoptischen Passionsberichten," in *Zur Bedeutung des Todes Jesu*, ed. Fritz Viering (Gütersloh: Gütersloher Verlagshaus Gerd Mohn, 1967), p. 48; Bultmann, *Synoptic Tradition*, pp. 272–273, 284.

have run counter to attempts by early Christians to depoliticize their faith in order to survive in the Roman world, especially if there had been no historical evidence of Jesus' having been tried and executed on political grounds.

B. Jesus' Cry of God-Forsakenness and the Identity of God

"The death of Socrates was a celebration of freedom" (R. Guardini).[97] Martyrs of all ages have died in the certainty that they represented a just cause and would receive an eternal reward. Both those who rebel against death in a defiant claim of immortality, and those who come to terms with it as human existence's own most distinctive possibility, experience death as a road to freedom.

But it was not so for Jesus. As Moltmann aptly puts it, his was not a "beautiful death." [98] This is true not only because crucifixion is one of the most agonizing and brutal forms of execution imaginable. It is also likely that Jesus faced his death with fear and trembling, doubt and sorrow, perhaps weakness and vacillation, as reflected by the scene in Gethsemane (Mk. 14:33–38 par.). According to ancient tradition, he died with "loud cries and tears" (Heb. 5:7), with a loud, inarticulate cry (Mk. 15:37 par.). Indeed, according to Mark and Matthew, the dying Jesus cried out with the words of Ps. 22:1, *"Eloi, Eloi, lama sabachthani*, My God, my God, why hast thou forsaken me?" (Mk. 15:34 par.). Scholars are divided as to the authenticity of this passage.[99] But even those who regard it as a product of early Christian tradition still believe that it represents an interpretation of one aspect of the historical reality of the death of Jesus, namely, that he "cried out" when he died. For it is difficult to believe that the early community would have created without any historical justification a tradition so

---

97. Quoted by Moltmann, *The Crucified God*, p. 145 (translation altered).
98. Ibid., pp. 146–147. The English text translates "schöner Tod" as "fine death."
99. Ellen Flesseman-van Leer supports its authenticity on the grounds that it is inconsistent with the stereotyped pattern by which the Evangelists have elsewhere introduced citations from the Psalms into the passion narrative, and that therefore it represents a historical kernel which legitimated the inclusion of other passages from Psalm 22 and other Psalms. "Die Interpretation der Passionsgeschichte vom Alten Testament aus," in *Zur Bedeutung des Todes Jesu*, pp. 79–95. Hartmut Gese argues that all the citations from Psalm 22 are constructions of the Evangelists. "Psalm 22 und das Neue Testament," *Zeitschrift für Theologie und Kirche*, 65 (April 1968): 1–22.

difficult to explain and so christologically embarrassing. The citation of Ps. 22:1 would be an attempt to interpret the death-cry of
Jesus by placing it in the context of an ultimate song of praise
(Ps. 22:19 ff.). Even so, attempts were made in the Western texts
and by the church fathers to modify this tradition, explain it away,
or deny it outright.

Jesus may have experienced (if not actually enunciated) the
abandonment of God at the moment of death in peculiarly acute
form just because his life had been lived in extraordinary immediacy to God. He had proclaimed the saving nearness of God's
kingdom and often spoke of God in familiar terms as "my Father."
To be abandoned by God in the full awareness of the gracious
nearness of God, and to be delivered up to the death of a criminal,
is the torture of hell; indeed Luther interpreted the tradition of
Christ's descent into hell as referring to his death in God-forsakenness. Hence in the cry it is not so much Jesus' personal existence
that is at stake but his theological existence, his whole proclamation of God as the one who is near in mercy. The divinity of God
and the fatherhood of the Father are at stake. God himself is
crucified in the death of the one who proclaimed the nearness of
God and lived in the immediate presence of God. Thus Moltmann suggests that Jesus' cry *also* means, "My God, my God, why
hast thou abandoned *thyself?*" God himself is on trial, is questioned, is seemingly at odds with himself in allowing Jesus to die
in this way. The crucifixion of Jesus demands a "revolution in
the concept of God." Either the God-concept itself must be
abandoned, or it must be discovered that only a "crucified God"
can overcome the power of death.[100]

Jesus himself did not answer this question. He clearly recognized that death itself cannot be a road to freedom. He refused to
venerate death in place of God, and in this paradoxical sense remained faithful to God even in the cry of God-forsakenness.[101]
But his life ended without excluding the possibility that there is
no road to freedom. The only possible source of true liberation

100. Moltmann, *The Crucified God*, pp. 147–153.
101. I have so interpreted the cry in *Jesus—Word and Presence*, pp. 211–214.

from death (and by implication from the other forms of bondage as well) must be God himself. But who and where is this God?

The answer of Christian faith is that God was there—in the depths of God-forsaken humanity, in the anguish of death, in the humiliation of crucifixion, in the sinfulness of a despairing death-cry. "The crucified God" does not actually *die;* rather he *suffers the death* of the dying Son.[102] Actual death can be experienced only indirectly: one experiences only one's own *dying,* not one's own *death.* One must remain alive in order to *experience* death, which is an all-the-more agonizing experience just because it is not one's own death but the death of another whom one loves. It was "necessary" that God experience this agony, that he suffer and undergo the death experience in the dying of his "beloved Son," that he share this final bondage of human existence—for only that which is suffered and undergone can also be overcome. God can negate the negative only if he takes the negative into or upon his very being, overcoming it there, transforming its negation into affirmation, its deadliness into life, its abandonment into communion. God suffers death—not to let death prevail, but to prevail over it, to liberate from it.[103]

This is of course already the meaning of faith in the resurrection from the dead. Hence the answer to the question, "Who and where was God in the death of Jesus?", points to a double identity. God is not only *the crucified God,* the one who suffers the death of his Son; he is also *the life-giving God,* the one "who gives life to the dead and calls into existence the things that do not exist" (Rom. 4:17).[104] In this double identity, God is *the liberating God, the God of freedom.* Primitive Christian faith had its origin in the experience that Jesus, having died, was not abandoned to death by God, but was raised from the dead, thereby gaining victory over death, entering *into* the final presence of God,

---

102. See Moltmann, *The Crucified God,* p. 243; cf. pp. 190–196, 242–246.
103. For a fuller development of this argument, see my *Jesus—Word and Presence,* pp. 214–217, 254–258.
104. Moltmann points to this double identification of God in primitive Christian tradition. *The Crucified God,* pp. 187–196.

entering *upon* his death-destroying work as the exalted Lord. The resurrection was both the vindication of Jesus by God—the vindication of Jesus' claim that God was near and gracious—and the empowerment of Jesus as the agent of God's liberating power in the world. For the risen Jesus was and still is experienced not as remote and inaccessible, but as present and active, calling and leading into a mission of freedom. The explication of this theme requires a transition from the historical figure of Jesus to the risen Christ, i.e., from "Jesus the Liberator" to "The Dialectics of Liberation," the next chapter. By way of approaching this transition I shall first consider, in the concluding section of this chapter, the liberation theologies of Paul and John.

5. SALVATION AS LIBERATION FOR PAUL AND JOHN

Thus far our discussion has drawn primarily upon material from the Synoptic Gospels in order to portray Jesus' radical freedom, his gospel of liberation, and questions about freedom raised by his death. But the two most creative theologians of the New Testament are the Apostle Paul and the anonymous author of the Gospel of John. Although they do not provide much information about Jesus that can be verified historically, they interpret the events comprising his life, death, and resurrection in a way that has decisively shaped the whole of subsequent Christian thought. It is not without interest that both Paul and John understand *salvation to mean liberation,* and they do so in formally similar ways, even though their specific concepts and outlooks are quite different. Of course they both use other symbols as well to express the meaning of the salvation event, but freedom (or liberation) is one of the basic symbols and can be used to integrate the others, thereby permitting the "construction" of a unified picture of both the Pauline and the Johannine theologies. For Paul, liberation is defined negatively as *redemption* from bondage and positively as self-divesting, upbuilding *love;* for John, it is defined as *unconcealment* of the truth and as eternal *life.*

A. Paul: Redemption and Love

We have already noted that "freedom" is a distinctively Pauline concept in the New Testament (since twenty-six of the forty-one occurrences of *eleutheria* are found in the Pauline corpus). Indeed, Paul was "an apostle of freedom" (1 Corinthians 9; Galatians 2). He had to defend the freedom of his apostleship against the Jerusalem Christians, who wanted to circumcise his Greek companions (Gal. 2:4–5), and to reaffirm it when confronted by the license of the Corinthian enthusiasts (1 Cor. 9:1, 19; 10:29). He was put in chains by the Romans on charges brought against him by the Jews, who were angered by his freedom from the law, and he probably died a political prisoner in Rome. Thus freedom was an intensely personal matter. It was also the central theme of his theology. At the same time, Paul was not entirely consistent when it came to the practice of freedom. Given the eschatological, apolitical character of his theology, he tended to be ambiguous about or even indifferent toward the political oppression of the Roman Empire, the institution of slavery, and the traditional subordination of women (while insisting upon the full freedom and equality of slaves and women within the eschatological community of faith).[105]

Käsemann has familiarized us with the fact that a conflict over the meaning of freedom and salvation existed in the early church. In its most extreme form, the conflict pitted the legalism of the Palestinian Jewish Christians against the libertinism of the Hellenistic Gentile Christians.[106] Paul was caught in the midst of this struggle and sought to define the meaning of "liberation." In this polemical context, his definition gained both a negative and a positive component. Against the legalists, Paul argued that Christ has indeed purchased our freedom (or "redeemed" us) from every form of bondage; against the enthusiasts, he argued that true freedom entails not only a divestment of self but also imposes a higher

---

105. I have discussed this matter above, pp. 199–202, and will not further consider it here.
106. Käsemann, *Jesus Means Freedom*, chaps. 2, 3; "The Beginnings of Christian Theology" and "On the Topic of Primitive Christian Apocalyptic," in *Journal for Theology and the Church*, 6 (New York: Herder & Herder, 1969): 17–46, 99–133.

law, that of love, whose purpose is to build up an integrated human community "in Christ."

The conceptuality and language of "redemption" do not occur frequently in Paul. *Apolutrōsis* ("redemption") is used in Rom. 3:24 (where it is directly associated with the expiatory sacrifice of Christ) and in Rom. 8:23; 1 Cor. 1:30. The image of a financial transaction is more clearly present in *(ex)agorazein,* a verb meaning "to redeem" in the sense of "to ransom," "to purchase or buy back one's freedom," which Paul uses in 1 Cor. 6:20; 7:23; Gal. 3:13; 4:5. The price is paid to the "powers" that hold humankind in thralldom, whether "heavenly" or "earthly," or to the law. Thus the term redemption can serve to stress the political significance of the work of Christ, as in 1 Cor. 7:23: "You were bought with a price; do not become slaves of men"—in other words, you have been set free from the established power structure because Christ has paid its price by his own death. Or it can be used as a counter-argument against the legalistic interpretation of salvation: *God* has paid the price for our sin through the death of Christ, freeing us thereby from the demand (or the price) of the law, which, when used as a means of attaining salvation, becomes a "curse," a form of bondage. This meaning is expressed in Gal. 4:5 and especially 3:13: "Christ redeemed us from the curse of the law, having become a curse for us." With the terms *apolutrōsis* and *exagorazein* Paul has taken over imagery from the cultic-juridical tradition, both Jewish and Hellenistic. The way that he uses these terms, however, breaks the entire framework in which freedom is won by meeting certain cultic or juridical conditions (offering a sacrifice, paying a debt, etc.). Hence it is not surprising that these terms play a secondary role in Paul's theology, although they have been inflated into terms of major significance for Christian piety, which tends therefore to overlook the way that Paul radicalized these concepts and then left them behind.[107]

The characteristic term for Paul is not "redemption" but "free-

---

107. Cf. Käsemann, "The Saving Significance of the Death of Jesus in Paul," in *Perspectives on Paul,* trans. Margaret Kohl (Philadelphia: Fortress Press, 1971), pp. 42–45; and Bultmann, *Theology of the New Testament,* I, 295–298.

dom" or "liberation" *(eleutheria)*,[108] which is used in both the
negative and the positive senses mentioned earlier. Negatively,
it means liberation from sin, law, death, and the powers (Rom.
6:18, 22; 7:3; 8:2; 1 Cor. 7:21–22, 39), thereby functioning as a
substitute for *apolutrōsis* and *exagorazein* that is free from cultic
and legalistic overtones. The transition from the negative to the
positive sense, and the beginning of the distinctively Pauline
theology of freedom, occurs in the great statement of Rom. 8:21:
". . . the creation itself will be set free from its bondage to decay
and obtain the glorious freedom of the children of God." (Rom.
8:23 makes it clear that this "liberation" is precisely the meaning
of "redemption.") The same imagery, which associates freedom
with a renewed relationship of creaturely human beings as "children" to the Creator God, recurs in Gal. 4:22–31, where Paul
concludes that "we are not children of the slave but of the free
woman"—Sarah, who symbolizes the true covenant and the new
Jerusalem. Here Paul has taken over and transfigured the conventional meaning of freedom as found in the Hellenistic world.
Freedom entails, to be sure, participation in a free or liberated
community—the *polis* for classical Greece, the family of a free man
or woman for both Romans and Greeks. But the free community
of which Paul speaks—the new Jerusalem—is no longer restricted,
exclusivistic, alienated; it is not based on blood, sex, race, inheritance, or property. It is rather based on the fact that all human
beings are *children of God*—children of the one Lord who clears
the earth of enthralling idols and sets his people free. We are
"children of freedom," not merely *"sons* of freedom" (cf. Matt.
17:26; Jn. 8:35), although our freedom is based on that of "the
Son." [109]

This freedom of the children of God is now viewed as an end
in itself rather than merely as a means to an end: *"For freedom
Christ has set us free"* (Gal. 5:1; cf. 2:4). Such freedom represents precisely the perpetuation of Jesus' radical freedom, which

108. Käsemann, *Perspectives on Paul*, p. 44. On Paul's interpretation of *eleutheria*,
see Leander Keck, "The Son Who Creates Freedom," *Concilium*, 93: 72–76.
109. See above, pp. 50–51. Cf. also the analysis of Matt. 17:25b–26 in n. 54. My
earlier study of black liberation makes use of the image "children of freedom."

becomes the property of all of God's children through his death and resurrection from the dead. Not only did Jesus' death result from the radical freedom with which he questioned and opposed the established orders, but also it climaxed his open, obedient, faithful sonship to God (Rom. 5:12–19; Phil. 2:8), whereby the disrupted relationship between creature and Creator was set right. The cross is his act of freedom par excellence; it is also the mediating link between the "radical freedom" of Jesus and the "glorious freedom of the children of God."

If liberation is linked to the death of Jesus (non-cultically and non-juridically), then freedom is gained precisely in the surrender of it—which is just the opposite of Adam, who lost his freedom by the attempt to seize it. This contrast is the central theme of the Christ-hymn in Phil. 2:5–11, which Paul adopted from the Hellenistic Christian community. Just as the essence of sin is idolatry, by which freedom is lost, so the essence of salvation is self-divesting love, by which freedom is gained. Unlike Adam, who was tempted to become "like God" (Gen. 3:5), Christ "did not count equality with God a thing to be grasped, but emptied himself, taking the form of a servant. . . . He humbled himself and became obedient unto death, even death on a cross" (Phil. 2:6–8). He did not take his *imago Dei* into claim for himself, perverting it thereby into a *sicut Deus*. He remained the Son because he divested himself of the rights of sonship; he gained his life by giving it up; he became free through obedience unto death, the final bondage. Hence the paradoxical relation between freedom and slavery, epitomized by 1 Cor. 7:22: slaves become free in Christ, those who are free become slaves of Christ.[110]

The self-surrender of Jesus, by which he gains his freedom, is the central meaning of *love* according to Paul (Gal. 1:4, 2:20; 2 Cor. 5:14–15). By means of the category of love, Paul appropriates and transforms the oldest of soteriological categories, the substitutionary formula, which has its roots in the Jewish expiation the-

110. Cf. Niederwimmer, *Der Begriff der Freiheit im Neuen Testament*, pp. 169–170; Käsemann, "A Critical Analysis of Philippians 2:5–11," *Journal for Theology and the Church*, 5 (New York: Harper & Row, 1968): 45–88; and Bultmann, *Theology of the New Testament*, I, 331–332.

ology.[111] It is not that one sacrifice substitutes for another, thus fulfilling the law's requirement of punishment. It is rather that Christ sets right the relationship between Creator and creature by means of his love "for others" even "unto death" (cf. Rom. 5:6–8; 14:15; 2 Cor. 5:14). *God* is loved, and all the commandments of the law are fulfilled, by loving one's neighbor as oneself (see Gal. 5:14 and especially Rom. 13:8–10, where the saying of Jesus in Matt. 19:18–19 is repeated almost verbatim).

If self-divesting love is the means by which the creation is "set free," then love is also the means by which the "freedom of the children of God" is sustained. Such freedom is not boundless, unstructured, libertinistic. Freedom has a structure, but it is not defined by the old law. Rather it is a new law, "the law of the Spirit of life in Christ Jesus" (Rom. 8:2; cf. 1 Cor. 9:21; Gal. 6:2), a liberating law ("where the Spirit of the Lord is, there is freedom," 2 Cor. 3:17), a law of love and freedom: "For you were called to freedom, brethren; only do not use your freedom as an opportunity for the flesh, but through love be servants of one another. For the whole law is fulfilled in one word, 'You shall love your neighbor as yourself' " (Gal. 5:13–14).[112] Love—the *nova lex,* the *nova oboedientia*—defines the structures of life in freedom, whereas duty defines the structures of life under bondage. Here, then, the link between law and freedom—which we have seen to be indispensable for the Greek world, but modified by Hebraic religion and radically dissolved by Paul, for whom the law had become a form of bondage—is reestablished at a higher level. There is no freedom without law, but the law in question is that of liberating love.

111. Käsemann, *Perspectives on Paul,* pp. 39–40, 42–43.
112. The expressions "law of love" and "law of freedom" do not actually occur in Paul, but the meaning is present in the passages cited. The expression "law of freedom" (*nomos tēs eleutherias*) is found in James 1:25; 2:12. See Martin Dibelius's commentary on this expression in *Der Brief des Jakobus* (7th ed.; Göttingen: Vandenhoeck & Ruprecht, 1921), pp. 110–113; also Käsemann, *Jesus Means Freedom,* pp. 86 ff. It most likely is of pre-Christian origin, both Stoic and Jewish. In James and the other Pastoral Epistles freedom has lost its Pauline radicalism and (in Käsemann's words, ibid., p. 99) has been domesticated or "churchified." On the Pauline understanding of the relation between law, freedom, and love, see Käsemann, ibid., chap. 3; Niederwimmer, *Der Begriff der Freiheit,* pp. 172–173; Bultmann, *Theology of the New Testament,* I, 336–337, 340–345.

Above all, this is a love that is upbuilding, that creates community, that dissolves a rampant, idolatrous, licentious individualism (cf. Gal. 5:13–26). The structure that love creates is that of a unified, liberated community—the one body of Christ—in which diversity is celebrated at the same time that all human differences are relativized (1 Cor. 12:4–13; cf. Eph. 4:1–16). In this community "there is neither Jew nor Greek, there is neither slave nor free; there is neither male nor female; for you are all one in Christ Jesus" (Gal. 3:28; cf. Col. 3:11). To be sure this is an eschatological community, and therefore part of the meaning of freedom for Paul is to be open for the future, letting oneself be determined by it rather than by the bondage of established structures; the Spirit that gives freedom (2 Cor. 3:17) and constitutes communion is (in Bultmann's words) "the power of futurity." [113] At the same time it is a reality that impinges upon the present, demanding of both Jew and Greek, slave and master, male and female, a fundamental, liberating alteration in human relationships so that all may become children of freedom. If Paul ultimately was reticent about drawing conclusions from this for the transformation of present social structures because of his expectation of the imminent end of history, we should not be.

B. JOHN: UNCONCEALMENT AND LIFE

Terms for "freedom" (derivatives of *eleutheria*) occur only four times in the Gospel of John (8:31–36), but the theme of freedom is nonetheless important for the theology and Christology of the Fourth Gospel. By means of this passage freedom is linked with other central Johannine symbols. Jesus is the *Revealer* whose means of *revelation* are his *words* (5:25; 8:38; 17:13–14). His revelation discloses the *truth* (8:31–32); and the truth brings about *freedom* (8:32)—above all, freedom from the bondage of sin, a freedom of the sons of God (8:33–36). The freedom to which we are set free by truth is ultimately identical with *life* (14:6); and Jesus, as the Revealer, is the *way* to both (14:6). Our

113. Bultmann, *Theology of the New Testament*, I, 335; cf. 330–340.

task now is to understand the connection between the *Revealer* (or "way"), *revelation, word, truth, freedom,* and *life.* The central Johannine theological symbols tend to be interchangeable; all are approximations at describing the underlying mystery of God's saving revelation in the world. Still, there is a certain progression or logical connection between them. If we wish to construct a Johannine theology of liberation, we may suggest that for John, as for Paul, liberation assumes both negative and positive forms. Negatively, it means *unconcealment* or *truth* (in the sense of unveiling, *alētheia*), i.e., liberation *from* the bondage of falsehood or darkness. Positively, it means freedom for life ("eternal life"), which is probably the most encompassing Johannine term for *salvation.* Viewed this way, the concept of freedom stands at the crux of Johannine theology, interrelating a number of symbols, although in quite a different fashion than for Paul.[114]

Jesus as the "Revealer" is the bearer of the truth that sets us free; in this sense he is the "Liberator." Thus liberation has a christological focus for John. The Christology of the Gospel is set forth in the discourses, where Jesus identifies himself as the one sent from God to bring light, truth, and life into the world (e.g., 5:19–47, and the Farewell Discourses, chs. 14–17). The means by which he reveals or liberates are his words, e.g., 5:24: "Truly, truly, I say to you, he who hears my word and believes him who sent me has eternal life." Words are the characteristic mode of Jesus' saving action in the world (cf. 8:28, 38, 43; 14:10; 15:22; 17:8, 14). The identity of his work and his word can be seen from the effect of the word: it bestows life (5:24; 6:68; 8:51) and freedom (8:31–32), it cleanses (15:3), it judges (12:47–48).[115] In 8:35–36 the Evangelist explicitly connects Jesus with the work of

---

114. On Jn. 8:31–36, see Rudolf Bultmann, *The Gospel of John,* trans. G. R. Beasley-Murray, et al. (Philadelphia: Westminster Press, 1971), pp. 433–437, 441; C. K. Barrett, *The Gospel according to St. John* (London: SPCK, 1956), pp. 285, 382; E. C. Hoskyns, *The Fourth Gospel,* ed. F. N. Davey (2d ed., London: Faber and Faber, 1947), pp. 337–340; Frederick Herzog, *Liberation Theology: Liberation in the Light of the Fourth Gospel* (New York: Seabury Press, 1972), p. 125; and Keck, "The Son Who Creates Freedom," pp. 76–77.

115. Cf. Rudolf Bultmann, *Theology of the New Testament,* vol. II, trans. Kendrick Grobel (New York: Scribner's, 1955), pp. 59–64.

liberation. Vs. 35 according to Bultmann may originally have been a parabolic saying of Jesus: "The slave has no permanent standing in the household, but the son belongs to it for ever" (NEB). But vs. 36 shows that the Evangelist intends that the "son" of vs. 35 be understood as Jesus himself: "If then the Son sets you free, you will indeed be free" (NEB).[116] Jesus is the Son who both "belongs for ever" and "sets [us] free"; he is both the "truth and the life" and the "way" (14:6).[117]

Is this Jesus a real human figure? According to Bultmann, the theme of the Gospel is "the word became flesh" (1:14a). Against the Gnostics, whose redeemer mythology the Evangelist has borrowed, it is necessary to stress the genuine humanity or "fleshly" character of the incarnate Logos.[118] Perhaps one may agree with Herzog, in referring to Jesus' statement concerning the "temple of his body" (2:21), that "the body is the proper context of freedom, man's entrance to a public space where he knows liberation." [119]

Against this, Käsemann contends that the real theme of the Gospel is found at 1:14b: "we saw his glory, such glory as befits the Father's only Son, full of grace and truth" (NEB). This is the glory of divinity, and therefore the Johannine Christ is docetic, "a god going about on earth." [120] Although there certainly are evidences of a *theios anēr* Christology in John, most scholars regard Käsemann's thesis as overstated. What sort of "glory" is this? What does "glory" symbolize? It might be suggested that the *glory* of the incarnate word of God is precisely the radical *freedom* of Jesus. The connection between freedom and glory is drawn

116. Bultmann, *The Gospel of John*, p. 440. Here there occurs the same connection between sonship and freedom as that reflected in Matt. 17:26: if the kings of the earth take tribute from "others," "then the sons are free" (see n. 54). Are these Johannine and Matthean fragments conceivably from the same lost parable?
117. Ibid., pp. 605–606.
118. Bultmann, *Theology of the New Testament*, II, 40–41; *The Gospel of John*, pp. 60–66.
119. Herzog, *Liberation Theology*, p. 59.
120. Ernst Käsemann, *The Testament of Jesus: A Study of the Gospel of John in the Light of Chapter 17*, trans. Gerhard Krodel (Philadelphia: Fortress Press, 1968), p. 9.

by Paul, who (to translate more literally) speaks of "the freedom of the glory *(eleutherian tēs doxēs)* of the children of God" (Rom. 8:21). Freedom is the essence of divinity, to be sure, but it is also the image of God in humanity. It is precisely Jesus' freedom that manifests the divine glory—a sovereign, transcendent freedom by which he overcomes the powers of bondage and darkness, bringing the light of truth to bear upon the falsity of the world, setting human beings free for unoppressed life (it is the miraculous "signs" of life—wine, water, healing, bread, raising from the dead —that reveal Jesus' glory, 2:11); a freedom that provokes the intention of Jesus' enemies to kill him (8:37).[121] To be sure, this portrait of Jesus is constructed by the Evangelist; but it need not be construed docetically, and it is not so far removed from the *exousia* or authoritative freedom of Jesus to which the Synoptic Gospels bear testimony.

Negatively, I have said, liberation means *unconcealment* or *truth* for the Fourth Gospel. The thematic statement occurs in 8:32: *"the truth will set you free"* (NEB). Truth *(a-lētheia)* means un-veiling, un-concealment, re-velation. The truth sets us free from the bondage of falsehood by unconcealing it, disclosing it for what it is, bringing the light to bear upon it. The truth about the falsehood of the world is the delusion that it can exist for and from itself, apart from God. This falsehood leads into bondage, the bondage of sin. In 8:34–36 sin is defined precisely as slavery, the loss of freedom consequent upon the world's self-deception.[122] In John a demythologization of the Devil has already occurred. He is not a supernatural person but human self-deception objectified and disguised: "When [the Devil] tells a lie he is speaking his own language, for he is a liar and the father of lies" (8:44, NEB).

---

121. Cf. Bultmann, *The Gospel of John,* pp. 67–72, 442–443; Herzog, *Liberation Theology,* pp. 39, 55–56. On *doxa,* see *Theological Dictionary of the New Testament,* ed. Gerhard Kittel, trans. G. W. Bromiley (Grand Rapids: Eerdmans, 1964), II, 233–252. On the connection between glory and freedom in Paul, see below, p.
122. Cf. Bultmann, *Theology of the New Testament,* II, 16, 27; *The Gospel of John,* pp. 438–439; Herzog, *Liberation Theology,* p. 128; C. H. Dodd, *The Interpretation of the Fourth Gospel* (Cambridge: Cambridge University Press, 1955), pp. 170–178.

Positively, liberation issues in *life (zōē):* "*I am the way, and the truth, and the life*" (14:6). "Life," says Bultmann, "is the redemptive good that is striven for"—not only in the Fourth Gospel, but also for Paul, indeed for biblical religion as a whole. But "life" becomes a special theme for John because it is precisely life that seems to be so lacking from this world, which has fallen into the bondage of death.[123] For this reason, John speaks of "life" as "eternal life" *(zōē aiōnios);* the terms are interchangeable. But to avoid the suggestion that this is an unearthly, heavenly, future life having nothing to do with the present quality of human existence, the term *zōē aiōnios* may be translated hermeneutically as "free life" [124]—i.e., life set free from this aeon's bondage to death.

"Life" characterizes the freedom of the *individual* who has been set free from the bondage of illusion and death. "God loved the world so much that he gave his only Son, that every individual who has faith in him may not die but have free life" (3:16, NEB paraphrased). "In very truth, any person who gives heed to what I say and puts his trust in him who sent me has hold of free life, and does not come up for judgment, but has already passed from death to life" (5:24–25, NEB paraphrased). In this sense, "life" is a way of designating symbolically what I have called *subjective freedom:* it is the freedom of subjectivity, of selfhood, the freedom to live as an authentic human person. Bultmann puts it existentially: "Life is for a man the illumination of existence in that authentic self-understanding that knows God as its Creator." [125] One could express it in a more contemporary idiom by saying that life entails a "liberation of consciousness" or "consciousness-raising." [126] At the same time, this is clearly a non-privatistic, non-autonomous subjectivity. It is non-privatistic because the Fourth Gospel portrays Jesus as drawing human beings out of privacy and isolation into a corporate selfhood; and it is non-autonomous because free

123. Bultmann, *Theology of the New Testament,* II, 11.
124. Herzog suggests "prevailing life" or "unoppressed life" as paraphrases of *zōē aiōnios* in *Liberation Theology,* pp. 70, 74, 107. I think "free life" comes closer to the actual intention of the symbol.
125. Bultmann, *The Gospel of John,* p. 435.
126. Cf. Herzog, *Liberation Theology,* p. 46.

life is purely the eschatological gift of God, which must be received in a stance of faith or openness.   In both respects, Jesus himself serves as the model.[127]

The famous "signs" of the Fourth Gospel, which the Evangelist has undoubtedly derived in some form from an earlier source,[128] are all *signs of life,* serving as "proof" that Jesus is the giver of life, the one who sets us free to live: the miracle at Cana (2:1–12); the gift of "living water" (4:7–26, especially 10, 14); the healing miracles (4:46–54; 5:1–9; 9:1–7); the multiplication of the bread, coupled with the saying, "I am the bread of life" (6:1–24, 35); and above all the raising of Lazarus from the dead (11:1–44), which anticipates Jesus' own resurrection (20:1–29).   In the context of the raising of Lazarus there occurs what might be taken as the central thematic statement of the Gospel.   Martha says that she knows her brother will rise again "in the resurrection at the last day."   But Jesus replies, "*I am* the resurrection and the life; he who believes in me, though he dies, yet shall he live, and whoever lives and believes in me shall never die" (11:24–26).   Resurrection is removed from the context of the apocalyptic expectation of the last days and is associated with the present life of Jesus: he is already "the resurrection" because of his radical openness to the Father, his corporate selfhood, and the saving, life-giving power of his personal presence.   It is the eschatological possibility made present and actual in the figure of the Liberator.[129]

127. I return to "life" as a symbol of subjective freedom, especially in its non-privatistic and non-autonomous aspects as portrayed by the Johannine theology, in Chap. VII, Sec. 4.
128. For recent discussion, see Robert Fortna, *The Gospel of Signs* (Cambridge: Cambridge University Press, 1970) ; and W. Nicol, *The Sēmeia in the Fourth Gospel* (Leiden: Brill, 1972) .
129. Cf. Bultmann, *The Gospel of John,* pp. 402–404; Herzog, *Liberation Theology,* pp. 247–249.

Chapter VI

The Dialectics of Liberation

1. THE ACTUALIZATION OF THE FREEDOM ENGENDERED BY JESUS

The freedom engendered by Jesus meant openness to God's future, by whose coming human beings would be liberated from oppressions of the past and gathered into a new self-identity, both individually and socially. Such freedom undoubtedly entails an inner, personal, psychic liberation: regardless of his external circumstances, Jesus was a radically free person. In this regard Christianity has found itself in accord with the Stoics and with Freud, with existentialism and the counter culture; and Paul was able to formulate his paradox that the slave is a free man (in Christ), and the free man a slave (of Christ).

But it is an unfortunate mistake to leave the matter there, as Paul tended to do and with him much of Christianity. Christians, like Stoics and Gnostics, retreated from the task of political revolution and social responsibility. Primitive Christianity could have benefited from an understanding of the political freedom that prevailed in the Greek city-states, and modern Christians could benefit from Marx's passionate recognition that without a revolution of structures nothing will really change—at least, not very much. The validity of Marx's insight is supported in a negative way by the fact that experimentation in psychic liberation meets with no real resistance in Christian churches, while strategies for social and political transformation are often considered anathema, and certainly not the business of religion and the churches. In other words, psychology is perceived as both personally beneficial and relatively harmless, whereas objective structural changes are likely to jeopardize underlying economic, social, and class interests.

We must not forget that Jesus was not only a radically free person. He also practiced a ministry of liberation, confronting thereby the bondage of disease and poverty, personal guilt and sin, religious and moral legalism, social injustice, patriarchal structures of authority, and economic and political exploitation. The kingdom that he proclaimed, whatever *more* it may be, is *at least* a political and historical symbol.

"Liberation" may be defined as "the actualization of freedom." For the reasons just indicated, when one asks how the freedom engendered by Jesus is to be actualized, made a concrete and efficacious reality for humankind as a whole, the answer must be framed in terms of the dialectics of the historical process, which includes *socioeconomic* and *political* as well as *personal* and *psychic* dimensions. I propose to address the question of actualization on two levels, one being a general theory of the historical-political-psychological process of liberation, the other representing an explicitly theological interpretation of the actualization of freedom. With regard to the historical process, I shall argue that freedom is actualized *both* as a goal to be accomplished by the human struggle for emancipation in the arenas of consciousness and politics (here the individual, subjective, psychic aspect of liberation is not ignored but included as a dimension within the historical), *and* as the advent of redemptive power, the inbreaking of the new over which persons have no control. The possibilities for freedom immanent in history become the bearers of the new birth of freedom as the liberating power of the future. According to Christian faith, the latter is understood to be the power of *God*, mediated in history through the agency of the *crucified and risen Jesus.* For Christians, the resurrection of Jesus from the dead is the energizing force in the dialectics of emancipation and redemption by which liberation occurs historically. The coming of the kingdom of freedom, and liberation from sin and death, law and the powers, are the work of the risen Jesus, who is now the agent of what he once proclaimed.

2. LIBERATION AND THE DIALECTICS OF HISTORY

A. THE PROBLEM OF MEANING IN HISTORY

The thesis I propose to argue in this section is that the process of human liberation constitutes the meaning of history. But is it legitimate to speak of the "meaning" of history at all? From what vantage point could one discern a universal process of history, which might conceivably furnish a context of meaning for individual events?

The basic reality of history appears to be its *ambiguity,* as Paul Ricoeur points out.[1] This ambiguity shows itself in many ways. On the one hand, there is undoubtedly a progressive accumulation of knowledge, technique, tools and instruments in history; but on the other, great civilizations rise and fall. This paradox engenders the ambiguity of progress versus crisis, of rationality versus irrationality. On the one hand, the underlying tendencies and unifying themes of historical epochs may be described; but on the other, the specific events and personalities of history manifest a multiplicity, contingency, and complexity that resist all explanatory systems. In addition, great achievements and tragic failures often seem closely linked: "Guilt only appears where history is the possibility for projects of greatness." [2]

From the point of view of Christian faith, suggests Ricoeur, there *is* a meaning in history, but it is a hidden, mysterious meaning—a meaning that provides a basis for hope but that does not nullify ambiguity and risk, a meaning based on the faith that God ultimately is the Lord of history, moving it in the direction of liberation (redemption, salvation) rather than allowing it to dissipate in absurdity, chaos, self-destruction.

> The Christian meaning of history is . . . the hope that [the ambiguity of] secular history is also a part of that meaning which

1. Paul Ricoeur, "Christianity and the Meaning of History," in *History and Truth,* trans. Charles A. Kelbley (Evanston: Northwestern University Press, 1965), pp. 81–97.
2. Ibid., pp. 86–92.

sacred history sets forth, that in the end there is only *one* history, that all history is ultimately sacred.

This meaning of history, however, remains an object of faith. If progress is the rational part of history, and if ambiguity represents the irrational part, then the meaning of history for hope is a surrational meaning—as when we say surrealist. The Christian says that this meaning is eschatological, meaning thereby that his life unfolds in the time of progress and ambiguity without his seeing this higher meaning, without his being able to discern the relation between the two histories. . . . He hopes that the *oneness of meaning* will become clear on the "last day," that he will understand how everything is "in Christ". . . .[3]

Similarly, Wolfhart Pannenberg argues that the whole of historical reality, in relation to which alone individual events have meaning, is not yet complete. This wholeness or totality, this "oneness of meaning," transcends the present moment not vertically but horizontally: it is constituted by the goal, the end, the future finality of history, which can now be glimpsed only proleptically and provisionally. Hence what is required, in place of a tight system of historical meaning, is a stance of openness to the power of the future, the power that determines past and present, drawing all finite events forward into its own mysterious fullness. Christians believe, on the basis of the resurrection of Jesus from the dead (*the* proleptic event), that the power of the future is the power of God, and that it is a liberating, saving power rather than enslaving and destructive.[4]

The question is whether this "surrational," eschatological meaning of history can shed any light on present historical experience. Even for the mundane events of day to day, ambiguity cannot be the sole or last word for Christian faith. "This is why the Christian," adds Ricoeur, "in the very name of this confidence in a hidden meaning, is encouraged by his faith to *attempt* to construct comprehensive schemata, to embrace the terms of a philos-

---

3. Ibid., pp. 93–94; quotation from p. 94, italics Ricoeur's.
4. Cf. Wolfhart Pannenberg, *Revelation as History*, trans. David Granskou (New York: Macmillan, 1968), pp. 1–22; "Hermeneutic and Universal History," in *Basic Questions in Theology*, vol. I, trans. George H. Kehm (Philadelphia: Fortress Press, 1970), pp. 96–136; *Theology and the Kingdom of God* (Philadelphia: Westminster Press, 1969), pp. 51–71.

ophy of history at least as an hypothesis"—despite his "instinctive distrust of systematic philosophies of history." [5] In this frame of mind, I wish to propose the possibility of an interpretation of the dialectical process of history that preserves (a) the hidden meaning that does in fact infuse history; (b) the reality of historical ambiguity, conflict, negation; and (c) openness to the future, which advances on its own terms, surprising and disrupting human projects. *Liberation* (the actualization of freedom) is the hidden meaning of history, occurring through the dialectics of negation, conflict, and "conscientization" (the raising of consciousness to a new level), engendered by the advent of future redemptive power.

A brilliant paradigm of this way of interpreting history is furnished by Hegel. In the Introduction to his *Lectures on the Philosophy of History,* he says that "world history is the progress of the consciousness of freedom." This is the case because history represents the process by which human spirit actualizes its own essence, and "the essence of spirit—its substance—is freedom." The subjective freedom of spirit can be "actualized," i.e., given objective form and reality, only through the dialectics of the historical process. This actualization of freedom—or what I am calling "liberation"—is the destiny and goal of world history. Description of this goal requires a religious affirmation: "Th[e] final aim [of history] is God's purpose with the world. But God is the absolutely perfect being and can, therefore, will nothing but himself, his own will. The nature of his own will, his own nature, is what we here call the idea of freedom." [6] In other words, God

5. Ricoeur, *History and Truth,* p. 95 (italics his) .
6. G. W. F. Hegel, *Reason in History: A General Introduction to the Philosophy of History,* trans. Robert S. Hartman (New York: Liberal Arts Press, 1953) , pp. 22–25. The translation by J. Sibree of the entire *Philosophy of History* has been reprinted by Dover Publications, New York, 1956. Generally I prefer the Hartman translation where the two texts overlap. On freedom as "the central idea in Hegel's thought," see Wolfhart Pannenberg, *The Idea of God and Human Freedom,* trans. R. A. Wilson (Philadelphia: Westminster Press, 1973), pp. 172–177; also Richard Schacht, "Hegel on Freedom," in *Hegel: A Collection of Critical Essays,* ed. Alasdair MacIntyre (New York: Anchor Books, 1972) , pp. 289 ff.; and Hegel, *Philosophy of Right,* trans. T. M. Knox (Oxford: Oxford University Press, 1952), §§ 4, 129, 149, 352; *Encyclopedia of the Philosophical Sciences* (for full bibliographical data on this work and its translation, see above, Chapter III, n. 23), §§ 160, 382–386.

himself *is* freedom, and his perfect freedom is the "idea" that activates history, drawing it toward its goal.

But freedom as the principle, aim, and goal of history and as the essence of human spirit remains hidden, mysterious, unconscious. The purpose of the historical process as a whole is to raise this unconscious principle into the full light of consciousness and political reality. Because the "idea" or "meaning" of history is hidden, another factor must be introduced in order to provide actuality and movement—the activity of humanity in the widest sense, whose motive power is will, desire, or interest. Hegel calls this second factor "passion." In a famous statement he proposes that the idea of freedom on the one hand and the passion of human beings on the other constitute "the warp [and] . . . the woof of the vast tapestry of world history. Their contact and concrete union constitute moral liberty in the state." [7] "Moral liberty in the state" is Hegel's way of referring to the actualization of freedom in moral, legal, social, economic, and ultimately political structures—a process analyzed most fully in the *Philosophy of Right*. Moreover, he suggests that the idea of freedom functions in history by means of the "cunning of reason," which "sets the passions to work for itself, while that through which it develops itself pays the penalty and suffers the loss." [8] The passions of human beings, their activity-producing desires, are constantly transcended and violated by the cunning, luring power of freedom. This freedom, this reason, "in its most concrete form is God. God governs the world; the actual working of his government . . . is the history of the world. . . . Before the pure light of this divine idea—which is no mere ideal—the phantom of a world whose events are an incoherent concourse of fortuitous circumstances utterly vanishes." [9]

It is evident from Hegel's description of the progressive actuali-

7. Hegel, *Reason in History*, pp. 25–29 (quotation from p. 29).
8. Ibid., p. 44.
9. Ibid., p. 47; translation from the Sibree edition of *The Philosophy of History*, p. 36.

zation of freedom[10] that this process is not *merely* the accomplishment of human spirit as it comes to consciousness of itself; it is *also* the gift and activity of divine spirit. The idea of freedom, which constitutes the meaning of history and enters into dialectical interplay with the passions, struggles, and conflicts of the human race, is a *divine* idea; and therefore it is *God* who governs the world, drawing or luring it forward, cunningly as it were, toward its goal. From the perspective afforded by the revealed religion (Christianity) and the final philosophy, it becomes apparent according to Hegel that the liberation of finite spirit through the dialectics of historical conflict (the rise of consciousness to the absolute, in the language of the *Phenomenology*) is *at the same time* the self-movement and self-revelation of absolute spirit—the movement by which God in perfect freedom constitutes his own fully concrete being, creates a world of nature and humankind, and liberates this world from estrangement and separation.[11] In other words, liberation is *both* a task to be carried out, a goal to be attained, by means of the ambiguous and often inconclusive struggles of history; *and* the gift of transcendence, the new birth of freedom as the power of the future, in relation to which persons and programs must remain open, receptive, expectant, ready to be disrupted, violated, drawn forward into the genuinely new.[12]

I now propose to take a closer look at these two aspects, which *together* constitute the "dialectics of liberation."

B. The Possibilities for Freedom Immanent in History: Emancipation through Negation, Conflict, and Conscientization

Rubem Alves, one of the leading theological voices from the third world, writes:

10. In the *Philosophy of History* he traces the actualization of freedom through three stages of world history: the Oriental, the Greco-Roman, and the Western (Christian). For summaries of the argument, see *Reason in History*, pp. 23–24, and *Philosophy of History*, pp. 103–110.
11. See especially *The Phenomenology of Mind*, trans. J. B. Baillie (rev. 2d ed.; London: George Allen & Unwin, Ltd., 1949), pp. 804–808; and Encyclopedia, §§ 567–571, 575–577.
12. On the latter aspect of Hegel in particular, see Martin Heidegger, *Hegel's Concept of Experience* (New York: Harper & Row, 1970), pp. 30, 40, 45, 48–49, 69, 77–80, 146–149.

. . . Freedom creates the new in history through a dialectical process. The new is not mediated directly. The reason for this is that the old, in history, resists and opposes the new. As a consequence, the Yes that freedom addresses to the new becomes historical only through and beyond the No with which it confronts, resists, and overcomes the power of the old that wants to perpetuate itself and abort the new. . . . When it confronts the power of the old, freedom assumes then the form of negation.[13]

But the negative form of freedom cannot be its final expression. In an image suggested by Nietzsche, the spirit of freedom must cease to be both a camel (the beast of burden) and a lion (the beast of prey), and become a child: "Why must the preying lion still become a child? The child is innocence and forgetting, a new beginning, . . . a sacred 'Yes.' For the game of creation . . . a sacred 'Yes' is needed."[14] Alves adds:

> Once the old is deprived of its power to enslave and paralyze, the world is made open for experimentation, for the creation of the new tomorrow. Freedom, accordingly, is not a movement emerging from or within the boundaries of the given system. It is rather the insertion of a new reality into history in such a way that the closed present is broken open for the new.[15]

This statement powerfully expresses *both* elements in the actualization of freedom that I have insisted must be brought into play. The present section is concerned with the *first* of these elements, the one in which freedom assumes the form of negation. Negation is necessary because the "consciousness in search of freedom"[16] comes into conflict with that which resists and opposes liberating change. When confronted by resistance and opposition, freedom takes the form of the "negation of the negative." Conflict and negation are intrinsic to the dialectical process by which history happens.

The word "dialectic" (*dia,* "separation," "transition" + *lektikē,* from *legein,* "to speak") describes a way of speaking and acting

13. Rubem A. Alves, *A Theology of Human Hope* (Washington: Corpus Books, 1969), pp. 104–105.
14. Friedrich Nietzsche, *Thus Spoke Zarathustra,* 1:1 (in *The Portable Nietzsche,* ed. and trans. Walter Kaufmann [New York: Viking Press, 1954], pp. 137–139).
15. Alves, *A Theology of Human Hope,* p. 105.
16. Ibid., p. 5.

that pits word against word, or force against force (*dia* as "separation," "asunder"), in order, by means of a necessary and mutually negating conflict, to find a way or to indicate a direction toward a mediating, synthesizing position (*dia* as "through," "transition").[17] True dialectic involves both separation (negation) and mediation (synthesis, negation of the negative). It entails a conflict and opposition for the sake of finding a way to a new form of consciousness, a closer approximation of truth, a more adequate political structure, in which the old forms are not lost but taken up into a higher unity. It was above all Hegel who used "dialectic" in this sense. True dialectic is based, not on what he called "pure" or "abstract" negation, which would come to a standstill in irresolvable, total, or violent conflict, but rather on "determinate" negation, "which cancels in such a way that it preserves and maintains what is sublated, and thereby survives its being sublated"—lending "determinacy" or content to the new form.[18] Conflict, of course, always entails the *risk* of violence, but violence itself is essentially *undialectical* because it has the effect of aborting the process of mediation which must follow that of negation. Therefore conflict and negation, if they are to become effective forces of historical liberation, must seek out nonviolent forms of action whenever possible, and avoid converting violence from a risk into a *policy* or calculated program.[19]

According to Hegel, it is precisely by means of the dialectic of determinate negation that freedom is actualized in the history of the world, that human beings engage in the unfinished quest for their own hidden and not-yet-realized essence, namely, to be conscious and to be free. The dialectic of determinate negation means that the reality of history is inescapably conflictual and ambiguous. Progress is made, novelty comes about, an advance toward liberation occurs by means of conflict, opposition, reversal,

17. This definition has been informed by Hans Urs von Balthasar's discussion of dialectic in *Karl Barth: Darstellung und Deutung seiner Theologie* (2d ed.; Cologne: Verlag Jakob Hegner, 1962), p. 80.
18. Hegel, *The Phenomenology of Mind*, pp. 137, 234.
19. I take up the issue of violence and nonviolence at the end of the chapter, pp. 319–321.

crisis, uncertainty. Such conflict and ambiguity are inevitable con-
comitants of the *finitude* and *fallenness* of history—a point that will
require fuller elaboration. Hegel contended that the conflictual
character of history is a matter of empirical observation: it is in
fact its most dominant characteristic. But it can also be discovered
by means of philosophical reflection, which means that the ambiguity and mystery of historical conflict are able to assume a certain
intelligibility, meaning, and purpose, the illumination of which is
the intent of any dialectical interpretation.

The dialectical actualization of freedom in history must occur
in two basic spheres or horizons, according to Hegel: that of
consciousness ("subjective spirit") and of *ethical* or *sociopolitical
actuality* ("objective spirit"). Hegel's treatment of the first
focuses on an analysis of the emancipation of self-consciousness
through the dialectics of the master-slave relationship. Consciousness is unable to become a true *self*-consciousness until the self
recognizes itself as reflected in another self. However, when
selves first encounter each other in history there ensues, instead of
a *mutual* recognition, a *struggle* for recognition—a violent, life-
and-death struggle in which one of the two is finally destroyed.
"It is solely by risking life that freedom is obtained." But victory
in a life-and-death battle for recognition (the "prestige battle")
is obviously an empty and illusory victory. Thus consciousness
takes an essential forward step when the prestige battle is replaced
by the master-slave relationship. Now instead of one self being
totally destroyed by the other, the one is oppressed, subjugated,
made dependent upon the other. This is a relationship of *unequal* rather than of mutual recognition, and as a consequence the
self-consciousness of each is only partially realized. The master
does not attain true self-recognition in the slave, for the slave's life
is reduced to the condition of a natural object, and the slave
merely loses himself in the master. Nonetheless, the slave is in a
superior position, dialectically speaking, for two reasons. First,
in virtue of his passivity before suffering and death, he becomes
aware of the finitude, determinacy, and limits of human life, which

is not to be recklessly squandered in a futile fight: the slave takes the first step toward nonviolence. Second, by means of his labor on behalf of another, the slave rises above his natural, selfish instincts. His activity thereby becomes a specifically human activity, a labor or work, which leads to the development of techniques and rationality. While the master remains imprisoned in his natural egotism, the slave becomes conscious of his freedom vis-à-vis nature, and he gains the means by which eventually to cast off his chains, thereby liberating both himself and the master. Thus the slaves of today are the bearers of tomorrow's history.[20]

The master-slave relationship may be taken as paradigmatic of every form of subjugation and inequality known to history. The forms of subjugation vary, including not only the institution of slavery itself (the harshest form), but also class divisions based on economic, political, and social factors, unjust distribution of income owing to the private ownership of capital, racial and sexual oppression, authoritarian family patterns, in general, all forms of hierarchically structured human relationships, which are as much a part of the bureaucracy of the modern corporate state as they were of preindustrial society. Progress in the liberation of consciousness occurs by means of the gradual movement toward equality and genuine mutuality of recognition in human relationships, and therewith toward full *self*-consciousness on the part of all. Such progress undoubtedly occurs, but it is slow, tortuous, and often checked, since new and sometimes more subtle forms of mastery and servitude seem capable of appearing once older ones have vanished.

Just because consciousness, in order to become self-consciousness, requires an intersubjective nexus of relationships, and because the various oppressive and conflictual forms of this nexus gain institutional reinforcement, the emancipation of consciousness requires for its actualization the emancipation of social and political structures as well. Otherwise the movement toward

20. Cf. Hegel, *Phenomenology of Mind*, pp. 231–239; *Encyclopedia*, §§ 430–435; and Alexandre Kojève, *Introduction to the Reading of Hegel*, trans. J. H. Nichols (New York: Basic Books, 1969), pp. 37–52.

equality and mutuality of recognition between individuals could never be consolidated or given "concrete ethical actuality [*Wirklichkeit*]," as Hegel says.[21] A purely subjective freedom would lapse into the "unhappy consciousness" of Stoicism and Skepticism, for it would realize that the self "cannot possess its freedom and truth independently of the conditions of the world." [22] Thus, says Hegel, "the absolute goal or . . . impulse of free spirit is to make its freedom its object, i.e., to *make freedom objective*" in the world.[23]

The possibilities for freedom immanent in history are most fully actualized, according to Hegel, in the "state." It is clear, however, from his description of the state,[24] that what is envisioned is not an empirical state but an ideal, an eschatological/utopian vision of a *Reich der Freiheit* in which the freedom and fulfillment of each is simultaneously the freedom and fulfillment of all, a community in which the needs of each become the needs of all, and the good of the social whole is identical with the good of the individual. A political structure that functioned in such a way would have several ancillary benefits: it would provide nonviolent, juridical, and legislative means of adjudicating conflicts, maximizing the quest for equality and mutuality of recognition; it would replace the institutionalized forms of bondage with institutions supporting freedom; and it would define the necessary limits of individual desire and consumption without constraint of spirit or denial of genuine needs—a critical exigency in view of the contemporary environmental and population crises. Most political systems achieve these goals to some extent, but all fall woefully short of the vision. In fact, with Hegel's description of the ideal state we find ourselves at the point of transition from the possibilities for freedom immanent in history to the advent or new birth of free-

21. Hegel, *Phenomenology of Mind*, pp. 457–461.
22. Ibid., pp. 241–267; the quotation is from Pannenberg, *The Idea of God and Human Freedom*, p. 149.
23. Hegel, *Philosophy of Right*, § 27. Hegel's analysis of the sociological structures by which freedom attains objective actualization is described in Chap. III, Sec. 4B, and need not be repeated here.
24. *Philosophy of Right*, § 260. This passage is quoted above, p. 151. On a similar description in Marx, see above, pp. 58–59.

dom as future power. For the kingdom of freedom is not an immanent human, historical possibility; it transcends as the infinite goal and depth of history.

Before making this transition, however, we should note that the several liberation movements of our time—black, woman's, third world—attest to the accuracy of Hegel's analysis. They show for example that emancipation occurs by means of conflict, by resistance against and negation of dominating, oppressive modes of consciousness or social structure—white racism and apartheid, in the case of blacks; male sexism and the myth of female weakness, in the case of women; the exploitative practices of the industrialized nations of the capitalist West and the communist East, in the case of the third world (including the under-classes within the wealthy countries).

Moreover, the liberation movements confirm that emancipation must occur in two dialectically related spheres: in Marxist terms, both the cultural-ideological superstructure (what Hegel referred to as "consciousness") and the socioeconomic and political infrastructure.[25] Emancipation of the first through a "raising" or transformation of consciousness has become a key initial strategy for all of the liberation movements—a recognition of the real situation of oppression and exploitation, a discovery of one's own true identity and potential as black, brown, red, feminine, etc.[26] But the new consciousness must lead to a program of action that will bring about concrete structural changes—in law, economics, social

25. Cf. Paulo Freire, "Education as Cultural Action," in *Conscientization for Liberation*, ed. Louis M. Colonnese (Washington: United States Catholic Conference, 1971), pp. 109–122.

26. Among blacks, this has been a central theme of many of the great leaders and writers: Frederick Douglass, W. E. B. DuBois, Malcolm X, Martin Luther King, Richard Wright, Frantz Fanon. See especially Fanon's *Black Skin, White Masks*, trans. Charles Markmann (New York: Grove Press, 1967). I have dealt briefly with the quest for a black identity in *Children of Freedom: Black Liberation in Christian Perspective* (Philadelphia: Fortress Press, 1974), pp. 65–70. Among women, the work of Simone de Beauvoir and Germaine Greer has been of special importance. See also Elizabeth Janeway, *Man's World, Woman's Place: A Study in Social Mythology* (New York: Dell Publishing Co., 1971); and Letty M. Russell, *Human Liberation in a Feminist Perspective—A Theology* (Philadelphia: Westminster Press, 1974), chap. 4. For third world liberation movements, see the works by Paulo Freire referred to below. Among neo-Marxists, Herbert Marcuse has argued that a new, aesthetic sensibility must precede revolutionary social changes: *An Essay on Liberation* (Boston: Beacon Press, 1969), chap. II.

relations, and distribution of political power. This of course is the significance of the black power movement, of feminism as a political force, and of the insistence upon the necessity for social revolution on the part of growing numbers of Latin American church leaders, some of whom propose to follow the example of Camilo Torres and other militant priests.[27]

The Brazilian philosopher of education Paulo Freire has proposed the concept of "conscientization *(conscientização)* to designate the key factor in the human struggle for freedom.[28] Conscientization embraces the two basic aspects that must be dialectically related: (1) perception and clarification of the reality of an oppressive or dehumanizing situation ("consciousness-raising"); (2) effective action to change the situation, to transform reality. Freire describes these two aspects as *reflection* and *action,* which he understands to be based on the use of *language* leading into *praxis*—another fundamental concept, encompassing not only action but also theory. In a passage of great significance for an understanding of the "politics" of human liberation (we should recall that according to Hannah Arendt the two distinctively political activities are *praxis* and *lexis,* action and speech),[29] Freire writes:

> There is no true word that is not at the same time a praxis. Thus, to speak a true word is to transform the world. An unauthentic word, one which is unable to transform reality, results when a dichotomy is imposed upon its constitutive elements. When a word is deprived of its dimension of action, reflection automatically suffers as well; and the word is changed into idle chatter, into *verbalism. . . .* On the other hand, if action is em-

27. See James Cone, *Black Theology and Black Power* (New York: Seabury Press, 1969), chap. I; Eleanor Flexner, *Century of Struggle: The Woman's Rights Movement in the United States* (Cambridge, Mass.: Harvard University Press, 1959); Gustavo Gutiérrez, *A Theology of Liberation,* trans. Caridad Inda and John Eagleson (Maryknoll, N.Y.: Orbis Books, 1973), pp. 88, 90–91, 111–112; Rubem Alves, *A Theology of Human Hope,* pp. 5–17; Philip Wheaton, "From Medellin to Militancy: The Church in Ferment," in *Conscientization for Liberation,* pp. 281–302.
28. See his *Pedagogy of the Oppressed,* trans. Myra Bergman Ramos (New York: Herder and Herder, 1972), p. 19 et passim; and *Education for Critical Consciousness* (New York: Seabury Press, 1973), pp. 41 ff.
29. Hannah Arendt, *The Human Condition* (Chicago: University of Chicago Press, 1958), p. 25.

phasized exclusively, to the detriment of reflection, the word is converted into *activism*. The latter—action for action's sake— negates the true praxis and makes dialogue impossible. . . . Human existence cannot be silent, nor can it be nourished by false words, but only by true words, with which men transform the world. To exist, humanly, is to *name* the world, to change it. . . . Men are not built in silence, but in word, in work, in action-reflection. . . . Dialogue is the encounter between men, mediated by the word, in order to name the world.[30]

It follows, accordingly, that the dialogical use of language is the key to conscientization. Freire places great stress upon the importance of dialogue and genuine communication between leaders and people, teachers and students, developing this in contrast to the "banking" concept of education, which "deposits" information in students, who thus remain dependent upon what they are told by others and do not learn to think and act for themselves. "Attempting to liberate the oppressed without their reflective participation in the act of liberation is to treat them as objects which must be saved from a burning building." [31] The relativization and even reversal of roles between leaders and people, teachers and students, are critically important in Freire's view because so often oppressed persons internalize the oppressor's attitude toward them. The oppressor becomes "housed" in the oppressed; and the latter either fear freedom because they can only think of themselves as subjugated, or, if they gain freedom, are likely to become oppressors themselves. What is needed, then, is a way of eliminating the whole destructive system of oppressors and oppressed: this is the task of conscientization, of liberating dialogue, of discovering the truth about oneself (whether oppressor or oppressed), and of determining to change the power-arrangements of the world in which one lives.

> Liberation is thus a childbirth, and a painful one. The man who emerges is a new man, viable only as the oppressor-oppressed con-

30. Freire, *Pedagogy of the Oppressed*, pp. 75–76 (italics his); cf. pp. 89–91, 119–121. In the last sentence the translation reads "mediated by the world . . .," which I assume to be a misprint.
31. Ibid., p. 52; cf. pp. 53–67, 76–80, 122, 130, 170–171.

tradiction is superseded by the humanization of all men. Or to
put it another way, the solution of this contradiction is born in
the labor which brings into the world this new man: no longer
oppressor, no longer oppressed, but man in the process of achieving freedom.[32]

C. The New Birth of Freedom as Future Liberating Power: The Dialectics of Emancipation and Redemption

The language of "new birth" draws us once again toward the
second major factor in the dialectics of liberation, to which the
words of Alves, quoted earlier, call attention: "Freedom . . . is
not a movement emerging from or within the boundaries of the
given system. It is rather the insertion of a new reality into history
in such a way that the closed present is broken open for the
new." [33] Why should this be the case? Why can the "kingdom
of freedom" not evolve from purely immanent historical possibilities? Why can humanity not finally succeed in emancipating
itself from the bondage of self and society? If the "new reality"
represents an other-than-human possibility, how then can it
become available to human experience?

To answer these questions, certain arguments developed in
Chapters III and IV must be reviewed. First, the *finitude* of
human freedom, its embodied, contingent status, means that experiences of the voluntary can be sustained in relation to the seemingly crushing force of the involuntary—bodily needs and capacities, the social system, the fundamental necessities that comprise
the conditions of life itself—only if persons are open to a future,
liberating power that transcends all their physical and social environments. Such openness is a structural component of human

32. Ibid., pp. 33–34; cf. pp. 28, 30, 32–33, 169. Freire describes in some detail how
he developed the methods of conscientizing education by working with illiterate and
deprived peasants in Latin America (see pp. 86–118; also *Education for Critical
Consciousness*, pp. 41–58). Conscientization is not restricted to the culturally deprived but is equally relevant for the middle and upper classes of the "developed"
nations: so argues John DeWitt, "From Schooling to Conscientization," in *Conscientization for Liberation*, pp. 145–162. The emphasis upon the birth of "a new
man" (but what of a new woman?) is characteristic of Latin American thinkers: cf.
Gutiérrez, *A Theology of Liberation*, p. 91; Alves, *A Theology of Human Hope*, pp.
96, 105, 122 ff. and Luís Ambroggio, "The Latin American Man and His Revolution," in *Conscientization for Liberation*, pp. 3–22.
33. Alves, *A Theology of Human Hope*, p. 105.

freedom as described phenomenologically. Because of this openness to a transcendence that cannot be confused with their own finite reality, human beings can never be finally satisfied by intrahistorical fulfillments.[34]

Second, the *fallenness* of human freedom means that it can be actualized historically only in *alienated* and *ambiguous* form. Hegel seized upon this factor in accounting for what he regarded as a necessary movement beyond the dialectic between consciousness and society (subjective and objective spirit) to a third dimension, which he called absolute spirit, the transsubjective and transobjective foundation of freedom. In the *Phenomenology* he called attention to the inability of achieving a true mediation between subjective and sociopolitical forms of freedom because of a profound alienation between the individual and the social whole (an alienation that characterizes contemporary culture as much or even more than it did Hegel's); and in the *Philosophy of Right* he argued that the ambiguity of empirical states means that they can never be identified with the kingdom of freedom, and that therefore art, religion, and philosophy must transcend the state.[35]

The underlying reason for the failure of human beings to attain the freedom for which they search in history lies in the paradoxical fact that they are responsible for their own captivity. They cannot liberate themselves because the powers that enslave them are ultimately of their own making. When they attempt to seize freedom, they disfigure it and enslave themselves all the more deeply. Ricoeur expresses this paradox with the concept of the *servile will:* "That freedom must be delivered and that this deliverance is deliverance from self-enslavement cannot be said directly; yet it is the central theme of 'salvation.'"[36] I have argued that an original and continuing act of *self-deception*—a delusion as to the proper limits of human existence—accounts for the servile will and explains why humankind cannot escape from its own

34. See Chap. III, Secs. 5B, C.
35. See Chap. III, Sec. 5A.
36. Paul Ricoeur, *The Symbolism of Evil,* trans. Emerson Buchanan (Boston: Beacon Press, 1969), pp. 101–106, 151–157 (quotation from p. 152).

fallen condition.[37] We cannot escape because we deceive ourselves
about our own deception. Moreover, this interior act of bondage
is objectified and demonically reinforced by the institutions, structures, norms, and powers of social existence, where we are confronted by what Moltmann calls the "vicious circles" of poverty,
force, racism and alienation, pollution, and a general sense of
cultural and personal malaise, from which there appears to be no
escape.[38]

For these reasons, the language of humanism, which understands
liberation to be a goal attainable by human effort, must be dialectically transfused (not replaced) by the language of faith.
Although characterized by the same revolutionary passion for
human deliverance, the language of faith, in Paul Lehmann's
words, "insists that the achievement of humanization comes by
the reality and power of a deliverance which occurs in history
from beyond history and refuses to abandon history." [39] In his
recent book, *The Transfiguration of Politics,* Lehmann argues
that the revolutionary struggles of history must be "transfigured"
by the power of "the presence of Jesus of Nazareth in the human
story." Otherwise revolutions, which are "born of the passion for
humanization," will end by "devouring their own children"—primarily by the conversion of revolutionary violence from a risk
into a policy, and by the reversal of roles between oppressors and
oppressed.[40] Hannah Arendt, whose analysis of revolution has
deeply influenced Lehmann, points out that revolutionaries have
been "curiously insensitive to reality in general and to the reality
of persons in particular, whom they felt no compunctions in sacri-
ficing to their 'principles,' or to the course of history, or to the
cause of revolution as such." [41]

37. See Chap. IV, Sec. 2.
38. Jürgen Moltmann, *The Crucified God: The Cross of Christ as the Foundation
and Criticism of Christian Theology,* trans. R. A. Wilson and John Bowden (New
York: Harper & Row, 1974) , pp. 329–332. See also above, Chap. IV, Sec. 3.
39. Paul Lehmann, *Ideology and Incarnation* (Geneva: John Knox Association,
1962) , p. 26. Cf. Alves, *A Theology of Human Hope,* pp. 85–87, 98.
40. Paul Lehmann, *The Transfiguration of Politics* (New York: Harper & Row,
1975), pp. xiii, 3, 7, 79–102, 271–274, 278–279.
41. Hannah Arendt, *On Revolution* (New York: Viking Press, 1965) , p. 85. Arendt
suggests that the American Revolution has been the only one "which did not
devour its own children" (p. 37).

Although I agree profoundly with Lehmann that revolutions, indeed all forms of the human struggle for liberation, must be saved from impotence and/or self-destruction, I detect in his analysis a tendency toward an apocalyptic or suprahistorical way of understanding how God acts redemptively in human affairs. The relation between what he calls "humanistic messianism" and "messianic humanism" or "messianic politics" is not a genuinely dialectical one. The only category by which he is able to describe political change is "revolution," which for him must remain an apocalyptic, suprahistorical category, always dependent upon God's transfiguring power to prevent it from dissolving into *Realpolitik* and succumbing to its own fate.[42] God acts in history, as it were, only on an apocalyptic threshold, impinging from "beyond history," keeping revolutions open and fluid, but not really energizing the human struggle for freedom from within, actualizing both revolutionary and nonrevolutionary possibilities for political emancipation. This is too narrow and undialectical a model for understanding the process by which liberation occurs in history.[43]

It is possible, I think, to find a philosophical basis for understanding the "new birth" of freedom as a supremely historical event rather than as an apocalyptic or suprahistorical phenomenon, but without thereby emasculating the genuine novelty and transcendence of future liberating power vis-à-vis past and present historical possibilities. According to Hegel, for example, the actualization of freedom is not merely the accomplishment of human spirit as it comes to consciousness of itself; it is also the gift and activity of divine spirit, which, as it were, pulls or lures history toward its future goal.[44] The rise of finite consciousness to the absolute is *at the same time* the return of absolute spirit to itself, and history is at once a divine-human process. This Hegel-

---

42. Cf. Lehmann, *The Transfiguration of Politics*, pp. 259–270.
43. A similar difficulty is evident in some of the earlier writings of Jürgen Moltmann, although for different reasons. Cf. *Religion, Revolution, and the Future*, trans. M. Douglas Meeks (New York: Scribner's, 1969), pp. 190, 196–198; and *Theology of Hope*, trans. James Leitch (New York: Harper & Row, 1967), pp. 179, 302.
44. See above, pp. 269–271.

ian vision has been preserved, varied, enriched in recent philosophy by the work of Ernst Bloch, Karl Jaspers, Alfred North Whitehead, and Martin Heidegger. In these more recent thinkers, however, the theistic assumptions are for the most part either deeply hidden or the mask of a latent humanism.

The latter is the case with Ernst Bloch and other humanistic Marxists who have been influenced by him (Roger Garaudy, Vitězslav Gardavský). In all of his works Bloch strongly emphasizes the hiddenness, mystery, and novelty of the future, but ultimately he identifies the *novum* with what is latent in the hidden human essence, rather than understanding it as something that radically transcends immanent historical possibilities. The great value of religion in his view is its recognition of the depth, mystery, and futurity of *humanum*. "The idea of *Deus absconditus* alone helps to maintain the *problem* of the legitimate mystery called *homo absconditus*. . . . It takes total Otherness to give the appropriate measure of depth to everything that has been longed for in deifying man." The unknown human future was religiously expressed by the word "God." "Thus God appears as the hypostasized ideal of the human essence which in reality has not yet come to be." [45]

Karl Jaspers contends that, although the future is concealed in the past and present, it is not accessible to research, cannot be planned with any precision, and always surprises us when it comes, creating events that are incalculable, unrepeatable, and irreplaceable. Because unique and creative events in history cannot be explained causally nor deduced as necessary, "they are like revelations from some other source than the mere course of happening." They come "toward us from out of the future, astonishing, simple, and overwhelming." Nevertheless, once they occur they become part of the matrix of history, forming the basis for new possibilities. [46] Jaspers's views tend to be confirmed by analyses of the

45. Ernst Bloch, *Man on His Own*, trans. E. B. Ashton (New York: Herder and Herder, 1970), pp. 154–155, 213, 216 ff.
46. Karl Jaspers, *The Origin and Goal of History*, trans. Michael Bullock (London: Routledge & Kegan Paul, 1953), pp. 141, 149–150, 183–188, 220–223, 242, 251.

element of incalculability in making predictions of alternative futures as the basis of scientific planning.[47]

Although Jaspers is correct in contending that total knowledge is impossible because of "the non-objective nature of the comprehensive whole," it is important nonetheless to emphasize that the element of incalculability is not the consequence of our present limited state of knowledge, so that what seems to be incalculable is merely the result of inadequate predictions based on imperfect data. If it is calculable in principle though not in fact, then in principle it is not an astonishing, overwhelming, arriving power that places persons at its disposal and draws them forward into genuine novelty. Even from the point of view of secular humanism and nontheistic philosophy, it is possible to affirm that human beings do have such experiences, indeed that these experiences are the real fund of being and life. The argument I am developing is not based on the "gaps" in scientific knowledge. Rather I am contending that the liberating power of the future is an essential, constitutive, and ever-present element in the dialectical structure of history, without which historical life would petrify.

Theistic assumptions are more evident in Alfred North Whitehead's vision of something beyond ourselves and our past that calls us forward in each moment into a yet unsettled future, luring or persuading with new and richer possibilities of being. That something is an ever-changing possibility which impinges upon us as the relevant ideal for each new moment. It is the power that makes for novelty, creativity, and life. Whitehead believes that these ideal possibilities cannot be credited with their own agency. Rather they are founded in an agency that is actual and unitary, a conscious subject of experience that is universal in scope and everlasting in duration: "God." [48]

47. See Fred Iklé, "Can Social Predictions Be Evaluated?" and Martin Shubik, "Information, Rationality, and Free Choice in a Future Democratic Society," in *Toward the Year 2000, Daedalus*, 96 (Summer 1967) : 733–758, 771–778.
48. See John B. Cobb, Jr., *God and the World* (Philadelphia: Westminster Press, 1969), pp. 54–55, 81–83, 88–90. Wolfhart Pannenberg has appropriated elements of the Whiteheadian vision in his own theology of the future; see especially *Theology and the Kingdom of God*, pp. 59, 61, 64–65, 70, 128–132, 134–136, 138–143.

Finally, the philosophy of Martin Heidegger provides a basis for understanding "God" (or the "word of God") as the power of the future, although Heidegger himself has resolutely refused to draw theological conclusions from his work. On Heideggerian grounds it may be argued that the unity, purpose, and liberation of history derive from its goal, not its origin. The end enters into the constitution and dynamics of history in a way that the beginning does not. It is transcendent, yet not beyond history or above history in a supernatural sense. History happens by the coming of the future through the past into the present, gathering and liberating by its coming. Because the modes of time—past, present, and future—are unified by the power of the future, the future is preeminent among the temporal ecstases. It is out of the future that we live: human existence requires openness to the future. Yet the future comes through the past, by means of which we understand. Past possibilities serve as the basis of a present project in which the future comes anew. Thus we understand out of the past and live out of the future, but we do both in the present. The present is the fulcrum of the historical process, whose energizing force is the future.[49] The *means* by which the future comes, according to Heidegger, is *language.* The future is now present with its liberating power by means of word or speech, i.e., linguistic images that manifest symbolically a new reality, hidden from sight. Thus, speaking theologically, one may say that the *word of God,* as it comes to speech in human praxis (word-action), is the power of the future that calls us forward— into freedom.[50]

The point toward which I have been moving in this analysis is that in every historical event a dialectical interaction takes place between the striving to bring freedom to birth out of possibilities

49. Martin Heidegger, *Being and Time,* trans. John Macquarrie and Edward Robinson (New York: Harper & Brothers, 1962), pp. 371–379, 384–388, 401, 434–438. See also Ray L. Hart, *Unfinished Man and the Imagination* (New York: Herder and Herder, 1968) , pp. 11, 272, 307–309.
50. Cf. the argument developed in my book, *Jesus—Word and Presence: An Essay in Christology* (Philadelphia: Fortress Press, 1971) , chap. III. The present work seeks to move beyond a Heideggerian conceptual framework, but without repudiating the latter.

contained in the past (the human struggle for emancipation in both revolutionary and nonrevolutionary modes) and the advent or new birth of freedom as the power of the future that creates new and unexpected possibilities (the divine gift of redemption). Freedom is actualized, or *liberation* occurs, in the dialectics of *emancipation* and *redemption*.[51]   Freedom may be defined precisely as that which happens when human beings come up against the limits of their own resources, yet somehow find it possible to go on, discovering that the future for which they are striving is already there as a gift, giving itself, drawing them on when all objective and subjective possibilities immanent in history have been exhausted.   Freedom is actualized in history, or liberation occurs, when the future comes into the present as redemptive gift, exerting its forward call in the context of an emancipatory project based upon past and present possibilities.   To put it in Whiteheadian language, every occasion of human experience is constituted by the interaction between the causal influence of the past and novel possibilities for the future, which lure it beyond mere repetition of past experiences.   In some events the element of human achievement and continuity with the past prevails, but never to the exclusion of the power and spontaneity of the liberating future vis-à-vis the present.   In other events the element of discontinuity, the revolutionary power of the *novum,* prevails, but never to the exclusion of the past, the regularities of a causal nexus, and humanity's projects for the future.   All events in history exhibit the influence of both these forces, and the distinctive character of each event is determined by the way they interact in it.   Rubem Alves describes the actualization of freedom in this dialectic quite vividly: "The past that was about to determine the present is penetrated by freedom.   Through this act the unfolding

51. For the terminological distinction, see Jürgen Moltmann, "Die Revolution der Freiheit," *Perspektiven der Theologie: Gesammelte Aufsätze* (Munich: Chr. Kaiser Verlag, 1968), p. 207.   Moltmann cites Hans Hoekendijk, "Feier der Befreiung," *Kontexte,* 4 (1967): 124–131.   In *Jesus—Word and Presence,* pp. 288–290, I described the same distinction in terms of two aspects of the reality of the future: the future as *futurum* (that which develops out of what has been in the past and now is) and as *adventus* (that which comes, the *novum,* the not-yet, the *parousia,* which shatters present expectations and calls or pulls the present forward into new possibilities).

of the immanent possibilities of 'what was' is interrupted and the new is inserted into the present." As a result of this insertion, this penetration, the present becomes pregnant with the possibilities of a new future, to which history will give birth by means of suffering, struggle, negation, and the constant labor to build a better tomorrow.[52]

Verification of the foregoing analysis may be found in the liberation movements, past and present. These movements, while engaged in a passionate, often revolutionary struggle for emancipation from oppressive conditions, have at the same time been open to the occurrence of liberation as a surprise, a redemptive gift, an event over which they ultimately have no control. This consciousness is most highly developed in the black experience, where the powerlessness of the slave or of the victim of segregation made it necessary to remain open to and reliant upon a power not at the oppressed person's disposal. The future is in God's hands, yet paradoxically one must move toward it by every means available. The paradox was powerfully expressed in the black spirituals, which also captured the eschatological imagery of Christian faith, using it both as a principle of criticism of present injustice and as a hope for a new tomorrow; and it has been preserved in the writings of black leaders down to the present day, notably W. E. B. DuBois, Howard Thurman, Malcolm X, and Martin Luther King.[53]

The dialectics of emancipation and redemption are captured by Gustavo Gutiérrez with a theoretical precision characteristic of the best Latin American liberation thinkers. He describes this dialectic in terms of a reciprocity between the historical process of liberation (what I am calling the struggle for emancipation) and the coming of the kingdom of God (the gift of redemption).

Without liberating historical events, there would be no growth of the Kingdom. But the process of liberation will not have con-

52. Alves, *A Theology of Human Hope*, p. 96; cf. pp. 97, 122–123. The imagery of penetration and pregnancy is found in Marx and Engels, *Die deutsche Ideologie*, in *Frühschriften*, ed. Siegfried Landshut (Stuttgart: Alfred Kröner, 1953).
53. I have discussed this aspect of the black experience in *Children of Freedom*, pp. 76–80.

quered the very roots of oppression and the exploitation of man by man without the coming of the Kingdom, which is above all a gift. Moreover, we can say that the historical, political liberating event *is* the growth of the Kingdom and *is* a salvific event; but it is not *the* coming of the Kingdom, not *all* of salvation. It is the historical realization of the Kingdom and, therefore, it also proclaims its fullness. This is where the difference lies. It is a distinction made from a dynamic viewpoint, which has nothing to do with the one which holds for the existence of two juxtaposed "orders"....

Salvation, says Gutiérrez, is "the inner force and the fullness" of the process of human self-generation.[54]

Gutiérrez also describes the human, historical, emancipatory side of this dialectic as "utopian" in character. He notes that the concept of utopia has come for many to be synonymous with "illusion, lack of realism, irrationality," whereas in point of fact it expresses a *"relationship to present historical reality,"* serving both as the *denunciation* of an intolerable state of affairs and as the *annunciation* of what is not yet, but can be and will be. Moreover, true utopian thinking is not illusory but rather verified by historical praxis. Finally, utopias are not irrational; rather, they emerge when scientific reason reaches its limits, and they are the product of a creative, imaginative use of reason both to unmask present reality and to envision genuine alternatives. As Karl Mannheim pointed out in *Ideology and Utopia* (1929), ideology advances a pseudoscientific version of reality and sanctions the status quo by irrational means, whereas utopian thinking transforms what exists by a creative and probing use of imagination.[55] Utopia, thus understood, enters into dialectical relationship with the kingdom of God, which together generate the process of liberation as a divine-human event.

In human love there is a depth which man does not suspect: it is through it that man encounters God. If utopia humanizes economic, social, and political liberation, this humanness—in the light

54. Gutiérrez, *A Theology of Liberation*, pp. 177 (italics his), 159. We have already observed that this dialectic is a central theme of Rubem Alves's *A Theology of Human Hope*.
55. Gutiérrez, *A Theology of Liberation*, pp. 232–235 (italics his).

290 New Birth of Freedom

of the Gospel—reveals God. . . . Christian hope opens us . . . to the gift of the future promised by God. It keeps us from any confusion of the Kingdom with any one historical stage, from any idolatry toward unavoidably ambiguous human achievement, from any absolutizing of revolution. In this way hope makes us radically free to commit ourselves to social praxis, motivated by a liberating utopia and with the means which the scientific analysis of reality provides for us. . . . The Gospel does not provide a utopia for us; this is a human work. The Word is a free gift of the Lord. But the Gospel is not alien to the historical plan; on the contrary, the human plan and the gift of God imply each other.[56]

3. THE LIBERATING POWER OF GOD IN HISTORY

A. God as "Liberating Power"

That which finally distinguishes biblical faith from all forms of political and existentialist humanism is its identification of the "future liberating power" by which freedom is newly born in history as *the power of God*. "Liberating power" becomes an attribute or definition of God, designating the distinctive way that he is known and experienced in history. God *is* "the event of suffering, liberating love";[57] he is "the God who breaks into human history to liberate the oppressed." [58] This designation of the identity of God is one of the central themes of the Old Testament. The commandments of the Decalogue begin with the pronouncement upon which all else depends: "I am Yahweh your God, who brought you out of the land of Egypt, out of the house of bondage. You shall have no other gods before me . . ." (Ex. 20:2–3). In both the Yahwist (Ex. 3:7–14) and the Priestly (Ex. 6:2–8) traditions, this decisive liberating action is linked with the divine name:

> God said to Moses, "I am Yahweh. I appeared to Abraham, to Isaac, and to Jacob, as God Almighty (*El Shaddai*), but by my name Yahweh I did not make myself known to them. . . . I have heard the groaning of the people of Israel whom the Egyptians hold in bondage and I have remembered my covenant. Say there-

---

56. Ibid., p. 238; cf. pp. 236–237.
57. Moltmann, *The Crucified God*, p. 252; cf. pp. 248–249, 255.
58. José Miranda, *Marx and the Bible*, trans. John Eagleson (Maryknoll, N.Y.: Orbis Books. 1974), p. 77.

fore to the people of Israel, 'I am Yahweh, and I will liberate you from the burdens of the Egyptians, and I will deliver you from their bondage, and I will redeem you with an outstretched arm and with great acts of judgment, and I will take you for my people, and I will be your God; and you shall know that I am Yahweh your God, who has liberated you from the burdens of the Egyptians. . . .' "

—Ex. 6:2–7[59]

This theme is taken up and echoed repeatedly by the Deuteron-omist and the prophets, especially Second Isaiah, with reference not only to the Exodus from Egypt but also to other historical experiences of deliverance of the Hebrew people. In the New Testament, the equivalent identification and naming of God is linked to another liberating action, the raising of Jesus from the dead: God is the one "who raised Christ Jesus from the dead" (Rom. 8:11; cf. Gal. 1:1), the one "who gives life to the dead and calls into existence the things that do not exist" (Rom. 4:17).[60] Exodus and resurrection: these are the two central events of "liber-ating love" by which the God of Moses, the prophets, and Jesus are known and identified—in the first instance, liberation from his-torical oppression; in the second, from the ultimate bondage of death.

Not only is God defined as the event of liberating love; con-versely, liberating power in history is defined by reference to God. Such power is not immanent and humanistic, the self-generating and self-emancipating historical potentiality of the human species; rather it is the power *of God,* who is the *Lord* of history, the *Creator* of the heavens and the earth. This is the significance of the fact that the Genesis account of creation serves as a prologue to the Exodus liberation-event;[61] similarly, creation and resurrec-

---

59. In place of the RSV "brought out from under" I have substituted "liberated from." For an analysis of this and similar passages, with extensive citations of the critical literature, see Miranda, *Marx and the Bible,* pp. 78–88. On the theme of God as the "Power of Liberation" in the Old Testament, see also Hans-Joachim Kraus, *Reich Gottes: Reich der Freiheit. Grundriss systematischer Theologie* (Neukirchen-Vluyn: Neukirchener Verlag, 1975), pp. 113–125. Kraus notes the close connection between this attribute and the divine name.
60. Cf. Moltmann, *The Crucified God,* pp. 188–189.
61. Citing von Rad and others, Miranda makes a good deal of this point, *Marx and the Bible,* pp. 78–79, 88–89.

tion are linked by Paul in Rom. 4:17. Liberation (from the "powers," from death, from sin) takes on a special determinacy when it is understood to be the work of God the Creator rather than of man and woman, the creatures. The historical praxis of the latter serves as the *mediation* of liberating power, but is not its ultimate source and determination.

B. The Crucified and Life-Giving God

Lest the rhetoric about the "liberating power" of God take on a triumphalistic note, we must recall that according to Christian faith the resurrection-event is inseparably linked with the crucifixion-event. In history, God's liberating power undergoes suffering and defeat. "God himself is dead," wrote Hegel, using the words of the Lutheran passion hymn—not in the sense that God actually ceases to be, but rather in the sense that he suffers the death of his Son, upon whom all the world's oppressions have been laid. God must undergo this "deepest anguish"—the indirect experience of death in the dying of a beloved Son—because only that which is suffered and undergone can also be overcome. In the cross of Christ the multiple forms of bondage—sin, law, death, the worldly powers—were quintessentially concentrated: Jesus was condemned as a sinner (Mk. 14:64 par.; Rom. 8:3) according to Jewish law; he was crucified by the Roman imperial power, and for him the agony of dying was intensified by the experience of God-forsakenness. Because God experienced this condemnation, crucifixion, and agony along with Jesus, he took the forms of bondage into or upon his own being, overcoming them there, depriving them of their very essence, converting their oppression into liberation. Hence, dialectically speaking, this "deepest anguish" is at the same time the "highest love"—the "suffering, liberating love" of God. What appeared to the eyes of the world as a tragic defeat was in fact a post-tragic victory: it was a victory *through* defeat, which is the only way that true and lasting victories are won in the real world. "Suffering," writes Ricoeur, "is a moment in divinity; that moment of abasement, of annihilation of the divine life, both completes and suppresses tragedy. Tragedy is consummated, for the evil is in God. . . . But tragedy is suppressed because it is inverted." [62]

Therefore the *crucified God* is also the *life-giving God* (Rom. 4:17), the God who raises from the dead (Rom. 8:11). He is the latter *because* he is the former, and he is the former in order to be the latter. Because he is both together, he is the *liberating God*. His work of liberation does not consist in mighty, visible, miraculous incursions into history, after the fashion of a *Deus ex machina,* which a literalistic reading of the Exodus and resurrection stories alone—apart from the defeats suffered by God's people throughout history—might lead one to suppose. God's liberating power occurs more dialectically than that: it is the power of weakness, and it entails the negation of negation. It is available only in and through the ambiguities and relativities of the *not-yet-consummated* human struggle for freedom. God shares in this history, empowering it and moving it toward its goal, but also suffering its setbacks and defeats. The history of freedom is the history of God.

God can undergo crucifixion, yet give life to the dead, because he is the triune God—the one whose very being consists of this dialectical process of death and life, of self-divestment and self-redintegration. The triune God is not a static, unchanging, eternal ground, or a highest, sovereign, heavenly being, but rather a *historical event*—the event of suffering, liberating love, an event that takes place between the Father, the Son, and the Spirit, encompassing the whole of human history. The Christian doctrine of the Trinity did not arise from Greek metaphysics (although metaphysical categories were later used to explicate it) but from the experience of God in the crucifixion and the resurrection of Christ. Moltmann has made this forcefully clear in his

62. Paul Ricoeur, *The Symbolism of Evil*, p. 328. For this paragraph as a whole, see G. W. F. Hegel, *Vorlesungen über die Philosophie der Religion*, ed. Georg Lasson (Hamburg: Verlag von Felix Meiner, 1966), II/2, 157–158, 163–167, 172; Eberhard Jüngel, "Vom Tod des lebendigen Gottes," *Zeitschrift für Theologie und Kirche*, 65 (April 1968): 93–116; Moltmann, *The Crucified God*, pp. 190–196, 242–246, 278; Hodgson, *Jesus—Word and Presence*, pp. 213–217, 254–258. See also the discussion above of "Jesus' Cry of God-Forsakenness and the Identity of God," Chap. V, Sec. 4B.

chapter on "The 'Crucified God' " in the book of the same title. His interpretation is best epitomized by the following statement:

> If . . . the believer understands the crucifixion as an event of the love of the Son and the grief of the Father, that is, as an event between God and God, as an event within the Trinity, he perceives the liberating word of love which creates new life [the Spirit]. By the death of the Son he is taken up into the grief of the Father and experiences a liberation which is a new element in this de-divinized and legalistic world. . . . He is in fact taken up into the inner life of God, if in the cross of Christ he experiences the love of God for the godless, the enemies. . . . In that case, if he lives in this love, he lives in God and God in him. If one conceives of the Trinity as an event of love in the suffering and death of Jesus . . . then the Trinity is no self-contained group in heaven, but an eschatological process open for men on earth, which stems from the cross of Christ.[63]

It has long been recognized that both monotheism and trinitarianism hold political implications. In his classic essay, "Monotheism as a Political Problem," [64] Erik Peterson argued that, even before Constantine, monotheism functioned as a political ideology supporting imperial interests because of its emphasis upon the oneness, authority, and supremacy of God: one God, one Logos, one Emperor, one Church, one Empire. In his view, with the development of the doctrine of the Trinity these identifications were shattered and a political theology became impossible in principle. More recent theologians, notably Moltmann and J. B. Metz,[65] have argued that a trinitarian theology is not apolitical but offers the basis for a new, critical political theology that understands the crucified and life-giving God as engaged in the struggle for human liberation from all forms of oppression, including that based on the idolatry of state religions. These insights have been taken up

63. Moltmann, *The Crucified God*, p. 249; cf. pp. 235–256. I shall attempt a formulation of the doctrine of the Trinity under the theme of "the God of Freedom" in Chap. VII, Sec. 2. Sec. 1 of that chapter considers the distinction between the work of the Son and the Spirit.
64. Erik Peterson, "Der Monotheismus als politisches Problem" (1935), in *Theologische Traktate* (Munich: Kösel Verlag, 1951), pp. 45–147.
65. See Moltmann, *The Crucified God*, pp. 325–326; "Political Theology," *Theology Today*, 28 (April 1971): 6–23; J. B. Metz, J. Moltmann, W. Oelmüller, et al., *Religion and Political Society* (New York: Harper & Row, 1974); J. B. Metz, *Theology of the World*, trans. William Glen-Doepel (New York: Herder and Herder, 1969), chap. V.

and developed by Juan Luís Segundo in the third volume of his *Theology for Artisans of a New Humanity,* titled *Our Idea of God.* He suggests that the Latin American experience offers a basis for criticizing the occidental image of God as an abstract, distant, privatistic Dominator, an image reflected in the socioeconomic structures of Western society. Against this, Segundo proposes an understanding of God as triune, as a society of persons of love, engaged in the fashioning of a human society in history, which, like the divine society, would be "concordant by virtue of community, neither confused nor divided, in such a way that the good of one is the good of all, because the needs and hopes of one touch upon the needs and hopes of all." [66]

C. GOD AS LIBERATOR IN THE EXPERIENCE OF OPPRESSED
    PEOPLES: THE QUESTION OF THEODICY[67]

The identity of God as Liberator, or as the liberating power of history, has been powerfully experienced by oppressed peoples. Indeed, if God were the Oppressor, or neutral to the facts of oppression, or powerless to change them, he would have to be rejected as a false deity. In a sense, then, liberation becomes the basis for a theodicy—a vindication of the justice of God in the face of evil, and a verification of belief in him. Only if liberation is in fact experienced, and experienced in such a way that is accountable by reference to a reality that cannot be identified with human self-emancipation, does language about "God" become relevant. Rubem Alves formulates the logic of this position in describing how an ancient "oppressed" people, the Israelites, came to speak of God:

> If the liberating event could neither be related to the people's vocation for freedom, as the effect to its cause, nor explained as an accident of historical circumstances, the people came to understand it as an act of a power from beyond history. The liberating facts were proclaimed then as God's acts. They were not simply

66. Juan Luís Segundo, *Our Idea of God,* trans. John Drury (Maryknoll, N.Y.: Orbis Books, 1974), esp. pp. 34–36, 63–69, 73, 101–102, 114–115. See also Francis P. Fiorenza, "Latin American Liberation Theology," *Interpretation,* 28 (October 1974): 447–450.
67. On the question of theodicy, see also the discussion of tragedy and existentialism, Chap. II, Sec. 4.

the result of circumstance but expressions of a transcendent freedom. . . . Israel, therefore, did not have an a priori idea of God
and from this dogmatic idea conclude as to his action in history.
On the contrary, it found itself determined to be free, in spite of
itself. This was its most fundamental historical experience. From
the historical reality of the liberating facts, a new language emerges
as something a posteriori that speaks about God as the power of
human liberation which expressed itself in and through the formative events of the life of the community.[68]

The question is whether such an experience and the argument
based upon it continue to be efficacious. Each of the contemporary liberation movements has had to face the question of theodicy,[69] none more centrally or fundamentally than black theology
of liberation. Recently this theology has been subjected to a
powerful critique by William R. Jones.[70] Jones points out that
the major black theologians writing today—Joseph Washington,
Albert Cleage, Major Jones, J. Deotis Roberts, James Cone—all
start with the fact of black suffering and oppression. They must
show that this suffering is not willed or caused by God, indeed
that God is efficaciously committed to its destruction. They must
be able to demonstrate, in other words, that God is not a "white
racist" but a "black liberator." However, this demonstration is
rendered unusually difficult by two distinguishing characteristics
of black suffering: it is an *ethnic* suffering, i.e., suffering is mal-
distributed and blacks seem to have been singled out as a racial
group in order to suffer, which could lead to the hypothesis of
divine disfavor toward blacks; and the suffering has assumed an
enormity and *perpetuity* that outstrip ordinary causal relations in
history and disrupt conventional theodicies.[71]

68. Alves, *A Theology of Human Hope*, pp. 89–90.
69. Mary Daly's *Beyond God the Father* (Boston: Beacon Press, 1973) could be
viewed as a theodicy from a feminist perspective that comes to negative conclusions.
Her critique of the biblical-doctrinal understanding of God has not yet been
adequately rejoined by a theology of woman's liberation. Alves, Gutiérrez,
Miranda, and Segundo, in works cited in this chapter, all develop understandings
of God that include elements of a theodicy from a third world perspective.
70. *Is God a White Racist? A Preamble to Black Theology* (New York: Anchor
Books, 1973).
71. Ibid., pp. xiv, xvii–xx, 72–75. On the question of theodicy in relation to the
radical evil of the modern world, see Jürgen Moltmann, "God and Resurrection:
Resurrection Faith in the Forum of the Question of Theodicy," *Hope and Planning*,
trans. Margaret Clarkson (New York: Harper & Row, 1971), pp. 31–55, esp. pp.
31–37.

In the face of these difficulties, a number of alternative strategies have been devised, none of which in Jones's view can be regarded as satisfactory logically or theologically. Washington, for example, argues that blacks are God's contemporary suffering servants and that they are suffering vicariously in order to redeem the world from the worst of sins, white racism. According to Cleage, God himself is literally black and is punishing his (black) people for their acquiescence and quietism in the face of white oppression. Major Jones and Roberts assert in different ways that the psycho-religious needs of oppressed blacks require a belief in the goodness and consolation of God, whose true function, then, is to enable those who must suffer to endure their hardship. It is evident that none of these arguments is able to explain why blacks have been singled out to suffer, and none of them really portrays God as a liberator of oppressed peoples. Rather he comes across as venge-ful (requiring the vicarious sacrifice of an innocent people), or as an accuser and punisher (the wrathful black God), or as a consoler and compensator (the God who satisfies religious and psychosocial needs). But these traditional ways of viewing God are precisely the "rotten points" of religious belief to which Paul Ricoeur has called attention in accounting for the rise of modern atheism.[72]

Clearly, the only viable black theodicy is one which would argue that blacks (and other oppressed peoples) have experienced and are experiencing the liberating action of God. The work of James Cone comes closest to representing this form of theodicy.[73] But Jones criticizes Cone by contending that it is impossible to prove that the decisive event of liberation for blacks has in fact taken place. When Jones's critique is analyzed more closely, it becomes evident that what he requires of black theology is something that neither it nor any theology can provide with integrity: namely, a *Deus ex machina,* a miracle-working God, who will set blacks free

72. Paul Ricoeur, "Religion, Atheism, and Faith," in P. Ricoeur and A. MacIntyre, *The Religious Significance of Atheism* (New York: Columbia University Press, 1969), pp. 59–98. For Jones's critique of Washington, Cleage, M. Jones, and Roberts, see *Is God a White Racist?*, pp. 79–97, 121–165.
73. Notably in his *A Black Theology of Liberation* (Philadelphia: Lippincott, 1970), and *The Spirituals and the Blues* (New York: Seabury Press, 1972).

all at once, in one "mighty act" such as the Exodus of the Israelites from Egypt.

> How can blacks know that God disapproves of black suffering except by His *elimination* of it, except *by His bringing it to an immediate halt?* . . . Cone must identify what he regards as *the definitive event of black liberation.* . . . The scandal of the particularity of black suffering can be answered only by an appeal to the particularity of God's liberating activity—*an Exodus-type event for blacks.*[74]

Obviously, such a "definitive event of black liberation" has not occurred and will not occur. God does not act that way in history, and to require him so to act is to erect a straw God who is easily demolished. The Bible does not represent God as acting that way, the Exodus story to the contrary notwithstanding, for this story must be interpreted as a symbolic representation of what was obviously a long and difficult odyssey on the part of the Hebrew people. Nor did God act that way in the case of Jesus, who died on the cross at the hands of the Roman oppressor. God does not intervene supernaturally in human affairs to bring about "definitive" or "immediate" or "total" liberation. The theological alternatives demanded by Jones (either God intervenes supernaturally or he is not a liberating God) cannot tolerate the dialectical insight that liberation is taking place in a not-yet-redeemed world, that liberation entails conflict, struggle, suffering, defeat, death-and-resurrection. But this insight is the profoundest meaning of Christian faith, which knows that the liberating God is also the crucified God, the God who gives life through death and who dies in order that we may live. God's liberating action, I have argued, is part of an ongoing historical process that takes place by means of the dialectical interaction between the advent of new possibilities for the future and the binding, oppressive powers of the old order. Such an interaction generates conflict, suffering, setbacks, and advances, but never superficial, unambiguous progress. Cone has a more realistic understanding of the place of suffering

---

74. Jones, *Is God a White Racist?*, pp. 115–117 (italics mine) .

in the process of liberation, an understanding he has learned from the black spirituals.[75]

Given these qualifications, however, it is still necessary to be able to affirm that blacks "have experienced and are experiencing the liberating action of God." If that assertion has no content or is in no sense verifiable, then there is no basis for a theodicy. Here it would be necessary to show that freedom has in fact been experienced, affirmed, and sung about in the black community, not only as a human product but also as a divine gift, not only after emancipation but also before it in the days of slavery, not only in the struggle for civil rights or the black power movement but also in the period of Reconstruction and segregation. This is not to downgrade the enormous significance of such events as the end of slavery, or the gradual dismantling of the legal structure of segregation, or the movement toward equal educational opportunity. But it is to say that God's liberating action is not *limited* to such historical breakthroughs as these, and that God can set and hold a people free even in the midst of historical bondage and reversals. Black theologians, preachers, and civil leaders have provided ample testimony to such experiences,[76] although admittedly theirs is an interpretation of data that is subject to other interpretations (nontheistic, nonemancipatory) as well. There are no simple proofs in this matter, and one's own mode of existence and praxis are at stake in the wager of belief or disbelief.

Jones himself finally settles for a humanistic existentialism that surrenders any belief in God and places the struggle for liberation solely on human shoulders. However, he is reluctant to embrace it openly, elaborating instead a "humanocentric theism" as a kind

75. See Cone, *The Spirituals and the Blues,* chap. 4, "God and Black Suffering."
76. See, e.g., the writings of Richard Allen, Henry Highland Garnet, Daniel Payne, Frederick Douglass, W. E. B. DuBois, Booker T. Washington, Malcolm X, Martin Luther King, James Cone, Vincent Harding, Charles Long, Howard Thurman, Benjamin Mays, Joseph Johnson. In Chapters III–IV of *Children of Freedom,* I have attempted to summarize this testimony and thus to provide some account of the way in which freedom has been experienced in the black community—indeed experienced in such a way as to provide a basis for an affirmation of the liberating power of God.

of way-station to a thoroughgoing nontheistic humanism.[77]   His
reluctance here is revealing, for he may sense that such a position
unintentionally hands a victory to the white segregationist, who
has argued all along that God is in effect a "white racist," that he
created the black race as inferior and intended it to be separated
from other races and subjugated, if not destroyed entirely.   The
black humanist would be conceding that the white racist was correct about God, whose existence or goodness must therefore be
denied—along with the black religious heritage in America.   The
situation is perhaps analogous to that of contemporary Judaism.
Against Richard Rubenstein's denial of the God of Israel "after
Auschwitz" (a denial of great significance for Jones), Emil Fackenheim has argued that now the command for the Jew, perhaps the
very meaning of Auschwitz, is *not* to deny God, for that would be
to hand Hitler a posthumous victory, the destruction of the Jewish religion and ultimately of Judaism.[78]   This is a hard word,
and of itself a scant basis for a theology of liberation, but it is a
beginning.

4. THE LIBERATING AGENCY OF THE CRUCIFIED
AND RISEN JESUS

A. The Resurrection as the History of the Praxis of Freedom[79]

In order to address the question of theodicy more concretely, it
is necessary to ask *how* God's liberating, life-giving power is historically *mediated*.   By whose agency, and in what specific and
determinate ways, does it become efficacious for human beings
here and now?   According to Christian faith, the *crucified and*

---

77. Jones, *Is God a White Racist?*, chaps. II, XI, XII, esp. pp. 171–172.   Jones stands
in a significant tradition of black humanism (including Countee Cullen, James Wel-
don Johnson, Langston Hughes, Carter Woodson, Nella Larsen, James Baldwin),
which has rebelled against God in the face of radical evil—"the only serious
atheism," in Moltmann's judgment (*The Crucified God*, p. 252).   Jones has also
been heavily influenced by French existentialism.

78. Emil L. Fackenheim, *God's Presence in History: Jewish Affirmations and Philosophical Reflections* (New York: New York University Press, 1970), chap. 3.

79. This phrase has been suggested by Jürgen Moltmann.   See also Wolf-Dieter
Marsch, *Gegenwart Christi in der Gesellschaft: Eine Studie zu Hegels Dialektik*
(Munich: Chr. Kaiser Verlag, 1965), chap. I.

risen Jesus has become the "agent" or "representative" of God's liberating power in history, in consequence of which the latter takes on a new determinacy or modality. It is determinate not as to its scope and content, but as to its means and form.[80]

The New Testament uses two terms to interpret the Easter experience of the living presence of the crucified Lord: *egeirein* (more common in the verb form, "to rise [from the dead]"), and *anastasis* (more common in the noun form, "resurrection"). The image of awakening and rising from sleep is not central to the biblical usage of these terms, and it is not necessary therefore to assume that the New Testament writers construed them in the metaphorical sense of awakening and rising from death in a revivified body. More likely the extension of meaning was along the lines of installation in a function, rising to an action, sending a historical figure, or inaugurating a course of affairs, which is the more characteristic way these terms were used in the Septuagint and elsewhere in the New Testament, and which would entail the creation of a new, transfigured body, not the resuscitation of an old one. This is especially the case with the noun *anastasis,* which means etymologically "standing up to" a function or action, or more figuratively, "coming to stand *(stasis)* in the midst of or throughout *(ana)*." That in the midst of which the "risen" Jesus stands is the world. Thus to say that Jesus is "raised from the dead" means that he "comes to stand" in the world as the "agent" or "representative" of God, engaged in the work (praxis) of liberation. Jesus' agency is not exercised in some remote realm or other-worldly "heaven," or in some transcendent dimension of "salvation history." Rather it is exercised in our midst, here and now, "on earth under heaven," which is where human beings dwell in this "world" *(kosmos).* Resurrection means his coming, his presence, his efficacious agency in behalf of liberation, not his departure or removal from the scene.

80. Some of the material in this section is a condensation and restatement of an interpretation of the resurrection developed more fully in Chapter 5 of *Jesus—Word and Presence,* esp. pp. 241–254, 265–287. The reader is referred to these pages for a more technical statement of the thesis and citations of biblical texts and critical literature.

The "body" by which his action is embodied is no longer his old, now dead and decayed physical corpse, but the ongoing human community, more specifically, the community of those who recognize and acknowledge his empowering presence. This community, the community of faith, becomes fully and truly "the body of Christ" insofar as it engages in a mission of liberating praxis toward the world (a praxis that includes words as well as deeds, cultic celebration and personal renewal as well as social action). Jesus himself is personally present and active as the "head" of this "body" (Eph. 1:22–23); his words and actions are mediated through those of the community. He cannot act in the world today without *us,* who are *his* agents or deputies (just as he is the representative of God); our action, insofar as it becomes truly liberating, is not ours alone but his—he is its source, empowerment, and criterion.

This *functional* way of defining the resurrection is concerned especially with its benefits "for us" and our involvement in it. If it is meaningful to ask what the resurrection meant for Jesus, we should have to say it meant that God vindicated him and his message, did not in fact abandon him to everlasting death, and remained true to his covenantal promise as Lord over all things. It is noteworthy that Paul and John stressed the functional aspect of the resurrection and did not speculate about its meaning "for Jesus." In Pauline usage, the title *kyrios* (Lord) refers to Jesus' work of salvation as the Risen One (Rom. 1:4–5; 4:24; 10:9; 2 Cor. 4:14). Salvation is linked with resurrection in such passages as Rom. 8:34; 10:9; 2 Cor. 5:15. The event of salvation, in turn, includes two elements for Paul: justification and newness of life, both of which are closely associated with the resurrection of Jesus from the dead, as for example in Rom. 4:25 and 6:4–9. Likewise, for John, the resurrection is linked with the gift of eternal life, which has already been actualized in Jesus' earthly ministry and is evidenced by his life-giving power (cf. Jn. 11:25–26).

The agency of the risen Jesus on behalf of God has to do above all with the liberation of enslaved, oppressed, broken, sinful, death-bound men and women; it has to do with the coming of a realm or kingdom of freedom and the transfiguration of this earth. There are, of course, other aspects of the work of the risen Jesus, but they can be interpreted as modalities of the praxis of freedom. The early church experienced the presence of the Lord precisely in the formation of a new praxis—not only cultic (the breaking of the bread, Lk. 24:13–35), but also social and political. The account of the Last Judgment in Matt. 25:31–46, and other sayings in the Synoptic tradition as well (e.g., Mk. 9:37 par.; Matt. 10:40–42; Lk. 10:16), represent an affirmation by primitive Christian faith of the presence of the risen Jesus in deeds of mercy and brotherly/sisterly love directed toward conditions of hunger, poverty, estrangement, disease, and imprisonment. As such, they represent forms of social liberation. The immediate actors, of course, are men and women who find themselves drawn into a discipleship to Jesus. This discipleship need not be explicit, but if it is, they know that it is *he* who is at work in their midst, calling them forward to new tasks, giving them the means and the vision to accomplish what otherwise would go unattended. Through them his resurrection constitutes a history of the praxis of freedom. He is the energizing force in the dialectics of emancipation and redemption, the means by which the liberating power of the future breaks into the present and a new birth of freedom can occur in the midst of the human struggle to be free.

Ernst Käsemann connects the realities of resurrection and freedom as follows:

> The power of Christ's resurrection becomes a reality, here and now, in the form of Christian freedom, and only in that. That reality is opposed on earth by anything that stands in the way of Christian freedom, and only by that. . . . Christ's resurrection means Jesus' sovereignty, and such sovereignty becomes an earthly reality only in the realm of Christian freedom. The earth has no scarcity of lords, and they all demand obedience. . . . Christ differs from the other lords in that he effects freedom. He does not just call to it; that would be the law of which there are innumerable characteristic forms. Jesus gives freedom. That is what

makes him unmistakably Lord and inseparably unites the earthly
with the exalted Lord.[81]

Likewise Rubem Alves:

> The word [resurrection] was borrowed from Jewish apocalypti-
> cism to express the community's experience that the One who had
> been crucified was alive in history, as a power of liberation.
> Through this language Jesus could no longer be referred to simply
> as a fact of history, finished, plunged in the past. . . . He was not
> a *fact,* simply, but rather the *factor* of history, the power of free-
> dom that creates the facts of liberation. Jesus was now historically
> experienced as an informing power in history. . . . Resurrection
> meant accordingly that the Suffering Slave, the One who had the
> secret and power of human liberation, was making history free.
> He is, therefore, the Lord of history.[82]

The risen Jesus is *able* to liberate from the powers of bondage
by having undergone them in his own suffering and death. As the
Crucified One, he participates in the ambiguities, fragmentation,
conflicts, and negativities of history, and only this Crucified One
is risen.[83] Thus, as the bearer of the future, he is able to enter
into the struggle to bring freedom to birth in conflict with the
powers that resist it. He is the agent of historical praxis because
he has entered into the dialectics of history; his death and resurrection are the fulcrum on which, according to Christian faith,
this dialectic turns. A "Crucified God" can be represented historically only by a "Suffering Slave." Such an identity has made
this Liberator relevant to oppressed peoples everywhere. He once
stood where they now stand and vice versa; he has taken upon
himself their suffering, making it his own, easing their burden,
empowering them in their struggle for freedom.

These themes were poignantly portrayed by the black spirituals.

> Were you there when they crucified my Lord?
> Oh! Sometimes it causes me to tremble, tremble, tremble.
> Were you there when they nailed Him to the tree?

81. Ernst Käsemann, *Jesus Means Freedom,* trans. Frank Clarke (Philadelphia:
Fortress Press, 1970) , pp. 154–155; cf. pp. 151, 153.
82. Alves, *A Theology of Human Hope,* pp. 130–131.
83. Ernst Käsemann, "The Saving Significance of the Death of Jesus in Paul,"
Perspectives on Paul, trans. Margaret Kohl (Philadelphia: Fortress Press, 1971) ,
pp. 32–59, esp. p. 57.

> Were you there when they pierced Him in the side?
> Were you there when He bowed His head and died?
>
> He arose, he arose from the dead,
> An' de Lord shall bear my spirit hom'.
>
> Children, we shall be free.
> When the Lord shall appear.
> Give ease to the sick, give sight to the blind,
> Enable the cripple to walk;
> He'll raise the dead from under the earth,
> And give them permission to talk.

The "appearance" of the Lord was an eschatological reality for the slaves, referring to the Second Coming of Jesus when the whole of creation would be set free. But the risen Jesus had also already appeared to the slaves, as he had to the first Christians. He was with them now as friend, fellow-sufferer, comforter, healer, savior, deliverer. They knew that the Risen One had been crucified and that there are no miraculous rescues in history, but they also knew that the Crucified was risen and that therefore they would not be slaves forever.

> The finality of Jesus lies in the totality of his existence in complete freedom as the Oppressed One, who reveals through his death and resurrection that God himself is present in all dimensions of human liberation. His death is the revelation of the freedom of God, taking upon himself the totality of human oppression; his resurrection is the disclosure that God is not defeated by oppression but transforms it into the possibility of freedom.[84]

I have argued thus far that the resurrection of the Crucified constitutes a history of the praxis of freedom. But one might still ask why this connection between the risen Jesus and freedom is necessary. Why must *Jesus* give freedom? Why is *his* agency required? Why can we not simply set ourselves free, or at least gain access to divine liberating power without the mediation of a historical Redeemer? From the perspective of Christian faith, three reasons may be set forth.

84. James Cone, *A Black Theology of Liberation*, pp. 210–211 (the first sentence is italicized by the author); cf. *The Spirituals and the Blues*, pp. 36, 47–57, 93; also my brief discussion of the meaning of the resurrection for the black experience in *Children of Freedom*, pp. 57–62.

(1) Without the "model" afforded by Jesus, the experience of freedom is in danger of issuing in enthusiastic self-delusion. According to Käsemann, this was the chief danger confronted by Paul in the church at Corinth.[85] The experience of freedom can readily be interpreted on the basis of an ideology of human self-deliverance, and it can issue in a libertinism that knows no limits, no structure, no obedience. Freedom is a dangerous commodity. When men and women engage upon the effort to liberate themselves and to live without limits, they only enslave themselves the more deeply. The model and agency of Jesus afford a check against this. For Paul, this meant above all the death of Jesus, and he drew the themes of crucifixion and resurrection together into the closest unity (cf. Rom. 4:24–25; 8:34; 1 Cor. 15:3–4; 2 Cor. 5:15; 13:4), insisting that the cross remains (in the words of Käsemann) "the signature of the Risen One." In Paul's view, "only the Crucified is risen, and the dominion of the Risen One today extends only so far as the Crucified is served." [86] Hence his death functions as a constant reminder that freedom is possible only as a gift of God and in the form of self-giving love.

(2) Not only the death but also the historical life and ministry of Jesus provide criteria for recognizing authentic freedom and distinguishing it from inauthentic. Jesus defines the meaning of freedom vis-à-vis the rival possibilities at stake in the ancient and modern worlds. This is true both of his person and of his ministry of proclamation and praxis. From his personal identity we have learned that true freedom entails openness to God (faith), non-separated, non-alienated community (love), and non-privatistic, non-autonomous subjectivity (life)—a matter to be pursued more fully in Chapter VII. From his proclamation and parabolic enactment of the advent of God's kingdom, we have learned that freedom is actualized in the realms of law and religious piety, social and political existence, and ultimately life and death itself.

85. Käsemann, *Jesus Means Freedom*, pp. 48–51, 59–65; cf. Alves, *A Theology of Human Hope*, p. 92.
86. Käsemann, "The Saving Significance of the Death of Jesus in Paul," *Perspectives on Paul*, pp. 56–57 (translation altered) .

These realms of liberation, which may be distributed into two main divisions—liberation of the self from sin and death, and of sociopolitical structures from law and the powers—will be the subject of concern in the concluding section of this chapter. A resurrection theology must turn to the life, ministry, and death of Jesus for the concrete filling-out of details, and conversely, of course, a historically oriented Christology must issue in a dialectics of liberation if the data concerning the earthly Jesus are to gain existential and practical meaning. Without Jesus the Proclaimer, the Healer, the Crucified and Risen One, there would be no determinate meaning of freedom for Christian faith, and Christianity would not be the "religion of freedom."

(3) God transcends us as the future, the end, the "whither" toward which all life is oriented. God's word is the power of the future that calls us forward. Freedom is experienced as the gift of the future, liberating humanity from past burdens and oppressions. To be radically open *for* the future *by the power of* the future is the essence of freedom. Now, Jesus is the agent by whom the power of the future ingresses. Without his present agency, God as the source and goal of freedom would remain an incomprehensible, impenetrable, unattainable mystery. There would be no advent of freedom, no actual *new birth* of freedom, and thus no dialectics of liberation. History would remain statically dominated by the oppressive legacy of the past and the iron law of cause and effect; liberation would come, apocalyptically, only at the end of time. If God is to remain God, he must be transcendent as well as immanent, hidden as well as revealed, absent as well as present. For this reason he "needs" an agent, a representative, a deputy,[87] who, by entering into history, can set it moving toward its goal by bringing that goal into productive, indeed volatile encounter with the negative and positive possibilities of his-

---

87. This concept has been developed by Dietrich Bonhoeffer, *Ethics*, 2d ed., ed. E. Bethge, trans. N. H. Smith (New York: Macmillan, 1965); *Letter and Papers from Prison*, rev. ed., ed. E. Bethge, trans. R. H. Fuller, F. Clarke, et al. (New York: Macmillan, 1967); and Dorothee Soelle, *Christ the Representative*, trans. David Lewis (Philadelphia: Fortress Press, 1967).

tory. Thereby God is not undialectically absent but rather dialectically present in the liberating praxis of his agent.

B. LIBERATION FROM THE POWERS OF BONDAGE

(1) Liberation of the Self from Sin and Death

The risen Jesus' work of liberation may be divided into two spheres, corresponding to a distinction made in our earlier discussion of the dialectical actualization of freedom in history, namely, the liberation of the *self* (or of consciousness), and the liberation of *sociopolitical structures*. Here we confront a perennial and irresolvable question: Which comes first? Liberation of persons or of structures? Which is more basic, psychic reality or social reality? Simple, undialectical answers to this question must be resisted. More important than establishing a priority, one way or the other, between self and structure, is the recognition that the two constitute an inseparable unity, and that concentration on the one to the neglect of the other cannot achieve lasting liberation. It does not matter where one starts, only that one makes and remakes the circuit between the two.

> Personal, inner change without a change in circumstances and structures is an idealist illusion, as though man were only a soul and not a body as well. But a change in external circumstances without inner renewal is a materialist illusion, as though man were only a product of his social circumstances and nothing else.[88]

This dialectical insight is confirmed by the insistence of Latin American leaders that social and political revolution must be directed toward a transformation and liberation of individual persons, perhaps even, as Dom Helder Cámara has put it, "that before we have a revolution in structures we need a cultural revolution—a sort of personal conversion, a change in attitude, a metanoia." [89] It is also confirmed by the biblical understanding of bondage (the dialectic between subjective and objective forms of

---

88. Moltmann, *The Crucified God*, p. 23. Leander Keck makes the same point in "The Son Who Creates Freedom," *Jesus Christ and Human Freedom* (*Concilium*, vol. 93; New York: Herder and Herder, 1974), pp. 80–81.
89. Quoted by Luís Ambroggio, "The Latin American Man and His Revolution," in Louis M. Colonnese, ed., *Conscientization for Liberation*, p. 7, cf. pp. 9 ff.; also Gustavo Gutiérrez, *A Theology of Liberation*, p. 91.

sin), and by the way the liberating action of the historical and risen Jesus has actually been experienced.

Liberation of *the self* means a liberation from *sin* and from *death* (two of the four forms of bondage distinguished by Paul). The two basic dimensions of *sin* are *idolatry* (pride) and *flight* (sloth, apathy). On the one hand, we venerate and absolutize ourselves or other finite things in place of God, thereby justifying patterns of exploitation and domination; on the other, we take flight from life, venerating death instead, or indulging in a general apathy toward conditions over which we assume that we have no control.[90] In both cases, our free and responsible creaturehood is disrupted. Now, idolatry and flight, pride and apathy, correspond precisely to the distortion of human consciousness in the form of the master-slave relationship to which reference was made in analyzing the dialectics of emancipation. The master embodies the sin of idolatry, for he becomes a god or "lord" to the slave and remains imprisoned in his own egotism; the slave embodies the sin of flight, for he is willing to surrender his freedom and equality out of fear of death or timidity in face of the master. Thus liberation from sin means overcoming the master-slave relationship in all of its historical manifestations—chattel slavery, class divisions, racial prejudice and oppression, sexual discrimination, authoritarian family patterns, the hierarchy and apathy engendered by modern bureaucracy and technology, the inequitable distribution of income and ownership. These patterns are to be replaced by a movement toward equality and genuine reciprocity in human relationships, therefore toward full selfhood on the part of every individual. Whenever and wherever such a movement takes place, Christian faith discerns the liberating work of the risen Jesus.

The *historical* and *crucified* Jesus set human beings free by reconstituting their creaturehood in true obedience to God. Likewise the *risen* Jesus liberates from the master-slave relation-

90. See Chap. IV, Sec. 2b. Dorothee Soelle argues that, from the point of view of a political interpretation, sin may be understood primarily as collaboration with and apathy toward "a structurally founded, usually anonymous injustice." *Political Theology*, trans. John Shelley (Philadelphia: Fortress Press, 1974), pp. 89–92.

ship by bringing a saving openness or obedience to God into play: this is the new "factor" that he brings on the scene in the dialectics of liberation. I am unable to transcend my self-mastery and self-servitude by further efforts of my own, for that simply deepens either my idolatry or my apathy: radical, self-saving autonomy is sin *par excellence.* I can be liberated, paradoxically perhaps, only by obedience—but not by obedience to a human master, rather by obedience to the God of freedom, who slays the finite, enslaving deities. The real God, unlike the idolatrous gods, does not oscillate between domination and protection; rather he liberates precisely by granting persons their creaturehood and suffering with them in that creaturehood. Paul designated the dying Jesus as the obedient one (Rom. 5:19; Phil. 2:8) because by his death he restored all people to the righteousness of true obedience—an obedience that acknowledges God to be the Creator and men and women to be creatures, who renounce all pious and rebellious attempts at self-salvation, but who at the same time exercise the responsibility of their created freedom, refusing to lapse into servitude or apathy. "Obedience," says Käsemann, "is the sign of regained creatureliness" [91]—and thus of liberation from the bondage of idolatry and flight.

Death is the second form of bondage of the self. I argued earlier for a distinction between physical mortality *(thnētos),* which as one of the conditions of finitude is not evil, and death *(thanatos),* which is the form mortality assumes when it becomes a binding, destructive power in the lives of individuals.[92] Mortality-as-death represents the objectification of our sinful flight from life and freedom. The writers of the Gospels, especially Mark, believed that the earthly Jesus was already locked in combat with the destructive power of death, which for them was symbolized by possessing demons, terrible diseases such as leprosy, and other incapacitating illnesses such as blindness and paralysis. It is important to note, however, that it was not believed that Jesus made

91. Käsemann, "The Saving Significance of the Death of Jesus in Paul," *Perspectives on Paul,* p. 41.
92. See Chap. IV, Sec. 3B.

people immortal, incapable of dying. Rather he freed them from premature, abnormal, disease-ridden death; he worked to heal their lives of physical and social wounds, and thus to save them from dying in the process of living.

But in the final analysis, mortality is *not* binding and "deadly" only if it does *not* have the power of cutting the individual off from a life-sustaining relationship with God. If mortality can ultimately thwart God's saving power in relation to the destiny of the individual, then it is in fact the enemy. That it does not have this power, that God alone is the victor over all that can stand between him and us, including our mortality and finitude, is based on the confession that Jesus has been raised—raised *from the dead (ek nekrōn)*, which means, not that he did not die, but that even his death was unable to destroy the life-giving presence of God upon which he had staked his entire existence and mission. Human beings are not immortal, incapable of dying, for they do in fact always die. Their mortality is both preserved and transfigured by the resurrection from the dead. It becomes a moment in the life of God. Thus it is no longer capable of being converted into "death," and in this sense the power of death (its "victory" or "sting," 1 Cor. 15:55) is destroyed. It is true that Paul uses the language of immortality in 1 Cor. 15:50–54, but he does not say that we are already immortal and thus deathless in the Greek or Gnostic sense. Rather in consequence of resurrection precisely from the dead, "we shall be changed." What is mortal must be "clothed with" or "put on" immortality. First mortality, then and only then, immortality. It is in this sense that after death and resurrection, mortality itself is transfigured—not lost but transformed as to its essence, both annulled and preserved in eternal life with God. Death is undergone only once: being raised from the dead, we shall never again die, and death has thus lost its dominion over us (Rom. 6:9); death is swallowed up in victory (1 Cor. 15:54), mortality in life (2 Cor. 5:4). The identity of the individual is not lost but taken up into a higher unity, a new "spiritual" body (1 Cor. 15:44), the *sōma Christou*.

Jesus' liberating action in relation to death is not so much his own action, except in an anticipatory way (the acts of healing, etc.), as it is the action of God.   God alone is the Liberator from death; Jesus mediates that action, not by what he does but by what is done to him and through him.   Still, his resurrection-presence in the praxis of freedom is the promise of victory over this ultimate form of bondage.   The victory will be complete only when God has put all enemies—including death—under his feet and has become "all in all" in a new creation (1 Cor. 15:22–28).

(2) *Liberation of Sociopolitical Structures from Law and the Powers*

The individual forms of bondage already have sociopolitical ramifications.   This is clearly the case with the sin of idolatry and flight, which in the form of the master-slave relationship stamps all human social institutions.   Likewise, it can be argued that death, as the ultimate and universal bondage, casts its shadow upon the whole of civilization, locking it into a self-destructive dialectic.   Hence the liberation from sin by an obediential openness to God, and from death by God's life-giving power, means that *in principle* the forms of social bondage are broken as well.

But sin gains social and institutional objectification, which is resistant to individual conversions of the heart and must be confronted on its own terms.   Hence we may speak of a liberation from *estrangement* (or "law") and from the oppressive *powers* (ideological and economic-political)—the other two forms of bondage distinguished by Paul.   We have confronted *estrangement* as the consequence of civilization's inability to achieve a true reconciliation between the individual and the social whole, an inability which means among other things that the attempt to attain freedom from purely intrahistorical possibilities cannot finally succeed.   For the New Testament and Paul in particular, the law becomes a symbol of cultural estrangement—the estrangement that exists between the legal demands of religious, political, and social institutions, and either the inability or the unwillingness of individuals to obey or to keep the law. The law is an objectification of my sense of responsibility and guilt, but now it stands over against me as an alien, enslaving, convicting power.[93]

Jesus' conflict with and fulfillment of the law is one of the central themes of the Gospels. Most of the conflict pericopes are concerned with some aspect of religious life or cultic practice: the laws of purification, the temple tax, modes of piety, the sabbath laws. By challenging these laws, Jesus liberated from the most alienating forms of religious practice. But on the other hand he came not to abolish the law and the prophets but to complete them (Matt. 5:17 par.). This "completion" is understood by Paul as part of the atoning, redemptive work of Christ, who has released us from the burden of the law by fulfilling its demand "in our place," "on our behalf," a theme especially prominent in Galatians and Romans.

> "No human being can be justified in the sight of God" for having kept the law: law brings only the consciousness of sin. But now, quite independently of law, God's justice has been brought to light. . . . All alike have sinned, . . . and all are justified by God's free grace alone, through his act of liberation in the person of Christ Jesus. For God designed him to be the means of expiating sin by his sacrificial death, effective through faith. God meant by this to demonstrate his justice, because in his forbearance he had overlooked the sins of the past. . . .
>
> —Rom. 3:20–26 (NEB)

Although Paul here employs the categories of expiation, the foundation of his argument is not the juridical notion of substitution by which the law's requirement of punishment is satisfied. Rather it is that Christ has set right the relationship between Creator and creature by his love for others, even unto death: *thereby* "God's justice has been brought to light," "quite independently of law." An ancillary benefit is that we sinners are released from the estranging and accusing demands of the law and experience a liberation from the burdens and legacy of the past.

93. See above, Chap. IV, Sec. 3A. On the relations between law, civilization, estrangement, and guilt, see Miranda, *Marx and the Bible*, pp. 178, 182–185, 187; Ricoeur, *The Symbolism of Evil*, pp. 100–150; and Gibson Winter, *Being Free: Reflections on America's Cultural Revolution* (New York: Macmillan, 1970), chap. II.

Paul also makes it clear that redemption from the law is not meant to issue in a libertinism or lawlessness but in a higher law, a law of love, freedom, and justice, a *novus ordo caritatis*. It is the law of love which in a positive way overcomes social estrangement, building up instead a community of reconciliation—an "emancipated society" in which all are free to participate, but in which particularity, uniqueness, and pluralism are preserved. This comes close to defining what is meant by "cultural revolution" in the terms of the counter culture. The risen Christ is at work, engaged in a praxis of freedom, in the struggle to build up a new human community, to create an emancipated society. Cultural revolution cannot be achieved by human power alone, but only by that power which overcomes alienation in principle. By engendering that power, the risen Jesus perpetuates the process, initiated during his earthly ministry, of "abolishing" and "completing" the law.[94]

The second form of social bondage consists of the institutionalization of *oppressive powers* in ideological as well as economic and political structures. *Ideology* represents a way of sanctioning unjust or traditional practices by an uncritical set of beliefs or doctrines that usually reflect psychological and/or sociological factors. Religion, it has often been argued, functions ideologically in society, as, for example, when it promotes the doctrine of individual conversion and insists that religious belief has nothing to do with politics, or when it espouses such social myths as that "the poor will always be with us" (a myth incorporated unfortunately into the Gospel of Mark), or that class divisions are inevitable, or when it provides a religious sanction for racism, slavery, sexism, classism. Rather than having anything to do with Christian faith, these ideologies are really expressions of privileged bourgeois (male) groups, who are content with the status quo and want to

94. On the Pauline theology of law, redemption, and love, see Chap. V, Sec. 5A; on Jesus' relation to the law, Chap. V, Sec. 3B; on the concept of cultural revolution, Winter, *Being Free*, chap. IV; on the "dialectic of love in estrangement," Moltmann, *Perspectiven der Theologie*, pp. 51–53; on "emancipated society and the presence of Jesus Christ," Marsch, *Gegenwart Christi in der Gesellschaft*, chap. I; on law as the instrument of interhuman justice, Miranda, *Marx and the Bible*, pp. 137, 152, 156, 159.

avoid disruptive changes. Therefore Dorothee Soelle argues that the critique of ideology must now replace demythologizing as the major theological task. The ideological fixations of Christianity are more dangerous today than its mythological world view.[95]

Earlier I suggested that Paul's notion of the "spirit powers" might be somewhat akin to modern-day ideologies. The earthly Jesus was of course engaged in a ministry of exorcism against such "demonic" powers, which are psychological as well as physical. Illusions, moreover, are the essence of ideology, and Jesus battled the power of illusion in the whole of his proclamation, which was intended (according to Johannine imagery) to allow the light of truth to shine in a deceitful and darkened world. The parables in particular were events of disclosure, by which their hearers were (and are) forced to see the truth about themselves and their relationship to God. Ideological illusions can become godlike, demonic powers that seem to possess us, and Jesus sets us free from this possession—not only the earthly Jesus, the healer and proclaimer, but also the risen Lord, who carries forward the fight against the powers.

> The other gods are in fact always the objectivations of our longings and fears, our pleasures and our wantonness. They are born in our hearts, and then, from the man who creates them, they gain power over him and over the earth. What influences our hearts always makes itself felt outside, acquires influence over our surroundings, and finally enslaves us and others, so that it comes at us again from outside. Thus the world's great forces of evil arise from human illusions which we cannot shake off, and which grow stronger than we, our society, and the efforts of the nations. . . . Where there is a real church, the world is, within a larger or smaller radius, cleared of demons, and God's sovereignty over his creatures begins in a new way.[96]

"Where there is a real church," the risen Jesus is present, the "head" of the "body," gathering, upbuilding, sending into mission, "abolishing every kind of domination, authority, and power" (1 Cor. 15:24, NEB).

95. Soelle, *Political Theology*, pp. 6–9, 61, 74–77. See the discussion of ideology in Chap. IV, Sec. 3c (1).
96. Käsemann, *Jesus Means Freedom*, p. 77.

The "powers" that Paul has in mind are not merely "spiritual" but also "earthly" or political. Therefore the powers abolished or destroyed by the rule of the risen Christ include socioeconomic and political forms of oppression. Although this emphasis was muted in Paul, it was not so in the case of the earthly Jesus, who condemned human injustice and engendered a critical partisanship on the side of the poor, the powerless, the outcasts and marginals, calling into question the established structures of domination and control.[97]

It is this side of the historical ministry of Jesus in particular that has attracted the attention of contemporary liberation movements. He identifies with their bondage, calling them forth into freedom as the agent of liberation. For blacks he is the Black Messiah, because as Cone says, "black" symbolizes "what the world means by oppression and what the gospel means by liberation." For women he is the one who challenged and broke up the patriarchal dominance of society, and who included women, who were religiously and socially ostracized, within his intimate following. For the third world he is the one who identified with the victims of economic and social discrimination, challenging the hypocrisy and greed of those with access to power who have used it to enhance their own wealth.[98] The "he" in each instance refers not merely to the historical Jesus but more especially to the crucified and risen Lord, who is now efficaciously present and at work in the movements for liberation. The liberation theologies are all resurrection theologies, whether consciously so or not, for otherwise the connection could not be made between determinate situations of bondage and liberation and Christian confession of Jesus as the Christ.

The involvement of the historical and risen Jesus in the struggles for human liberation means that any partisanship must be *critical.* Jesus himself did not join the Zealot resistance movement because the kingdom whose coming he proclaimed was the work

97. On the concept of "critical partisanship," see above, pp. 238–239.
98. See Cone, *A Black Theology of Liberation,* p. 217; Soelle, *Political Theology,* pp. 65–66; Russell, *Human Liberation in a Feminist Perspective,* pp. 137–139; Gutiérrez, *A Theology of Liberation,* pp. 172–178.

of God, not of a violent seizure of power. He did not indulge in the rhetoric of hatred, thereby enflaming partisan passions, for he must have realized that few areas of human endeavor are more beset by alienation, idolatry, legalism, and a taste for vengeance than movements of liberation and revolution.[99]

The model of a critical partisanship means that it is inappropriate for Christians to embrace *unqualifiedly* any particular political form or economic system in the struggle for sociopolitical freedom. For example, an absolute or dogmatic choice between capitalism and socialism is uncalled for from a Christian perspective, although relative judgments are unavoidable. Each of these systems has been and is capable of severe forms of social injustice—capitalism, through unrestrained competition and profit, great concentrations of property and wealth in private hands, and exploitation of human and natural resources; socialism, through unmanageable and dangerous concentrations of power in organs of the state and party, and restrictions on individual freedom of thought, expression, style, and movement. The Christian must remain a partisan of human liberation within a given system and set of circumstances, determining whether reforms of the existing structure are possible, or whether a revolutionary transition is necessary, calculating in each instance what the human and social costs will be. Time is running out, and more humane and equitable modes of socioeconomic organization must soon evolve if civilization is to survive on this planet. My own view is that a form of democratic socialism, one which abjures the use of violence, guarantees a significant distribution of power, and achieves a sensitive balance between individual liberties and exigencies of the social and environmental whole, represents the most promising option for the future. In any event, the bourgeois phase of Western culture, with which capitalism has been historically associated, is drawing to a close, and it seems unlikely that capitalism can survive a cultural revolution of this magnitude. What will replace it is not clear; if it is to be socialism in some form, hope-

99. Cf. Moltmann, "Political Theology," *Theology Today*, 28: 16–19, 22–23.

fully the latter will prove capable of transcending the empirical
manifestations with which we have become familiar during the
past century. The dialectics of emancipation and redemption as
described in this chapter ought to serve as a crucible in which new
forms can be shaped, tested, and refined. In this process the kingdom of freedom remains a utopian vision that can never be fully
actualized, although it energizes the process at every critical moment.[100]

The dangers of an *uncritical* partisanship are evident from some
of the unguarded statements of the black theologian James Cone.
Cone is so concerned to argue that God has "taken sides" in the
black struggle for freedom and justice that he is led to assert that
God is exclusively and unqualifiedly identified with black people,
that whiteness is intrinsically evil and the object of divine wrath,
and that violence and destruction are justified in the struggle
against oppression. Perhaps his most unguarded statement is the
following:

> Black Theology cannot accept a view of God which does not rep-
> resent him as being for blacks and thus against whites. Living in
> a world of white oppressors, black people have no time for a
> neutral God. . . . There is no use for a God who loves whites the
> *same* as blacks. . . . What we need is the divine love as expressed
> in Black Power which is the power of black people to destroy their
> oppressors, here and now, by any means at their disposal. Unless
> God is participating in this holy activity, we must reject his love.[101]

The alternative to a vengeful, destructive partisanship is not neutrality but rather what Moltmann has called "the dialectic of siding with the humiliated" for the sake of effecting the liberation

100. On the partisan yet critical involvement of Christians in the struggle for
social and political liberation, see Kraus, *Reich Gottes: Reich der Freiheit*, pp. 403–
413. On socialism as an option, see William R. Coats, *God in Public: Political
Theology Beyond Niebuhr* (Grand Rapids: Eerdmans, 1974), esp. chap. 8; and Juan
Luís Segundo, "Capitalism—Socialism: A Theological Crux," in *The Mystical and
Political Dimension of the Christian Faith*, ed. C. Geffré & G. Gutiérrez (*Concilium*,
vol. 96; New York: Herder and Herder, 1974), pp. 105–123.
101. Cone, *A Black Theology of Liberation*, pp. 131–132. Although similar rhetoric
is scattered through this, Cone's angriest, book (e.g., pp. 17–18, 25–29, 108, 118,
120–122, 130–134, 136–137, 176, 192–193), I think he has allowed himself to make
statements that do not reflect his own best judgment and are not consistent with
the logic of Christian faith as he understands it. Cone has been sharply criticized
on this score by the black writer Julius Lester in "Be Ye Therefore Perfect,"
Katallagete, 5 (Winter 1974): 24–25.

and humanization of all [102]—including white racists, who need to be emancipated from their white racism, not robbed of their humanity. Cone has allowed himself to be swayed too much by an essentially pagan view of God as one who takes vengeance upon the enemies of his chosen, righteous people. This is not the God of the prophets or of the crucified and risen Jesus. The presence of the latter in the praxis of freedom demands of us all a critical, iconoclastic, humanizing, reconciling partisanship in the struggle against the oppressive powers.

But the question remains as to whether even a critical partisanship can work effectively for liberation without engaging in acts of violence, especially when confronted by the violence of the established structures. It seems clear that Jesus himself practiced *nonviolence*[103] in an *active,* not a passive way. He did not avoid conflictual situations, but he sought to resolve conflicts without destroying the enemy. He did not cooperate with the arresting and accusing authorities, but he died without resisting them violently. For him, perhaps unlike the Zealots, violence was not an end in itself, nor could it become a policy or a calculated means to an end. He recognized that the kingdom he proclaimed could not help but enter into conflict with the conditions of this world (cf. Matt. 10:34–36; 11:12). He must have known that the use of power and force is not only unavoidable in conflictual situations (cf. the cleansing of the temple, Mk. 11:15–19 par., and the advice to purchase a sword, Lk. 22:35–38), but also that it always

102. Moltmann, *Religion, Revolution, and the Future,* pp. 140–143; see also Gutiérrez, *A Theology of Liberation,* pp. 273–275, 287–302.
103. The literature on this subject is enormous. A good survey of it is provided by James F. Childress, "Nonviolent Resistance and Direct Action: A Bibliographical Essay," *Journal of Religion,* 52 (October 1972): 376–396. Given the limitations of this book and of my own competence on the subject, the following brief discussion can do no more than raise certain questions and give hints of a direction toward finding answers. My reflections have been assisted not only by Childress's article but also by Paul Lehmann, *The Transfiguration of Politics,* pp. 259–274; Hannah Arendt, *On Revolution,* pp. 1–52, 85–87, 109–110, 215; Rubem Alves, *A Theology of Human Hope,* pp. 111–114; Jürgen Moltmann, *Religion, Revolution, and the Future,* pp. 143–145; Reinhold Niebuhr, *Moral Man and Immoral Society* (New York: Scribner's, 1932), chaps. VII–IX, esp. pp. 252–253; Rosemary Ruether, *Liberation Theology* (New York: Paulist Press, 1972), pp, 184–186; Martin Hengel, *Victory Over Violence: Jesus and the Revolutionists,* trans. David E. Green (Philadelphia: Fortress Press, 1973); and Leander Keck, "The Church, the New Testament, and Violence," *Pastoral Psychology,* 22 (October 1971): 5–14.

runs the risk of violence. At the same time he admonished those who followed him not to engage in acts of violence, retaliation, or resistance (Matt. 5:38–42), and he insisted that they must love their enemies as well as their friends (Matt. 5:43–44). However, as Gutiérrez points out, the love of enemies

> does not mean avoiding confrontations; it does not mean pre-serving a fictitious harmony. . . . In the context of class struggle today, to love one's enemies presupposes recognizing and accepting that one has class enemies and that it is necessary to combat them. It is not a question of having no enemies, but rather of not ex-cluding them from our love. But love does not mean that the oppressors are no longer enemies, nor does it eliminate the radi-calness of the combat against them. "Love of enemies" does not ease tensions; rather it challenges the whole system and becomes a subversive formula.[104]

Conflict, struggle, the active and even revolutionary use of power, yes; but violence as a calculated policy or end in itself, no. Violence may be defined as "direct, intentional, and unauthorized harm which is against the will of the one harmed." [105] Violence subverts the essence of political institutions, which is to provide a forum for speech and action and hence for the nonviolent adjudi-cation of conflicts. Violence, especially against persons, like the primitive prestige battle (which ended with the death of one or both of the combatants), of itself precludes the possibility for further development because the relational structures by which such a development might have been sustained are destroyed. In other words, *violence is a highly undialectical act.* Instead of keeping history open and moving, it has a deadening, paralyzing effect. It does not represent a new birth but an abortion. The purpose of the presence of the risen Christ at the point of inter-section between the possibilities for freedom immanent in history and the new birth of freedom as liberating power is to keep the conflicts and resistances generated by this interaction open, pro-ductive, and volatile but nonviolent.

---

104. Gutiérrez, *A Theology of Liberation*, pp. 275–276. See also Milan Machoveč, *Jesus für Atheisten* (Stuttgart: Kreuz Verlag, 1972), pp. 126–133.
105. Childress, "Nonviolent Resistance and Direct Action," p. 378.

Nonviolence rather than violence, then, must serve as a *policy* or *way of life*. But even as a policy it must not be absolutized, for it cannot eliminate the *risk* of violence that every struggle for human liberation entails.[106] There are certainly occasions when the use of power generates violence, or when violence itself becomes an uncalculated and unavoidable necessity, as for example when conditions grow so inhuman, degrading, or totally threatening that it is better to die than not to resist violently or to act in self-defense. Under such circumstances it may still be possible to engage in nonhomicidal forms of violence, such as the urban riots of the late sixties, which were spontaneous outbursts of rage against outrageous conditions, directed against property rather than persons. Here at least a degree of dialectical openness is retained. But even when violence takes the form of killing, as in wars and revolutions, it cannot be denied that in the clearing created by violence new possibilities may sometimes emerge.

Indeed, it is not beyond the power of God to use revolutionary violence as an occasion for a dialectical transfiguration. Within human politics, violence remains an undialectical act. It occurs at the limits and the point of breakdown of human power; in this sense it is an "apocalyptic phenomenon," as Paul Lehmann rightly says.[107] Yet in the vacuum, the abyss, the abortion of possibility occasioned by violence, God—and God alone—can act, engendering history anew, bringing life out of death. The risen Christ is *also* present in wars and revolutions, which serve as the locus of his *opus alienum*.[108] His *opus proprium* is that of the nonviolent actualization of freedom through the dialectics of emancipation and redemption. The fact that even violence cannot finally abort this dialectic indicates that God is the Lord of history, not the human passion for liberation.

106. The distinction between the risk and the policy of violence is one of Paul Lehmann's important contributions to the discussion. See *The Transfiguration of Politics*, pp. 264–265, 271–274.
107. Ibid., p. 262.
108. This expression is used by Karl Barth in a slightly different sense in *Church Dogmatics*, ed. G. W. Bromiley and T. F. Torrance, III/4 (Edinburgh: T. & T. Clark, 1961), 456 ff.

PART FIVE
FINAL FREEDOM

Chapter VII

The Symbolics of Freedom

1. THE SPIRIT AND FREEDOM'S NEW BIRTH

Having completed an investigation of *how* the freedom *engendered* by Jesus is *actualized* (the question of liberation), we are now confronted by a final question, which concerns the *meaning* and *structures* of the freedom thus engendered and actualized. *"For freedom* Christ has set us free" (Gal. 5:1). What is this freedom? The answer can no longer be oriented to the forms of bondage (freedom *from* sin, law, death, and the powers), for then the logic of freedom would be dominated by the logic of bondage. Rather, a positive, constructive definition of life-in-freedom must be fashioned from the distinctive way that freedom has been experienced and symbolized by Christian faith.

An initial orientation is suggested by Bultmann,[1] who argues that, by contrast with the timelessness of the Greek world view, freedom for Christian faith means *openness to the future.* Human beings, says Bultmann (following Heidegger), exist toward the future; they are always in process of becoming what they might be. Yet the sinful, death-bound person is enthralled by the unalterable, unrepeatable past and is not free to decide in response to the call of the future. Thus freedom is experienced as the *gift* of the future, liberating from the past—a future that stands in sharp antithesis to and judgment upon the past, calling humanity forward into a new world out of the old (here the apocalyptic contrast between two aeons is appropriate); yet a future that is not distant but is now breaking into and indeed constituting the present with its transforming power, *a future whose advent engenders a new birth of freedom.* Freedom, says Bultmann, "means possessing genuine future, whereas man under the power of death,

1. Rudolf Bultmann, *Primitive Christianity in Its Contemporary Setting,* trans. R. H. Fuller (New York: Meridian Books, 1956), pp. 144–145, 180–188, 204–205, 208; *Theology of the New Testament,* vol. I, trans. Kendrick Grobel (New York: Scribner's, 1954), pp. 330–335.

as he formerly was, had no future. . . . Freedom is nothing else than being open for the genuine future, letting one's self be determined by the future." [2]

Following this clue, and on the basis of the symbols, images, and events of Christian experience, we may construct a *symbolics of freedom* in which the *essential structures* of human existence undergo a reversal of priorities and a transfiguration of meanings. This reversal and transfiguration is refracted through the figure of *Jesus as the radically free person,* as the following schema illustrates.

The symbolics of freedom has its *initial* orientation, no longer to power, self-determination, autonomy (as in all humanistic views—Greek, Stoic, Freudian, existentialist), nor to objective social structures (as in Marxism, behaviorism, and technocracy), but to *openness*—openness to future liberating power, which, on the basis of the symbols of Christian experience, may now be identified with *God* as the One whose essential being *is* freedom. In place of the neutral phenomenological category of openness (which lends itself to "pagan" interpretations as well—tragic, naturalistic, existentialist), we may introduce the biblical symbol of *faith*—a symbol based on the Hebraic experience of God, yet one whose meaning was intensified or radicalized by its use in the sayings of Jesus and early Christian rhetoric. From the perspective of what is now the basic horizon of freedom, the other two

2. Bultmann, *Theology of the New Testament, I,* 332. 335.

structures may be redefined symbolically as *love* (non-separated, non-alienated community), and *life* (non-privatistic, non-autonomous subjectivity).   Finally, the three symbolic structures coalesce in an encompassing image, that of the *kingdom of freedom* as a liberated communion of free subjects founded upon the power of God's free grace.   The advent of this kingdom is fragmentary and incomplete under the conditions of history, and therefore the liberated community remains an eschatological, postpolitical vision, a vision that should infuse political action but not be confused with it.   Our proper relation to the kingdom is one of *hope* rather than of scientific calculation or political utopianism (although the coming kingdom may interact dialectically with utopian expectations and struggles for liberation).

I have taken the Pauline triad *faith, hope,* and *love,* adding to it the characteristically Johannine symbol of *life,* subsuming them all under the image central to the proclamation of Jesus, the *kingdom.*   Hopefully this procedure will not appear too contrived. Freedom is a rich and complex reality, encompassing many of the central Christian symbols.   It provides one way, and for the time being an appropriate way, of ordering the diversity of the biblical and doctrinal tradition into a coherent whole.

The elaboration of a Christian symbolics of freedom requires a transition from Christology to Pneumatology as its theological foundation, for the Spirit is the empowering source and eschatological norm of the new birth of freedom.   According to the Gospel of John, the Spirit is the power by which one is "born anew" *(gennēthē anōthen,* Jn. 3:3–7).   If the "life" into which one is newly born is a symbol of freedom for the Fourth Gospel (as I shall argue in Sec. 4), then the connection among "Spirit," "new birth," and "freedom" is at least implicit in the Johannine theology.   The saying of Jesus to Nicodemus in this passage might be paraphrased as follows: "Unless one is born anew into freedom through the Spirit, he cannot enter the kingdom of freedom" (cf. Jn. 3:3, 5).

What I am proposing under the rubric of a "symbolics of freedom" might be described in Catholic terms as a "spirituality of liberation," [3] or in Protestant terms as "sanctification"—a new life of inward freedom imparted to the believer by the Holy Spirit, based on the justifying act of God in Christ.[4] Sanctification, as the completion of the process of justification, is an irrefragably eschatological event, which explains the expression "final freedom" to designate Part Five of the argument, containing the present chapter. Christian "perfection" (the new life-in-freedom to be described by our "symbolics") refers to a future possibility, not a present reality (as Pietism and John Wesley contended), although it is a possibility that ought to infuse, illumine, and stucture the present.

"Sanctification by the Spirit" (*en hagiasmō Pneumatos*, 2 Thess. 2:13; 1 Pet. 1:2) entails the consummation or "perfection" of the "freedom" for which Christ has set us free. Hence the work of the Spirit, like that of Christ, is a work of freedom. Paul makes this explicit in the third chapter of 2 Corinthians. Just as Moses removed the veil that covered his face when he came before the Lord (Ex. 34:34), so also the veils that cover our minds will be removed when we turn to the Lord (2 Cor. 3:15–16). But the Lord is no longer to be sought on Mount Sinai but in his presence in the Spirit.[5] "Now the Lord is the Spirit, and where the Spirit of the Lord is, there is freedom" (3:17). We are thus liberated from the bondage of the written code and of a particular (holy) place as the conditions for knowing God. The Spirit is "the Spirit of the *living* God" (3:3); "the Spirit *gives life*" (3:6), which is a new life-in-freedom (3:17). The "splendor" or "glory" *(doxa)* that attends the dispensation of the Spirit (3:8), and that is iden-

---

3. Cf. Segundo Galilea, "Liberation as an Encounter with Politics and Contemplation," in *The Mystical and Political Dimension of the Christian Faith*, ed. C. Geffré & G. Gutiérrez (*Concilium*, vol. 96; New York: Herder and Herder, 1974), p. 20.
4. Cf. Van A. Harvey, *A Handbook of Theological Terms* (New York: Macmillan, 1964), pp. 214–215. On the relation between justification and sanctification, see Karl Barth, *Church Dogmatics*, IV/2, trans. G. W. Bromiley (Edinburgh: T. & T. Clark, 1958), 499–511. Book III of John Calvin's *Institutes of the Christian Religion* sets forth the doctrine of sanctification in classical Protestant terms. It is noteworthy that this book contains the well-known chapter "On Christian Liberty" (*Inst.*, III, xix).
5. George S. Hendry, *The Holy Spirit in Christian Theology* (Philadelphia: Westminster Press, 1956), p. 24.

tical with the very being of the Lord (3:18), is undoubtedly the
glory of freedom (cf. the *eleutheria tēs doxēs* of Rom. 8:21).
"Freedom" could be read for "glory" in 2 Cor. 3:18: "And we all,
with unveiled face, beholding the freedom of the Lord, are being
changed into his likeness from one degree of freedom to another;
for this comes from the Lord who is the Spirit." [6]

But if the work of the Spirit, like that of Christ, is a work of
freedom, how then is the Spirit to be distinguished from Christ?
The "Lord" to whom Paul refers in 2 Corinthians 3 is not only the
Lord of Israel but also "the Lord Jesus Christ," for it is only
through Christ that the veil has been taken away (3:14). Therefore "the Spirit of the Lord" (3:17) is also "the Spirit of Christ."
Paul says as much in Rom. 8:9; Gal. 4:6; Phil. 1:19; and in fact
the expressions "in Christ" and "in the Spirit" are used inter-
changeably in the Pauline epistles (cf. Rom. 8:1, 9; 14:17–18;
Phil. 2:1). In Rom. 8:2, the Spirit whose law "has set [us] free
from the law of sin and death" is identified as "the Spirit of life
in Christ Jesus." The distinction between Christ and the Spirit
is obviously a dialectical one, not only for Paul but for Christianity as a whole. "In the experience of the Church," writes
Hendry, "the presence of the Holy Spirit was known, not as an
alternative to, but as a mode of, the presence of the living Christ
which forms the constitutive fact of Christian faith. . . . The
presence of the Spirit does not supersede the presence of Christ:
that is the spiritualist heresy which has plagued the Church repeatedly from the time of Montanus onward." [7]

Paul distinguishes between the modes of activity of Christ and
the Spirit primarily in terms of what might be called *objective* and

---

6. On the association of the Spirit, freedom, and life in Paul, see Bultmann, *The-
ology of the New Testament,* vol. I, § 38, "Freedom from Sin and Walking in the
Spirit," esp. pp. 333–336; Kurt Niederwimmer, *Der Begriff der Freiheit im Neuen
Testament* (Berlin: Verlag Alfred Töpelmann, 1966), pp. 168 ff.; and Joseph
Haroutunian, *God with Us: A Theology of Transpersonal Life* (Philadelphia: Westminster Press, 1965), chap. 2 (the title of this chapter, "The Spirit of the Living
God," is from 2 Cor. 3:3, and in it Haroutunian argues that the Spirit constitutes
the Christian life-in-freedom, which must be understood as a communal or transpersonal life).
7. Hendry, *The Holy Spirit in Christian Theology,* p. 41.

subjective spheres of operation. "The Spirit is the subjective complement or counterpart of the objective fact of Christ, and it is the function of the Spirit to bring about an inner experience of the outward fact in the hearts of men."[8] The objective fact or action of Christ is not to be limited to his past, "earthly" ministry (as Hendry tends to construe the matter), but includes also his present agency as risen Lord on behalf of liberation. The modality of his "objective" presence obviously differs when he is no longer physically present in an individuated body but is rather mediated by the collective body of the faithful. But the action of the risen Christ remains "objective" in the sense that it functions as a "factor" in the actualization of freedom through the dialectics of the historical process (see Chap. VI, Secs. 2, 4), and because it is mediated by and issues in the transformation of objective sociocultural structures. The work of the Holy Spirit, by contrast, is "subjective" in the sense that the Spirit acts from within the subjectivity of believers and the intersubjectivity of the community to bring about a personal/interpersonal appropriation of and response to the saving gift of freedom. Thus the risen Christ and the Spirit work "simultaneously," in different modalities or spheres— from "without" and from "within"—to effect freedom.

The simultaneity, however, is not undialectical. The Fourth Gospel and to a lesser extent Luke–Acts lay great stress on the fact that the gift of the Spirit comes only at the end of the historical ministry of Jesus.[9] This distinction between temporal dispensations must, however, be construed symbolically, at least for the Gospel of John. According to the latter, the earthly Jesus is *already* "the resurrection and the life" (Jn. 11:25), and with the imparting of the Spirit by the risen Lord (20:22) the eschatological

---

8. Ibid., p. 25; cf. pp. 24–26, 34–35, 41–42. The "subjective" work of the Spirit has been stressed by many recent theologians, notably Karl Barth, *Church Dogmatics,* vol. I/1, trans. G. T. Thomson (Edinburgh: T. & T. Clark, 1936), pp. 515–523; vol. I/2, ed. G. W. Bromiley and T. F. Torrance (Edinburgh. T. & T. Clark, 1956), § 16; also Karl Rahner, *The Trinity,* trans. Joseph Doncell (New York: Herder and Herder, 1970), chap. III, esp. pp. 92–93; and Paul Tillich, *Systematic Theology,* vol. III (Chicago: University of Chicago Press, 1963), pp. 283 ff.
9. See Hendry, *The Holy Spirit in Christian Theology,* pp. 21–23.

age has begun. The temporal distinction between Christ and the
Spirit is maintained by the Fourth Evangelist within the framework of a view of time for which past, present, and future fuse
into each other through the presence of eternity. What seems
valid from the Johannine way of thinking is a distinction between
the *historical* presence of God in Christ (understanding "history"
to include both past and present) and the *eschatological* presence
of God in the Spirit (understanding "eschatology" to describe the
future that constitutes history by its dynamic in-breaking).[10]

Summarizing the argument thus far, we may say that the liberating work of the crucified and risen Jesus is *objective* and *historical,* whereas that of the Spirit is *subjective* and *eschatological.* To
this twofold way of distinguishing the work of the Spirit correspond two of the traditional names or titles: as the subjective presence of God, the Spirit is the *Paraclete* (Advocate, Comforter,
Intercessor); as the eschatological presence of God, the Spirit is the
Sanctifier (and as such the Consummator). It remains to examine
the liberating action of the Spirit in these two modalities a bit
more closely. Regarding the first, the main point to stress is that
the subjective working of the Spirit is at the same time intersubjective. The locus of the Spirit's activity is not merely the individual heart of the believer but the *community* of believers, i.e.,
the church as a "communion of saints," a sanctified community
and as such a liberated community. The Spirit works "from
within" to build up a liberated communion of free subjects and
thus to actualize the kingdom of freedom. Through the testimony of the Spirit, the needs of each become the needs of all, and
each person finds fulfillment through the fulfillment of the other.
For this reason the Spirit has often been interpreted on the
Augustinian model as the love that kindles communion between
the Father and the Son, between God and humankind, and between individual men and women. The bearers of the Spirit,
suggests Haroutunian, are my brothers and sisters, not a ghost or
a fire, or wind or breath. "The Spirit interdwells my brother and
myself for our communion with God and with one another in
10. This distinction is suggested by Rahner, *The Trinity,* pp. 91–92, 96–97.

Christ Jesus." [11]

The sanctifying work of the Spirit is *eschatological* because the kingdom of freedom represents an eschatological possibility that can be only fragmentarily actualized here and now; and because from the point of view of trinitarian theology the Spirit represents God's self-redintegration following his self-divestment in the world, and therewith the final overthrow of the enslaving powers and the return of all creaturely things to the Creator. Bultmann notes that according to Paul

> the power of the Spirit is manifested in the fact that it gives the believer freedom, opens up the future, the eternal, life. For freedom is nothing else than being open for the genuine future, letting one's self be determined by the future. *So Spirit may be called the power of futurity.* The expression of this conception is the fact that the Spirit is the eschatological gift: the "first-fruit" (Rom. 8:23), or the "guarantee" (II Cor. 1:22; 5:5).[12]

This motif is reflected in Ephesians (probably a deutero-Pauline writing), where the Holy Spirit is described as "the Spirit of promise" *(pneuma tēs epaggelias,* Eph. 1:13), "the pledge that we shall enter upon our heritage, when God has redeemed what is his own, to his praise and glory" (1:14, NEB). "Do not grieve the Holy Spirit of God," the author continues, "for that Spirit is the seal with which you were marked for the *day of our final liberation" (eis hēmeran apolutrōseōs,* 4:30, NEB).[13] This suggestive

11. Haroutunian, *God with Us,* p. 77. The intersubjective or transpersonal presence of the Spirit is a major theme of Haroutunian (see pp. 74–78), as it is of Dietrich Bonhoeffer in *Sanctorum Communio* (London: Collins, 1963), pp. 115–150. Behind Bonhoeffer stands Hegel's famous statement that the Spirit is "God existing as community," *Vorlesungen über die Philosophie der Religion,* ed. Georg Lasson (Hamburg: Verlag von Felix Meiner, 1966), II/2, 180, 198.
12. Bultmann, *Theology of the New Testament,* I, 334–335. Italics mine.
13. Cf. Karl Barth's commentary on these passages in *Church Dogmatics,* I/1, 530–531. It is well-known that the latter three volumes of the *Church Dogmatics* correlate a trinitarian and salvation-historical structure: the doctrine of creation is associated with God the Father, the doctrine of reconciliation with the Son, and the doctrine of redemption with the Holy Spirit. (For an anticipation of this structure, see I/1, §§ 10–12.) However, Barth rarely thematized the eschatological aspect of the Spirit clearly implied by this structure, describing rather the work of the Holy Spirit in terms of the "subjective reality and possibility" of revelation (I/2, § 16). Of course vol. V of the *Dogmatics,* the Doctrine of Redemption, remained unwritten, so Barth's intentions at this point are uncertain. I have argued, for what I hope are sufficient reasons, that "liberation" or "redemption" should be associated with the work of the Son, while "sanctification," in the sense of the completion of redemption (or "final liberation," Eph. 4:30), is properly reserved for the Spirit.

passage (suggestively translated) forms the basis for my designating
Part Five of the argument as "final freedom," and for associating
with it the work of the Holy Spirit, whose eschatological "fruits"
or "spiritual gifts" include precisely the symbols of freedom to be
considered in this chapter: faith, hope, love (1 Corinthians 13),
and life (2 Cor. 3:6).[14] By means of the Spirit the freedom newly
born through the cross and resurrection of Christ is not only
rendered subjectively efficacious but is also brought to eschatological completion.

2. FAITH: OPENNESS TO THE GOD OF FREEDOM

In describing "the radical freedom of Jesus" (Chap. V, Sec. 2), I
argued that the definitive horizon of his life was that of a relationship to God, which was characterized by the Gospels and primitive
Christian faith as a relationship of "sonship" and "obedience."
Neither of these categories is especially available or helpful today:
"sonship" suggests a privileged sexual relationship, while "obedience" has an authoritarian, repressive, punitive ring for many
people.[15] For this reason I am suggesting the symbol of "faith" as
a better way of translating the neutral phenomenological category
of "openness." Although "faith" was not a self-referential term
for Jesus (with the possible exception of his use of the formula
amēn legō humin, "faithfully I say to you . . ."), the New Testa-

14. The qualities enumerated in 1 Cor. 13 are clearly intended by the context of
the discussion as spiritual gifts (cf. 1 Cor. 12:1, 31; 14:1). The most encompassing
of the gifts of the Spirit for both Paul and John is "life." Another enumeration of
the fruits of the Spirit, including not only love and faith but also joy, peace,
patience, kindness, goodness, etc., which are here considered marks of freedom, is
found in Gal. 5:22–23. I shall consider the category of joy under the discussion of
life. It is noteworthy that in the three part-volumes of vol. IV of the *Church Dogmatics,* ed. G. W. Bromiley and T. F. Torrance (Edinburgh: T. & T. Clark, 1956,
1958, 1961–62), Barth designates the work of the Holy Spirit in correspondence to
that of the Son by the terms faith, love, and hope (§§ 63, 68, 73) .

15. This is true despite the obvious fact that the terms were not intended in this
sense by the New Testament. Dorothee Soelle suggests that "obedience in the proclamation of Jesus" means rather a "liberated spontaneity" (*Beyond Mere Obedience: Reflections on a Christian Ethic for the Future,* trans. Lawrence Denef [Min-
neapolis: Augsburg Publishing House, 1970], pp. 36–42) ; and Jürgen Moltmann
writes: "The so-called *new obedience* is *new* only when it is no longer obedience
but free, imaginative, and loving action" (*Theology of Play,* trans. Reinhard Ulrich
[New York: Harper & Row, 1972], p. 48) .

ment writers occasionally used it to designate who Jesus was, namely, the truly faithful one, or as Heb. 12:2 puts it, "the pioneer and perfecter of our faith"; and of course the category of faith became one of great significance for Paul and John in designating a saving, liberating relationship of believers to God "in Christ."[16]

This early Christian usage is legitimated by the fact that Jesus spoke *about* faith in an extensive and significant way, although not in relation to himself. In *Jesus—Word and Presence,* I sought to summarize the varied references to faith *(pistis)* in the Synoptic tradition under the three headings *power, wholeness,* and *openness.* Faith possesses an improbable *power* like that of a grain of mustard seed, a power that derives ultimately from God himself (although God is rarely mentioned directly). It is a power that makes life *whole* by integrating personal existence, freeing it from anxiety and uncertainty, and by healing physical affliction and social cleavage. Faith is a *liberating power* that "saves" life, giving it wholeness and efficacy, in the midst of bondage, estrangement, and guilt. This liberating power is founded, moreover, on a relationship of *openness* to God and his coming kingdom, in which we now participate "by faith." [17]

Faith means to be open to God by the power of God, and thereby to experience a transformation of the personal and social dimensions of existence. To live faithfully is to orient one's life away from oneself to the transcendent ground, horizon, or source of life. The Protestant Reformation caught this meaning and expressed it powerfully. The legacy of the Reformation, suggests Gerhard Ebeling, may be summed up by the formula, "free by

---

16. On the latter point, see Rudolf Bultmann's discussion of *pistis* in general Christian usage and in Paul and John (with extensive citations of texts) in *Theological Dictionary of the New Testament,* ed. G. Kittel and G. Friedrich, trans. G. W. Bromiley, (Grand Rapids: Wm. B. Eerdman, 1964–1974), VI, 205–228.

17. See the summary statement of this thesis in *Jesus—Word and Presence: An Essay in Christology* (Philadelphia: Fortress Press, 1971), p. 151, and the detailed exegesis that follows, pp. 168–188. See also Gerhard Ebeling's excellent essay, "Jesus and Faith," in *Word and Faith,* trans. James W. Leitch (Philadelphia: Fortress Press, 1963), pp. 201–246.

faith"—meaning thereby above all that persons are free in relationship to God, free from themselves, free to turn to God in certainty and without satisfying prior conditions based on "works"
or piety. To be free *from* God would be the deepest bondage, for
then we should have to judge and save ourselves, which is an
impossibility. [18]

Hope qualifies faith by designating its essentially temporal-
eschatological character. The transcendent ground to which faith
is open is the creative-liberating power of the future, which calls
us forward out of the bondage of the past into a redeemed present
and an open future. God transcends us and reveals himself to
us as the power of the future; he is the one who is always before
us, luring, calling forward into new possibilities of being. Thus
we may speak of "hopeful faith." But the formula may be reversed to read "faithful hope," for hope without faith is a piteous
condition (1 Cor. 15:19): if there is no basis in present experience
for trusting in the saving, liberating power of God, then hope is
empty or illusory. Theologies of faith (e.g., Ebeling) and of hope
(Moltmann) must come to realize that the two qualities cannot be
separated, for they symbolize the two essential components of any
human relationship to God. Moreover, true faith *(hopeful faith)*
by its own dynamic issues in a renewed community *(love)* and a
transformed subjectivity *(life)*. Thus the symbols of freedom
may be encompassed and integrated from the point of view of
faith, which specifies the *definitive* horizon of human existence—
namely, an openness to the God of freedom.

But who is this "God of freedom?" At scattered points throughout this book I have intimated that "God" and "freedom" are co-
constitutive themes; now these intimations must be expanded into
a theological proposal. Karl Rahner argues that God is the transcendent ground, possibility, or horizon of human freedom: the
reality of human freedom presupposes the reality of a transcendent, divine freedom as the sole context or "horizon" in which the

18. Gerhard Ebeling, *Frei aus Glauben* (SgV no. 250; Tübingen: J. C. B. Mohr,
1968), esp. pp. 3–5, 16–17.

former can flourish. This argument, which has been advanced in similar form by Wolfhart Pannenberg, is summarized by the following statements:

> True freedom is born from the transcendence of man, hence it is freedom before and towards God. Even if God is not known or not expressly visualized in the free act: wherever freedom is really exercised, this happens in silently stretching beyond all individual data into . . . infinity . . . in an anticipation of God. *Thus we experience precisely in freedom what is meant by God,* even if we do not name or consider this ineffable, incomprehensible, infinite goal of freedom, which makes possible the distance to the object of our choice, the actual space of freedom. God is . . . the infinite horizon which alone makes the free choice of individual things possible.[19]

> *The reality of God,* on which man is dependent in the structure of his subjectivity, *is encountered only where,* in the context of his world, [*man*] *receives himself as a gift in the experience of freedom.* . . . Theology should think of God . . . as the origin of freedom, as the reality which makes possible the subjectivity of man.[20]

If the reality of God is encountered where we experience freedom, and if we experience in freedom what is meant by God, then God must in some sense *be* freedom. My proposal is that the most intrinsic of the divine attributes, the one that designates God's *divinity,* is freedom. This means that God cannot be a static, hypostatized "supreme being," but an open, free event. He is *the Free One,* the One who "has" freedom absolutely; his freedom is the event or power that clears a free realm in which

19. Karl Rahner, *Grace in Freedom,* trans. Hilda Graef (New York: Herder and Herder, 1969) , pp. 226–227 (italics mine) ; pp. 206–210, 218–219, 228. The grounds for this argument are both Heideggerian (see n. 21 below) and Kantian. For Kant's proposal that God and freedom are co-constitutive postulates of practical reason, see the *Critique of Practical Reason,* trans. Lewis White Beck (New York: Liberal Arts Press, 1956), pp. 128–137, 143–144.

20. Wolfhart Pannenberg, *The Idea of God and Human Freedom,* trans. R. A. Wilson (Philadelphia: Westminster Press, 1973) , pp. 96, 110 (italics mine); cf. pp. viii, 92–93, 109–114. On the Hegelian foundation of Pannenberg's view of freedom, see pp. 144–177; see also the discussion of Hegel in Chap. III above, esp. Sec. 5, where arguments similar to those of Rahner and Pannenberg are adduced.

human beings can dwell.[21] As *the* event of freedom, because he
has freedom absolutely, God is *both* eternally finished, self-suffi-
cient in his internal relationships, independent or free of everything outside himself; *and* eternally open or unfinished, the future
power that calls all things forward into new and richer possibilities
of being, free therefore to relate to all things that come into being
and to incorporate them into his own increasingly enriched life
without becoming more or less than God. Precisely because he is
free *from* the world in a way that no creature can be, God is also
radically free *for* the world. Or as Karl Barth expresses it, God
is "free also with regard to his freedom," [22] free to enter into communion with the world, free to be conditioned by his relationship
with human beings, free to co-create the historical future with
them without ceasing to be the Creator,[23] free to liberate his
creatures through *their own* personal and social struggles for freedom such that his grace does not cancel but rather undergirds
their humanity, free finally to suffer and to be crucified in history
without thereby giving himself up.

   This discussion leads back to the doctrine of the Trinity, which
is concerned to understand God as one who constitutes himself
and the world through an ongoing dialectic of relationships *ad*

21.This language is suggested by Martin Heidegger, who, in several of his later
writings, uses the term *das Freie* ("the Free") as one of the names to designate
the "event" (*Ereignis*) of Being (*Sein*) by which all beings (*Seiendes*) exist, the
"clearing," "dimension," or "region" that brings things into the open and gives them
free rein. Human beings, we are told, are the mortals that dwell within the free
sphere cleared by the Free. See especially "Building Dwelling Thinking," in *Poetry,
Language, Thought*, trans. Albert Hofstadter (New York: Harper & Row, 1971), pp.
149–151; also "The Nature of Language," in *On the Way to Language*, trans.
Peter D. Hertz (New York: Harper & Row, 1971), pp. 91, 106–108; "Die Frage nach
der Technik," in *Vorträge und Aufsätze* (Pfullingen: Neske, 1954), I, 24–25; *What
Is Called Thinking?*, trans. J. Glenn Gray (New York: Harper & Row, 1968), pp.
132–133. That such language may be intended by Heidegger in some sense to refer
to God (or "the God") is suggested by ". . . Poetically Man Dwells . . .", in *Poetry,
Language, Thought*, pp. 213–229. See also William J. Richardson, "Heidegger and
the Quest of Freedom," *Theological Studies*, 28 (June 1967) : 301–303, 305. On the
expression, "the One who has freedom absolutely," which reflects Karl Rahner's
definition of God as "the Being that 'has being' absolutely" (*Hörer des Wortes*, ed.
J. B. Metz [Munich: Kösel-Verlag, 1963], pp. 66, 69), see *Jesus—Word and Presence*,
pp. 116–119 (where, however, the category of "word" rather than of freedom is
employed).
22. *Church Dogmatics*, ed. G. W. Bromiley & T. F. Torrance, vol. II/1 (Edinburgh:
T. & T. Clark, 1957), p. 303; cf. pp. 297–321.
23. On this point, see Rubem Alves, *A Theology of Human Hope* (Washington:
Corpus Books, 1969), p. 144.

intra and *ad extra*.   It was above all St. Augustine in *De Trinitate*
who developed a model for understanding the triune structure of
God's being in terms of a "subject" that constitutes itself as subject by an act of self-distinction (in which the subject becomes the
"object" of its own knowledge by entering into relation with objects other than itself) and of self-redintegration (in which the
subject returns to itself "enriched" by its mediation through
otherness).   Augustine found analogies for this model in human
experience, and when applied to the being of God it yielded the
following pattern: God as "Father" is the divine *memory* or subjectivity; God as "Son" is the divine *knowledge* or *wisdom* in
which God becomes an object to himself, his own other; and God
as "Spirit" is the divine *love* that serves as the medium of relationship between Father and Son.[24]

Karl Barth has modified the Augustinian model by proposing
that the divine act of self-distinction or divestment, by which God
becomes an object *for* himself (both within the divine life and in
the world), should be understood as love rather than as knowledge;
and that the divine act of self-redintegration, God's being *in and
for* himself, is *freedom* rather than love.[25]   By introducing freedom as a mode of divine being and substituting love for knowledge, Barth has attempted to adjust Augustinian "intellectualism"
in the direction of a more dynamic, voluntaristic conception of
God, whose divinity or freedom is to be affirmed against the
intellectualism of Western (Latin) theology.   In a sense, then,
freedom becomes the most adequate, unrestricted symbol for the
divine life, rather like Tillich's proposal that "Spirit" (closely

24. Augustine, *De Trinitate*, IX–XV, esp. IX, 2–4.   The Augustinian view is represented by Karl Rahner, who proposes that God exists triunely in three modes of
subsistence and in a twofold structure of self-communication, each comprised of four
aspects: origin-history-invitation-knowledge,   and   future-transcendence-acceptance-
love.   See *The Trinity*, chap. III, esp. pp. 87–99, 109–113.
25. Karl Barth, *Church Dogmatics*, II/1, § 28.   Barth's discussion of the Trinity
bears many similarities to that of Hegel.   See the latter's treatment of the Kingdoms
of the Father, Son, and Spirit in *Vorlesungen über die Philosophie der Religion*,
II/2, chaps. 2–5; also his *Encyclopedia of the Philosophical Sciences* (for full
bibliographical data see above, Chap. III, n. 23), §§ 161, 163, 213–214, 236); and Emil
Fackenheim's discussion of the "double Trinity" in *The Religious Dimension in
Hegel's Thought* (Bloomington: Indiana University Press, 1967), pp. 149–154,
193–206, 218–219.

associated with freedom by the tradition, as we have seen) is the most embracing and unrestricted of the trinitarian symbols.[26]   But the freedom of God is not purely indeterminate, spontaneous, or capricious.   It is determined by the objective of God's love, which is to create distinction without separation, otherness without alienation, and thus to constitute communion both within himself and between himself and the world.   Barth therefore rightly intends to hold *love* and *freedom* in dialectical relation as the two fundamental divine perfections.   God is *the One* (Father) who *loves* (Son) in *freedom* (Spirit).[27]   In this sense he is the Free One, the event of freedom—or, to use Moltmann's more adequate expression, *the event of suffering, liberating love.*[28]

In the triune being of God love and freedom define each other. *(a)* The divine love is a *free* love, for it is not necessitated by the creature but is purely gratuitous: God does not need the world to be God (nor is he merely a projection of human desires), and therefore he is free to be God for the world in a quite radical fashion.   The divine love is also a *liberating* love, for it sets the creation free from its self-imposed bondage and reestablishes rightful relationships, both intrahuman and divine-human.   *(b)* The divine freedom is a *loving* freedom: it is not sheer indeterminacy or caprice but a freedom determined by and bound to the world, for the sake of which God undergoes self-divestment, becoming an object to himself in the otherness of the world, suffering and dying at the hands of the world to effect its redemption. The divine freedom is also a *compassionate* freedom, which does not leave love hanging in the anguish of death and separation but completes love by overcoming estrangement and reestablishing unity.

26. Paul Tillich, *Systematic Theology,* vol. I (Chicago: University of Chicago Press, 1951), pp. 249–252.
27. This is the formula that Barth introduces in § 28 of the *Church Dogmatics.* The dialectic between the perfections is developed at great length in §§ 29–31. In *Church Dogmatics,* vol. I/1 (Edinburgh: T. & T. Clark, 1936), pp. 352–353, Barth directly identifies God's self-revelation as Lord ("the root of the doctrine of the Trinity") with *freedom:* God is "the alone Free [One]."
28. Jürgen Moltmann, *The Crucified God,* trans. R. A. Wilson and John Bowden (New York: Harper & Row, 1974), p. 252. For reasons that cannot be elaborated here, God's being is personal (in a conceptual, not merely a metaphorical, sense) because personhood is constituted precisely by the event of liberating love. I have made the same point in a different way in *Jesus—Word and Presence,* pp. 123–128.

With this formulation of the doctrine of the Trinity we have, I believe, an adequate basis for responding to the twofold challenge of modern atheism, which is after all an atheism based on rival perceptions of human freedom.[29]   In place of the God who protects, rewards, and compensates (Marx's "opium of the people," Freud's "future of an illusion"), we may affirm the God who *loves,* and who by his suffering love provides real consolation for human suffering.   In place of the God who dominates, accuses, and punishes (Marx's religion of oppression, Freud's genealogy of the Father-figure), we may affirm the God who *liberates,* who sets his people free from their oppressions and repressions, giving them faith, love, life, and hope.

3. LOVE: NON-SEPARATED, NON-ALIENATED COMMUNITY

The discussion of love may be brief, since what is mainly needed is to recapitulate themes already addressed at various points in earlier chapters.   For much of human history, as we observed at the outset, "freedom" has designated those who belong to a privileged class, clan, or caste.   The Greek word *eleutheria* distinguished the male citizens of the *polis* from slaves, women, and foreigners; and the same has been true, in one form or another, of most ancient and many modern societies.   Moreover, all human communities experience a greater or lesser degree of alienation and estrangement.   Bondage takes root in and is demonically intensified by the social involuntary.

Jesus of Nazareth, by both word and deed, envisioned the possibility of a non-separated, non-alienated community—a free brotherhood and sisterhood for which the single best term is "love." He himself practiced love in the strong sense of "compassion" toward "the crowds" (people in the mass) and toward those who suffered individually.   He gathered about himself a table fellowship that excluded no one—tax collectors, sinners, poor laborers,

29. See Chap. II, Sec. 7A; and Paul Ricoeur, "Religion, Atheism, and Faith," in P. Ricoeur and A. MacIntyre, *The Religious Significance of Atheism* (New York: Columbia University Press, 1969) , pp. 59–98.

Zealots, women, the sick. He spoke of love *(agapē)* relatively infrequently, but what he said challenged traditional assumptions.
He linked the love of God and the love of neighbor (Mk. 12:29–
31 par.), making it clear that the love of God takes the form of
doing justice to the neighbor (cf. Matt. 6:24; 19:16–19; Lk. 11:
42). Moreover, he extended neighbor-love to include not only
one's compatriots, indeed not only those in need (Lk. 10:29–37),
but also precisely one's enemies (Matt. 5:43–46)—which means,
not that there are no longer any enemies, but that they too are
included within the human community and that their needs must
in some sense also become ours. The radicalism of this demand
becomes comprehensible only in light of the fact that Jesus also
proclaimed God's mercy or forgiveness, which is the form that his
love *for us* primarily assumes, and which provides the condition
for the possibility of fulfilling the demand.[30]

Paul recognized that in the case of Jesus himself love assumed
the form of suffering, self-giving, and existence for others even
unto death. In this form love was to become a "law of freedom"
(cf. Gal. 5:13–14)—a *novus ordo caritatis*—which would provide
the structure by which a unified and liberated community could
be "built up" (1 Cor. 8:1; cf. Eph. 4:16) in such a way as to exclude licentious individualism (Gal. 5:15–26), but without con-
stricting genuine diversity or a variety of gifts (1 Cor. 12:4–31).
The Apostle clearly understood love as one of the eschatological
gifts of the Spirit. It is through the Holy Spirit that "God's love
has been poured into our hearts" (Rom. 5:5); the Spirit is the
Spirit of love (Gal. 5:22; cf. Rom. 15:30; 1 Cor. 4:21). "The
pneuma liberates man for supreme activity in love," writes Stauffer. But this

> *agapē* stands under the sign of the *telos*. This is the great truth
> of I Cor. 13. For this reason love is the heavenly gift surpassing
> all others, the "more excellent way" [1 Cor. 12:31], which not
> only stands at the heart of the trinity of faith, love and hope but

30. Cf. *Theological Dictionary of the New Testament*, I, 47, cf. 44–48. See our discussion of "Brotherhood/Sisterhood" in Chap. V, Sec. 2B.

is also greater than the other two. . . . With love the power of
the future age already breaks into the present form of the world.[31]

"Love" might be defined as eschatological freedom, perfect or
final freedom; whereas "faith" designates the relationship of openness to God that makes intrahuman love a possibility; and "hope"
defines the modality by which we love here and now. In this
sense, love stands in the middle between faith and hope,[32] serving
to encompass and integrate the symbols of freedom. Or more
precisely, because of the dialectical interplay between these symbols, each can stand at the center and each at the periphery.

In the analysis of community as a structure of freedom, I proposed that "communion" has a co-intentional structure (Chap.
III, Sec. 4A). In the reciprocal co-intentionality of communion,
we intend each other for the sake of the other, putting ourselves
at the other's disposal, making his or her needs our own, yet
knowing that we will not thereby be lost or destroyed but rather
fulfilled. In the liberated community, both particularity and
participation, both subjectivity and intersubjectivity, are accomplished. Although grounded in the ontological constitution of
human (inter)subjectivity, full actualization of this reciprocity is
an eschatological possibility only because of the privatism, separation, and alienation that infect all forms of social existence. Paul
Ricoeur, who was reluctant to discuss intersubjectivity within the
framework of an eidetics of the will because he believed it must
already presuppose a teleologically oriented poetics of freedom,
nevertheless at one point in *Freedom and Nature* provides an
intimation of what is meant by free communion:

> The community is my good because it leads towards making me
> whole within a "we" where the lacuna of my being would be
> filled. In some moments of precious communion I sense tenta-
> tively that the isolated self is perhaps only a segment torn from
> such others who could have become a "thou" for me. . . . There

31. Ethelbert Stauffer, ibid., I, 50–51. On the relation between freedom and love
in Paul, see above, Chap. V, Sec. 5A.
32. As in 1 Thess. 1:3; 5:8; Col. 1:4–5. The order of the triad in 1 Cor. 13:13
appears to be an exception; cf. ibid., I, 51–52.

are some encounters . . . which truly function as a conversion of
the heart of willing and have the force of a genuine spiritual rebirth. Such encounters create freedom. They set me free.
Friendship or love between two people can be like that.[33]

Love means existing for the sake of the other, by means of which
the identity of the individual self is not lost but fulfilled, taken
up into a higher unity. Such love entails a "spiritual rebirth"—
a new birth of freedom.

4. LIFE: NON-PRIVATISTIC, NON-AUTONOMOUS SUBJECTIVITY

The New Testament uses two terms meaning "life" in a broad
range of connotations, *zōē* and *psychē*. Although both are quite
common and well-distributed through the literature, *zōē* (including derivative forms) occurs more frequently. Basically it designates the natural life of the human being, meaning the "operative
power" that is the essence of life itself. Even this life, however,
is not autonomously self-constituted but is given by God through
his Spirit, which is known as *zōopoioun,* the "life-giver" (Jn. 6:63;
1 Cor. 15:45). At the same time, the term *zōē* designates what
Bultmann calls "true life" (referring to the connection between
alētheia and *zōē* in the Gospel of John). "True life," by contrast
with provisional life or life "in the flesh" (Gal. 2:20), which is
subject to death, refers to the future life after death that is based
on the resurrection of Christ. Since it is indestructible it can
also be called "eternal life" *(zōē aiōnios).* Although the full
reality of this life is something for which we still hope, in some
sense it is already a present possession—a theme that was stressed
by Paul and even more so by the Fourth Evangelist.[34]

Pychē, the basic category of Greek psychology, is used by the
Septuagint to translate *nephesh,* which is the central term in the

33. Paul Ricoeur, *Freedom and Nature: The Voluntary and the Involuntary,* trans.
Erazim V. Kohák (Evanston: Northwestern University Press. 1966), p. 128. See also
Ricoeur's "The *Socius* and the Neighbor" in *History and Truth,* trans. Charles A.
Kelbley (Evanston: Northwestern University Press, 1965), pp. 98–109.
34. Rudolf Bultmann, in *Theological Dictionary of the New Testament,* II, 861–866.

anthropological vocabulary of the Old Testament. It means "life," "living being," "person," "soul," "psyche." The classic text is Gen. 2:7: "Then Yahweh formed humankind *('adham)* of dust from the ground, and breathed into its nostrils the breath of life; and humankind became a living being *(nephesh chayyah)"* (RSV modified). *Nephesh* refers to the whole person as a psychosomatic unity, designating the individual subject who is free and responsible. Again, this is not an autonomous subjectivity, for without God's Spirit *(rûach)*, which "breathes" life into the human being, the *nephesh* could neither come into existence nor sustain itself as a living being.[35]

Psychē as used in the New Testament builds upon this Hebraic understanding. It refers to natural physical life given by God, designating not mere physicality *(sarx)* but the individual as a responsible subject or self existing before God and in relation to other *psychai*. There can be no *psychē* apart from the body (in this sense the Greek duality between mortal body and immortal soul is rejected), but on the other hand *psychē* means something more than simply being physically alive. It entails a distinctive quality of life ("true life"), based on an authentic, saving relationship to God. This is the meaning of the saying of Jesus found variously in all four of the Gospels: "Whoever would save his life *(psychē)* will lose it; and whoever loses his life *(psychē)* for my sake and the gospel's will save it" (Mk. 8:35 par.). Life that has been "saved" (not through human effort but by a giving of oneself up to the gospel) is set free from the bondage of death, but it is not free of embodiment, for it is only through the body that individual uniqueness is preserved. However, after death embodiment is secured not by reincarnation in the old physical body (or for that matter a new physical body) but by entering into a spiritual body *(sōma pneumatikon,* 1 Cor. 15:44), which is a collective body, the *sōma Christou.*[36]

The symbol of "life" attains a special prominence in the Gospel

---

35. Edmond Jacob, in ibid., IX, 617–632.
36. Eduard Schweizer, in ibid., IX, 637–656.

of John,[37] where it is linked to the power of the Spirit through
the imagery of "new birth" (Jn. 3:3–7), and to the event of freedom through the category of "truth" (cf. Jn. 8:32; 14:6). *True*
life for the Fourth Gospel is in fact *eternal* life *(zōē aiōnios)*—or,
as I suggested earlier, *free* life, life that has been set free from the
bondage to death that prevails in "this world." [38] The usage of
the terms *zōē* and *zōē aiōnios* (among the most common in the
Johannine vocabulary) makes it clear that they describe a reality
that applies primarily to the existence of individual persons: the
gift of free life creates a new subjectivity, liberated from the past
and open to the future, manifesting itself outwardly in love (15:9–
17; 1 Jn. 3:14–15) and inwardly in confidence (1 Jn. 3:21; 5:14)
and joy (Jn. 15:11; 16:20–24; 17:13).[39]

This subjectivity is above all *non-autonomous,* because it is
based on the "free life" brought into the world and made a presently efficacious reality by the One who *is* the resurrection and the
life (11:25). Just as Jesus gained or actualized life by losing it,
so also must we. This is the significance of the saying in Jn. 12:25,
which as we have noted has parallels in all three Synoptic Gospels
(Mk. 8:35 par.; Matt. 10:39; Lk. 17:33): "He who loves his life
(psychē) loses it, and he who hates his life *(psychē)* in this world
will keep it for free life *(zōē aiōnios).*" Here the key terms *psychē*
and *zōē* are conjoined and systematically related. Our earthly,
physical life *(psychē)* will become the true, free life *(zōē aiōnios)*

---

37. This is not to suggest that life is not also an important category for Paul, but
the limitations of this chapter require selectivity. For Paul the operative term is
zōē. Psychē occurs rarely in the Pauline corpus and is not significant as a theological term, except for the *contrast* Paul wants to draw between *psychē* (physical
life) and *pneuma* (the new life given by God through the resurrection of Christ)
in 1 Cor. 15:44–47. *Psychē* was apparently too strongly Hellenistic in connotation
to be used by Paul constructively. (Ibid., IX, 648–650.) Concerning *zōē* (which
with related forms occurs many times in his epistles), Paul stresses the *present*
reality of the "true life" given through Christ, the Spirit, and the Word. We are
even now to live by the Spirit and walk by the Spirit (Gal. 5:25; cf. Rom. 6:4;
8:12–13), whose first fruit is love (Gal. 5:22). True life (or "newness of life")
entails a liberation from sin, law, and death. Moreover, the "law" of this life is
not *auto-nomous* but the law of the Spirit (Rom. 8:2). (Cf. Bultmann, in ibid.,
II, 866–870.)
38. See above, Chap. V. Sec. 5b.
39. Bultmann, in *Theological Dictionary of the New Testament,* II, 870–872.

that is already a present reality, if we seek the center of our life not in ourselves but in the One who has gone before us. We are thus freed from attempts at self-preservation and experience a new and liberating openness to God and the neighbor.[40]

The new subjectivity is also *non-privatistic,* as 1 Jn. 3:14–16 (cf. 4:7–11) makes clear in a pregnant statement:

> We know that we have passed out of death into life (*zōē*), because we love the brethren. He who does not love remains in death. Anyone who hates his brother is a murderer, and you know that no murderer has free life (*zōē aiōnios*) abiding in him. By this we know love (*agapē*), that he laid down his life (*psychē*) for us; and we ought to lay down our lives (*psychai*) for the brethren.

Here again *zōē* and *psychē* are conjoined, this time to show that free life manifests itself in a "laying down" of life for our brothers and sisters in an act of self-giving love. In the Gospel of John, the other occurrences of *psychē* (in addition to 12:25) make precisely the same point: in 10:11–17, we are told that "the good shepherd lays down his life for the sheep"; in 13:37–38, Peter promises to lay down his life for the Lord; and 15:13 sums up the matter in the Johannine version of the great commandment: "Greater love has no man than this, that a man lay down his life for his friends." [41]

I shall now address the category of "life" as a symbol of freedom in a more contemporary idiom. Human life entails at least three basic actions or functions: *(a)* presence to oneself in a personal body; *(b)* creativity, celebration, joy, play; and *(c)* openness to and participation in that which transcends finite existence ultimately. Such a distinction is formally similar to Paul Tillich's designation of self-integration, self-creativity, and self-transcendence as the

---

40. On this interpretation of Jn. 12:25, cf. Schweizer, in ibid., IX, 642, 644.

41. The non-privatistic character of life in the Gospel of John is stressed by Frederick Herzog, *Liberation Theology: Liberation in the Light of the Fourth Gospel* (New York: Seabury Press, 1972) , pp. 63, 86, 123, 195 et passim.

three basic functions of life in the process of self-actualization.[42] Since the third of these has already been considered under the symbol of faith (as well as being central to the biblical usage of *zōē* and *psychē*), the discussion here will be limited to the first two.

Above all, true vitality entails *presence-to-oneself*, or in Tillichian terms, self-integration through the principle of centeredness,[43] in both temporal and spatial dimensions. Subjectivity, I proposed earlier (Chap. III, Sec. 3), may be defined as a temporal integration of conscious experience by means of language, which gathers the modes of time into a living, meaningful presence. Human temporality is integrated by an intentional projection of future action, based on the heritage and causal nexus of the past, lending coherence and direction to the present moment. Without temporal integration life would disintegrate into an irredeemable past, an unachievable future, and a meaningless present, which would be a form of living death, a total bondage to time. Subjective freedom entails an openness to an available future, which engenders temporal integration and presence to oneself. *Spatial* integration or presence—the other dimension of subjectivity—is a function of the *body*, which serves as the spatial locus of the temporal focus that I am. My body makes me available to myself and to others, both permitting a necessary distance through physical differentiation, and providing the medium by which communication can take place. Language, of course, is the most supple means of human communication, and it is an indivisibly psychosomatic function. By means of language the body becomes a personal body, the body of a subject, an "I." This personal body, which

---

42. Paul Tillich, *Systematic Theology* (3 vols.; Chicago: University of Chicago Press, 1951–1963), III, 30–163. According to Tillich, these life-functions are expressions of the ontological polarities intrinsic to the structure of essential being: individualization and participation, dynamics and form, freedom and destiny (I, 174–186). Under the conditions of existence, these polarities become conflictual and estranged from each other (II, 62–66). However life, according to Tillich, is neither essential nor existential but ambiguous (III, 32). Therefore a quest for unambiguous life may be discerned running through the functions of integration, creativity, and transcendence. The three main symbols for unambiguous life are Spirit of God (or Spiritual Presence), Kingdom of God, and Eternal Life (III, 107–110) —symbols that are also central to our symbolics of freedom, although they are not developed within the conceptual framework of Tillichian theology.
43. Ibid., III, 30–41.

represents the sphere of "my own," serves as the locus of my receptivities and is at my disposal in ways that other bodies are not.

In describing humanity's "freedom for life," Rubem Alves focuses upon the body, which establishes our solidarity with the world. Nature is not an alien entity but rather the home of men and women, to be enjoyed and respected. Through our bodies we are able "to fertilize and transform the world." The body makes the human being a person; it is the precondition of both communion and self-relatedness; we are both social and sexual. Salvation does not entail an escape from the world or the body; liberation has to do not with the negation but with the emancipation of the body from all that represses it.

> It is because life is so good, the body so full of possibilities, the world so inviting, that suffering is so painful. . . . Suffering emerges as a result of, and as a protest against, whatever, in our present historical reality, makes the fulfillment of the erotic sense of life impossible and therefore aborts the project of agape.[44]

The resurrection "of the body" means its liberation from all forms of social and physical bondage (above all that of death). It does not entail the resuscitation of the old corpse but the creation of a "new body," an imperishable body no longer subject to the corruption of death and other forms of bondage, a body that is now intrinsically a social body (1 Cor. 15:42–57).

The *creativity, celebration, joy,* and *playfulness* of life have been important themes of the recent "theologies of play." These theologies at their best have not ignored pain and suffering but rather have argued that "only those who are capable of joy can feel pain at their own and other people's suffering. . . . Where freedom is near, the chains begin to hurt." Moltmann, the author of this statement, adds: "*Life* as *rejoicing* in liberation, as *solidarity* with those in bondage, as *play* with reconciled existence, and as *pain* at unreconciled existence demonstrates the Easter

44. Rubem Alves, *A Theology of Human Hope*, pp. 147–153 (quotation from p. 151). Cf. also *Tomorrow's Child: Imagination, Creativity, and the Rebirth of Culture* (New York: Harper & Row, 1972), pp. 158–161; and Jürgen Moltmann, *Theology of Play*, p. 34.

event in the world." [45]   It is in virtue of their "playing creativity"
that women and men image God and celebrate their God-given
freedom.   The higher animals too are able to play, and their play
is a rudimentary cipher of freedom; but human beings alone
among the animals are able to play freely, i.e., creatively, imaginatively, linguistically.   Yet humankind's creativity is distinguished
from that of God: it is not a *self*-creation but a finite, responding
creativity engendered by God's grace.   Thus human freedom is
located between that of the animals, whose play is at best a pro-
totype of freedom, and that of God, whose creativity is *ex nihilo,
de libertate Dei*.[46]

Joyful fulfillment in the *present* is an essential element of subjective freedom, even though human life is intrinsically future-
oriented.   Just because according to Christian faith the future is
assured by God's promise, we are set free to celebrate and enjoy
the present.   Alves makes this point as well as anyone I know.

> On the way toward the new tomorrow man receives the gift of the
> present, the time of enjoyment, the time that does not exist for the
> sake of any other time.   There is a time of rest, a contemplation,
> of pure joy.   On the way toward the promised land man learned
> that there is a time when he has to stop, to abdicate all attempts
> to build the future, to remain in pure receptivity and in a total
> abandonment of calculation.   His today was God's gift.   He could
> rest because the politics of liberation was not carried on by the
> power of man alone, but rather by the passion and activity of
> God.   Therefore, it was not only possible to rest in the present
> without losing the future but rather necessary to rest in the pres-
> ent in order not to lose the future.[47]

The symbols of freedom may all be integrated from the point of
view of "life."   It presupposes a faithful openness to the God of
freedom, who is the creator and sustainer of life; it issues in a self-
giving love for one's sisters and brothers; it hopes in confidence for
the coming of God's kingdom, and therefore is set free to enjoy
and celebrate the goodness of present existence.   The imagery of

---

45. Moltmann, *Theology of Play*, p. 31   (italics his).
46. Ibid., pp. 23, 47–49, 70.
47. Alves, *A Theology of Human Hope*, p. 156; cf. pp. 145–158.

"new birth," with which I have been working throughout this theology of freedom, is closest to the symbol of life: it is precisely "life" that dies through sin, law, death, and the powers; and it is "life" that is newly born through the incarnation, death, and resurrection of Christ. A "new birth of freedom" means above all a redeemed and liberated *life*.

5. HOPE: THE KINGDOM OF FREEDOM

An association of "hope" and "freedom" occurs in 2 Cor. 3:4–18, a passage to which I referred earlier in describing the work of the Spirit as a work of freedom. Paul makes it clear that the "hope" *(elpis)*, "boldness" *(parrēsia)*, and "confidence" *(pepoithēsis)* to which he alludes as characterizing his work among the Corinthians (3:4, 12) are not based on a self-sufficiency but on the sufficiency given by God, "who has qualified us to be ministers of a new covenant, not in a written code but in the Spirit; for the written code kills, but the Spirit gives life" (3:5–6). The same Spirit gives freedom (3:17), which makes it possible to remove the veil of the old covenant, dependent as it is on the law and on the holy place (i.e., Sinai), and to behold the glory or sovereign freedom *(doxa)* of the Lord directly (3:18). Hope, then, is based upon the freedom that liberates from law and death, and that epitomizes the new covenant, the "dispensation of righteousness," which far exceeds the old in a splendor *(doxa)* that is permanent (3:9–11).[48] Freedom manifests itself in hope as well as in life, love, and faith.

The same point can be made by examining more closely the connections among faith, love, life, and hope as symbols of freedom. On the one hand, hope defines the "modality" of the other symbols. It is only "by hope" that faith is able to remain open to a God who is not seen, or that the eschatological reality of love can be experienced here and now, or that life can survive in the midst of a dying world. Hope entails a confidence that is eschatolog-

48. Bultmann points out the connection between *elpis* and *eleutheria* in this passage in *Theological Dictionary of the New Testament*, II, 531–532.

ically oriented, not empirically based on the "visible" evidence of
this world. "Hope that is seen is not hope. For who hopes for
what he sees? But if we hope for what we do not see, we wait
for it with patience" (Rom. 8:24–25; cf. 2 Cor. 4:18). Such hopeful confidence is characterized by expectation, patience, and above
all *imagination,* which according to William Lynch, "is the gift
that envisions what cannot yet be seen, the gift that constantly
proposes to itself that the boundaries of the possible are wider
than they seem." Imagination, by contrast with fantasy, is not
oriented to illusory wish-projections but to *reality,* which it evokes
in the mode of image or symbol rather than of objective, visible
data.[49] Rubem Alves also stresses the imaginative realism of hope:
"It is the *presentiment* that *imagination is more real* and *reality
less real than it looks.* It is the *hunch* that the overwhelming
brutality of facts that oppress and repress is not the last word. It
is the suspicion . . . that in a miraculous and unexpected way life
is preparing the creative event which will open the way to freedom and resurrection." [50]

But hope is not merely the modality of the other symbols. It
also specifies the intrinsically most appropriate relationship to "the
pure nondisposability of God," as Karl Rahner puts it, and to
God's kingdom of freedom, which transcends the present as the
nondisposable, noncalculable future. True or final freedom—
the freedom that constitutes God's being and rule—can never be
controlled or manipulated, for it remains invisible precisely as it
makes itself available for salvation. Hope, then, is the symbolic
form in which God's freedom becomes a liberating reality in our
midst.[51] From this point of view hope becomes the central symbol of freedom, and it is in this light that the programmatic statement by Moltmann seems appropriate: "From first to last, and
not merely in the epilogue, Christianity is eschatology, is hope.

---

49. William F. Lynch, *Images of Hope: Imagination as Healer of the Hopeless*
(New York: Mentor-Omega Books, 1965), pp. 26–28, 127–128, 161, 209–210 (quotation from p. 27).
50. Alves, *Tomorrow's Child,* p. 194 (italics his).
51. Karl Rahner, "On the Theology of Hope," *Theological Investigations,* vol. X,
trans. David Bourke (New York: Herder and Herder, 1973), pp. 250–255.

... The eschatological is not one element *of* Christianity, but it is the medium of Christian faith as such, the key in which everything in it is set, the glow that suffuses everything here in the dawn of an expected new day." [52]

Correlative with *hope* as a symbol of freedom is its eschatological content, the rule and realm of God, the *basileia tou theou,* which I have interpreted as a *kingdom of freedom,* arguing that it was the central symbol of Jesus' proclamation, and that it has inspired many of the struggles for human liberation within the ambiance of biblical faith, including the vision of a new birth of freedom in America (a vision that has been flawed and distorted but never wholly lost). The kingdom of freedom may be defined as a *liberated communion* of *free subjects* founded upon the power of *God's free grace.* Thereby the three symbolic structures of freedom—faith as openness to God, love as non-separated, non-alienated community, and life as non-privatistic, non-autonomous subjectivity—are encompassed, reconciled with each other, and fulfilled. In the kingdom, the freedom of the individual and of the social whole are no longer at odds with each other but become mutually reinforcing, because it is *God* who rules or empowers the kingdom, not sinful human beings or alienating social structures. Precisely the relation to transcendence engenders and liberates existential and sociopolitical relations.

The image "kingdom of freedom" *(Reich der Freiheit)* was first used by Hegel to designate the sociopolitical world in which humankind ought properly to dwell by contrast with the "kingdom of nature," which is the realm of necessity.[53] As such it is reminiscent of Aristotle's definition of the *polis* as the "community of the free" *(koinōnia tōn eleutherōn),*[54] and it prefigures Marx's employment of the same image to describe the future classless

---

52. Jürgen Moltmann, *Theology of Hope: On the Ground and the Implications of a Christian Eschatology,* trans. James W. Leitch (New York: Harper & Row, 1967), p. 16 (italics his).
53. G. W. F. Hegel, *The Philosophy of Right,* trans. T. M. Knox (New York: Oxford University Press, 1967), § 4. See above, p. 149.
54. *Pol.,* III, 4, 1279a21.

society based on "free human production." [55] This understanding
of the expression "kingdom of freedom," as well as the biblical
usage of *basileia,* make it clear that "kingdom" is a political image,
not a cosmological, existential, or vitalistic one. In its broadest
sense, *basileia* refers to the *rule* of a political figure, a "king," and
it describes the *realm* or political entity constituted by this rule.
The terms *basileia* and *polis* are used as synonymous parallels
several times in the New Testament (e.g., Matt. 12:25 par.; Rev.
11:13, 15; 17:18; 21:23–24). It is not inappropriate, therefore,
that Karl Barth should write:

> Of one thing in the New Testament there can be no doubt:
> namely, that the description of the order of the new age is that
> of a *political* order. Think of the significant phrase: the King-
> dom of God, or of Heaven, that it is called *Kingdom* of God or
> Heaven, and remember, too, the equally "political" title of the
> King of this realm: *Messias* and *Kyrios.* And from Revelation 21
> we learn that it is not the real church (*ecclēsia*) but the real city
> (*polis*) that truly constitutes the new age. Or, to put it other-
> wise, the Church sees its future and its hope, not in any heavenly
> image of its own existence but in the real heavenly *State.* . . .
> This "politicizing" of the earthly Church is "from above," af-
> firmed from the point of view of the ultimate reality, of the "last
> things". . . .[56]

At the same time, as Barth stresses (and as is already implicit
from Hegel and Marx), the political imagery of the kingdom functions in an *eschatological* or *postpolitical* context.[57] Strictly speaking, the kingdom is not a historical *reality* or *phenomenon,* but it
is a *factor* in history, with profoundly political as well as personal
implications. It might be described as a *utopian political image,*
which functions both as a principle of protest against present conditions and as the image of a fulfilled human community—a community of justice and love, freedom and equality—which does *not*
yet exist but which *could* and *should* exist and one day *shall*

55. Karl Marx, *Capital,* vol. III, trans. Ernest Untermann (Chicago: Charles H. Kerr & Co., 1909), p. 954. See above, Chap. II, Sec. 2ʙ, esp. p. 59.
56. Karl Barth, "Church and State," in *Community, State, and Church* (New York: Anchor Books, 1960), pp. 124–125 (italics his); cf. p. 154.
57. On the dialectic between the political and the postpolitical in Jesus' parables of the kingdom, see above, pp. 230–232.

exist.[58] The mode of reality or "ontological status" of this utopian image is postpolitical or eschatological because it refers ultimately to the rule and realm *of God,* not to the work of human beings, although it is precisely the human work on behalf of liberation that serves as the vehicle of divine action. The kingdom "comes" or "draws near" *(ēggiken,* Mk. 1:15 par.) at the point of intersection between the striving to bring freedom to birth out of possibilities contained in the past (the human struggle for emancipation) and the advent or new birth of freedom as the power of the future that creates new and unexpected possibilities (the divine gift of redemption, the *basileia* proper).[59] We do not yet know how to describe concretely what lies "beyond politics," but we do know that in the kingdom political aspirations and struggles will be transfigured, not negated. The kingdom is *more,* not less, than political because it symbolizes *God's* liberating power by which a *new polis* (cf. Rev. 21:2) is constituted. It properly belongs to the *symbolics* (or poetics), not the *politics,* of freedom. As such, it furnishes the critical symbolic principle by which historical and political struggles for liberation can be measured, but without being confused with any concrete historical actualization.

The *Christian church*—the community of faith, love, life, and hope—properly exists at the point of juncture between the human struggle for liberation and the advent of the kingdom of freedom. The church is not the kingdom itself, but it is a historical anticipation or *avant-garde* of the kingdom in the sense that it ought already to be a *community of the liberated.* This is what Gutiérrez means by contending that, as the "sacrament of history," church "in its concrete existence ought to be a place of libera-

58. On utopian political thinking, see above, pp. 289–290; also Paul Tillich, "The Political Meaning of Utopia," in *Political Expectation,* ed. James Luther Adams (New York: Harper & Row, 1971), pp. 125–180. On this aspect of the kingdom of God, see Wolfhart Pannenberg, *Theology and the Kingdom of God* (Philadelphia: Westminster Press, 1969), pp. 79–81, 84, 111–113, 116–124; Moltmann, *Theology of Hope,* pp. 21–22, 25, 213–214; and "The Revolution of Freedom," in *Openings for Marxist-Christian Dialogue,* ed. Thomas W. Ogletree (Nashville: Abingdon Press, 1969), pp. 66–71.
59. See the elaboration of this point above, pp. 286–289, with special reference to the insights of Gustavo Gutiérrez in *A Theology of Liberation,* trans. Caridad Inda and John Eagleson (Maryknoll, N.Y.: Orbis Books, 1973), pp. 177, 236–238.

354   *New Birth of Freedom*

tion";[60] or what Moltmann suggests by referring to it as "a testing ground of the kingdom of God";[61] or what Pannenberg intends by defining it as "an eschatological community pioneering the future of all mankind";[62] or finally what Alves envisions by describing it as "the future actually taking place in the present," "the *aperitif* of a banquet still to come." [63]

Thus understood, the church has both a critical and a constructive function, or as Gutiérrez expresses it, the task of both denunciation and annunciation.[64] Its *critical*, denunciatory task is to expose and pronounce judgment upon the injustices and inadequacies of present political forms of society, to criticize the conventional social role of religion (which tends to reinforce the status quo by providing a means for the "disburdening" of subjective alienation without addressing structural or systemic oppression), to serve as a constant reminder that the world is not yet the kingdom of God, and to provide criteria for distinguishing between true and false liberation.[65]

Its *constructive,* annunciatory, prophetic function is, above all by *being* the community of the liberated, to "produce signs of the anticipated wholeness and integrity of human life." [66] But beyond that, it must engage in a "world-transforming, future-seeking missionary practice." [67] The annunciation of the gospel, writes Gutiérrez, has a "conscientizing" or "politicizing" function. "But this is made real and meaningful only by living and announcing the Gospel from within a commitment to liberation, only in concrete, effective solidarity with people and exploited social classes." [68] In other words, the church, after the model of Jesus himself, must engage in a *critical partisanship* on behalf of those

60. Ibid., pp. 255–279, esp. 261.
61. Moltmann, *Theology of Play*, pp. 58–61.
62. Pannenberg, *Theology and the Kingdom of God*, p. 75; cf. pp. 76–78.
63. Alves, *Tomorrow's Child*, p. 201; cf. pp. 202–203. On the "ambiguous" relation between the church and the kingdom of God, see Tillich, *Systematic Theology*, III, 374–382.
64. Gutiérrez, *A Theology of Liberation*, pp. 265–272.
65. Cf. Moltmann, *Theology of Hope*, pp. 22, 305–306, 310–321, 324; Pannenberg, *Theology and the Kingdom of God*, pp. 81–85.
66. Pannenberg, *Theology and the Kingdom of God*, p. 86; cf. pp. 87–93.
67. Moltmann, *Theology of Hope*, p. 288, cf. pp. 289, 327–330.
68. Gutiérrez, *A Theology of Liberation*, p. 269; cf. pp. 270–279.

who suffer most at the hands of the world—the poor, the oppressed, the sick and hungry, the old and the young, the minority groups and *marginales* of every society—not for their sake alone but for the liberation of all people. In the final analysis the forms of bondage —sin, law, death, the powers—are no respecters of persons and afflict all social classes. The church's mission is a truly universal one, but this mission requires concrete commitments and priorities in the way that the gospel of liberation is proclaimed and practiced.

Everyone knows how far short of this vision, in both its critical and constructive dimensions, the Christian churches in America have fallen. But a theology of freedom should not merely belabor this fact or allow it to have a paralyzing effect, which can only lead to privatism and despair. For what is urgently needed in America today is an image or a vision that can engender a true spiritual reawakening. Lincoln's image of "a new birth of freedom" offers such a vision. The responsibility of theology is to provide resources that might enable the churches to contribute to the actualization of this vision.

INDEXES

Index of Biblical References

Index of Names

Index of Subjects